Liberalization, Financial Instability and Economic Development

Anthem Frontiers of Global Political Economy

The **Anthem Frontiers of Global Political Economy** series seeks to trigger and attract new thinking in global political economy, with particular reference to the prospects of emerging markets and developing countries. Written by renowned scholars from different parts of the world, books in this series provide historical, analytical and empirical perspectives on national economic strategies and processes, the implications of global and regional economic integration, the changing nature of the development project, and the diverse global-to-local forces that drive change. Academics featured in the series extend earlier economic insights to provide fresh interpretations that allow new understandings of contemporary economic processes.

Liberalization, Financial Instability and Economic Development

Yılmaz Akyüz

ANTHEM PRESS
LONDON · NEW YORK · DELHI

Anthem Press India
An imprint of Wimbledon Publishing Company India Private Limited (WPCIPL)
WPCIPL is a subsidiary of Wimbledon Publishing Company Limited (UK)

This edition first published in India 2014
by ANTHEM PRESS INDIA
www.anthempress.co.in

First published in UK and USA 2014
by ANTHEM PRESS
www.anthempress.com

A copublication with
South Centre
POB 228
Chemin du Champ d'Anier 17
1211 Geneva 19
Switzerland

Cover image: Peter Stuckings / Shutterstock.com

ISBN-13: 978 93 80601 86 1 (Hbk)
ISBN-10: 93 80601 86 7 (Hbk)

To Bernie

CONTENTS

Chapter VII
The Global Economic Crisis and Asian Developing Countries: Impact, Policy Response and Medium-Term Prospects

Chapter VIII
The Staggering Rise of the South?

INTRODUCTION[1]

Globalization is understood and promoted as absolute freedom for all forms of capital, above all financial capital, while restrictions continue to shape the markets for goods, labor and technology. This has reduced the power of nations to regulate and control their own economic space, shifted the playing field against labor and industry, and led to growing financialization of the world economy. Two important consequences are increased instability and inequality. Moreover, for developing countries (DCs) the benefits of unleashed finance have proved to be highly elusive. It has not only meant loss of crucial policy tools for industrialization and development, but has also exposed them to severe global financial cycles, as seen once again during the recent turmoil originating in the US and Europe. Thus, the belief that DCs have decoupled from the North and become new engines of global growth has turned out to be a myth.

This book urges DCs to be as selective about globalization as advanced economies (AEs), better manage their integration into an inherently unstable international financial system, rebalance domestic and external sources of growth, and manage market forces by strengthening public control. It brings together several papers written since the mid-2000s, except the first one which goes back two decades. It is organized in two parts. Part One examines the impact of financial liberalization on stability and growth in DCs and national, regional and global policy options in reducing instability. Part Two focuses on the current financial crisis in AEs, its spillovers to DCs and consequences for their medium-term prospects.

Chapter I, on the pitfalls of financial liberalization, was written in the heydays of globalization and the Washington Consensus and addresses the kind of issues that have become hotly debated since the onset of the financial crisis in AEs. It examines potential risks associated with domestic financial deregulation and capital account liberalization that were widely pursued by DCs at the time. Its main message is that the focus of financial policies in DCs should be stability, industrialization, growth and development, noting that in all modern examples of industrialization, finance was made to serve industry and trade not the other way round. This necessitates a considerable degree of public intervention and control over financial institutions and markets. While in some cases interventions may have been misguided in the past, the waste and inefficiencies they generated cannot be compared with enormous damages and misery resulting from the operation of unfettered financial markets, as seen time and again during recurrent crises in emerging and mature economies since the great waves of liberalization in the 1980s and 1990s. Ironically and for the same reason, liberalization has not diminished but significantly increased public intervention in finance, though in different forms – to clean the mess and repair the damages that financial crises create, including bailouts and nationalization of insolvent financial institutions.

The chapter starts with a critical examination of orthodox propositions on the benefits of financial liberalization, notably removal of control over interest rates and credit allocation, recommended as a remedy to many ills of DCs including poor savings, investment and productivity. It is argued that there are no compelling theoretical reasons for a shift to a regime of higher real interest rates to raise aggregate savings and investment. On the other hand, while liberalization often leads to financial deepening, this does not always result from higher savings or a shift from unproductive assets to productive investment. A shift into financial assets does not necessarily improve efficiency because financial markets and institutions often fail to direct resources to their socially more productive uses. Market signals governing resource allocation do not always reflect fundamentals. This is a main reason why DCs need government intervention in the form of directed and preferential credits to support socially productive investment and accelerate industrialization, as successfully practised in late industrializers such as Japan and Korea. Nor are financial institutions always productively efficient. Liberalization may reduce intermediation costs by creating competition, but can also raise the risk premium and hence the cost of finance by leading to greater instability and uncertainty.

Stability is an essential attribute of an efficient financial system and this is what governments strive to achieve through prudential regulations. However, the record in this respect is quite dismal. There has been a constant battle between regulators and the market, with the latter successfully innovating and introducing new practices to escape restrictions or moving business to unregulated segments of the system. Regulations are often designed to fight the last crisis not the next one, thereby falling behind market practices. The international community has now landed on "macroprudential policy" – not an altogether reliable or well-developed tool to curb excessive risk taking (Elliott et al. 2013).

The efficiency and stability of the financial system also depend on how it is organized. Traditionally a distinction is made between two systems. In the Anglo-American market-based system of finance, banks focus on short-term lending and hence need only adequate reserves and access to lender-of-last-resort financing to avert liquidity crises, while corporate investment depends mainly on share and bond issues in the capital market. By contrast, the German–Japanese bank-based system involves long-term lending by banks and hence necessitates substantial own capital to safeguard solvency. Historically the latter is found to be more stable. It reconciles the Keynesian dilemma of the need of the society for productive investment with the desire of individuals to remain liquid without leading to short-termism and instability.

However, there are a number of prerequisites for an efficient and stable bank-based system and these are not always fulfilled in practice. Thus, important instances of severe banking instability and crises are found not only in DCs but also in AEs. Moreover, not only are there variations within the bank-based and market-based systems, but also the distinction between the two has become hazy over time. For instance with the repeal of the Glass–Steagall Act in 1999, the US moved toward a system of market-based banking with a significantly increased role for banks (Hardie and Howarth 2013). Overall, the benefits claimed for market-based systems are unsubstantiated and DCs are well advised to strengthen their banking system to suit their needs rather than emulate the market-based model. However, it should not be forgotten that under a hands-off approach, any system of finance can go awry.

Chapter I finally turns to financial openness. It is argued that the mainstream view, widely held at the time of the writing of the chapter, that capital account liberalization may cause difficulties only if there are imbalances and distortions elsewhere in the economy, has no sound theoretical or empirical basis. This is also true for the benefits claimed for international capital flows in the allocation of global savings. The bulk of gross flows of capital are motivated by prospects of short-term gains rather than real investment opportunities and considerations of long-term risks and return. Rather than securing greater fiscal and balance of payments discipline they tend to support inappropriate policies with potentially very damaging consequences for economic and social welfare.

The chapter goes on to examine the recovery of capital inflows to Latin America in the early 1990s, after a ten-year drought during the preceding debt crisis, and finds parallels with the surge to the Southern Cone in the 1970s, which had culminated in a severe crisis. It thus anticipates a series of subsequent crises in emerging economies (EEs) beginning in Mexico in 1994–95.[2] While the ideal response to such a surge is to raise investment in traded goods sectors, the conditions attracting foreign money such as high interest rates and currency appreciations do not favor such investment. Nor could this always prevent an eventual crisis because of maturity mismatches due to the financing of long-term investment with short-term and highly fickle foreign money. Thus, there is a need to exercise considerable control over capital inflows.

Chapter II focuses in greater detail on policy options in managing financial instability in EEs, noting that boom–bust cycles in such economies are closely related to global financial cycles and international capital flows. In the past two decades in the developing world currency and balance of payments crises have occurred under varying conditions with respect to current account and budget balances, inflation, currency appreciations, public or private indebtedness, consumption or investment booms, and regulatory oversight of financial institutions. This experience casts serious doubts on the orthodox thinking that such crises arise mainly from domestic policy shortcomings and inconsistencies and exposes the dogma that price stability is necessary and sufficient for macroeconomic and financial stability. The endogenous unstable dynamics analysis developed by post-Keynesians, notably Hyman Minsky, goes a long way in providing a framework for understanding boom–bust cycles driven by international capital flows in EEs.

Keynesians do not have much faith in monetary policy in restraining bubbles or fighting debt deflation and recessions. Bubbles can better be checked by controlling the growth of bank assets through regulatory instruments. During downturns, the "Big Bank," the lender-of-last-resort, can deal with debt deflation while a "Big Government," a spender-of-last-resort, can stimulate income and employment. However, as the chapter warns, such interventions could sow the seeds of the next crisis. For instance, the monetary policy response to the bursting of the dot-com bubble in the early 2000s played an important role in the subsequent subprime bubble while the response to the subprime crisis through zero-bound rates and quantitative easing (QE) now risks creating yet another bubble.

In EEs, where boom–bust cycles are closely intertwined with swings in capital flows and external debt is denominated in reserve currencies, stabilization is much more complicated than in the US and other major reserve-currency issuers. In these economies during downturns and capital flight, the "Big Government" cannot borrow abroad in reserve currencies and the "Big Bank" cannot print international liquidity. Even a straightforward liquidity crisis can thus lead to widespread insolvencies among banks and other private debtors, as seen in Asia in the 1990s. For these reasons, it is all the more important to start countercyclical policy in good times and manage surges in inflows and avoid the build-up of fragility.

However, under capital account openness the erosion of monetary policy autonomy goes well beyond what is portrayed in the standard theory of the impossible trinity.[3] There are limits to how effectively macroeconomic policy can be used to simultaneously overcome currency and payments imbalances and credit and asset bubbles caused by a surge in capital inflows and without compromising domestic policy objectives. Still, in its latest institutional view on capital controls the Fund insists that in managing capital flows "a key role needs to be played by macroeconomic policies, including monetary, fiscal and exchange rate management" while capital controls should be used in exceptional circumstances, only as a last resort and on a temporary basis.[4] However, there is no practical or theoretical reason for any economy with judiciously designed policies to attain stability and growth, and debt and balance of payments sustainability to alter the mix and stance of its macroeconomic policies when faced with an externally generated unsustainable surge in capital flows. For such an economy, capital controls can be the first best measures to insulate domestic conditions from external financial pressures.

In reality many governments in EEs use interventions in currency markets to deal with surges in capital inflows and accumulate reserves as self-insurance against sudden stops and reversals. Indeed, contrary to expectations that the need for reserves would diminish as DCs gained access to international capital markets, there is a strong correlation between reserve holding and capital inflows. Interventions and reserve accumulation could no doubt prevent appreciations and deterioration of the current account, but they cannot always be fully sterilized. Nor can they prevent currency and maturity mismatches in private balance sheets. They, in effect, provide public insurance against private risks with the full carry costs, estimated to be in the range of $100 billion per annum in 2007, borne by governments. There is little rationale to allow hot money to enter the economy and invest it in low yielding reserve assets as self-insurance against its exit.

The chapter concludes that a central and permanent role should be played by financial regulations and capital controls in managing surges in inflows. Prudential rules appropriately extended to foreign exchange positions and transactions including quantitative limits, special loan loss provisions, and liquidity, reserve and capital requirements can help mitigate maturity and currency mismatches and exchange-related credit risks. But, since a very large proportion of capital inflows are not intermediated by the banking system, there is a need to go beyond such measures and introduce market-based and/or direct controls over portfolio and FDI inflows and foreign borrowing.

Chapter III reviews the record under globalization, as of 2006, on capital formation and job creation, focusing on the role played by liberalization of capital flows as well as macroeconomic policy. Its main message is that increased international capital flows have served to redistribute investment and jobs among countries rather than leading to a generalized acceleration of capital formation and employment generation. Capital has become increasingly footloose in all its forms and this, together with a large global reserve army of labor, has created opportunities for labor arbitrage for transnational corporations. However, this has not produced a significant convergence of wages between DCs and AEs, but swung the playing field in favor of capital, reducing the share of labor income in world output – a trend that has continued unabated since the writing of the chapter (UNCTAD TDR 2013; Stockhammer 2012). Increased concentration of incomes has not resulted in faster accumulation of productive capital. Indeed, a distinct feature of the period since the 1980s is that investment typically generates more profits while profits are invested less and less in productive capital.

In DCs in the past two decades, inward FDI as a percentage of GDP has shot up but the investment ratio has shown no tendency to rise. A large proportion of FDI, as conventionally defined, constitutes financial operations involving transfer of ownership of existing assets rather than expansion of productive capacity. As the chapter shows, the record of DCs that embraced a strategy of reigniting capital accumulation and growth through a combination of rapid external liberalization, increased reliance on foreign capital and reduced public investment is particularly dismal.

Macroeconomic and financial policies have played a major part in the paucity of productive accumulation and jobs. Governments in many AEs have shifted to fiscal orthodoxy and abandoned fiscal policy as a tool of macroeconomic management whereas procyclical policy has been widespread in DCs, except for a brief period after the collapse of Lehman Brothers in 2008. However, despite the growing aversion to Keynesian fiscal management, chronic public deficits emerged and public debt has grown faster than output in most major AEs, in large part due to supply-side tax policies and financial bailout operations. In DCs, although external sovereign debt generally declined, there has been an unprecedented accumulation of domestic liabilities an increasing proportion of which has been acquired by nonresidents.

Almost all financial bubbles are associated with excessive investment, not only in property but also in industry, which cannot be sustained with the return to normal conditions, leading to prolonged underutilization and even destruction of productive capacity. This is a main reason why investment is the most unstable component of aggregate demand and why its volatility has increased in the recent period of financial liberalization. Typically, it falls a lot faster under financial busts than it rises during booms. This is also true for wages and employment.

Recoveries from recessions brought about by financial crises are weak and protracted because it takes time to repair balance sheets – to remove debt overhang and unwind excessive and unviable investments generated during the bubbles that culminate in such crises. They also tend to be jobless and yield little investment as increases in incomes are used to pay off debt. This was the case in the US during recoveries in the early 1990s and 2000s from recessions brought about by the bursting of credit and asset bubbles. It has been even more so in the current recovery from the subprime recession – the precrisis income had been restored by the second quarter of 2011, but employment was lower by some 6.5 million. In this latter case policy shortcomings regarding debt restructuring and fiscal stimulus have also played a major role in delaying recovery, thereby leading to unnecessary losses of output and employment (Akyüz 2014). A similar pattern of sluggish job and investment growth is also a common feature of recoveries in DCs following financial crises.

Chapter IV turns to exchange rate management, noting that it occupies a central position in the policy debate in DCs for two reasons. First, as a result of the increased emphasis on export-led growth and reduced barriers to trade, the exchange rate has gained added importance. Second, because of growing integration of DCs into international financial markets, exchange rate gyrations have become a major source of macroeconomic and financial instability.

Trade is the main link between the exchange rate and economic growth but this is not always adequately accounted for in the literature. The conventional trade theory emphasizes supply-side linkages between trade and growth while the Keynesian analysis focuses on the demand-side and the balance of payments constraint. However, since growth cannot be sustained without accumulation, any link between trade and growth should encompass investment. Successful examples of late industrializers in East Asia suggest a virtuous link between exports and investment, or a dynamic "export–investment nexus," incorporating both supply and demand linkages. While there are limits to what the exchange rate can achieve on its own, stable and competitively valued exchange rates are an essential part of industrial development and call for a judicious management of capital flows.

It is the capital account regime not the exchange rate regime that holds the key to success in maintaining stable and appropriately aligned exchange rates. Under a hands-off approach to capital flows, neither fixed nor freely floating rates can work. Stable and competitively valued exchange rates would require occasional adjustments in the nominal value of the currency in order to realign them and avoid gyrations. A viable system thus combines a certain degree of flexibility in the exchange rate regime and a considerable degree of control in the capital account regime.

While most East Asian DCs use considerable discretion in the management of capital flows and exchange rates, there have been large swings in intraregional exchange rates during the boom–bust cycles in capital flows in the new millennium. This instability owes a great deal to inconsistencies in the exchange rate regimes pursued by the countries in the region, spanning the whole spectrum between the two corners of independent floating and the currency board, with the intermediate regimes also showing significant variations with respect to how tightly the pegs are managed. The coexistence of a variety of regimes entails significant intraregional swings at times of large movements of the dollar against other reserve currencies. This is a matter of concern at a time of rapid economic integration of the region and provides a strong rationale for intraregional exchange rate cooperation.

The scope for replicating the European Monetary System (EMS) by pegging bilaterally and floating collectively faces a number of hurdles. Fixing all regional currencies to the dollar (or any other reserve currency) would secure intraregional stability, but this would imply loss of monetary policy autonomy as well as wild fluctuations against third currencies. Such an option might be appropriate for countries looking for a credible external anchor but not for East Asia which has a better record of monetary and fiscal discipline than the US. A viable option could be a crawling peg vis-à-vis a common basket of reserve currencies with agreed central parities and bands. This would have to be supported by regional institutions and mechanisms designed to prevent the emergence of imbalances and crises. A number of lessons can be learned from the EMS, including its shortcomings in areas such as macroeconomic policy coordination, currency adjustment, market regulation and surveillance, the capital account regime and intraregional lending.

Regional arrangements are second best, defensive mechanisms against systemic global financial instability. Addressing the root causes of the problem requires a major overhaul of the international financial architecture to establish its key missing ingredients. These include effective multilateral disciplines over misguided policies in systemically important, reserve-issuing countries whose macroeconomic and exchange rate policies and financial institutions exert a disproportionately large impact on international monetary and financial conditions. Effective rules and regulations needed to bring inherently unstable international financial markets and capital flows under control are also lacking.

As discussed in Chapter V, the IMF holds a central position in this undertaking.[5] However, it has increasingly moved away from its central task of prevention of imbalances and crises toward crisis lending as well as areas which fall outside its mandate and expertise. The IMF needs to go back to its core objectives and stay out of development finance and policy and poverty alleviation. Its main task is crisis prevention not crisis lending. The more it has failed to prevent instability and crises, the more it has become involved in crisis lending; so much so that it has come to depend on crises to remain relevant. IMF bailouts tend to add to systemic instability by undermining market discipline and creating moral hazards for lenders. They also distort the balance between creditors and debtors. There should be strict limits to IMF crisis lending and ways and means should be found to involve private creditors in crisis resolution through voluntary and involuntary mechanisms and orderly debt workouts. Temporary debt standstills and exchange restrictions should become legitimate ingredients of multilateral financial arrangements.

To bring greater authority and legitimacy to the IMF, any reform should address shortcomings in its governance system. The IMF cannot be an impartial institution if it continues to rely on a handful of its members for funds needed to lend to others in payments difficulties and if its financial operations remain linked to bilateral debtor–creditor relations among its members. Consideration should be given to using special drawing rights to fund the resources needed. This would also help move away from the dollar-centered international reserves system and the problems associated with it (Akyüz 2012a).

Part Two has three overlapping papers written at different points of time during the crisis in AEs. Chapter VI, written in the early months of 2008 before the collapse of Lehman Brothers, focuses on the causes and depth of the subprime crisis and its potential impact on DCs, notably in Asia. It traces the subprime crisis back to financial deregulation that started in the early 1980s.

The US banks lost their cost advantage as a result of removal of control over deposit rates in the early 1980s, at a time when deposits were losing importance as a source of funds for financial intermediation and growth of markets for commercial papers and increased securitization put a downward pressure on lending rates. They responded by going into riskier areas of lending, including for property and leveraged buyouts, and expanding their fee-based off-balance-sheet activities in the capital market through subsidiaries and affiliates. Simultaneously, securities firms and insurance companies started engaging in traditional banking activities without being subject to conventional prudential oversight.

All these strengthened the link between credit and asset markets, with credit expansions increasingly translated into asset bubbles and the bubbles leading to credit growth thanks to the practice of mark-to-market valuation. Rather than adapting regulatory policies to the new financial environment, the US authorities submitted to pressures for further deregulation, effectively demolishing the firewalls between commercial banking and investment banking in the late 1990s. This, together with sharp cuts in interest rates made in response to the bursting of the dot-com bubble in the early 2000s, allowed rapid expansion of speculative lending and investment which culminated in the subprime crisis.

The chapter maintains that a vigorous monetary policy response to the crisis would be helpful, but would not be able to overcome the difficulties since the crisis was one of solvency rather than liquidity. In the absence of measures directly addressing the debt (mortgage) overhang in the household sector, the recovery would be slow since market-driven balance sheet restructuring is a protracted process.

The vulnerability of DCs to adverse financial spillovers from the crisis varied according to their prevailing macroeconomic and financial conditions which, in turn, depended largely on how the precrisis surge in capital flows was managed. Most Asian countries had been successful in avoiding unsustainable currency appreciations and balance of payments positions and were able to accumulate sufficient reserves through interventions in currency markets to counter any sudden stops and reversals in capital flows. However, they had not been able to prevent the surge of inflows from generating asset, credit and investment bubbles, in large part because of their reluctance in imposing sufficiently tight controls. As a result, they were exposed to certain risks from a reversal of capital flows, but not of the kind that had devastated the region during 1997–98.

The chapter argues that a sudden stop and reversal in capital inflows could happen as a result of a widespread flight toward quality, with investors taking refuge in the safety of government bonds in AEs, and/or of a growing need to liquidate holdings in EEs in order to cover mounting losses and margin calls – something that indeed happened later in the year after the collapse of Lehman Brothers. However, this was not expected to create serious payments difficulties in Asian DCs, but several countries in Central and Eastern Europe with large current account deficits and high levels of external debt. On the other hand, it was also recognized that capital flows to Asian DCs could accelerate if

Europe joined the US in easy monetary policy – as indeed happened after the Lehman collapse.

The prevailing view before the Lehman collapse was that Asian DCs would not be affected very much by the subprime crisis, partly because the severity of the crisis was underestimated and partly because exports to the US were seen to constitute a relatively small percentage of GDP in both China and other Asian DCs. However, the chapter argues, this did not account for the dependence of intraregional trade and domestic manufacturing investment on exports. Furthermore, the impact would deepen significantly with a possible spread of the crisis to Europe. Even then, however, sound macroeconomic conditions in the region would allow a strong countercyclical policy response to counter the contractionary impulses from the crisis. Nevertheless, China needed more than a countercyclical policy response – a durable shift from exports toward domestic consumption – since the crisis was expected to bring a sizeable and possibly durable external adjustment in the US.

Chapter VII, written in 2010, two years into the crisis, returns to these themes and makes an ex post assessment of the impact of the crisis on Asian DCs, their policy response, performance and prospects. Like many other regions, these countries too did not feel the adverse impact of the financial turmoil and economic contraction in the US until the collapse of Lehman Brothers. Subsequently, as a result of a combination of financial and trade shocks, several Asian economies including Taiwan, Malaysia, Thailand, Singapore and Turkey had negative growth in 2009 while China, India and Korea experienced significant slowdown compared to precrisis years.

On the financial side, despite increased holdings of foreign assets, the region did not incur heavy losses on the so-called toxic derivatives because of a relatively small share of such assets in total portfolios. However, the impact of the sudden stop and reversal of capital inflows were felt strongly in asset, credit and currency markets, in large part because in the aftermath of the 1997 crisis many Asian countries had liberalized foreign entry to domestic securities markets, resulting in a sharp increase in foreign presence. Thus, equity markets came under heavy pressure, losing more than half of their values in most countries in the region. Booms in several Asian property markets also came to an end. Redemption by highly leveraged hedge funds from the US and UK played a major role in the withdrawal of nonresident investment. In effect, Asian EEs started to provide liquidity to portfolio managers and institutional investors in mature markets in order to cover their losses and margin calls and allow them to reduce debt. Coming on top of a cutback in cross-border interbank lending and local lending by foreign banks' affiliates, this resulted in a sharp contraction in domestic credit. Finally, even though most countries had ample reserves and strong payments positions they chose not to defend their exchange rates in view of weakening export prospects.

In most Asian DCs contraction in exports caused much bigger dislocations than financial spillovers. After having seen double digit growth for several years, exports fell by similar rates in the course of 2009. Even without accounting for spillovers to domestic demand, this shaved five to six percentage points off growth. The more successful East Asian exporters of manufactures, deeply integrated into global production networks supplying consumables to the US and Europe, were hit particularly hard, whereas others including India, where domestic demand was a more dynamic component of precrisis growth, suffered relatively less.

Policy response to fallouts from the crisis diverged significantly from earlier episodes of capital flight with almost all countries implementing countercyclical measures. There was no recourse to interest rate hikes in defense of currencies, except for a brief period in Indonesia. However, several countries extended deposit insurance to external liabilities of banks in an attempt to boost confidence. As capital flows stabilized within a few months after the Lehman collapse, interest rates were lowered in an attempt to stimulate domestic demand.

The countercyclical fiscal response was unprecedented, especially in East Asia, and the spending packages introduced were far greater, as percentages of GDP, than those in AEs, including the US where the crisis originated. China, however, missed an opportunity to design a stimulus package so as to address underconsumption. Rather than boosting household incomes and private consumption, it focused on investment in infrastructure, property and industry, pushing its investment ratio toward 50 percent of GDP. This aggravated the problem of excess capacity in several sectors and left a legacy of a large stock of debt in public enterprises and local governments – problems that China is still grappling to overcome.

While countercyclical measures were quite effective in stabilizing output and promoting recovery, the paper argued, growth momentum in the South could not be sustained in the absence of a strong recovery in AEs. In the event, this is ultimately what happened. As the effects of stimulus packages of DCs faded, the US recovery remained sluggish and the eurozone went into a second dip, DCs could not avoid recoupling, slowing considerably from 2011 onwards.

Over the medium term DCs are unlikely to go back to the unprecedented economic performance they had enjoyed in the years preceding the financial crisis. This would require a return to "business as usual," with the US acting as a locomotive to major surplus economies (China, Germany and Japan) and growing running deficits. This would eventually wreak havoc on the international monetary system. Global growth and stability will depend not only on rebalancing between China and the US, as was popularly emphasized at the time, but also on an expansionary adjustment in the two other major surplus economies, Germany and Japan, that have been relying on exports for growth. In particular, the German policy of "competitive disinflation" is seen not only as a major source of global imbalances but also a key destabilizing force in the eurozone – something which has contributed significantly to the deepening of the financial turmoil and prolonged the decline in the region.

The final chapter was written at a time when US recovery was well underway but sluggish, there was considerable uncertainty about the depth of the eurozone crisis, and DCs were enjoying a strong upswing after an initial dip. It provides a critical examination of the myth, widely entertained until the recent loss of growth momentum in the South, that major EEs are "decoupled" from the North and have become new engines of global growth.

In one interpretation, decoupling is understood as desynchronization of business cycles. At a time when global interdependence has been deepening, decoupling in this sense could only mean increased capacity of DCs to sustain growth independent of cyclical positions and strengths of AEs by pursuing appropriate domestic policies and adjusting them to neutralize any shocks from the North. However, the evidence cited in the chapter shows that deviations of economic activity from underlying trends continue to be highly correlated between the North and the South. In another sense, decoupling could mean a shift in the trend (potential) growth of DCs relative to AEs. In such a case, even when business cycles are synchronized, growth in the South would exceed that in the North by a larger margin. However, the chapter sees no evidence of such an upward shift in potential growth in DCs.

The decoupling thesis first appeared when DCs started to enjoy exceptionally rapid growth in the years before the outbreak of the crisis while growth in AEs remained weak. In the early days of the crisis there were also widespread expectations that growth in the South would be little affected by the difficulties facing AEs. The thesis came back with full force when DCs recovered rapidly after a short-lived downturn in 2009, while recovery in the US remained weak and Europe went into a second dip. This hype about the "rise of the South," together with the policy of easy money in AEs, was a major factor in the surge of international lending and investment in DCs both before the outbreak of the crisis and after the Lehman collapse. Governments in major EEs also subscribed to the view that they had become key autonomous players in the global economy since this, in effect, meant that their policies were on the right track.

The IMF has been a major advocate of the decoupling thesis. It underestimated not only the depth of the financial crisis, but also its impact on DCs, maintaining that the dependence of growth in the South on the North had significantly weakened (IMF WEO April 2007 and April 2008). After 2011 it has constantly overprojected growth in DCs. But eventually it has had to recognize the possibility that "recent forecast disappointments are symptomatic of deeper, structural problems" revising downward the medium-term prospects of these economies (IMF WEO April 2013, 19). In a more recent report submitted to the St Petersburg meeting of the G20, the IMF "has dropped its view that EEs were the dynamic engine of the world economy" in a "humbling series of U-turns over its global economic assessment" (Giles 2013). Its latest verdict is that the "world's economies moved much more in lockstep during the peak of the global financial crisis than at any other time in recent decades [...] The increased co-movement was not confined to the advanced economies, where the global financial crisis was centered, but was observed across all geographic regions and among advanced, emerging market, and developing economies" (IMF WEO October 2013, 81).

These "U-turns" reflect the failure of the IMF to develop a sound understanding of growth fundamentals in DCs and their global linkages. Looking at such fundamentals as savings, investment, productivity and industrial growth, the final chapter concludes that the growth surge in DCs in the run-up to the crisis owes a lot more to exceptional but unsustainable global economic conditions than improvements in their underlying fundamentals. Until the global crisis, the credit, consumption and property bubbles in AEs, particularly the US, produced a highly favorable global environment for DCs in trade and investment, capital flows and commodity prices and these accounted for much of the acceleration of growth in the South. China also played a key role in the commodity price surge, but its own growth was driven by exports to AEs.

Again, some special external conditions played a major role in the resilience of DCs to the crisis. With the subprime crisis the international economic environment deteriorated in all areas that had previously supported expansion in DCs, capital flows and commodity prices were reversed and exports to AEs collapsed. However, for three reasons most DCs were able to rebound quickly. First, as noted, a strong countercyclical policy response was made possible by favorable payments, reserves and fiscal positions built up during the preceding expansion and this has allowed DCs to turn to domestic demand for growth. Second, capital flows recovered briskly thanks to sharp cuts in interest rates and QE in AEs. Third, China launched a massive stimulus package in infrastructure and property investment and this gave an even stronger boost to commodity prices than the precrisis export-led growth because of the very high commodity intensity of such investments compared to exports of manufactures.

However, the chapter concludes, the pace and pattern of domestic-demand-driven growth that EEs enjoyed after 2009 cannot be sustained. First, the risk–return configuration that has created the surge in capital flows to DCs, notably the historically low interest rates and rapid liquidity expansion in AEs, cannot last forever. Second, China could not keep on creating investment bubbles in order to fill the demand gap left by the slowdown of its exports to AEs and act as a locomotive to commodity-dependent DCs. Nor could it go back to the precrisis pattern of growth. It needs to shift to consumption-led growth, but this faces political hurdles because it would require a significant redistribution of income. Even a moderate slowdown in China could bring an end to the commodity boom. The most vulnerable DCs are those which have enjoyed the twin booms in commodity prices and capital flows since the early years of the millennium.

These considerations have been corroborated by developments since the final chapter was written. With continued instability and slowdown in AEs, structural weaknesses in DCs have been exposed. Although conditions in global financial and commodity markets have remained generally favorable since 2009, the strong upward trends in capital flows and commodity prices that had started in 2003 have come to an end and exports to AEs have slowed considerably. The prospects of the exit of the US Federal Reserve Bank from ultra-easy monetary policy have already triggered considerable instability in capital inflows, with several major EEs, notably those with large current account deficits, facing outflows and considerable pressures in their currency and asset markets. Growth in the South, including China, has decelerated considerably. In Asian DCs as a whole, the most dynamic developing region, it is five percentage points below the rate achieved before the onset of the crisis; in Latin America less than half of the precrisis rate.

Five years into the crisis, growth in the US is still below potential, Europe is struggling to get out of recession and major EEs are slowing rapidly after a temporary resilience. Longer-term prospects are not much brighter largely because the key problems that gave rise to the most serious postwar crisis, income inequalities, external imbalances and financial fragilities, remain unabated and have indeed been aggravated. On the one hand, the jury is still out on the survival of the eurozone, at least as currently constructed

(O'Rourke and Taylor 2013). On the other hand, in the US a renewed bout of instability remains a real possibility not only because the underlying issues that caused the debacle have not been fixed and financial market and institutions have not been brought under adequate regulatory discipline and oversight (Blinder 2013), but also because of the way the crisis has been managed.

The US has relied excessively on monetary policy, including unconventional means for an extended period, because of its reluctance to directly address the debt overhang and provide adequate fiscal stimulus. The ultra-easy monetary policy has created financial fragility by promoting search-for-yield in risky assets and leverage and posed serious policy dilemmas.[6] On the one hand, if the Fed persists much longer with historically low interest rates and QE, it could generate another boom–bust cycle. On the other hand, exit and normalization of monetary policy could trigger a severe shock to markets accustomed to plenty of cheap money. A Goldilocks scenario in which the Fed engineers an orderly exit without endangering financial stability or choking off growth looks an implausible fairy tale.

Thus, five years since the collapse of Lehman Brothers, developing economies are again exposed to severe shocks with a potentially devastating impact on their stability, growth and development.[7] Ten years ago Goldman Sachs identified the BRIC countries as the "emerging markets" with the brightest economic prospects. A few years later it became BRICS with the addition of South Africa. Now, in September 2013, three of them, Brazil, India and South Africa, are listed among the countries dubbed the "fragile five" by Morgan Stanley (Lord 2013), with the addition of Turkey and Indonesia, again countries among the rising stars of recent years.

***

A fundamental issue raised by systemic instability and recurrent crises in mature and emerging economies is how to put financial markets and institutions in the service of economic and social development. The inherent instability of the international monetary and financial system, and the resistance of major AEs to a genuine reform, pose particularly difficult policy challenges to DCs, since instability and crises in the South are now increasingly produced by global financial cycles and the associated surges and reversals of capital flows. DCs need to use all possible policy tools to control the financial system and international capital flows in order to prevent build-up of financial fragility and reduce the likelihood of crises.

However, attention should be paid not only to how best to regulate the existing financial institutions and markets, but also how to restructure and reorganize them. A rebalancing between state intervention and market forces in search of greater stability and sustained industrialization and growth is both necessary and urgent. In this context at least five key issues need to be re-examined, drawing on the recent experience of both mature and emerging economies: the pros and cons of bank-based and market-based financial systems; the role of state-owned banks; public intervention in private banking, including in the allocation and cost of credit; the impact of foreign banks on the efficiency and stability of the financial system; and the capital account regime.[8]

Greater financial and macroeconomic stability also requires action on other fronts. Despite growing disillusionment in the South, the Washington Consensus is dead only in rhetoric. There is little rollback of policies pursued and institutions created on the basis of that consensus in the past two decades. On the contrary, the role and impact of global market forces in the development of DCs has been greatly enhanced by continued liberalization of trade, investment and finance unilaterally or through bilateral investment treaties and free trade agreements with AEs, and this has narrowed the policy space of DCs and heightened their exposure to external shocks.

DCs need to be as selective about globalization as AEs and reconsider their integration into the global economic system, in recognition that successful industrialization is associated neither with autarky nor with full integration, but strategic integration designed to use foreign finance, markets and technology in pursuit of industrial development. This implies rebalancing external and domestic forces of growth and reducing dependence on foreign markets and capital. The role of the state and markets needs to be redefined, not only in finance but also in all key areas affecting industrialization and development, keeping in mind that rapid industrialization and catch-up is not possible without active policy.

Notes

1 I am grateful to Michael Lim Mah-Hui and Richard Kozul-Wright for comments and suggestions. The usual caveat applies.
2 The paper, in effect, constitutes an initial contribution to the collective wisdom developed in the Trade and Development Report of UNCTAD in the early 1990s about the vulnerability of DCs to boom–bust cycles in capital flows. For a concise account, see UNCTAD TDR (1995, 76–77).
3 For a more recent account, see Rey (2013).
4 IMF (2012, 1). The IMF now includes sterilized interventions among the macroeconomic policies that should be employed even though, as noted in the chapter, for years it maintained that they were ineffective.
5 These themes are further developed in a more recent paper (Akyüz 2012a), drawing also on the lessons from the financial crisis in the US and Europe and their adverse spillovers to DCs.
6 BIS (2013, 1) warns that the recent "strong issuance of bonds and loans in the riskier part of the spectrum [is] a phenomenon reminiscent of the exuberance prior to the global financial crisis."
7 For the implications of ultra-easy monetary policy and the problems that exit could cause for DCs as well as the US, see Akyüz (2013).
8 For a brief discussion of the key issues involved in these areas, see Akyüz (2012b).

References

Akyüz, Y. 2012a. "Why the IMF and the International Monetary System Need More than Cosmetic Reform." In Y. Akyüz, *The Financial Crisis and the Global South: A Development Perspective*. London: Pluto Press.

———. 2012b. "National Financial Policy in Developing Countries." South Centre Policy Brief 14, December.

———. 2013. "Waving or Drowning: Developing Countries after the Financial Crisis." South Centre Research Paper 48, June. Geneva.

______. 2014. "Crisis Mismanagement in the United States and Europe: Impact on Developing Countries and Longer-Term Consequences." South Centre Research Paper 50, February. Geneva.

Blinder, A. 2013. "Five Years Later, Financial Lessons Not Learned." *Wall Street Journal*, 11 September.

BIS. 2013. *Quarterly Review. International Banking and Financial Market Developments*, September.

Elliott, D. J., G. Feldberg and A. Lehnert. 2013. "The History of Cyclical Macroprudential Policy in the United States." US Department of Treasury, Office of Financial Research Working Paper 8, May.

Giles, C. 2013. "IMF Changes Tune on Global Economic Assessment." *Financial Times*, 4 September.

Hardie, Iain, and David Howarth. 2013. *Market-Based Banking and the International Financial Crisis*. Oxford: Oxford University Press.

IMF. 2012. *The Liberalization and Management of Capital Flows: An Institutional View*, 14 November. Washington, DC.

IMF WEO (various issues). *World Economic Outlook*, Washington, DC.

Lord, James. 2013. "EM Currencies: The Fragile Five." Morgan Stanley Research, August 2001. http://www.morganstanleyfa.com/public/projectfiles/dce4d168-15f9-4245-9605-e37e2caf114c.pdf. Accessed 30 October 2013.

O'Rourke, K. H., and A. M. Taylor. 2013. "Cross of Euros." *Journal of Economic Perspectives* 27 (3).

Rey, H. 2013. "Dilemma Not Trilemma: The Global Financial Cycle and Monetary Policy Independence." Paper presented at the Jackson Hole Symposium, Wyoming, August.

Stockhammer, E. 2012. "Why Have Wage Shares Fallen? A Panel Analysis of the Determinants of Functional Income Distribution." ILO, Conditions of Work and Employment Series 35. Geneva.

UNCTAD TDR (various issues). *Trade and Development Report*. Geneva: United Nations.

Part One

LIBERALIZATION, STABILITY AND GROWTH

Chapter I

FINANCIAL LIBERALIZATION: THE KEY ISSUES[1]

A. Introduction

In recent years financial policies in both industrial and developing countries have put increased emphasis on the market mechanism. Liberalization was partly a response to developments in the financial markets themselves: as these markets innovated to get round the restrictions placed on them, governments chose to throw in the towel. More importantly, however, governments embraced liberalization as a doctrine.

In developing countries, the main impulse behind liberalization has been the belief, based on the notion that interventionist financial policies were one of the main causes of the crisis of the 1980s, that liberalization would help to restore growth and stability by raising savings and improving overall economic efficiency; greater reliance on domestic savings was necessary in view of increased external financial stringency. However, these expectations have not generally been realized. In many developing countries, instead of lifting the level of domestic savings and investment, financial liberalization has, rather, increased financial instability. Financial activity has increased and financial deepening occurred, but without benefiting industry and commerce.

In many industrial countries the financial excesses of the 1980s account for much of the sharp slowdown of economic activity in the 1990s. Financial deregulation eased access to finance and allowed financial institutions to take greater risks. The private sector accumulated large amounts of debt at very high interest rates in the expectation that economic expansion would continue to raise debt servicing capacity while asset price inflation would compensate for high interest rates. Thus, when the cyclical downturn came, borrowers and lenders found themselves overcommitted: debtors tried to sell assets and cut down activity in order to retire debt, and banks cut lending to restore balance sheets. Thus, the asset price inflation was replaced by debt deflation and credit crunch.

The recent experience with financial liberalization in both industrial and developing countries holds a number of useful lessons. This chapter draws on this experience to discuss some crucial issues in financial reform in developing countries. The focus is on how to improve the contribution of finance to growth and industrialization; developing the financial sector and promoting financial activity is not synonymous with economic development.

B. Interest Rates and Savings

One of the most contentious issues in financial policy is the effect of interest rates on savings. There can be little doubt that short-term, temporary swings in interest rates have little effect on private savings behavior since that is largely governed by expectations and plans regarding current and future incomes and expenditures: they alter the level of savings primarily by affecting the levels of investment and income. However, when there is a rise in interest rates that is expected to be permanent (for instance, because it is the result of a change in the underlying philosophy in the determination of interest rates), will consumer behavior remain the same, or will the propensity to save rise? The orthodox theory expects the latter to occur, and thus argues that removing "financial repression" will have a strong, positive effect on savings (Shaw 1973, 73).

Empirical studies of savings behavior typically do not distinguish permanent from temporary changes in interest rates. Recent evidence on savings behavior in a number of developing countries that changed their interest rate policy regimes shows no simple relation between interest rates and private savings. This is true for a wide range of countries in Asia and the Middle East (Indonesia, Malaysia, Philippines, Sri Lanka, Republic of Korea and Turkey: Cho and Khatkhate 1989; Amsden and Euh 1990; Lim 1991; Akyüz 1990), Africa (Ghana, Kenya, Malawi, Tanzania and Zambia: Nissanke 1990), and Latin America (Massad and Eyzaguirre 1990) that undertook financial liberalization, albeit to different degrees and under different circumstances.

But this should come as no surprise:

- Even according to the conventional theory, the personal propensity to save from current income depends on the relative strength of two forces pulling in opposite directions, namely the income and substitution effects. Moreover, if current income falls relative to expected future income, a rise in interest rates can be associated with a fall in savings. This often happens when interest rate deregulation occurs during rapid inflation and is accompanied by a macroeconomic tightening that results in a sharp decline in employment and income.
- A large swing in interest rates can lead to consumption of wealth, especially when noninterest income is declining. This is true especially for small savers who can react to increases in interest rates by liquidating real assets and foreign exchange holdings in order to invest in bank deposits in an effort to maintain their standard of living, consuming not only the real component of interest income but also part of its nominal component corresponding to inflation. This tendency is often reinforced by "money illusion" or the inability to distinguish between nominal and real interest incomes, something that tends to be pervasive in the early stages of deregulation. Thus, the initial outcome of deregulation can be to lower household savings, particularly if it is introduced at a time of rapid inflation. For instance in Turkey high deposit rates in the early 1980s allowed a large number of small wealth-holders to dissave.
- The behavior of households may be quite different from that assumed in conventional theory. For instance, they may be targeting a certain level of future income or wealth. Higher interest rates may then lower household savings by making it possible to attain the target with fewer current savings. For instance, in the Republic of Korea and Japan

low interest rates combined with high real estate prices have tended to raise household savings (Amsden and Euh 1990).

- Financial liberalization can lower household savings by allowing easier access to credit and relaxing the income constraint on consumption spending. In many countries financial liberalization has, indeed, given rise to a massive growth in consumer loans (such as instalment credits for cars and other durables, credit card lending, etc.). This appears to have been one reason why the household savings rate declined and the debt/income ratio rose in the 1980s in the United States – something which is at the heart of the current debt deflation process (UNCTAD TDR 1991, part 2, chaps 1–2; 1992, part 2, chap. 2). An inverse correlation between household borrowing and savings ratios has also been observed in most other OECD countries since the early and mid-1980s (Blundell-Wignall and Browne 1991).
- Even if financial liberalization and higher interest rates do not lower personal savings, they can reduce total private savings and aggregate domestic savings by redistributing income away from debtors – a category which typically includes corporations and the government. In many developing countries undistributed corporate profits are an important part of private savings and the most important source of business investment. Generally, the savings rate is higher than for households: corporate retentions are high, ranging between 60 to 80 percent of after-tax profits, because ownership is usually concentrated in the hands of families and there is no outside pressure to pay out dividends (Honohan and Atiyas 1989; Akyüz 1991). The redistribution of income from corporations to households through higher interest rates can thus reduce total private savings even if it raises household savings. In developing countries this effect can be particularly strong because firms operate with high leverage, loan maturities are short and corporate debt usually carries variable rates. Thus, a rise in interest rates not only raises the cost of new borrowing but also the cost of servicing existing debt. Evidence from the studies already mentioned suggests that in a number of countries (e.g., Philippines, Turkey, Yugoslavia), sharp increases in interest rates were a major factor in the collapse of corporate profits and savings that took place particularly in the early phases of financial liberalization.

Such adverse effects are especially marked when interest rates are freed under rapid inflation. There is a widespread agreement that financial liberalization undertaken in an unstable environment may make things worse, and that such reforms should be undertaken only after macroeconomic balances are attained (World Bank 1989; Edwards 1989). Nevertheless, many countries have resorted to liberalization as part of shock therapy against stagflation.

Thus, interest rate increases are not a reliable instrument for raising domestic savings, but can damage macroeconomic stability and investment. The crucial question is how to design interest rate policies compatible with sustained stability and growth.

The historical experience of major industrial countries holds some useful lessons. Until the 1980s real short-term interest rates in these countries were slightly negative and real long-term bond rates slightly positive; i.e., about 1 to 2 percent below and above inflation respectively. Until the oil shocks of the 1970s, there was sustained growth and price stability. But since the beginning of the 1980s (for reasons to be discussed later) real interest rates have been, on average, more than twice their historical levels. Nevertheless, these countries enjoyed one of the longest periods of economic expansion in the postwar period with low inflation. This generated a widespread perception that high real interest rates do not impede investment and growth, but help price stability. However, the subsequent debt-deflation-cum-recession has clearly shown that economic expansion attained at very high real interest rates eventually depresses income, investment and growth.

C. Financial Liberalization and Deepening

It is generally agreed that financial liberalization raises financial activity relative to the production of goods and nonfinancial services. However, there is much less consensus on the causes and effects of this "financial deepening." According to the financial repression theory (McKinnon 1973; Shaw 1973) financial deepening represents increased intermediation between savers and investment because higher interest rates raise savings and shift them from unproductive assets toward financial assets, thereby raising the volume of productive investment.

While it is true that financial liberalization can shift existing savings toward financial assets, **reallocation** is not the only and even the most important reason for financial deepening. Financial liberalization can also lead to deepening by **redistributing** savings and investment among various sectors, and by creating greater opportunities for **speculation**. Since these can worsen the use of savings, financial deepening is not necessarily a positive development.

The prime role of the financial system in the savings/investment process is to intermediate between deficit and surplus sectors rather than to transfer aggregate savings into aggregate investment. Deficit sectors (typically the corporate sector and the government) save as well as invest, while surplus sectors (households) invest as well as save. Thus, redistribution of savings and investment among sectors can, by changing sectoral surpluses and deficits, result in financial deepening without any change in aggregate savings and investment – for instance, as already noted, when higher interest rates redistribute income and savings from debtors to creditors. Even when this does not alter the volume of aggregate savings (i.e., lower savings of debtors are compensated by higher savings of creditors), it increases deficits and surpluses and, hence, the amount of financial intermediation. Indeed, financial intermediation can increase while aggregate savings and investment fall (Akyüz 1991). This can happen even under the orthodox assumptions that saving rates are positively related to the interest rate and that savings determine investment and growth (Molho 1986, 112).

In such cases financial deepening is a symptom of a deterioration of the finances of the corporate and public sectors, reflecting an accumulation of debt in order to finance the increased interest bill rather than new investment. Financial deepening driven by such Ponzi financing has been observed in a number of countries (e.g., Turkey, Yugoslavia and New Zealand) where financial liberalization redistributed income in favor of creditors and encouraged distress borrowing.

Similarly financial deepening can be the result of a redistribution of a given volume of aggregate investment, when, for instance, higher interest rates induce households to reduce investment in housing and shift to bank deposits. Then, the increase in the household surplus and in the volume of deposits represents a decline in household investment, not a rise in savings.

Financial liberalization often raises holdings of both financial assets and liabilities by firms and individuals at any given level of income, investment and savings. This tendency to borrow in order to purchase assets is driven by the increased scope for capital gains generated by financial liberalization. Liberalization increases the instability of interest rates and asset prices, thereby raising prospects for quick profits through speculation on changes in the market valuation of financial assets. It also allows greater freedom for banks and other financial institutions to lend to finance activities unrelated to production and investment, and to firms and individuals to issue debt in order to finance speculation. These can generate considerable financial activity unrelated to the real economy, and lead to financial deepening – as in the United States in recent years through leverage takeovers, mergers, acquisitions and so on (UNCTAD TDR 1992, part 2, chap. 2).

Deepening can also result from the impact of changes in interest rates on the form in which savings are held. Indeed, one of the main reasons why savings do not in practice strongly respond to increases in real interest rates is the existence of a range of assets with different degrees of protection against inflation; for, returns on such assets also influence savings decisions. The greater the influence of interest rates on the allocation of savings among alternative assets, the smaller the influence on the volume of savings.

Whether shifts of savings into financial assets improve the use of resources depends on where they come from and how efficiently the financial system is operating. Clearly, a switch from commodity holdings can improve the use to which savings are put. But, contrary to widespread perception, there is very little evidence of extensive commodity holding in developing countries as a form of savings. Such holdings entail substantial storage and transaction costs, making their own real rate of return typically negative. Moreover, there is considerable uncertainty regarding the movement of prices of individual commodities even when the general price level is rising rapidly. These factors, together with the existence of more liquid, less costly inflation hedges (such as foreign currency or gold) reduce the demand for commodities as a store of value. The large commodity holdings that exist in African countries typically reflect the nature of production and nonmonetization of the rural economy. Consequently, increases in deposit rates are often unable to induce liquidation of commodity stocks (Aryeetey et al. 1990; Mwega 1990; Nissanke 1990).

An increase in domestic interest rates can induce a shift from foreign currency holdings to domestic assets, and repatriation of flight capital. Many governments, however, have found it necessary to legalize foreign currency holdings and introduce foreign currency deposits for residents and to offer very high interest rates in order to attract foreign currency holdings to the banking system. Certainly, in both cases the portfolio shifts can increase the resources available for investment and deepen finance. However, as discussed in Section H, capital flows and dollarization resulting from such policies often prove troublesome for macroeconomic stability, investment and competitiveness.

Freeing interest rates in the formal sector can also trigger a shift away from informal markets. However, the scope of such shifts may be limited since the reason for informal markets is not always interest rate controls and credit rationing. They often provide services to small and medium producers who do not have access to bank credits. Since financial liberalization does not always improve their access to banks, informal markets continue to operate after the deregulation of interest rates. As savings placed in the informal sector assure these producers some access to credit, they are not always willing to shift to banks when deposit rates are raised (Chipeta 1990; Aryeteey et al. 1990; Mwega 1990). On the other hand, when funds are shifted to banks, the cost of finance for informal market borrowers can rise considerably. Moreover, such shifts can result in financial "shallowing" because informal markets provide more financial intermediation due to the absence of liquidity and reserve requirements (van Wijnbergen 1983; Owen and Solis-Fallas 1989).

It can thus be concluded that financial deepening brought about by liberalization is not necessarily associated with a higher level and/or better use of savings. Indeed, the empirical evidence does not support the claim that financial deepening is associated with faster growth (Dornbusch and Reynoso 1989). The degree of financial deepening is therefore not a good measure of the contribution of finance to growth and development.

The relevant issue in financial reform is efficiency rather than deepening. There are various concepts of efficiency of financial markets and institutions (Tobin 1984), but from the point of view of the role of finance in economic growth and development, the conventional notions of **allocative** and **productive** (i.e., **cost) efficiency** are the most relevant ones.

D. Allocative Efficiency

1. Market failure

Financial markets and institutions can be said to be **allocatively efficient** if they direct resources to their more socially productive use, i.e., if they finance investment with the highest social rates of return. This concept broadly corresponds to what Tobin (1984, 3) calls functional efficiency and provides a rationale for devoting resources to financial activity.

Allocative efficiency is closely related to the extent of "the accuracy with which market valuations reflect fundamentals" ("fundamental-valuation efficiency," Tobin 1984, 5). Prices of financial assets provide market signals for resource allocation. Speculative bubbles in securities markets influence investment and consumption decisions as well as financing plans of corporations while exchange rate misalignments cause misallocation of resources between traded and nontraded goods sectors.

There is ample evidence that in industrial countries financial liberalization has resulted in a considerable increase in the volatility of interest rates, equity prices, exchange rates and the prices of real estate, gold, silver and collectable assets, and caused large and sustained deviation of these from their fundamental values (e.g., Cutler, Poterba and Summers 1990; Miller and Weller 1991; Kupiec 1991). Similarly, "(t)akeover mania, motivated by egregious undervaluations, is testimony to the failure of the market on this fundamental-valuation criterion efficiency" (Tobin 1984, 6). These deviations reflect the pervasiveness of speculative forces: "the similarity of patterns in a wide range of asset markets suggests the possibility that they are best explicable as a consequence of the speculative process itself" (Cutler, Poterba and Summers 1990, 36).

Quite apart from the distorting effects of speculation on asset prices and resource allocation, financial markets also fail to allocate resources efficiently because of a number of imperfections not attributable to government intervention. These include missing markets, asymmetric and incomplete information, and various externalities not mediated by markets (Stiglitz and Weiss 1981; Greenwald and Stiglitz 1986; Stiglitz 1989a; Datta-Chaudhuri 1990). Such market failures are more serious in developing than in developed countries and tend to obstruct the learning process which plays a key role in modern industrialization. "Learning [...] means that it will not be optimal to pursue myopic policies; one cannot use current comparative advantage as the only basis for judgments of how to allocate resources. Moreover, it may be optimal to initially incur a loss; the imperfections of capital markets thus may impose a more serious impediment on LDCs taking advantage of potentials for learning" (Stiglitz 1989a, 199).

2. *Successful intervention*

Governments in many countries have therefore acted to influence the allocation and pricing of finance as part of their industrial policy. Indeed, almost all modern examples of industrialization have been accompanied by such intervention. Directed and preferential credits have been the most important instruments of some successful industrializers in East Asia (Amsden 1989; Bradford 1986; Cho and Khatkhate 1989; Hanson and Neal 1985; Westphal 1990). As noted by a recent report, in Japan an important instrument of intervention was policy-based finance, used through the Japan Development Bank "to induce the private sector to achieve specified policy objectives." It was based on the recognition that "if the private financial market were perfect (in terms of competition, information and freedom of transactions) policy-based finance would be unnecessary. In reality, however, there are limits to the perfect fulfillment of these conditions in the financial market. Thus, one can understand the significance of policy-based finance as one means of compensating for these market limitations" (Kato et al. 1993, 28).

In the Republic of Korea "government intervention was necessary not just to steer credit in the right direction but to underwrite production during the learning process that was far more involved than what is commonly meant by 'infant industry protection.' Subsidized credit meant the difference between establishing new industries or not, rather than the difference between high and low profits" (Amsden and Euh 1990, 31). Thus, "extensive intervention by the government with South Korea's financial system can be viewed as an internal capital market and, consequently, it could have led to a more efficient allocation of credit than possible in a free-market financial system" (Lee 1992, 187).

But many countries have directed credit with much less success. The differences between successful and unsuccessful intervention have been partly due to skill in "picking winners." While it is true that governments are not necessarily better equipped to do this than markets, the experience strongly suggests that whether a firm (or an industry) is a winner depends on how it is managed. A number of factors seem to separate success from failure in this respect:

- The ability of governments to prevent the interventionist finance from degenerating into inflationary finance, to resist excessive credit expansion and to ensure fiscal discipline: macroeconomic stability appears to have been a more important factor in growth than financial liberalization and deepening (Dornbusch and Reynoso 1989).
- To make provision of support conditional upon good performance, and to see that government support and protection are actually used for the purposes intended rather than simply as a handout.
- To design objective, well-defined and market-based performance indicators –namely, competitiveness in world markets and export performance – in order to assess the nature and extent of the support needed, and whether it is being used effectively (Amsden 1989; Westphal 1990).
- To attain social consensus on the purpose and modalities of government intervention. As noted by a recent report this was particularly important in the success of the policy-based finance in Japan: "when the government does intervene in private economic activities, or carries out economic activities itself in place of private actors, it must not merely give some abstract reason, but rather clearly explain the concrete need for and obtain social agreement on those activities" (Kato et al. 1993, 28). This has been achieved through "extensive participation of the private sector in the policy-formation process based on the public-private cooperative system," i.e., in the advisory councils including "industry leaders and general citizens" as well as bureaucrats, which are still widely used (Kato et al. 1993, 85).

3. Measuring efficiency

As noted above, the main impulse to financial liberalization in developing countries has come from the frustration with ineffective and wasteful intervention and the belief that liberalization would raise allocative efficiency. Thus, many countries have chosen to liberalize finance rather than reform their industrial policies and state intervention. However, this has not always resulted in a better allocation of credits.

In the orthodox theory better allocation means a tendency toward equalization of rates of return on investment in different sectors. Similarly, a more efficient credit allocation is expected to reduce the variation of the cost of finance across borrowers on the assumption that profit maximization requires equalization of marginal cost of borrowing and marginal rate of return on investment (Cho 1988).

These measures, however, are highly inappropriate. First of all, as discussed below, one important determinant of the rate of return and cost of capital is risk. When projects carry different risks, an optimal allocation must reflect these differences in rates of return and borrowing costs. More important, when capital markets are short-sighted, equalization of profit rates typically means discriminating against those firms and industries with dynamic comparative advantages and learning potentials that have to incur initial losses. Since financial liberalization is often associated with a shortening of time horizons, a tendency toward equalization of rates of profit and cost of capital could worsen allocation.

Financial liberalization normally reduces or eliminates credits on preferential terms and hence diminishes variations in cost of capital across sectors. Therefore, measuring the effect of financial liberalization on allocative efficiency in terms of reduced variations in cost of capital is tautological. On the other hand, a successful industrial policy could reduce variance in borrowing cost by diminishing the number of industries requiring special treatment. For instance, it has been argued that the decline in the inter-industry variance of borrowing costs in the Republic of Korea in the 1980s compared to the 1970s reflects the success not of financial liberalization as suggested by some authors (e.g., Cho 1988), but of industrialization policies (Amsden and Euh 1990, 43–44).

Financial liberalization in developing countries often changes significantly the sectoral allocation of credit. Evidence suggests that typically the shares of service sectors, consumer loans and property-related credits tend to increase at the expense of industry. This may result from a reduction in directed credit allocation, which often favors industry and does not necessarily indicate a deterioration of resource allocation. However, it is important to note that these changes are often associated with shortening of maturities and declines in demand for manufacturing investment credits, when liberalization takes place in an unstable environment and results in very high and volatile interest rates.

Perhaps more important indicators of the effects of financial liberalization on allocative efficiency are the number of nonperforming loans, loan default rates and bank failures. Evidence from a number of countries (e.g., the Southern Cone countries, Indonesia, Philippines, Turkey and Yugoslavia) indicates that deregulation of interest rates and elimination of restrictions on financial activities have almost always been followed by increases in the proportion of nonperforming loans in bank portfolios and in bank failures. Again, resort to liberalization to cure instability and stagnation has often played an important role. These, together with external shocks, had already greatly weakened the balance sheets of the corporate sector and financial institutions. Deregulation of interest rates, often accompanied by monetary tightening, further disrupted the financial position of the highly leveraged corporate sector, leading to increased loan default rates and eventually to bank failures.

E. Productive Efficiency and Cost of Finance

The traditional concept of productive efficiency refers to microeconomic efficiency of firms in producing goods and services with given prices for their inputs. When applied to the financial system, this concept would simply be translated into intermediation cost or interest spread. However, one must approach productive efficiency from a broader perspective and define it as the ability of the financial **system** to provide finance at the lowest possible cost. This depends not only on the extent to which financial intermediaries minimize the cost of intermediation between the ultimate lender and the ultimate borrower, but also on the ability of the entire financial system to minimize the interest paid to the ultimate lender (the lender's interest rate).

1. Risk, uncertainty and interest rates

The Keynesian notions of **lender's** and **borrower's** risks provide an appropriate framework for discussing the determinants of cost of finance and the effects of financial liberalization on productive efficiency (Keynes 1936, 144). An important determinant of the lender's interest rate is the risk due to the possibility of default by the borrower, i.e., the lender's risk. First, there is the risk of voluntary default, or what Keynes calls the moral risk: the lender must make an allowance for the possibility of dishonesty of the borrower. Second, involuntary default arising from imperfect foresight, i.e., from uncertainties over factors outside the control of the borrower which affect profitability. This risk, called the borrower's risk or the pure risk, is inherent in all investment decisions and cannot be eliminated. However, it can be reduced by the access of the borrower to better information and more stable economic conditions. The pure risk is closely related to allocative efficiency. When finance is not efficiently allocated, the probability of involuntary default increases. This raises the lender's risk and the cost of finance: allocative inefficiency thus aggravates cost inefficiency.

The lender also runs a risk regarding the capital value of his assets due to uncertainties over future interest rates and asset prices (as well as the price level). The capital-value uncertainty increases with the volatility of asset prices and interest rates, as well as with the increased frequency of bank failures. These raise liquidity preference and lower the demand for capital-uncertain assets, thereby shortening the maturities of financial assets and pushing up interest rates, especially long term. The degree of productive efficiency of the financial system therefore depends in part on its ability to attain stability and reduce capital-value uncertainty.

The search for greater allocative efficiency through financial liberalization can greatly reduce the productive efficiency of the financial system by giving rise to increased financial instability and raising the cost of finance to investors. This is a systemic influence, quite independent of any rise in interest rates that may result from eliminating ceilings. Indeed, the financial instability and bank failures stemming from financial liberalization in the major industrial countries, especially the United States, in the 1980s played a major role in considerably raising long-term interest rates and reducing their sensitivity to changes in short-term rates (Akyüz 1992, 59–60).

2. Intermediation margin

The second component of cost of finance, namely the intermediation margin, reflects the microeconomic efficiency in the use of resources devoted to financial activity. This is particularly important in bank finance even though mark-ups of intermediaries in stock exchanges are not negligible (Tobin 1984, 4). The spread between lending and deposit rates is influenced by operating expenses, legal reserve and liquidity requirements as well as by the pressure of competition on profit mark-ups. Reserve and liquidity requirements are typically lowered as part of financial liberalization. Similarly, operating expenses and profit mark-ups tend to fall as entry barriers are dismantled.

However, financial liberalization also tends to increase the spread by raising the rate of default on loans since banks often pass the cost of bad loans onto other borrowers. Therefore, erroneous investment and financing decisions and allocative inefficiency can lead to cost inefficiency by raising not only the lender's interest rate, but also the spread. The increase in the cost of finance, in turn, can push sound borrowers into insolvency, thereby increasing loan default rates and pushing up the lender's risk and the lender's interest rate further. This often leads to Ponzi financing whereby banks increasingly lend to high-risk, speculative business at very high interest rates in order to cover high deposit rates and defaults. Such a process is unsustainable, but it can nevertheless cause considerable waste.

F. Regulation of Finance and Financial Stability

The preceding discussion has shown that stability is an essential attribute of an efficient financial system. After many episodes of turmoil in financial markets in both developing and developed countries, there now appears to exist a consensus on the need for prudential regulations in order to attain stability. But, can such regulations and supervision prevent financial instability when interest rates are allowed to fluctuate freely and banks are left free to compete for deposits by bidding up interest rates?

1. Risk taking by banks

The theory of finance suggests that because information is imperfect and asymmetric (the borrower knows more about his investment than the lender) and contracts are incomplete (lenders cannot control all aspects of the borrower's behavior), banks implement their own quantity rationing by imposing credit ceilings, and restrict deposit and loan rates in order to avoid excessive risk taking (Stiglitz and Weiss 1981; Davis 1993, 13–16). Since higher interest rates tend to reduce the average quality of loans through adverse selection (lending to high-risk borrowers willing to pay high interest rates) and moral hazard (inducing "good" borrowers to invest in riskier projects), the expected rate of return net of default will decline once the loan rate has reached a certain level. This implies that even in the absence of prudential regulations, there will be limits to price competition and risk taking in the banking sector.

However, self-restraint cannot always be relied on to prevent financial instability, particularly in developing countries. Banks tend to engage in speculative financing and excessive risk taking provided that failure does not have serious consequences for their shareholders and managers. This happens when they can easily acquire deposit insurance, enjoy implicit or explicit guarantees for bailout and have easy access to the lender-of-last-resort facility, and when sanctions and penalties for failing bank managers are inadequate. This is often the case in developing countries where governments are often all too ready to rescue banks in trouble. The moral hazard that results is made worse by the existence of deposit insurance schemes designed to give protection to depositors and attract funds into banks. Banks often have to pay very little for the insurance coverage while having all the incentives to raise deposit rates to mobilize funds to invest in high-return, high-risk, and often speculative projects.

Furthermore, in developing countries large nonfinancial corporations are often able to exert strong influence over banks, causing bank lending to be concentrated on a small number of firms, at the cost of increasing their own vulnerability. Corporate distress borrowing and Ponzi financing tend to be much more common in developing countries, and these become particularly visible and problematic during episodes of financial liberalization. The intense competition that banks in many developing countries face from unregulated financial markets can also lead to higher interest rates and greater risk taking.

2. Prudential regulations

Evidence from both developed and developing countries shows that a judicious combination of effective prudential and protective regulations is necessary to prevent financial instability. In many developing countries, however, regulations restricting excessive risk taking and/or covering such risks are absent. In some countries government restrictions on lending to a single firm and the acquisition of real estate or shares in nonfinancial corporations are strict but not implemented. Legal provisions against bad assets are either absent or ignored, and capital requirements are either inadequate or nonexistent or unimplemented. There is a widespread noncompliance even with legal reserve requirements, not always because they are especially high, but because the monetary authorities are unable to impose sufficient penalties.

However, prudential regulations, while necessary, may not always be sufficient to prevent financial instability. With the freeing of deposit rates considerable competition can build up between the newly deregulated and unregulated financial sectors, giving rise to sharp increases in deposit rates, thereby raising the loan rates and deteriorating the quality of bank assets as high-yield, high-risk lending replaces safer but lower-yielding portfolios. It is not always possible to check this process through prudential regulations on the asset side of banks' balance sheets. Pressures can develop to allow banks to enter into new lines of business in order to restore their profitability and viability in the face of higher deposit cost. Such pressures will often find favor with the liberalist view underlying interest rate deregulation, and hence result in the relaxation of constraints on types of bank lending and investment.

The experience of the United States in the 1980s illustrates how easily such a process can develop (UNCTAD TDR 1992, part 2, chap. 2). As the Fed moved away from targeting interest rates to monetarism in order to reduce inflation, and the Regulation Q ceilings on deposit rates were lifted, banks with long-term portfolios with fixed interest rates (particularly mutual savings banks and Savings and Loan Associations, S&Ls) experienced serious difficulties. Considerable pressure developed for the introduction of legislation to attract deposits to these institutions (e.g., raising deposit insurance limits) and to allow them to invest in high-yield, high-risk assets. Thus, these institutions, and subsequently commercial banks, increasingly financed consumer and credit card loans, high-yield noninvestment grade (junk) bonds, leverage buy-outs, real estate acquisition, and development and construction loans. A large amount of debt was accumulated by households and firms while banks acquired high-risk assets. This process ended with the collapse of the S&Ls with an estimated cost of about $200 billion, and was replaced by a debt-deflation process already mentioned.

Stricter capital adequacy requirements of the type recently introduced by BIS (UNCTAD TDR 1992, part 2, annex 1) could have helped to slow down this process but would probably not have prevented it. As there was simultaneously a speculative bubble in the stock market, banks would have had no difficulty in raising capital at very favorable terms to cover their high-risk investment, but would have remained exposed to risks on both sides of their balance sheets. Indeed, this is exactly what happened in Japan where banks can account as capital almost half of accrued but unrealized capital gains on equities and use them to offset potential loan losses. As the stock market was rising rapidly in the 1980s, banks counted on these gains instead of setting aside reserves against potential losses on high-risk, property-related lending. The subsequent decline in stock prices, together with the fall in property prices, thus created difficulties for banks from both sides of their balance sheets.

There are also other instances of boom and bust where rapid expansion of some banks through high-risk, high-return lending increased their stock prices sharply and allowed them to raise capital at costs lower than the prudent banks. "In such cases neither public scrutiny of bank balance sheets, nor capital ratios would have prevented the propagation of the crisis" (Kregel 1993, 10).

3. Interest ceilings

In short, competition among financial institutions can easily result in escalation of interest rates and/or excessive risk taking either because prudential capital requirements become ineffective or pressures build up for relaxing controls over bank asset portfolios. Such risks are greater in developing countries. This, together with the fact that stability of interest rates and asset prices is essential for an efficient financial system, constitutes a strong case in favor of controlling interest rates as well as bank lending.

An effective way of doing this is to impose statutory ceilings on deposit and/or loan rates. Such ceilings have been widely used in industrial countries until recent years. In Japan, for instance, interest rate regulations played a crucial role throughout the postwar period and have not yet been abolished totally. Again, the recent legislation in the United States regarding the depository institutions (the Federal Deposit Insurance Corporation Improvement Act of 1991, Jones and King 1992) stipulates mandatory restrictions on deposit interest rates for undercapitalized banks in the context of capital-based policy of prompt corrective action. Since undercapitalization is widespread among banks in developing countries, the scope for the application of such restrictions must be much greater.

Regulation of short-term interest rates through intervention in interbank markets is also essential for attaining greater financial stability and preventing frequent bank failures, particularly when there is considerable maturity mismatching between banks' assets and liabilities. Under such conditions, large swings in interest rates can create serious dilemmas for banks. If banks respond to an unexpected increase in market interest rates by raising deposit rates, their profits can be sharply reduced and their solvency threatened. If they do not, or if they are prevented to do so by deposit ceilings, they may suffer a considerable deposit drain. Banks can respond to increased swings in short-term rates with variable rate loans or by shortening the maturities of their assets, as they have indeed done in many countries, but when done on a large enough scale this simply transfers the interest rate risk onto the borrower and replaces it with greater credit risk.

It should be kept in mind that control over interest rates through ceilings and intervention does not eliminate the need for certain types of prudential regulations to reduce financial fragility, i.e., vulnerability to default in the corporate and household sectors (Minsky 1982, 1986; Davis 1993). This is particularly true in developing countries where the level of economic activity is much more variable. When activity is buoyant, banks tend to lend increasingly against assets which carry considerable capital risk, including not only illiquid assets such as property but also securities; they also expand consumer credits and invest directly in securities and property. But when the expansion comes to an end and incomes and asset prices start to fall, the quality of bank assets can deteriorate rapidly, and even set off a debt-deflation process and credit crunch. Reducing the fragility of the financial system thus calls for prudential regulations designed to prevent excessive investment and lending with considerable capital risk arising from their susceptibility to changes in the pace of economic activity.

G. Options in Financial Organizations

The discussions above suggest that the efficiency of the financial system crucially depends on the way it is organized because that influences the nature and the degree of risk, uncertainty and instability. On the other hand, the experience of industrial countries shows that there is no single way of organizing finance. Consequently, an important issue in financial reform in developing (and Eastern European) countries is what types of financial institutions and markets need to be promoted.

1. Bank-oriented and market-oriented finance

It is possible to distinguish between two broad types of financial arrangements according to whether or not banks and capital markets serve distinct functions. In an ideal-type **differentiated** system banks act primarily within the monetary system, arranging payments and extending short-term commercial credits. Corporations obtain investment finance in the capital market by direct security issues, often via the intermediation of investment banks for underwriting and brokerage. Ownership of companies is highly fragmented: an important part of corporate securities is held by households and institutional investors in diversified portfolios. Such a segmentation is the essence of the Anglo-American system which we will call, for brevity, the **market-oriented** system.[2]

In the German-type of **universal banking** (the **bank-oriented** system), on the other hand, commercial banks play a much greater role at all stages in the process of corporate investment. They provide investment finance and function also, like investment banks. They also have considerable control over firms both through their own equity holding and proxy votes for private investors, and by appointing representatives on the boards of firms. They lend primarily to firms in which they hold equity interest. Household financial wealth tends to be held in banks rather than direct securities, and bank credits account for a larger proportion of external financing of corporate investment

There are certainly a number of variants combining elements of both systems. In the United Kingdom commercial banks do not have much control over corporations, but there is no legal separation between commercial and investment banking In Japan commercial banks hold corporate equities but are prevented from playing a major role in the underwriting of corporate securities. Individual ownership of stocks is much smaller than ownership by financial and nonfinancial corporations, and corporate equity is controlled through interlocking shareholding within industrial groups where banks play a central role. Banks also control other financial institutions (e.g. pension funds) that invest in equity. Lending by banks and insurance and pension funds usually takes place within the same groups and involves purchase of company bonds as well as loans. In Japan bank credits have played a much more important role in financing business growth than in the other countries discussed here, although recently there has been a shift to securities markets.

2. *Efficiency of alternative systems*

In recent years many developing countries have been seeking to institute and promote capital markets, often as part of the structural adjustment programs. One of the main reasons for privatizing public enterprises has been precisely to promote capital markets. Similarly, access to equity markets has been granted to nonresidents in order to boost demand.

There are a number of arguments in favor of developing capital markets as a way of overcoming the paucity of investment finance in developing countries. The bank-oriented system of investment finance has traditionally been viewed as inherently problematic because of the risks associated with maturity transformation in a volatile economic environment. Such a system increases the vulnerability of firms to financial shocks since the cost and availability of bank credit often undergo sharp and unexpected changes. By contrast, capital markets are expected to provide firms with more predictable, longer-term finance, while secondary markets in securities accord savers liquidity. It is also often argued that they would exert better financial discipline over firms through shareholder action and the threat of being taken over by other firms.

While there are often serious problems and weaknesses in bank-oriented finance in developing countries, the benefits claimed for a market-oriented system are unsubstantiated. It is often overlooked that the financial systems in Germany and Japan have not only proved to be remarkably stable, but also in the major respects discussed in Sections D and E are more efficient than the Anglo-American system. Historically, financial asset prices and interest rates in Germany and Japan have been less volatile than in the United States, bank deposits more stable, and financial disruptions and bank failures less frequent. Moreover, the cost of finance to industry has been much lower in Germany and, more particularly, in Japan. Evidence suggests that high capital costs have contributed to declining competitiveness both in industry and international banking in the United States. Lower capital costs and a more predictable supply of finance appear to have enabled Japanese firms to undertake longer-term projects, including investment in research and development, whereas United States firms have been deterred (McCauley and Zimmer 1989; Poterba 1991; Zimmer and McCauley 1991).[3]

One of the main reasons for the greater stability and efficiency of the financial systems in Germany and Japan is their ability to overcome the dilemma posed by modern capital markets. As noted by Keynes (1936, chap. 12), modern capital markets reconcile the social need for investment with the preference of individual investors for liquidity. This is a necessity since "if individual purchases of investment were rendered illiquid, this might seriously impede new investment." However, while secondary markets in securities accord savers liquidity, they also open up prospects for speculation whereby most of the players "are, in fact, largely concerned, not with making superior long-term forecasts of the probable yield of an investment over its whole life, but with foreseeing changes in the conventional basis of valuation a short time ahead of the general public." Thus, these markets tend to operate like "casinos" where players speculate on the speculations of other players.

The pattern of shareholding and ownership that characterizes the German and the Japanese systems has allowed them largely to overcome this dilemma. The fact that banks and business groups with a long-term stake in the corporations hold the controlling interest means not only that secondary markets tend to be less active and volatile, but also that the managers do not need to pay much attention to how the market values their assets from day to day, and can concentrate instead on the long term. This also helps reduce liquidity preference and short-termism on the part of individual investors and portfolio managers.

The bank-oriented system can exert a different and more efficient financial discipline over enterprises than the market-oriented system. Banks in Germany and Japan (and banking groups) are often in a position to monitor the performance of management by direct access to information through their close and long-term relations with firms as shareholders and creditors, and to intervene when needed in order to prevent failure. By contrast, in the Anglo-American system of fragmented shareholding, individual investors have neither the means nor the incentive to monitor and control corporate management. In extreme cases, market discipline is exercised through hostile takeovers, but these are often disruptive and wasteful. More importantly, since markets tend to value the enterprise largely on the basis of short-term financial performance, the takeover threat creates pressures and incentives for the management to think short term.

Furthermore, the internal capital market organized within banks and firms connected by cross shareholding also improves enterprise performance by reducing the borrower's risk by permitting economies of scale in collecting, processing, evaluating and disseminating information. For the same reason, there is less credit rationing in a bank-based system (Fama 1985; Driscoll 1991). Such a system also permits to reduce considerably the lender's risk and the rate of interest since it provides deposit holders the liquidity they seek at a smaller risk of capital uncertainty by pooling and institutionalizing the risk associated with individual investment projects, and by reducing erroneous investment decisions.

A financial system with a close interface between banks and corporations tends to lower the rate of return required by investors to undertake investment. The expected rate of return on investment must be high enough to cover both the borrower's risk and the rate of interest received by the lender. However, as noted above, the borrower's risk is an important determinant of the lender's risk. The effect of this duplication of the borrower's risk on the rate of interest can be reduced by increasing the degree of the lender's involvement in the borrower's investment and other managerial decisions, since the lender is then better able to assure himself that pure risk is being properly weighed by the borrower: indeed both components of the lender's risk (i.e., the moral risk and the pure risk) would disappear if the lender and the borrower were the same person. The bank-oriented system thus reduces the extent to which the borrower's risk is duplicated in the lender's risk and the interest rate, and, hence, lowers the cost of investment.

3. Requirements for an efficient bank-oriented system

These are particularly important considerations to be taken into account in reforming the financial system in developing countries where the cost of finance needs to be kept low and firms must be able to take the long view in order to succeed in "learning by doing." However, the experience of many developing countries shows that the concentration of ownership in the hands of inside investors and close relations between banks and corporations are not necessarily conducive to good enterprise performance and financial stability. Indeed, in many developing countries the equity control of corporations is in the hands of families or business groups, and interlocking ownership between corporations and banks is widespread. Such arrangements have often resulted in corruption, collusive behavior, speculation and inefficiency. Moreover, financial instability and short-termism in bank and corporate behavior are common features of these countries because a number of conditions essential for an efficient bank-oriented system are not always met.

First of all, for the reasons already explained, price stability is essential for a bank-oriented system. This calls for, above all, fiscal and monetary discipline and a viable and relatively stable external payments position. Prudential regulations and effective supervision are also essential in a bank-oriented system. In particular, firms should not be allowed to own and control banking organizations since this will transfer the elements of the safety net to them, and burden the monetary authorities with tasks they cannot undertake (Corrigan 1991). In the German system prudential limits on long-term lending and individual loans, capital adequacy requirements, and effective supervision of banks' risk exposure by an agency separate from the central bank play a central role.

One argument against market-oriented finance is that "competition in ownership is no substitute for competition in product markets" (Corbett and Mayer 1991, 20). This is also true for the bank-oriented system; namely, it does not make up for lack of competition in the markets for goods and services. Thus, such a system too needs to be combined with policies depending on competition as a spur to efficiency. In those developing countries where the bank-oriented system with widespread interlocking ownership has failed, the markets for goods and services were generally highly oligopolistic and protected from competition. By contrast, in countries where corporations were encouraged and forced to compete in export markets, a similar financial organization made a major contribution to industrialization.

Finally, new firms should have access to finance and entry into new lines of financial activity should not be impeded. This calls for some competition in the banking sector. However, competition policies should be designed to prevent monopoly power rather than to allow completely free entry into the banking sector and unlimited price competition among banks – practices that have often led to financial instability in both developed and developing countries. Furthermore, specialized banks for industrial development and controls over credit allocation can play an important role in providing finance to new entrants.

4. Control and regulation of stock markets

While reform efforts need to concentrate in these areas, it is also true that capital markets are a reality in a number of countries and they also need to be improved. While most developing countries regulate primary issues and stipulate a number of conditions regarding their size, maturity and redemption and disclosure of information there is very little effective control over secondary markets. Irregularities such as insider trading and fraud are widespread and administrative capacity to undertake effective supervision weak.

Stock prices in many of the so-called emerging markets have been extremely erratic and subject to very large swings. By removing credit constraints financial liberalization has often triggered an increase in speculative activity by institutions and individuals. In many such countries, increased speculative activity in the secondary market caused stock prices to rise before 1987 even faster than in most of the world's major stock markets, and to fall, again far more than elsewhere, after October 1987 (Singh 1992). Most of these markets have again shown large swings over the last few years.

Since the size of these markets is relatively small, the direct effects of sharp falls in stock prices on the economy are negligible. However, the state of expectations in the equities market influences the exchange rate and capital flows since, as discussed in the next section, these markets are open to foreigners and/or provide alternative investment for holders of foreign currency assets. Greater stability is thus essential to prevent destabilizing feedbacks between equity and currency markets.

One way of reducing volatility is through the so-called "circuit breakers" introduced in the United States after the October 1987 crash (Kupiec, 1991). These consist of predetermined price floors: when prices fall to the floor, trading is suspended for a predetermined period. Such measures can be particularly helpful in reducing intra-day bandwagon-type declines in stock prices. Another is through the financial transactions tax long advocated by Keynes (1936, 160–61). Such a tax may help reduce speculative instability by deterring short-term trading, improve the efficiency of the stock market and lengthen the time horizon of corporate managers (Stiglitz 1989b; Summers and Summers 1989).

Public or semi-public agencies with large holdings of securities can also play an important role in bringing greater stability to stock prices. For instance, in Turkey the agency dealing with privatization has operated both as a buyer and a seller in the market for the shares of privatized public companies, exerting a significant influence on prices, even though its objective has not been to stabilize the market. Institutional investors and particularly provident funds can both provide the Japanese/German-type of shareholding and control over enterprises, and help to attain greater stability.

H. External Liberalization and Financial Openness

Recent years have witnessed the increased integration of developing countries into the international financial system in large part due to widespread external financial liberalization. Most of these countries have also liberalized imports and increasingly relied on exports for growth, but the degree of internationalization of finance has gone much further than trade. Indeed in many countries the share of transactions with international characteristics in the financial sector is far greater than the share of trade in GDP.

1. The concept of financial openness

By external financial liberalization we mean policy actions that increase the degree of the ease with which residents can acquire assets and liabilities denominated in foreign currencies and nonresidents can operate in national financial markets, i.e., financial openness. Three broad types of transaction can be distinguished in this respect. First, **inward** transactions: allowing residents to borrow freely in international financial markets, and nonresidents to invest freely in domestic financial markets. Second, **outward** transactions: allowing residents to transfer capital and to hold financial assets abroad, and nonresidents to issue liabilities and to borrow in domestic financial markets. Third, **domestic transactions in foreign currencies**: allowing debtor–creditor relations among residents in foreign currencies such as bank deposits and lending in foreign currencies.

Our definition of financial openness is wider than capital account liberalization because it includes financial transactions among residents denominated in foreign currencies. These are an important part of banking and finance, and affect the national economy in much the same way as cross-border financial transactions (Bryant 1987, chap. 3).

2. The extent of financial openness in developing countries

Widespread liberalization has occurred on all three fronts. Inward transactions are virtually free in a large number of countries, particularly in Latin America where external borrowing by the private sector, often **via** the intermediation of resident banks, is not subject to approval, except for capital market issues. Similarly, there are few restrictions on the access of nonresident investors to domestic capital markets. The debt crisis has played an important role in this respect: the "market-based menu" has generated new prospects for arbitrage and windfall profits and significantly raised the amount of equities and domestic currency debt assets held by nonresidents (UNCTAD TDR 1989, 105–107). More recently, access of nonresidents to national equity markets has been encouraged in the context of privatization programs.

As for outward transactions, an increasing number of developing countries have adopted capital account convertibility in recent years – some to an extent not found in most industrialized countries. Liberalization of transactions among residents in foreign currency, however, has gone much further. Indeed, there has been a tendency to encourage residents to hold foreign exchange deposits with banks at home, increasing the importance of foreign currency in the economy, i.e., dollarization. The share of foreign currency in total deposits in recent years reached 50 percent in a number of developing countries in Latin America as well as in Asia (e.g., Philippines), the Middle East and Europe (e.g., Turkey and Yugoslavia). This figure is well above the levels found in some international financial centers such as London where the share of total bank claims (including interbank claims) on residents in foreign currencies barely exceeds 20 percent (Bryant 1987, chap. 3; Akyüz 1992).

3. Nature of capital flows

The consequences of financial openness in developing countries have not been adequately treated in the literature primarily because this is a very recent phenomenon. Mainstream thinking is largely an extrapolation of "open economy macroeconomics," and treats the issue in the context of "sequencing of economic reforms." This literature emerged in large part from an ex post attempt to explain why the Southern Cone liberalization experiment failed (Corbo et al. 1986; Corbo and de Melo 1987; Diaz-Alejandro 1985; Dornbusch 1983; Frankel 1983; McKinnon 1982). It takes it for granted that external financial liberalization is desirable on efficiency grounds: it is said to have positive effects on the level and allocation of investment, and these efficiency gains more than compensate for the loss of policy autonomy, i.e., reduced ability of governments to achieve national objectives by using the policy instruments at their disposal (Bryant 1980, chap. 12).

According to this view, external financial liberalization may give rise to perverse results only if there are problems elsewhere in the economy, e.g., budget deficits, monetary instability, and distortions and imperfections in goods and labor markets. On the other hand, since it is not possible to correct these at once, external financial liberalization must be properly sequenced. Although it is sometimes argued (e.g., Krueger 1984) that it may be difficult to control inflation without liberalizing the economy, the majority view is that domestic financial markets and the current account should be liberalized before the capital account, and that fiscal balance and monetary stability should be attained before any liberalization (Dornbusch 1983; Edwards 1984, 1987 and 1989; Fischer and Reisen 1992; Frankel 1983; McKinnon 1982).

The benefits claimed for financial openness are generally based on the assumption that the internationalization of finance allows savings to be pooled and allocated globally through movement of capital across countries in response to opportunities for real investment, thereby improving the allocation of resources internationally and equalizing rates of return on investment everywhere. Accordingly, external financial liberalization in developing countries is expected to give rise to capital inflows provided that it comes after domestic financial markets have been liberalized and interest rates raised. This is seen as a one-off phenomenon of adjustment of domestic interest rates to world levels as capital scarcity is reduced through an increase in the underlying capital flows.

However, the evidence strongly suggests that international capital flows do not in practice improve the international allocation of savings. There has been no narrowing of differences in rates of return on capital investment in the major industrial countries, or in real long-term interest rates; nor has the link between the levels of savings and investment in individual countries been considerably weakened (UNCTAD TDR 1987; Kasman and Pigott 1988; McCauley and Zimmer 1989; Akyüz 1992). The main reason is that most international financial transactions are portfolio decisions, largely by rentiers, rather than business decisions by entrepreneurs. The bulk of capital movements is motivated primarily by the prospect of short-term capital gains, rather than by real investment opportunities and considerations of long-term risk and return. The speculative element is capable of generating gyrations in exchange rates and financial asset prices by causing sudden reversals in capital flows for reasons unrelated to policies and/or the underlying fundamentals. Rather than penalizing inappropriate policies, capital flows can help to sustain them, as has been the case in recent years in the United States and Italy where inflows have helped to run chronic fiscal deficits.

Thus, financial openness tends to create **systemic** problems regardless of the order in which various markets are liberalized and distortions removed. The exposure to short-term, speculative capital flows is much greater for developing than for developed countries because their instability provides greater opportunities for quick, windfall profits on short-term capital movements while their ability to influence capital flows through monetary policy is much more limited.

While internal financial liberalization strengthens the link between inflation and interest rates, external financial liberalization (unlike trade liberalization) weakens that between inflation and the exchange rate, bringing the latter under the domination of capital flows instead of trade balances and the relative purchasing power of currencies: inflation differentials are more readily reflected in nominal interest rate differentials than in the movement of the nominal exchange rate. Thus, although short-term capital inflows motivated by the lure of quick, windfall profits are often associated with positive **real** interest rate differentials in favor of the recipient, such a differential is neither necessary nor sufficient in all cases. Capital inflows usually occur in response to a **nominal** interest rate differential that markets do not expect to be fully matched by a nominal exchange rate depreciation. Such differentials often emerge when domestic inflation is much higher than abroad and domestic financial markets have been liberalized. Since in many developing countries inflation rates close to those prevailing in the major OECD countries are very difficult to attain, the scope for big arbitrage opportunities to emerge is much greater. Similarly, an expectation that equity prices will rise faster than domestic currency depreciation can prompt an inflow of capital.

Both types of expectation can be self-fulfilling since the inflow of funds, if large enough, can itself maintain the value of the currency and boost equity prices.

Such inflows are typically initially a response to a favorable shift in market sentiment regarding the recipient country. This shift may result from external causes such as a sudden rise in export prices, or from internal ones such as reduced inflation, better growth prospects, and greater political stability and confidence in the government's policies. After the initial shift in market sentiment, a bandwagon develops and creates a speculative bubble where people are lending or investing simply because everybody else is doing so. The boom does not necessarily peter out smoothly: a recently liberalized, well-performing economy can suddenly find favor with foreign capital of all sorts, but if things go wrong for some reason, the capital can disappear just as rapidly. When the bubble bursts and the currency comes under pressure, even a very large positive real interest rate differential may be unable to check the capital outflow.

4. Recent capital flows to Latin America

That was the story of the liberalization episodes in the Southern Cone in Latin America in the 1970s, when high domestic interest rates, overvalued exchange rates, freedom to borrow abroad, and plentiful international liquidity combined to induce capital inflows. But there are strong signs that a similar process is again underway in a number of Latin American countries. It is estimated that the region as a whole received about US$40 billion in 1991, three times the level of 1990, the main recipients being Mexico, Brazil, Argentina, Venezuela and Chile. Not all the capital inflows have been for short-term uses, but much of them do appear to have been, particularly in Argentina and Brazil (Griffith-Jones et al. 1992, Tables 4 and 5; UNCTAD TDR 1992, part 2, annex 2). In the majority of these countries capital inflows continued at an accelerated pace in 1992. In Chile where "the monetary authorities adopted a cautious approach based on the assumption that the oversupply of foreign exchange was only temporary and was due to the unusually high price of copper and the low international interest rates" (ECLAC 1991, 41), short-term capital inflows slowed down considerably in 1992 thanks to various measures designed to reduce the arbitrage margin.

What is remarkable about recent capital inflows to Latin America is not only that the recipient countries are in very different positions compared to the 1970s, but that they also differ widely among themselves with respect to inflation, fiscal posture, and exchange rate and trade policies. Argentina, Chile and Mexico have liberal trade regimes whereas Brazil has tight controls. While Brazil has had a large fiscal deficit and very high inflation, others, particularly Chile and Mexico, have had balanced budgets or fiscal surpluses, and moderate inflation. Capital has been attracted by a combination of currency appreciation and high real interest rates in Chile, Mexico and particularly Argentina (and also a booming stock market in the latter two), but not in Brazil where the underlying factor has been very high real interest rates (about 4 to 5 percent per month). Currency appreciation is due to exchange rate policy in Argentina (which uses the exchange rate as a nominal anchor to reduce inflation), but not in Chile and Mexico where it is market generated. It has led to a considerable deterioration of the trade balance, especially in Argentina and Mexico.

The ideal response to such capital inflows is a corresponding increase in domestic investment in traded goods sectors. This not only prevents a sharp appreciation of the currency by raising capital goods imports, but can also enhance export capacity – something that may be needed especially when capital flows dry up or are reversed. But higher investment is not always possible when domestic interest rates are prohibitive and long-term investment with funds borrowed abroad at lower rates carries considerable exchange rate risk. In other words the high interest rates and/or currency appreciation that attract short-term capital also deter investment. In Latin America capital inflows resulted in a sharp swing in the transfer of resources abroad by about 4 percent of the region's GDP during 1990–91, but investment remained depressed: in Brazil and Argentina the investment ratio remained below the levels of the 1980s when these countries had been making large transfers on debt servicing.

The problems of macroeconomic management in the face of a massive capital inflow are well known. Sterilizing them by issuing domestic debt can impose a serious burden on the public sector, particularly when the arbitrage margin is large. In Brazil, for instance, the cost of carrying the extra US$5 billion of reserves purchased in this way amounted to about US$2 billion during 1991–92, adding considerably to domestic public debt (UNCTAD TDR 1992, part 2, annex 2; Junior 1992). Furthermore, by increasing the stock of government debt, sterilization itself tends to raise domestic interest rates and, hence, the arbitrage margin. If, on the other hand, the currency is allowed to appreciate, it can undermine the competitiveness of the domestic industry, possibly eventually triggering a sharp reversal in short-term capital flows.

5. *Opening stock markets to nonresidents*

Instability in short-term capital flows combined with the inherent volatility of investment in company equity exposes the economy to even greater risks. Since opening up domestic capital markets requires some form of currency convertibility for nonresident equity investors, a close link can develop between stock and currency markets even in countries where the capital account is not fully open. This may prove to be a serious problem in Latin America because of the increased presence of nonresidents in capital markets. In Mexico, for instance, equity holding by nonresidents is estimated to have amounted to more than $25 billion, or about a quarter of the market's capitalization, in the second quarter of 1992 (Latin American Economy and Business May 1992, 4), compared to about 5 percent in the major capital markets such as New York and Tokyo. The link between these two inherently unstable markets can be further strengthened by dollarization of the economy, when that occurs.

This link increases the potential for the emergence of foreign exchange and/or stock market crises. Since the return on investment to the foreign investor depends largely on the movement of the exchange rate, a serious shock (e.g., a terms of trade deterioration) that makes a devaluation appear inevitable can trigger both a sharp decline in equity prices and an outflow of capital. Similarly, the mood in equity markets can exert a strong influence on the exchange rate – e.g., bullish expectations can trigger capital inflow, leading to appreciation. By contrast, a bearish mood in the capital market and/or massive profit taking in dollars by nonresidents can not only prick the speculative bubble in the stock market, but also lead to a currency crisis. Recent evidence suggests that chaotic feedbacks between financial and currency markets can easily develop: for instance, when the bubble burst in the Tokyo stock exchange at the beginning of 1990, there was a massive shift out of yen-denominated assets, causing also considerable drops in the government bond index and the currency (Akyüz 1992).

6. Effects of volatile capital flows on investment and trade

One important consequence of sharp swings in the direction of capital flows and greater instability of exchange rates is to increase borrower's risk. For investors in traded goods sectors, the real exchange rate is the single most important relative price affecting profits. But firms in nontraded goods sectors are also affected depending on the imported inputs they use. Exchange rate gyrations produce considerable uncertainty regarding prospective yields of investment. By raising the average rate of return required by investors to undertake investment, particularly in the traded goods sectors, this will depress the level of investment corresponding to any given rate of interest.

The influence of the exchange rate on investment decisions increases with the share of foreign trade in the economy. It is thus of growing importance in the developing world because of widespread import liberalization and emphasis on export-led growth. It is therefore ironic that the exchange rate is becoming increasingly determined by purely financial forces delinked from trade and investment. Exchange rate instability can thus undermine "outward oriented" strategies by depressing investment in exports. The evidence suggests that such adverse effects have occurred even in industrial countries where firms are better equipped to hedge against unexpected swings in exchange rates, and that exchange rate stability has been characteristic of countries with sustained export growth (UNCTAD TDR 1987; UNCTAD TDR 1989, part 1, chap. 5).

The second **systemic** effect of volatile capital flows is through interest rates. As already noted, capital-value uncertainty and interest rates both rise as a result of increased borrower's risk as well as greater instability in interest rates and prices of financial assets, including equities, associated with volatile capital flows. More important, increased competition between domestic currency and foreign currency assets also tends to raise the cost of finance because of the greater risk and uncertainty in developing countries. The fact that most developing countries are economically and politically less stable than developed countries, with financial and legal systems that are less able to ensure enforcement of contracts, increases the hazards of financial investment. In a financially closed economy the safety premium on foreign currency assets is counter-balanced by the high transaction costs of shifting into them, at least for most small savers, but financial openness reduces these costs considerably. Consequently, domestic assets need to carry much higher rates of return than external assets. This can reduce investment and impair competitiveness.

7. Controlling capital flows

Complete isolation of the financial system in a developing country from the rest of the world is neither feasible nor desirable. Successful export performance requires close interaction of banks at home with world financial markets in order to provide trade-related credits and facilitate international payments. The ability to borrow in international capital markets allows diversification in corporate finance while foreign investment in capital markets can help broaden their equity base and reduce their leverage. Foreign banks can bring greater competition in the provision of banking services, thereby reducing the intermediation margin and the cost of finance.

Nevertheless, most developing countries need to exercise considerable control over external capital flows in order to minimize their disruptive effects and gain greater policy autonomy to attain growth and stability. There are a number of techniques to control capital flows with different degrees of restrictions and effects that were widely used in industrial countries in the 1960s and 1970s (OECD 1972, 71–77, 1981, 1982; Fleming 1973; Swidrowski 1975; Swoboda 1976). Quantitative measures to limit short-term capital inflows through banks include reserve requirements on foreign liabilities, limits on their net external or foreign currency positions, or on gross external or foreign currency liabilities, and minimum holding periods and blocking of foreign deposits for such periods. Similarly a number of measures may be applied to restrict external borrowings by nonbanks, including reserve requirements on their foreign liabilities, and exchange controls such as prohibition of borrowing other than commercial or supplier credits received by importers, control on domestic foreign currency credits to domestic importers and exporters, and regulations regarding the timing of export and import settlements. Of these, limits on banks' net external or foreign currency positions and exchange controls regarding nonbanks can also be applied to restrict outflows. Restrictions on interest payments on nonresident deposits and negative interest rates are also among the measures that can be used to deter capital inflows.

Taxes may also be used to reduce the arbitrage margin and discourage speculative capital flows. A tax designed to reduce interest differentials (like the interest equalization tax used in the United States in the past to check outflows) can also be especially effective in checking capital inflows in developing countries where inflation and interest rate differentials with developed countries tend to be large. The tax rate can be used flexibly according to the behavior of capital flows and the objective pursued. Similarly Keynes' proposal for a financial transactions tax may be extended to apply to international financial transactions in order to "throw some sand in the wheels" and "deter short-term financial round-trip excursions" (Tobin 1978).

Finally, various restrictions may be introduced on the access of nonresidents to capital markets. One common measure is to limit foreign ownership to approved country funds and allow transactions on such funds only among nonresidents in order to control the flow of foreign funds in and out of the country **via** capital markets. This can be combined with the requirement that such funds be managed by local managers who are generally more amenable to "moral suasion" by the authorities.

It should be kept in mind that in several industrialized countries capital markets have been opened to nonresidents only very recently. In Japan, for instance, they were largely closed until the 1984 agreement with the United States, and even in Europe, where an integrated financial market is seen as an important step in the completion of a single EEC market, restrictions on entry into capital markets still remain in a number of countries (e.g., France and Italy). Again, the Republic of Korea only recently opened up its capital market to nonresidents, but restricted foreign acquisition to 10 percent of total equity capital, and to 2 percent in some strategic industries.

Some of these techniques have recently been used in Latin America in order to slow down short-term capital inflows. These include reserve requirements for foreign currency liabilities (Chile and Mexico), compulsory liquidity requirements on the short-term forex liabilities of commercial banks (Mexico), minimum holding periods (Chile), extension of the fiscal stamp tax to foreign credits (Chile), restrictions on company borrowing abroad through stock and bond issues (Brazil), and limits on the dollar amounts that banks can raise in deposits abroad as a proportion of their total deposits (Mexico). However, such measures have generally had only limited success. Governments are often very shy in applying effective controls for fear of fending off genuine, long-term capital and investment. This is certainly a legitimate concern, particularly in Latin America, after a decade-long foreign exchange strangulation. However, experience shows that capital controls might have to be introduced anyway if the process develops into a payments crisis and capital flight. It may be easier to restrict short-term inflows and prevent debt accumulation early on than to check capital flight in a crisis.

Controls on capital flows are not always effective when there are large arbitrage opportunities. It is thus important to bear in mind that price stability is vital for a financially open economy, since high inflation and wide interest rate differentials with reserve currency areas often lead to large arbitrage opportunities and encourage unsustainable capital flows. Furthermore, exchange rate management plays an important role. Explicit or implicit exchange rate guarantees tend to reduce the risk involved in arbitrage and encourage capital flows. As noted above, this has been an important factor in attracting short-term capital to Argentina. In Chile, by contrast, "the monetary authorities moved to resist revaluation of the peso by introducing changes to create uncertainty concerning yields on short-term capital flows" (ECLAC 1992, 40). These measures included the ending of the practice of advance announcement of devaluation of the peso, widening of the currency band, and linking the peso to a basket of currencies instead of the US dollar. They appear to have played an important role in slowing down short-term capital inflows and securing greater real exchange rate stability by introducing uncertainty regarding the movement of the exchange rate. In Mexico too the authorities widened the differential points for the peso–US dollar exchange rate to allow larger fluctuations, although its effects on capital flows seem to have been limited (Banco de Mexico 1992, 144).

Historical experience clearly shows that capital controls are no answer when the underlying policies are not sustainable. For instance, measures to control capital inflows are generally ineffective against capital flight stemming from economic and political instability. Moreover, it is important to bear in mind that capital controls are needed not in order to pursue inappropriate policies and exchange rates, but to minimize the disruptive effects of short-term capital flows, and gain greater policy autonomy to attain growth and stability.

I. Conclusions

The focus of financial policies in developing countries should be industrialization and stability. A common feature of all modern examples of industrialization is that they have all succeeded in making finance serve industry and trade not the other way round. This has often necessitated a considerable amount of intervention and control over financial activities. On the other hand, despite widespread claims for efficiency of financial markets, financial liberalization in many countries in recent years has generated more costs than benefits. These have included persistent misalignment of prices of financial assets, resulting in inefficiencies in the allocation of resources; sharply increased short-term volatility of asset prices, resulting in greater uncertainty, shorter maturities and higher interest rates; excessive borrowing to finance speculative asset purchases and consumption, resulting in unsustainable stocks of debt, increased financial fragility and reduced household savings; and loss of autonomy in pursuing interest rate and exchange rate policies in accordance with the needs of trade and industry.

It is equally true that government intervention in finance has often been misguided, giving rise to inefficiency and waste. However, the appropriate response should be to reform the government and rationalize intervention rather than throw in the towel and simply "un-leash market forces." The main challenge is to determine where and how governments should intervene and to make sure that the intervention achieves its aims. The discussions so far suggest the following:

- Macroeconomic stability is of cardinal importance for the stability and efficiency of the financial system since excessive volatility of prices and economic activity tends to increase financial fragility, create uncertainty, raise interest rates and shorten the time horizon. While macroeconomic stability itself is influenced by financial policies, monetary and fiscal discipline is crucial.
- In cases where directed credits and financial subsidies are successfully used as part of industrial policy, winners are not picked by "bureaucrats," but through a process based on a close interaction between the government and the business, and the use of market signals to assess risks and opportunities. Success also depends on ensuring reciprocity between support and performance; use of controls, regulations and subsidies for the intended purposes; and readiness to revise them as necessary.
- Financial policies must take account of the dual nature of interest rates: the **return** aspect which primarily influences the distribution of asset holdings in different forms, and the **cost** aspect which determines the capacity of the corporate sector to generate

internal funds, to undertake investment and to compete in world markets. It is important to bear in mind that while high interest rates are not necessary to increase savings, low and stable capital cost is crucially important for investment and competitiveness.

- There is often a need for deposit ceilings and intervention in the money market in order to stabilize interest rates and asset prices, and prevent excessive risk taking and price competition in the financial sector. Such controls should be applied with flexibility and discretion, taking into account macroeconomic conditions as well as the needs of trade and investment. Rigid rules regarding the level of real interest rates are no more sensible than those about the rate of growth of money supply in the conduct of monetary policy.
- Prudential regulations and a strong bank supervision are also essential to prevent excessive risk taking and financing of speculative activities by banks. Measures such as capital requirements are not always enough to reduce fragility: it may also be necessary to act directly on the asset portfolios of banks and restrict lending against or investment in highly capital-uncertain assets such as securities and property, and exposure to a single firm. Firms should not be allowed to own and control banks. Protective regulations such as deposit insurance and lender-of-last-resort facilities should only be introduced in combination with prudential regulations.
- Most developing countries need to concentrate their energies in strengthening their existing bank-based financial systems rather than pin their hope on transplanting Wall Street. They also need to promote long-term equity holding via institutional investors such as provident funds, and permit banks to hold equities within prudential limits. Transfer taxes and "circuit breakers" may be used to deter short-term trading and reduce volatility in stock markets. Easy access to stock markets and readily available short-term financial instruments paying market returns tend to increase financial instability.
- Particular care needs to be given to the design of external financial policies since mistakes in this area tend to be very costly and difficult to reverse. Allowing residents uncontrolled access to international capital markets has proved damaging in many developing countries, and short-term speculative capital flows have proved extremely troublesome. Developing countries need to exercise a considerable degree of control over external capital flows through taxes, quantitative restrictions and exchange controls in order to minimize their adverse effects on macroeconomic equilibrium, exchange rates and trade; to control the pace of accumulation of external debt; and to gain greater autonomy in monetary policy. Access of nonresidents to domestic capital markets should be restricted since close links between the two inherently volatile markets can be very dangerous. It is also important to resist the temptation to dollarize the economy in order to keep capital at home: policies should address the root cause of the problem and eliminate the reasons for extensive demand for foreign currency.
- A pragmatic not a doctrinaire approach is needed toward financial control and liberalization in developing countries. Restrictions on financial flows and interest rates may be removed over time as they fulfil their functions. Financial liberalization undertaken as a result of a successfully implemented industrial policy is very different

from liberalization as a reaction to misguided and failed intervention. Has financial liberalization ever remedied stagnation and instability?

Notes

1 First published as an UNCTAD discussion paper in March 1993. This chapter draws upon various publications by the author including: "Financial Liberalization in Developing Countries: A Neo-Keynesian Approach," UNCTAD Discussion Paper 36, March 1991; "On Financial Openness in Developing Countries," in *International Monetary and Financial Issues for the 1990s*, vol. 2, UNCTAD, Geneva, 1993; "Does Financial Liberalization Improve Trade Performance?" in *Globalization, Regionalization and New Dilemmas in Trade Policy for Development*, edited by D. Tussie and M. Agosin, Macmillan, 1993; and "Financial Policies for Industrialization and Development: Reflections on Financial 'Deepening' and 'Efficiency,'" in *Economic Crisis in Developing Countries*, edited by M. Nissanke and A. Hewitt, London: Pinter/St Martin's Press, 1993. I have greatly benefited from comments and suggestions made by various people, including the participants of a Financial Globalization and Systemic Risk workshop at the Center on International Economic Relations, University of Campinas, Sao Paulo, 15–16 June 1992; the participants of an ECLAC/UNU–WIDER/UNCTAD seminar on Savings and Financial Policy Issues in African, Asian, Latin American and Caribbean Countries, ECLAC, Santiago, 5–6 October 1992, particularly Carlos Massad and Gunther Held; and my colleagues in UNCTAD, Shahen Abrahamian, Andrew Cornford, Detlef Kotte and Cem Somel. The examination of financial efficiency in terms of various concepts of risk in Section E owes a great deal to discussions with Jan Kregel. None of the persons mentioned are, of course, responsible for any errors.

2 The description of various systems here draws largely on Corbett and Mayer (1991), Kregel (1991) and Somel (1992). For a summary account of the structural aspects of these systems, see also Davis (1993, 23–26). We do not examine here how these different systems evolved, but there can be little doubt that government policies and regulations played a major role.

3 In conformity with contemporary trends and in response to outside pressure, Japan has been undergoing a transition toward a market-based and open financial system, which is not easy to reconcile with the policy of cheap finance. There have been severe fluctuations in share prices, interest and exchange rates, and a tendency for the cost of finance to rise (Martin 1992).

References

Akyüz, Y. 1990. "Financial System and Policies in Turkey in the 1980s." In *The Political Economy of Turkey: Debt, Adjustment and Sustainability*, edited by T. Aricanli and D. Rodrik. London: Macmillan.

______. 1991. "Financial Liberalization in Developing Countries: A Neo-Keynesian Approach." UNCTAD Discussion Paper 36, March.

______. 1992. "Financial Globalization and Instability." In *Change: Threat or Opportunity for Human Progress?* vol. 3, *Globalization of Markets*, edited by Üner Kirdar. New York: United Nations, 39–84.

Amsden, A. 1989. *Asia's Next Giant: South Korea and Late Industrialization*. New York: Oxford University Press.

Amsden, A., and Yoon-Dae Euh. 1990. "Republic of Korea's Financial Reform: What Are the Lessons?" UNCTAD Discussion Paper 30, April.

Aryeetey, E., Y. Asante, F. Gockel and A. Kyei. 1990. "Mobilizing Domestic Savings for African Development and Industrialization: A Ghanaian Case Study." Unpublished academic paper, Queen Elizabeth House, Oxford.

Banco de Mexico. 1992. *The Mexican Economy 1992*. Mexico City.

Blundell-Wignall, A., and F. Browne. 1991. "Macroeconomic Consequences of Financial Liberalization: A Summary Report." OECD Department of Economics and Statistics, Working Paper 98, February.

Bradford, C. I. 1986. "East Asian 'Models': Myths and Lessons." In *Development Strategies Reconsidered*, edited by J. P. Lewis and V. Kallab. New Brunswick, NJ: Overseas Development Council.

Bryant, R. 1980. *Money and Monetary Policy in Interdependent Nations*. Washington, DC: The Brookings Institution.

______. 1987. *International Financial Intermediation*. Washington, DC: The Brookings Institution.

Chipeta, C. 1990. "Mobilizing Domestic Savings for African Development and Industrialization: A Case Study of Malawi." Unpublished academic paper, Queen Elizabeth House, Oxford.

Cho, Yoon-Je. 1988. "The Effects of Financial Liberalization on the Efficiency of Credit Allocation: Some Evidence from Korea." *Journal of Development Economics* 29.

Cho, Yoon-Je, and D. Khatkhate. 1989. "Lessons of Financial Liberalization in Asia: A Comparative Study." World Bank Discussion Paper 50.

Corbett, J., and C. P. Mayer. 1991. "Financial Reform in Eastern Europe: Progress with the Wrong Model." CEPR Discussion Paper 603, September.

Corbo, V., and J. De Melo. 1987. "Lessons from the Southern Cone Policy Reforms." *The World Bank Research Observer* 2 (2).

Corbo, V., J. De Melo and J. Tybout. 1986. "What Went Wrong with the Recent Reforms in the Southern Cone?" *Economic Development and Cultural Change* 34 (3).

Corrigan, E. G. 1991. "The Banking–Commerce Controversy Revisited." *Federal Reserve Bank of New York Quarterly Bulletin*, Spring.

Cutler, D. M., J. M. Poterba and L. H. Summers. 1990. "Speculative Dynamics." NBER Working Paper 3242.

Datta-Chaudhuri, M. 1990. "Market Failure and Government Failure." *Economic Perspectives*, Summer.

Davis, E. P. 1993. *Debt, Financial Fragility and Systemic Risk*. Oxford: Clarendon Press.

Diaz-Alejandro, C. 1985. "Good-Bye Financial Repression, Hello Financial Crash." *Journal of Development Economics* 19 (1–2).

Dornbusch, R. 1983. "Panel Discussion on the Southern Cone." *IMF Staff Papers* 30 (1).

Dornbusch, R., and A. Reynoso. 1989. "Financial Factors in Economic Development." *American Economic Review: Papers and Proceedings*, May.

Driscoll, M. 1991. "Deregulation, Credit Rationing, Financial Fragility and Economic Performance." OECD Department of Economics and Statistics Working Paper 98, February.

ECLAC. 1991–92. *Economic Panorama of Latin America*. Santiago: UN.

Edwards, S. 1984. "The Order of Liberalization of the Balance of Payments." World Bank Staff Working Paper 7, 10.

______. 1987. "Sequencing Economic Liberalization in Developing Countries." *Finance and Development*, March.

______. 1989. "On the Sequencing of Structural Reforms." OECD Working Paper 70, September.

Fama, E. F. 1985. "What's Different about Banks?" *Journal of Monetary Economics* 15, January.

Fischer, B., and H. Reisen. 1992. *Towards Capital Account Convertibility*. OECD Development Centre, Policy Brief 4.

Fleming, J. M. 1973. "Problems of Disruptive International Capital Movements." In *Europe and the Evolution of the International Monetary System*, edited by A. K. Swoboda. Geneva: Sijthoff Leiden, Institut Universitaire de Hautes Etudes Internationales.

Frankel, J. A. 1983. "Panel Discussion on the Southern Cone." *IMF Staff Papers* 30 (1).

Greenwald, B., and J. E. Stiglitz. 1986. "Externalities in Economies with Imperfect Information and Incomplete Markets." *Quarterly Journal of Economics* 101 (2).

Griffith-Jones, S., A. Marr and A. Rodriguez. 1992. "The Return of Private Capital to Latin America: The Facts, an Analytical Framework and Some Policy Issues." In J. Williamson et al., *Fragile Finance: Rethinking the International Monetary System.* FONDAD, the Hague, the Netherlands

Hanson, J. A., and C. R. Neal. 1985. "Interest Rate Policies in Selected Developing Countries, 1970–1982." World Bank Staff Working Papers 753.

Honohan, P., and I. Atiyas. 1989. "Intersectoral Financial Flows in Developing Countries." World Bank Working Paper 164, March.

Jones, D., and King, K. K. 1992. "Implementation of Prompt Collective Action." Paper presented to the meeting of technicians of Central Banks of the American Continent, Barbados, 16–20 November.

Junior, P. A. 1992. "Política monetária e ingresso de divisas: o caso Brasileiro recente." Paper presented to the meeting of the technicians of Central Banks of the American Continent, Barbados, 16–20 November.

Kasman, B., and C. Pigott. 1988. "Interest Rate Divergence among the Major Industrial Nations." *Federal Reserve Bank of New York Quarterly Bulletin*, Autumn.

Kato, K., T. Shibata, K. Fukui, A. Mogi, Y. Miwa, Y. Niwa, N. Ichikawa and M. Furuta. 1993. "Policy-Based Finance: The Experience of Postwar Japan. Final Report to the World Bank." The Japanese Development Bank, January.

Keynes, J. M. 1936. *The General Theory of Employment, Interest and Money*. London: Macmillan.

Kregel, J. A. 1991. "Markets and Institutions in the Financing of Business." Paper prepared for the Jerome Levy Institute Conference: Restructuring the Financial System for Economic Growth, University of Bologna, 21–23 November.

_______. 1993. "Financial Fragility and the Structure of Financial Markets." Paper presented at the Allied Social Science Associations Meetings, Anaheim, California, 7 January.

Krueger, A. O. 1984. "Problems of Liberalization." In *World Economic Growth*, edited by A. Harberger. San Francisco: ISC Press.

Kupiec, P. 1991. "Financial Liberalisation and International Trends in Stock, Corporate Bond and Foreign Exchange Market Volatilities." OECD Department of Economics and Statistics, Working Paper 94, February.

Lee, Chung H. 1992. "The Government, Financial System, and Large Private Enterprises in the Economic Development of South Korea." *World Development* 20 (2).

Lim, J. Y. 1991. "The Philippine Financial Sector in the 1980s." UNCTAD Discussion Paper 35, March.

Massad, C., and N. Eyzaguirre. 1990. *Ahorro y formacion de capital: experiencias latinamericanos*. Santiago: CEPAL.

Martin, P. 1992. "Not the Time to Gloat over Japan's Shocks." *Financial Times*, 26 May.

McCauley, R. N., and S. A. Zimmer. 1989. "Explaining International Differences in the Cost of Capital." *Federal Reserve Bank of New York Quarterly Bulletin*, Summer.

McKinnon, R. I. 1973. *Money and Capital in Economic Development.* Washington, DC: The Brookings Institution.

_______. 1982. "The Order of Economic Liberalization: Lessons from Chile and Argentina." In *Economic Policy in a World of Change*, edited by K. Brunner and A. Meltzer. Carnegie-Rochester Conference Series on Public Policy, Amsterdam, Netherlands.

Miller, M., and P. Weller. 1991. "Financial Liberalisation, Asset Prices and Exchange Rates." OECD Department of Economics and Statistics, Working Paper 94, February.

Minsky, H. 1982. *Inflation, Recession and Economic Policy*. Armonk, New York: Wheatsheaf Books.

_______. 1986. *Stabilizing an Unstable Economy*. New Haven: Yale University Press.

Molho, L. E. 1986. "Interest Rates, Saving, and Investment in Developing Countries." IMF Staff Papers 33 (1).

Mwega, F. M. 1990. "Mobilizing Domestic Savings for African Development and Industrialization: A Case Study of Kenya." Unpublished academic paper, Queen Elizabeth House, Oxford.

Nissanke, M. 1990. "Mobilizing Domestic Resources for African Development and Diversification: Structural Impediments in the Formal Financial System." Unpublished academic paper, Queen Elizabeth House, Oxford.

OECD. 1972. *Economic Outlook* 12, December.

______. 1981. *Controls on International Capital Movements: Experience with Controls on International Portfolio Operations in Shares and Bonds.* Paris.

______. 1982. *Controls on International Capital Movements: The Experience with Controls on International Financial Credits, Loans and Deposits.* Paris.

Owen, P. D., and O. Solis-Fallas. 1989. "Unorganized Money Markets and 'Unproductive' Assets in the New Structuralist Critique of Financial Liberalization." *Journal of Development Economics* 31.

Poterba, J. M. 1991. "Comparing the Cost of Capital in the United States and Japan: A Survey of Methods." *Federal Reserve Bank of New York Quarterly Review*, Winter.

Shaw, E. S. 1973. *Financial Deepening in Economic Development.* New York: Oxford University Press.

Singh, A. 1992. "The Stock Market and Economic Development: Should Developing Countries Encourage Stock Markets?" UNCTAD Discussion Paper 49, October.

Somel, C. 1992. "Finance for Growth: Lessons from Japan." UNCTAD Discussion Paper 44, July.

Stiglitz, J. E., and A. Weiss. 1981. "Credit Rationing in Markets with Imperfect Information." *American Economic Review*, June.

Stiglitz, J. E. 1989a. "Markets, Market Failures, and Development." *American Economic Review: Papers and Proceedings*, May.

______. 1989b. "Using Tax Policy to Curb Speculative Short-Term Trading." *Journal of Financial Services Research* 3 (3).

Summers, L. H., and V. P. Summers. 1989. "When Financial Markets Work Too Well: A Cautious Case for a Securities Transactions Tax." *Journal of Financial Services Research* 3 (3).

Swidrowski, J. 1975. *Exchange and Trade Controls.* Essex: Gower Press.

Swoboda, A. K., ed. 1976. *Capital Movements and Their Control.* Geneva: Sijthoff Leiden, Institut Universitaire de Hautes Etudes Internationales.

Tobin, J. 1978. "A Proposal for International Monetary Reform." *The Eastern Economic Journal*, July–October.

______. 1984. "On the Efficiency of the Financial System." *Lloyds Bank Review*, July.

UNCTAD. 1987. "The Exchange Rate System." In *International Monetary and Financial Issues for the Developing Countries.* Geneva: United Nations.

UNCTAD TDR (various issues). *Trade and Development Report.* Geneva: United Nations.

Van Wijnbergen, S. 1983. "Interest Rate Management in LDCs." *Journal of Monetary Economics* 12, September.

Westphal, L. E. 1990. "Industrial Policy in an Export-Propelled Economy: Lessons from South Korea's Experience." *Economic Perspectives*, Summer.

World Bank. 1989. *World Development Report.* Washington, DC.

Zimmer, S. A., and McCauley, R. N. 1991. "Bank Cost of Capital and International Competitiveness." *Federal Reserve Bank of New York Quarterly Bulletin*, Winter.

Chapter II

MANAGING FINANCIAL INSTABILITY IN EMERGING MARKETS: A KEYNESIAN PERSPECTIVE[1]

A. Introduction

With widespread deregulation and rapid growth of financial wealth, business cycles in both advanced economies and emerging markets are increasingly dominated by the financial system.

It is true that there is not always a one-to-one correspondence between real and financial cycles, and recessions do not always go in tandem with financial crises. Nevertheless, the response of the financial system to impulses emanating from the real economy has become increasingly procyclical, and this tends to reinforce expansionary and contractionary forces and amplify swings in investment, output and employment, creating new dilemmas for macroeconomic policy.

With rapid liberalization of the capital account, international capital flows have become the driving force behind financial cycles in developing countries, capable of producing unsustainable expansions followed by financial crises and recessions. While country-specific (pull) and global (push) factors can both play important roles in determining their direction, size and nature, evidence shows that the most damaging episodes of financial crises in emerging markets are those associated with boom–bust cycles in capital flows driven by special and temporary global factors beyond the control of the recipient countries.[2]

Indeed, since the early 1990s currency and balance of payments crises have occurred under varying macroeconomic and financial conditions in Latin America, East Asia and elsewhere. They were seen not only in countries with large and widening current account deficits (e.g., Mexico and Thailand), but also where deficits were relatively small and presumed sustainable (Indonesia and Russia). A significant currency appreciation is often a feature of countries experiencing currency turmoil (Mexico, Russia, Brazil and Turkey) but this has not always been the case – appreciations in most East Asian countries experiencing speculative attacks during 1997 were moderate or negligible. In some cases crises were associated with large budget deficits, as in Russia, Turkey and Brazil, but in others (Mexico and East Asia), the budget was either balanced or in surplus. Crises occurred not only where capital flows supported a boom in private consumption, as in Latin America, but also in private investment, as in East Asia. Again, in some episodes of crises external liabilities were largely public (Russia and Brazil) while in others they were private (East Asia). Finally, most countries hit by balance of payments and financial crises are said to have been lacking effective regulation and supervision of the financial system, but Argentina could not avoid a payments crisis and default despite having one of the best systems of prudential regulations in the developing world and a financial system dominated by foreign banks.

Recurrent financial turmoil in emerging markets under varying conditions has raised serious questions about the mainstream economic thinking which has traditionally attributed currency and balance of payments crises to macroeconomic policy inconsistency, notably lack of fiscal and monetary discipline, and regarded price stability as both necessary and sufficient for financial stability.[3] In reality, in most countries financial boom–bust cycles, asset price and exchange rate gyrations, and credit surges and crunches have all occurred under conditions of low and stable inflation. In more extreme cases, as in Latin America, where price instability has traditionally been regarded as structural and chronic, single digit and stable inflation rates have been attained at the expense of increased financial fragility and instability through exchange-rate-based stabilization programs relying on short-term, unstable capital inflows.[4] The failure of the International Monetary Fund (IMF) to diagnose the nature of these crises and distinguish them from traditional payments difficulties caused by domestic demand expansion and inflation led to serious errors in policy response, notably in East Asia where procyclical monetary and fiscal tightening served to deepen the economic contraction caused by the reversal of capital flows.

There has been a proliferation of ex post hypotheses and ad hoc models designed to explain the causes and dynamics of these crises, incorporating various features of financial markets including herd behavior, collective action problem, moral hazard, asymmetric information and contagion. While bringing some valuable insights into cumulative financial processes, none of these could provide a fully fledged macrofinancial theory of instability integrating impulses emanating from both real and financial sectors. With its emphasis on such interactions, the Keynesian analysis of financial instability has thus emerged as a strong contestant, particularly as events have increasingly reaffirmed its fundamental proposition that the systemic problems facing modern market economies are unemployment and financial instability, rather than price instability.

This chapter examines the extent to which the Keynesian thinking could help understand the causes and dynamics of crises in emerging markets and provide policy prescriptions for managing financial cycles without sacrificing employment and growth. It is concluded that at the analytical level the endogenous unstable dynamics analyzed by post-Keynesians, notably Hyman Minsky, goes a long way in providing a powerful framework for explaining the boom–bust cycles driven by international capital flows in emerging markets. Its main policy conclusion that financial control rather than macroeconomic policy holds the key to financial stability is equally valid for managing capital flows. There is, however, a need to develop new instruments for stabilization, placing greater emphasis on countercyclical financial regulations and control than has hitherto been the case.

B. The Keynesian Instability Hypothesis and Financial Cycles

Keynes' analysis of financial instability in the *General Theory* is all too familiar, colored by several metaphors such as the beauty contest, musical chairs and the game of snap.

Nevertheless, in the *General Theory* Keynes was not very much occupied with the causes of financial instability but, rather, its effects on employment and income. Nor did he spend much time on examining the behavior of investment, income and employment over the entire business cycle, concentrating, instead, on underinvestment and unemployment and what to do about them. Even though he insisted that his was a theory of fluctuations in production and employment originating from financial markets and referred repeatedly to cycles, it remains true that the *General Theory* did not develop a fully fledged analysis of boom–bust cycles of the kind that pervades financial markets today. This we owe to Hyman Minsky, who analyzed and advanced financial instability as an intrinsic feature of market economies, following in the footsteps of Irving Fisher and Keynes – a hypothesis which he called "an interpretation of the substance of Keynes's 'General Theory.'"[5]

The essence of the financial instability hypothesis is the procyclical response of financial markets to impulses emanating from the real economy. This not only amplifies swings in investment, output and employment, but also generates endogenous fragility wherein periods of deep recessions associated with financial crises are the outcomes of financial excesses in the preceding booms. The procyclical effects of finance on real economic activity derive mainly from procyclical risk assessments by lenders and investors: namely, risks are underestimated at times of expansion and overestimated during contractions.

Minsky (1977 and 1986, chap. VII) explains this with the proposition that stability (tranquility), including that of an expansion, is destabilizing since it increases confidence, reduces the value placed on liquidity and raises the acceptable debt-to-equity ratios. The increased optimism and sense of security generated by an economic expansion often results in declines in risk spreads and provisions, and improved credit ratings.[6] Given the herd behavior intrinsic in modern financial markets and "mark-to-market" practices in the valuation of assets, these tend to produce a cumulative process of credit expansion, asset price bubbles and overindebtedness which, in turn, add to spending and growth. Asset prices at such times are driven not so much by improved prospects of income streams as by expectations of further price increases, pushing price earnings and price-to-rent ratios to unsustainable levels. Stock and property booms give rise to credit expansion by raising collateral values and reducing loan loss provisions. Faster growth in lending, in turn, adds fuel to increases in the market valuation of assets, making investment even more attractive.

However, as balance sheets adopt smaller margins of safety, the system develops endogenous fragility, and financing positions are increasingly translated from hedge to speculative and, eventually, to Ponzi finance.[7] With a cyclical downturn in economic activity and/or increased cost of borrowing, incomes on assets acquired can no longer service the debt incurred. Increased loan delinquency leads to a widening of risk spreads and falling asset prices and collateral values, producing a credit crunch. As risks are overestimated, even the borrowers that normally qualify for credit become unable to borrow. This in turn puts further pressure on debtors, forcing them to liquidate assets, setting off a process of debt deflation and deepening the contraction in economic activity.[8]

Minsky's financial instability hypothesis emphasizes the finance–investment link; it is built around "a financial theory of investment and an investment theory of the cycle"

(Minsky 1978, 31). Indeed, financial bubbles almost always give rise to excessive investment in certain sectors which become unviable with the return to normal conditions. This is true for investment not only in areas susceptible to speculative influences such as residential and commercial property, but also in machinery and equipment, as in Japan in the late 1980s, in the United States during the dot-com bubble of the second half of the 1990s, and in East Asia in the run-up to the 1997 crisis. However, with increased access of households to credit, the Keynesian link between income and consumption has also become weaker. As a result, consumption booms produced by asset price inflation and credit expansion can be a driving force of aggregate demand, reducing household savings and raising indebtedness in the course of expansion. This was the case in Latin America in the 1990s where surges in capital inflows were generally associated with booms in consumption. Similarly, much of the stimulus to growth in the United States' economy since the mid-1990s came from increased consumer spending encouraged by speculative booms in equity and property markets, and greatly facilitated by mortgage equity withdrawal.[9]

In the traditional Keynesian analysis, no special attention is paid to the role that may be played by international capital flows and exchange rates in financial cycles. With rapid capital account liberalization, however, international capital flows have increasingly dominated economic cycles in emerging markets because of extensive dollarization and widespread currency and maturity mismatches in balance sheets. The effect of capital flows on domestic spending tends to be procyclical: surges in capital flows and currency appreciations lead to increases in net worth in balance sheets, encouraging spending. This is reinforced by the real balance effect to the extent that nominal exchange rate stability or appreciation helps bring down inflation. Similarly, depreciations resulting from sudden stops and reversals add to contractionary impulses.[10]

The response of capital flows to domestic economic conditions is also procyclical. Economic expansion and booms in asset markets often attract foreign investment and lending which can, in turn, appreciate the currency, add to asset price inflation, and raise aggregate demand and growth, thereby making such inflows even more attractive. However, this process can also increase vulnerability to exchange rate swings by generating unsustainable trade deficits and currency and maturity mismatches in balance sheets. When capital flows stop as a result of the rapid accumulation of risks, or a negative shock to growth, or a deterioration in global financial conditions with respect to liquidity and risk appetite, or contagion from a crisis in another developing country considered in the same asset class by markets, this process could be rapidly reversed, resulting in sharp depreciations, credit crunch, debt deflation and economic contraction.

In a world of unstable capital flows, every financially open economy is vulnerable to sharp and unexpected swings in the external value of its currency. However, because of extensive dollarization and maturity mismatches in balance sheets and greater presence of foreigners in domestic asset markets, destabilizing feedbacks between domestic financial markets and capital flows are much stronger in developing than industrial countries. Exchange rate turbulence rarely spills over to domestic capital markets and the banking sector in industrial countries.[11] By contrast, in emerging markets major payments and currency crises are seldom contained without having a significant impact on domestic financial conditions and economic activity. This is a main reason why about 85 percent of all defaults in developing countries during 1970–99 were linked with currency crises (Reinhart 2002). Credit rating agencies often fail to anticipate currency crises, but they are pretty good in predicting defaults – downgrades follow, rather than lead, currency crises. Similarly, major banking and/or asset market crises in emerging markets often have adverse effects on capital flows and currency markets, but this is not always the case in industrial countries.[12]

C. Investment and Jobs over the Financial Cycle

Episodes of exceptionally rapid economic expansion driven by financial bubbles can no doubt bring greater prosperity than expansions where finance plays a more passive and accommodative role. But they are also susceptible to producing deeper recessions or longer periods of stagnation. Moreover, sharp swings in asset prices, exchange rates and aggregate demand cause a fundamental uncertainty regarding the return on capital, shorten planning horizons and promote defensive and speculative strategies in investment which can, in turn, exert a significant adverse influence on the pace and pattern of capital accumulation and result in the considerable waste of resources.[13]

Tracking the behavior of investment and employment over the entire expansion–recession–recovery cycle dominated by the financial sector shows that losses of investment and employment incurred at times of recessions are not fully recovered when the economy turns up from its trough, giving rise to the phenomenon of jobless recovery.[14] In this respect there are considerable similarities between emerging markets and advanced industrial countries, notably the United States where business cycles have been increasingly shaped by financial sector developments over the past three decades.

In the United States the dot-com expansion in the 1990s was characterized by asset price inflation, overindebtedness and overinvestment in certain sectors linked to information and communication. The recession that followed in Spring 2001 involved widespread financial difficulties. The subsequent recovery was the weakest in terms of investment since 1949. It was also jobless: it took 38 months for employment to recover whereas in a typical expansion in the period 1960–89, employment recovered its recessionary losses in eight months. Furthermore, there was an increased resort to flexible employment practices, including temporary and part-time employment and overtime (Schreft, Singh and Hodgson 2005).

Many explanations have been offered, but there is an agreement that financial factors played a significant role in job losses over the entire cycle.[15] The deflation-cum-recession following the dot-com bubble exposed the overindebtedness in the corporate sector, forcing them to focus on restoring the health of balance sheets during the subsequent recovery. Increased profits were thus used either for industrial restructuring or for reducing debt rather than expansion of production capacity and employment. The consequent downsizing and labor shedding resulted in a combination of falling employment and rising labor productivity and profits.[16] The industries that lost jobs during the 2001 recession were exactly those that saw rapid expansion during the dot-com bubble and these went on losing jobs in the subsequent recovery (Groshen and Potter 2003).

The continued tight conditions in financial markets during the recovery also impaired the ability of small-firms to create jobs, particularly in services which typically rely on equity financing and venture capital rather than debt. After the dot-com bubble burst, such financing almost disappeared because of heightened uncertainty, making it difficult for small firms to expand.[17]

There are often considerable uncertainties about the strength of a recovery from finance-driven recessions. This discourages firms from making long-term commitments to employment, promoting a wait-and-see attitude in hiring more permanent workers (Schreft, Singh and Hodgson 2005). Indeed, under conditions of increased uncertainty, even longer periods of growth may fail to generate jobs. This is noted in the case of Turkey: "the growth that did occur [during 1993–2004] was relatively 'jobless' as the volatility of the economy made employers less likely to hire new workers than to extend work hours of existing employees" (WB/IEG 2006, 4). One of the consequences of increased financial instability is the growing demand by firms for more flexible hiring-and-firing practices as a buffer against large and unexpected swings in economic activity. Such practices could also protect firms' profits against unexpected shifts in international competitiveness resulting from instability in exchange rates – a phenomenon which gains added importance in emerging markets.

The expansion–recession–recovery cycles driven by international capital flows in emerging markets produce even greater and more durable dislocations in investment and employment. Not only is the composition of investment distorted toward speculative activities, but its average level also falls over the entire cycle. In the four countries hit by the 1997 crisis in East Asia, the boom supported by capital inflows in the mid-1990s raised the average investment ratio by some 7 percentage points of GDP, while during the crisis the average decline was more than 16 percentage points. Investment stagnated in the subsequent recovery with the result that there was a sharp decline in the investment ratio over the entire cycle (UNCTAD TDR 2000).

In the labor market, booms generated by capital inflows often raise real wages, but the behavior of employment depends on several factors.[18] Employment in traded goods sectors tends to fall if the currency appreciates significantly and investment and productivity growth is sluggish, and this may be offset only partly by expansion in services. Evidence shows that in almost all emerging markets real wages rose during the boom phase but in Latin America, where productivity lagged, there was little change in unemployment, while in East Asia overall unemployment fell. In all these countries real wages fell and unemployment rose sharply during recessions, and in many of them unemployment rates exceeded the levels reached before the boom. Again in all these cases the subsequent recoveries were jobless; the unemployment rates remained above the rates attained during expansion by between 4 and 6 percentage points even after income losses had been fully recovered.

D. The Policy Problem

The task of managing financial cycles in order to mitigate their adverse consequences for investment and employment is overwhelming even for major advanced countries where domestic institutions are robust and financial conditions are relatively resilient to instability in international capital flows and exchange rates. It calls for more than macroeconomic fine-tuning or aggregate demand management à la Keynes. Minsky (1986, 287) knew this only too well when he remarked that "I feel much more comfortable with my diagnosis of what ails our economy and analysis of the causes of our discontents than I do with the remedies I propose," noting that a once-and-for-all resolution of the flaws of capitalism cannot be achieved because financial innovations introduce new mechanisms of instability.

In the Keynesian tradition not much faith is placed in monetary policy either in smoothing financial excesses at times of expansion or fighting unemployment during recessions. Minsky (1986, 304) views it as counterproductive for the former task and impotent for the latter: "Monetary policy to constrain undue expansion and inflation operates by way of disrupting financial markets and asset values. Monetary policy to induce expansion operates by interest rates and the availability of credit, which do not yield increased investment if current and anticipated profits are low." Instead, he favors a system of financial institutions designed to dampen instability, including by controlling the level and growth of bank assets through instruments such as capital adequacy requirements (Minsky, 1986, 320–21). However, like Keynes, he also focuses on preventing depression-cum-recessions and recommends a "Big Bank," a lender of last resort, to deal with debt deflations and credit crunches, and a "Big Government," a spender of last resort, to prevent economic contraction and unemployment. It is, however, recognized that "Big Bank" and "Big Government" can create moral hazard and this makes financial regulations all the more important.

In practice central banks in industrial countries do not generally respond to asset price inflation but tend to relax policy when the bubble bursts.[19] Certainly there are serious difficulties in identifying when asset price increases represent a bubble rather than improved fundamentals, but these are not insurmountable.[20] As argued by Kindleberger (1995, 35), monetary policy authorities would need to use judgment and discretion, rather than "cookbook rules of the game," when speculation threatens substantial rises in asset prices and exchange rates with possible subsequent harm to the economy. However, they often refrain from doing that in the belief that their task is to keep inflation under control, a monetary policy stance that maintains price stability would also promote financial stability, and financial markets do not need intervention as they regulate themselves. These explain why, for instance, the United States Federal Reserve refrained from acting during the dot-com bubble in the 1990s even when its chairman recognized that the United States economy was suffering from "irrational exuberance" or from using either monetary instruments or the regulatory authority it had been granted to stem speculative lending during the subprime bubble of the 2000s, despite repeated warnings.

In advanced countries the ability to respond to an eventual financial turmoil and recession by expanding liquidity and lowering policy interest rates mitigates the consequences of this indifference of monetary policy to credit and asset bubbles. The United States, for instance, responded to several instances of turmoil in financial markets and the threat of economic contraction by aggressive monetary easing and/or massive liquidity injections, including during the 1987 stock market break, the 1990–91 recession, the panic in the international bond market and the Long-Term Capital Management debacle triggered by the Russian crisis, the bursting of the dot-com bubble of the 1990s, and now the subprime crisis.

However, while such interventions are generally successful in averting deep and prolonged recessions, they often carry the risk of sowing the seeds of subsequent troubles. The response of the Fed to the bursting of the dot-com bubble by rapid liquidity expansion and historically low interest rates, as well as its reluctance to curb rapidly growing speculative lending, is clearly at the origin of the current subprime mortgage crisis.[21] Again, it is now increasingly argued that sharp cuts in policy interest rates and massive liquidity injection in response to the subprime crisis would only serve to compound the problems faced by the United States economy by preventing the much-needed correction in asset prices.[22]

Emerging markets do not generally have the option of a countercyclical monetary policy response to a financial crisis and economic contraction resulting from sudden stops and reversals in capital flows, because they cannot easily control outflows, stabilize the debt contracted in foreign currencies and undo the balance of payments constraint. In a credit crunch involving foreign lenders and investors, central banks cannot act as lenders of last resort to stabilize the exchange rate and avoid hikes in the debt burden. Nor is there an international lender of last resort to undertake this task.[23] Consequently, even when the problem is, in essence, one of lack of international liquidity, the collapse of the currency and hikes in interest rates could lead to the insolvency of otherwise sound debtors.

Even in industrial countries where balance sheets are largely insulated from the impact of large currency swings, monetary easing designed to weather difficulties in the domestic financial system can run up against external hurdles. It could weaken the currency and increase inflationary pressures, particularly when there is a large current account deficit that needs to be financed. This is exactly the dilemma that the United States Fed may now start facing in designing an effective response to the subprime crisis and the threat of recession – that is, its autonomy to run an independent monetary policy is now threatened in a big way, for the first time in the post–Bretton Woods world.

The problem is certainly more acute in developing countries where external obligations are in foreign currencies. In Korea, for instance, as in Japan, corporations had traditionally pursued aggressive investment strategies with a high degree of leverage, and the government often stood as a lender of last resort to bail out their creditors. This approach was underpinned by a strong government guidance of private investment to avoid moral hazard, speculation and excess capacity. However, in the 1990s when investment guidance was dismantled and corporations were allowed to borrow freely abroad, lack of an international counterpart to the domestic lender of last resort to smooth out liquidity problems drove a number of them into serious problems, including bankruptcy (Akyüz 2000).

This is why in emerging markets it is all the more important to start countercyclical policy during expansion and manage surges in capital inflows so as to prevent macroeconomic and balance sheet imbalances and exposure to a sudden stop and reversal of international capital flows. Here we focus on two main areas of response: countercyclical macroeconomic policy, notably monetary policy, and financial regulations, including direct (administrative) or indirect (market-based) restrictions over capital flows.[24] Reference will also be made to the role that fiscal policy may play in managing surges in capital inflows.

E. Capital Flows and Countercyclical Monetary Policy

It has long been recognized that the capital account regime has an important bearing on the scope and effectiveness of monetary and exchange rate policies. According to the standard economic theory, policymakers cannot simultaneously pursue an independent monetary policy, control the exchange rate and maintain an open capital account. All three are *potentially* feasible but only two of them could be chosen as *actual* policy – hence the dilemma known as the impossible trinity. Once the capital account is opened, a choice has to be made between controlling the exchange rate and an independent monetary policy. Using monetary policy as a countercyclical tool to stabilize economic activity could result in large cyclical swings in the exchange rate and the balance of payments. Conversely, if monetary policy is used to stabilize the exchange rate, it cannot act as a countercyclical macroeconomic tool and prevent large cyclical swings in economic activity.

However, in most developing countries with open capital accounts, the erosion of monetary policy autonomy is often greater than is typically portrayed in economic theory. It cannot always secure financial and macroeconomic stability, whether it is geared toward a stable exchange rate or conducted independently as a countercyclical tool. On the one hand, as already noted, because of large-scale liability dollarization, there are strong spillovers from exchange rates to domestic economic and financial conditions. Thus, using monetary policy as a domestic countercyclical tool does not guarantee stability when there are large swings in capital flows and exchange rates.

On the other hand, the effect of monetary policy on exchange rates is much more uncertain and unstable than is typically assumed in the theory of impossible trinity because of the volatility of risk assessments and herd behavior. During financial turmoil, hikes in interest rates are often unable to check sharp currency declines, while at times of favorable risk assessment a much smaller arbitrage margin can attract large inflows of private capital and cause significant appreciations.

Even when the authorities are prepared to use greater judgment and discretion in monetary policy, they may face serious trade-offs because domestic conditions may call for one sort of intervention and external conditions another. This is most clearly seen at times of rapid exit of capital when the liquidity expansion and cuts in interest rates needed to prevent financial meltdown and stimulate economic activity could simply accelerate flight from the currency. As a result, monetary authorities are often compelled to pursue procyclical policy in an effort to restore confidence. However under crisis conditions the link assumed in the traditional theory between the interest rate and the exchange rate also breaks down. When the market sentiment turns sour, higher interest rates aiming to retain capital tend to be perceived as increased risk of default. As a result, the risk-adjusted rate of return could actually fall as interest rates are raised. This is the main reason why procyclical interest rate hikes implemented as part of IMF support during several episodes of financial crises were unable to prevent the collapse of the currency, serving instead to deepen economic contraction.

Monetary policy also faces hurdles at times of economic expansion and asset bubbles associated with surges in capital inflows. Tightening monetary policy in order to check asset price bubbles and overheating could encourage external borrowing and short-term arbitrage flows, while lower interest rates would discourage such flows but lead to domestic credit expansion and overheating. A way out could be to employ countercyclical monetary tightening while intervening in the foreign currency market to resist appreciations and sterilizing its impact on domestic liquidity by issuing government debt. This can succeed when capital inflows are moderate in size and concentrated in the market for fixed-income assets. However, under surges across various segments of asset markets, sterilization could result in higher interest rates, attracting even more arbitrage flows. Furthermore, since interest earned on reserves is usually much lower than interest paid on public debt, there will be quasi-fiscal costs, which can be large when interest rate differentials are wide and the surge in capital inflows is strong.[25]

There are less costly methods of sterilization such as raising noninterest-bearing reserve requirements of banks. This would also increase the cost of borrowing from banks, thereby checking domestic credit expansion. However, it could also encourage firms to go to foreign creditors. Banks may also shift business to offshore centers and lend through their affiliates abroad, particularly where foreign presence in the banking sector is important. A certain degree of control over the banking system would thus be needed to prevent regulatory arbitrage and reduce the cost of intervention.

Countercyclical fiscal policy no doubt has a role to play in managing expansions. When the economy is overheating due to a boom in private spending supported by capital inflows, fiscal tightening would obviate the need for tighter monetary policy and higher interest rates and, hence, prevent encouraging further arbitrage inflows and appreciations. If budget revenues and expenditure structures are appropriately designed, much of this task could be done through automatic stabilizers. Furthermore, a budgetary surplus can also facilitate sterilization by absorbing excess liquidity without issuing government paper. But this would not eliminate the fiscal cost of sterilization since the surplus could be used to reduce the stock of public debt. In reality, governments in emerging markets often run procyclical fiscal policy, particularly in countries with chronic fiscal deficits and large public debt (Akyüz 2006).

During the recent surge in capital flows several developing countries have intervened in currency markets to absorb excess capital inflows and avoid sharp appreciations. Evidence from work in the Bank for International Settlements (BIS) (2005) suggests that sterilized intervention has generally been more successful in emerging markets than in advanced countries, particularly where the banking sector is closely controlled.[26] In China intervention has not only been successful in stabilizing the exchange rate but is also less costly to the government because of its control over the banking system.[27] This is also true for several other countries in East Asia, including those hit by the 1997–98 crisis, which have returned to quasi-dollar pegs, stabilizing their currencies within relatively narrow margins. There have also been examples of successful intervention in other parts of the developing world where capital inflows were relatively small.[28]

F. Reserve Accumulation as Self-Insurance

A policy of accumulating reserves through intervention in the foreign exchange market at times of strong capital inflows and using them during sudden stops and reversals appears to be a sensible countercyclical response to instability in international capital flows. When successful, interventions would prevent destabilizing currency appreciations and deterioration in the trade balance and, thus, lower the likelihood of currency turmoil, secure insurance against speculative attacks and reduce the degree of payments adjustment needed in case of such an event.

This strategy, however, lacks a strong rationale since it implies that a country should borrow only if the funds thus acquired are not used to finance investment and imports, but held in short-term foreign assets. Moreover, it does not prevent currency mismatches and exposure in private balance sheets. Finally, even when the quasi-fiscal cost of interventions is reduced by control over interest rates or higher reserve requirements, there could be a large transfer of resources abroad since the return on reserves is less than the cost of external borrowing.

Traditionally, reserves covering three months of imports were considered adequate for addressing the liquidity problems arising from time lags between payments for imports and receipts from exports. The need for reserves was also expected to lessen as countries gained access to international financial markets and became more willing to respond to balance-of-payments shocks by adjustments in exchange rates. However, capital account liberalization in developing countries and their greater access to private finance has produced exactly the opposite result. Private capital flows have allowed running larger and more persistent current account deficits beyond the levels that could be attained by relying on international reserves. But this has also resulted in an accumulation of large stocks of external liabilities. As a result, debtor countries have become increasingly vulnerable to sudden stops and reversals in capital flows, and this has increased the need to accumulate reserves to safeguard against currency turmoil and speculative attacks. Indeed, evidence shows a strong correlation between capital account liberalization and reserve holding, and a growing tendency to absorb capital inflows into reserves rather than current payments (Aizenman and Lee 2005; and Choi, Sharma and Strömqvist 2007).

After the East Asian crisis, emerging markets were strongly advised by the IMF to have adequate international reserves to cover their short-term debt – debt with a remaining maturity of up to one year – in order to reduce their vulnerability to sudden stops in capital flows.[29] Reserve accumulation accelerated with the strong recovery of capital inflows in the early years of the 2000s. It has gained further momentum as developing countries taken together started to run twin surpluses in their balance of payments; that is, on both current and capital accounts.[30] Since 2001 reserves have increased at an average rate of $500 billion per year, exceeding $4 trillion, or 6.8 months of imports, at the end of 2007.[31]

Of the $3.2 trillion additional reserves accumulated after 2001, two-thirds are earned and one-third borrowed.[32] Since in previous decades the current account of developing countries was in deficit, the entire stock of reserves held at the beginning of this decade was borrowed reserves. This means that almost half of the current stock of reserves in developing countries – that is, some $2 trillion – are borrowed reserves. This is about 250 percent of their short-term debt and 65 percent of their total debt to private creditors. Assuming a moderate 500 basis point margin between the borrowing rate and the return on reserves, the annual carry cost of these reserves would reach some $100 billion.[33] This constitutes a net transfer of resources to major reserve currency countries and exceeds the total official development assistance to developing countries.[34]

There is considerable diversity among developing countries in the sources of reserves. Outside China and fuel exporters, reserves in developing countries are entirely borrowed since, taken together, their current account has been in deficit. In both China and fuel exporters, current levels of reserves are very high, covering around thirteen and ten months of imports, respectively. China enjoys twin surpluses in its balance of payments and over a third of its reserves are borrowed, although in recent years reserves have been coming increasingly from its current account surpluses. By contrast, reserves in fuel exporters are entirely generated by oil surpluses; in these countries the current account surplus is partly used for net investment abroad, mostly through sovereign wealth funds (SWFs), and gross capital outflows exceed gross inflows.[35]

Some other countries such as Brazil generate relatively smaller amounts of current account surplus while at the same time receiving net inflows of capital. In Brazil, unlike in China, however, these are accompanied by sluggish growth. Because of a high degree of vulnerability to deterioration in the market sentiment and reversal of capital flows, monetary and fiscal policy are both kept tight, depressing growth and lowering import demand. Despite a strong appreciation, slow growth and favorable export markets have helped generate a small current account surplus. In most other emerging markets reserves are fully borrowed. This includes India where the currency has been kept relatively stable and the current account broadly in balance. There has been a rapid accumulation of reserves coming from net capital inflows, covering six months of imports and exceeding short-term debt by a large margin. Finally, a few emerging markets, including the most vulnerable ones, do not appear to have taken adequate self-insurance by translating capital inflows into additional reserves. These include Turkey, where reserves barely match short-term external liabilities, accumulated primarily by the private sector in recent years in search of cheap credit abroad, and Mexico, where they cover just over two months of imports. In both countries currencies have appreciated significantly. In Turkey this, together with relatively strong growth supported by unprecedented levels of capital inflows, has pushed the current account deficit to almost 8 percent of GDP, while in Mexico the deficit has been contained due to slower growth and strong oil revenues.[36]

G. Financial Regulations, Capital Controls and Risk Management

There are thus limits to monetary policy in emerging markets in managing surges of capital flows with a view to reducing vulnerability to sudden stops and reversals. While foreign exchange market interventions and reserve accumulation can succeed in preventing appreciations and trade deficits, these do not only entail significant costs, but also fail to check the build-up of fragility and exposure in balance sheets to external shocks and contagion. Under most circumstances, regulation and control of capital inflows would be the only viable option to address this problem.

In restraining the build-up of financial fragility at times of expansion, Minsky favors, as noted, controlling the level and growth of bank assets rather than interest rate hikes. Conventional prudential regulations, including capital and liquidity requirements and provisions for nonperforming portfolios, impose a certain degree of control over lending by banks while seeking to ensure their solvency. However, rather than reducing the cyclicality of the financial system, in reality risk assessment methods and prudential rules, including Basel I and Basel II, tend to aggravate procyclical behavior. Since rules about provisions are often based on current rates of loan delinquency, they result in inadequate provisioning and overexpansion of credit in boom times when asset prices and collateral values rise and loan performance improves. When the downturn comes, loan delinquency rises rapidly and standard rules on provisions can lead to a credit crunch. Similar difficulties apply to capital charges. Banks typically lose equity when an economy is hit by a massive exit of capital, hikes in interest rates, and asset price and currency declines. Enforcing capital charges under such conditions would only serve to deepen the credit crunch and recession.[37] Again, in determining capital adequacy, Basel I assigned low risk weights to interbank claims, encouraging short-term lending. But such loans driven by interest arbitrage were a major factor in exposure to short-term debt in the East Asian crisis. There are similar procyclical provisions in Basel II.[38]

It is possible to design prudential regulations in a countercyclical fashion to make them act as built-in stabilizers and reduce the cyclicality of the financial system.[39] Forward-looking rules may be applied to capital requirements in order to introduce a degree of countercyclicality. This would mean establishing higher capital requirements at times of financial booms, based on an estimation of long-term risks over the entire financial cycle, not just on the actual risk at a particular phase of the cycle. Similarly, not current but future losses can be taken into account in making loan loss provisions, estimated on the basis of long-run historical loss experience for each type of loan – a method practised in Spain. Again, long-term valuation rather than mark-to-market valuation may be used for collaterals in mortgage lending in order to reduce the risks associated with ups and downs in property markets, as done in many European countries. Finally, other measures affecting conditions in credit and asset markets, such as margin requirements, could also be employed in a countercyclical manner, tightened at boom times and loosened during contractions.

While appropriately designed prudential regulations could help smooth financial cycles and provide greater safeguards, they encounter limits in preventing financial instability and crises (Akyüz and Cornford 2002). This is clearly exemplified by the continued incidence of instability and crises in the United States, the country with the most sophisticated financial system in the world and state-of-the-art prudential regulation and supervision. Regulatory safeguards are pretty ineffectual in the face of macroeconomic shocks which can drastically alter the quality of bank assets. Furthermore, rules on the standards for risk assessment, capital requirements and provisions designed to check excessive risk taking and provide safeguards against such risks are constantly circumvented. This is often done by moving highly risky activities off balance sheets involving financial derivative products (such as structured investment vehicles widely used during subprime mortgage expansion in the United States) and guarantees and letters of credit that create contingent assets and liabilities. Until recently, this was increasingly facilitated in the United States by the deregulation of banks' activities that has the effect of removing firewalls between commercial and investment banking (Kregel 2007).

Since a large proportion of cross-border and cross-currency operations are intermediated by domestic financial institutions, notably banks, prudential rules no doubt have implications for international capital flows. Similarly, market-based (indirect) measures of control over capital flows, such as unremunerated reserve requirements, can be considered as part of prudential regulations in so far as they contribute to the solvency of these institutions. This means that measures to control capital flows cannot always be distinguished from prudential rules, and several measures that normally come under prudential policies can in fact be used for managing capital flows.

This overlap is sometimes taken to an extreme position that capital account liberalization should not be a cause for concern if it is accompanied by stronger and more comprehensive prudential regulations and effective supervision designed to manage risks associated with international capital flows and borrowing and lending in foreign currencies. Under capital account openness, prudential regulations become even less effective because of increased exposure to macroeconomic and exchange rate shocks. Furthermore, it is not always possible to regulate and control capital flows through prudential measures because they are not always intermediated by the domestic financial system – for instance, when local firms directly borrow or invest abroad, or nonresidents enter domestic securities markets. Therefore, direct restrictions over foreign borrowing and investment, and market access would need to complement prudential regulations appropriately extended to address the risks associated with capital flows through the banking system.

These risks could be addressed by applying more stringent rules for capital charges, loan loss provisions, and liquidity and reserve requirements for transactions involving foreign currencies. More specifically, banking regulations for the management of risks involving foreign exchange positions need to address three fundamental sources of fragility: maturity mismatches, currency mismatches and exchange-rate-related credit risks.

Maturity transformation is a traditional function of the banking system, but this should not be encouraged in the intermediation between international financial markets and domestic borrowers particularly since national monetary authorities cannot act as lenders of last resort in foreign currency. Banks tend to rely on central banks for the provision of international liquidity, trying to shift the cost of carrying large stocks of reserves onto them. This exposes them to exchange rate and interest rate risks since in the event of a sudden stop in capital inflows and inadequate central bank reserves, they may not be able to obtain international liquidity or do so only at very high costs. To reduce the liquidity risk, restrictions can be applied to maturity mismatches between foreign exchange assets and liabilities of banks with a view to preventing borrowing short in international markets and lending long at home, through stricter liquidity and reserve requirements and even direct limits.

Similarly it is important to restrict currency mismatches between banks' assets and liabilities and discourage banks from assuming the exchange rate risk. Banks with short foreign exchange positions (that is, where forex liabilities exceed assets) run the risk of losses from depreciations while those with long positions lose from appreciations. Furthermore, maturity mismatches between forex assets and liabilities can lead to exchange rate risks even when assets are matched by liabilities in the aggregate. Currency mismatches can be restricted through quantitative limits on short and long positions (e.g., as a proportion of equity or total portfolios) or minimum capital requirements on foreign exchange exposures. In most cases it may be more appropriate to prohibit currency mismatches altogether.

The third important risk associated with foreign exchange borrowing and lending by banks is the exchange-rate-related credit risk. Banks can eliminate currency and maturity mismatches by lending in foreign currency, but unless their borrowers have foreign exchange earning capacity, this simply implies the migration of the exchange rate risk to borrowers which, in turn, results in greater credit risk. This kind of lending is particularly common in economies where an important part of bank deposits is in foreign currencies. It also proved problematic in some countries in East Asia where banks lent heavily in foreign currency for investment in property as well as to firms with little foreign exchange earning capacity in the run-up to the 1997 crisis. Such practices could be discouraged by applying higher risk weights and capital charges for foreign assets and more stringent standards of provision for foreign currency loans, or prohibited altogether. However, evidence suggests that only a few emerging markets have addressed the vulnerabilities arising from currency-induced credit risks even though many of them appear to have taken measures to reduce exposure to foreign exchange risks (Cayazzo et al. 2006).

Emerging markets with stronger fundamentals regarding savings and investment, and current account and external debt positions, appear to be more willing to introduce measures of control over inflows at times of surges, while severely indebted countries highly dependent on foreign capital are more inclined to allow in speculative, short-term capital even when the potential risks they pose are clearly visible. In fact, in most of the latter countries the capital account appears to be financially more open than in those with stronger fundamentals.[40]

Naturally, the effects of the measures introduced depend, inter alia, on their nature.[41] In 1994 Malaysia imposed direct restrictions on acquisitions of short-term securities by nonresidents, and these were largely effective in improving the external debt profile, preventing asset bubbles, and allowing greater space for macroeconomic policy. By contrast, Chile used market-based unremunerated reserve requirements in a countercyclical manner, applied to all loans at times of strong inflows in the 1990s, but phased out when capital dried up at the end of the decade. This was effective in improving the maturity profile of external borrowing, but not in checking aggregate capital inflows, appreciations and asset price bubbles. Similar measures have been introduced in 2006 and 2007 in Thailand and Colombia, respectively.[42]

Periods of strong capital inflows also create the opportunity to strengthen controls over capital account measures so as to bring greater stability over the longer term. For instance, at the end of 2007 the Indian government adopted a proposal by the Securities and Exchange Board to restrict foreign buying of shares through offshore derivatives despite an adverse initial reaction from the stock market. This move was designed not so much to relieve the upward pressure on the rupee as to bring greater transparency by restricting the activities of the hedge funds (Kansara and Kansara 2007).

When capital inflows are excessive, it is also possible to adjust the regime on resident outflows to relieve the upward pressure on the currency. Chile followed this path in the 1990s for direct investment abroad. More recently China took a decision to permit investment by its residents in approved overseas markets for mitigating the pressure for appreciation and Brazil loosened restrictions on residents' outflows, allowing mutual funds to invest abroad up to 20 percent of assets. Chile and Korea have also liberalized rules limiting individual or institutional investments abroad.

Such a policy response is, in fact, an alternative to sterilized intervention, but does effectively nothing to prevent currency and maturity mismatches in balance sheets. Furthermore, liberalization of outflows may result in increases in inflows, particularly through the return of flight capital of residents.[43] Besides, once introduced for cyclical reasons, they cannot be easily reversed when conditions change. Therefore, greater attention would need to be paid to the longer-term implications of removing restrictions over resident outflows at times of temporary surges in capital inflows.

H. Conclusions

Real economic activity is increasingly shaped by developments in the sphere of finance both in advanced economies and in emerging markets. Boom–bust cycles in asset, credit and foreign exchange markets have become more frequent and damaging for productive investment and labor. These cycles are more difficult to manage in emerging markets since they are increasingly linked to boom–bust cycles in international capital flows determined by factors beyond their control, including monetary policies and conditions in major advanced economies. This is particularly true for countries with weak fundamentals with respect to external payments and asset positions and a high degree of dollarization. Since policy options during the rapid exit of capital are highly limited, emerging markets cannot afford to be complacent at times of booms in capital inflows and economic expansion. Rather, countercyclical policies should start in good times in order to reduce vulnerability to sudden stops and reversals.

The Keynesian analysis of financial instability provides considerable insights into understanding the dynamics of financial cycles in emerging markets, notably the interactions among asset, credit and currency markets and their impact on private spending and economic activity, which hold the key to determining the vulnerabilities involved. Its policy conclusion that financial regulation and control, rather than macroeconomic policy, provides the principal tool for securing financial stability is equally valid for managing capital inflows in emerging markets. There is a strong case for prudential regulations to be appropriately extended to address specific risks associated with international capital flows and borrowing and lending in foreign currencies. These should be combined with direct controls over access of foreign lenders and investors to domestic financial markets and over investment by residents abroad, and designed and used in a countercyclical manner – a conclusion that stands in sharp contrast with official advice to developing countries for dealing with surges in capital inflows.[44]

It should also be noted that financial regulations and direct and indirect control over capital flows are not foolproof. This means that monetary policy would need to be directed, from time to time, toward stabilization of the exchange rate, and this task would be easier if price stability is broadly assured and fiscal policy can be deployed as a countercyclical tool. These conditions are not always secured and there is considerable diversity among emerging markets in the space available for countercyclical macroeconomic policy. It is much more limited where there are structural savings, fiscal and foreign exchange gaps, high levels of sovereign and external debt, and excessive dependence on foreign capital. Such countries are systemically vulnerable to the whims of international capital flows and in need of much more fundamental changes than strengthening financial regulations and control or countercyclical macroeconomic policy.

Notes

1 First published in *METU Studies in Development* 1 (2008). An earlier version was presented in a conference "70 Years After the General Theory," organized by the Turkish Social Science Association, the Middle East Technical University, Ankara, on 1–2 December 2006.

2 The independent role of global factors is also recognized by the World Bank (2003, 26): "dynamics of net capital inflows and the changes of official reserves over the cycle do indeed indicate that the push factor is more important for middle income countries, while the pull factor dominates in high income countries." On postwar cycles in capital flows, see UNCTAD TDR (2003, Chapter II) and, for more recent episodes, IMF (2007b, Chapter III).

3 On the view that financial stability depends on price stability, see Schwartz (1995) and Bordo and Wheelock (1998).

4 See UNCTAD TDR (2003, chap. 6). See also Borio and Lowe (2002) on the emergence of financial imbalances and instability in a low inflation environment.

5 (Minsky 1992, 1). For Minsky's financial instability hypothesis, including its historical and intellectual background, see Papadimitriou and Wray (1998), De Antoni (2006) and Kregel (2007); and for its relation to Irving Fisher's debt deflation theory of the Great Depression, see Davis (1992).

6 For a survey of the evidence on procyclical behavior of risk assessments, credit and asset prices, see Borio, Furfine and Lowe (2001).

7 The hedge position describes a situation where expected cash flows are more than sufficient to meet all debt commitments now as well as in the future. In speculative finance there are short-term liquidity problems, requiring debt rollover, but over the longer term debt is likely to be payable. In the case of Ponzi finance there is no such likelihood – see Minsky (1986, 206–207).

8 For such episodes of financial and investment cycles in industrial and developing countries, see UNCTAD TDR (1992, chap. 2; 1998, chap. 3; 2001, chap. 1) and Davis (1992).

9 On the wealth effect of the equity boom on private consumption and savings in the United States during the second half of the 1990s, see Maki and Palumbo (2001).

10 For evidence on the procyclical effects of capital flows on economic activity in emerging markets, see Prasad et al. (2003).

11 A classic example is the 1992 EMS (European Monetary System) crisis which produced sharp drops in the lira and pound sterling without provoking financial crises in Italy and the United Kingdom. Similarly, at the end of the 1990s the dollar–yen rate was seen to change by over 20 percent within a matter of a week. Such swings were comparable to those experienced in East Asia in 1997 but did not produce widespread defaults and bankruptcies. A notable exception

is the 1987 stock market break which was closely linked to the instability of the dollar after the Plaza agreement.

12 For instance, despite persistent difficulties in the financial sector in Japan throughout the 1990s, the yen saw periods of strength as well as weakness. By contrast, the recent instability of the dollar is influenced, at least partly, by the subprime mortgage crisis.

13 For firms' investment and employment decisions under uncertainty, see Dixit and Pindyck (1994).

14 Here recovery refers to the phase of expansion where growth is only enough to make up for income losses during the preceding recession. It is jobless if the growth rate of employment is not positive.

15 For a discussion of various explanations offered, see Bernanke (2003), who emphasizes increased productivity, and Freeman and Rodgers (2005), who reject it.

16 UNCTAD TDR (2003, 6–9). For corporate debt, see Arestis and Karakitsos (2003).

17 According to Chichilnisky and Gorbachev (2005), such financing declined by 86 percent during 2001–2003. Earlier Groshen and Potter (2003, 5) had argued that "financial headwinds (particularly for risky new ventures) might arise from the collapse of initial public offering and venture capital financing," noting that "such 'financial headwinds' were blamed for extending the 1990–91 recession and cited as a reason for monetary easing at that time by Federal Reserve Chairman Alan Greenspan."

18 For the evidence on the evolution of employment and wages in boom–bust-recovery cycles in emerging markets, see UNCTAD TDR (2000, chap. 4), ILO (2004) and van der Hoeven and Lübker (2005), analyzed in greater detail in Akyüz (2006).

19 For a discussion of monetary policy and asset prices, see the papers in ECB (2003); and Detken, Masuch and Smets (2003) for a summary of the issues raised.

20 According to Borio and Lowe (2004, 19), "identifying **in a timely way** the development of financial imbalances with potential unwelcome implications for output and inflation, while very hard, is not impossible."

21 For the reasons behind the subprime crisis, including the role of deregulation, see Kregel (2007) and Kuttner (2007).

22 It is notable that such warnings are also coming from financial markets – see Roach (2007).

23 On why establishing an international lender of last resort could bring a host of other problems and may not be the appropriate response, see Akyüz and Cornford (2002).

24 For a discussion of policy options available in managing capital inflows, see Williamson (1995).

25 The fiscal cost of each dollar of reserves can be written as: $ig - ir = (ig - ix) + (ix - ir)$, where ig, ir and ix are the rates, in common currency, on government domestic debt, reserve holdings and external borrowing, and typically $ig > ix > ir$. The margin between ix and ir is determined mainly by the credit risk and between ig and ix by the exchange rate risk. When nonresident claims are only in foreign currencies, the first term on the right-hand side of the equation is captured by the holders of public debt at home and the second term is the net transfer abroad – what Rodrik (2006) calls the social cost of foreign exchange reserves. For the distinction between the two types of transfers and costs, see UNCTAD TDR (1999, chap. 5). Mohanty and Turner (2006) provide some estimates of the fiscal cost of intervention in emerging markets.

26 See, notably, Disyatat and Galati (2005) and Mihaljek (2005); and for a general survey of the issues involved, see Sarno and Taylor (2001). However, examining several episodes of surges in capital inflows since the early 1990s, the IMF (2007b, 124) concludes that "a policy of resistance to exchange rate pressures does not seem to be associated with lower real appreciation, while countercyclical fiscal policies have had the desired effect," and that sterilized intervention is likely to be ineffective when the influx of capital is persistent. According to Mohanty and Turner (2006), over the period 2002–2006, most central banks in Asia eased monetary policy and lowered interest rates as they were building reserves without losing control over inflation. This stands in sharp contrast to the conclusion reached by the IMF (2007b, 122) that "the policy of sterilized intervention [...] often tends to be associated with higher inflation." It is notable that the IMF does not make a single reference to work undertaken at the BIS in these areas.

27 In China, where over 80 percent of central bank securities are held by banks, reserve requirements were raised from 7 percent in 2003 to 15 percent in early 2008, and the share of central bank bills in total assets of banks more than doubled.

28 In Argentina, for instance, sterilization has been successful in keeping the real exchange rate within a target range and absorbing resulting excess liquidity through emission of central bank paper since 2002–03, despite opposition from the IMF – see Damill, Frenkel and Maurizio (2007).

29 This is known as the Greenspan–Guidotti rule. A problem with such rules is that vulnerability is not restricted to short-term debt; what matters in this respect is liquidity rather than maturity of liabilities: see UNCTAD TDR (1999, chap. 5). For an attempt to empirically determine the optimum level of reserves based on welfare criteria, see Jeanne and Rancière (2006).

30 Here capital account refers to nonreserve financial account as defined in IMF (2007a).

31 These figures, derived from the IMF *World Economic Outlook Database*, exclude the first tier newly industrialized economies – Korea, Taiwan, Singapore and Hong Kong.

32 Borrowed in the sense that they accompany increased claims by nonresidents in one form or another, including direct and portfolio equity investment, which generate outward income transfers.

33 The average spread of emerging market bonds exceeded 700 basis points during the 1990s and never fell below 400 basis points. It reached 1400 basis points after the Russian crisis, falling by half toward the end of the decade. Until 2002 it was over 600 basis points, falling rapidly afterwards and hovering around 200 basis points in recent months (World Bank 2007).

34 The method used here to estimate the cost of reserves differs from the procedure applied in the literature (e.g., Rodrik 2006) in making a distinction between borrowed and earned reserves. Polak and Clark (2006) also refer to borrowed reserves in their estimation of the cost to the poorest developing countries.

35 According to some estimates, total assets of SWF in fuel exporters now exceed $1.5 trillion, with an important part invested in equity abroad: see IMF (2007c, annex 1.2) and Truman (2007). But there is considerable hostility in the United States toward investment by SWF, sometimes seen as cross-border nationalization (Weisman 2007).

36 For currency movements and current account balances in emerging markets in recent years, see UNCTAD TDR (2007, chap. 1).

37 This happened in Asia when the IMF tried to strengthen regulatory regimes in the middle of the 1997 crisis – see UNCTAD TDR (1998, chap. 3, box 3).

38 On the procyclicality of Basel I and Basel II, see Akyüz and Cornford (2002), Cornford (2005) and Francis (2006).

39 This approach is finding considerable support in the BIS (2001, chap. 7); see also Borio, Furfine and Lowe (2001) and White (2006).

40 In various measures of financial openness, most economies in South and East Asia are classified as partially or largely closed while Latin American economies with weaker fundamentals are generally found to be more open; see, for example, Dailami (2000), notwithstanding the caveat in the next endnote.

41 The effectiveness of capital control measures is a highly contentious issue and is not addressed here. Cross-country comparisons of capital account regimes and their economic impact are generally based on indices constructed on the basis of on/off dummies according to whether or not there is a restriction in a particular area, without consideration of the nature of the restrictions and their enforcement – for a description of such measures, see Miniane (2004) and Eichengreen (2001). According to the IMF (2007b, 114), "episodes characterized by tighter controls on inflows are associated with narrower current account deficits and lower net private inflows."

42 For an assessment of the experiences in the 1990s, see Epstein, Grabel and Jomo (2003), and for the more recently introduced capital account measures, see IMF (2007b and 2007c).

43 For evidence on this effect, see Reinhart and Reinhart (1998).

44 Although according to a recent report by the Independent Evaluation Office "the IMF has learned over time on capital account issues" and "the new paradigm [...] acknowledges the usefulness of capital controls under certain conditions, particularly controls over inflows" (IMF/IEO 2005, 11), the IMF continues to be ambivalent even toward market-based measures to stem speculative inflows, advocating instead fiscal tightening and exchange rate flexibility even though, as noted in the same report, none of these standard measures recommended by the fund is a panacea, and each involves significant costs or dilemmas (IMF/IEO 2005, 60). For a critique of the IMF's approach to capital account issues, see Akyüz (2005).

References

Aizenman, J., and J. Lee. 2005. "International Reserves: Precautionary vs. Mercantilist Views, Theory, and Evidence." IMF Working Paper 05/198.

Akyüz, Y. 2000. "Causes and Sources of the Asian Financial Crisis." Paper presented at the Host Country Event: Symposium on Economic and Financial Recovery in Asia, UNCTAD X, Bangkok, 17 February. Reprinted in TWN Global Economy Series 1.

______. 2005. "Reforming the IMF: Back to the Drawing Board." UNCTAD, G-24 Discussion Paper 38.

______. 2006. "From Liberalization to Investment and Jobs: Lost in Translation." ILO Working Paper 74. Geneva.

Akyüz, Y., and A. Cornford. 2002. "Capital Flows to Developing Countries and the Reform of the International Financial System." In *Governing Globalization*, edited by D. Nayyar. New York: Oxford University Press.

Arestis, P., and E. Karakitsos. 2003. "The Conditions for Sustainable U.S. Recovery: The Role of Investment." The Levy Economics Institute of Bard College, Working Paper 378.

Bernanke, B. S. 2003. "The Jobless Recovery." Remarks made at the Global Economic and Investment Outlook Conference, Carnegie Mellon University, Pittsburgh. 6 November.

BIS (Bank for International Settlements). 2001. *Annual Report.* Basel.

______. 2005. "Foreign Exchange Market Intervention in Emerging Markets: Motives, Techniques and Implications." BIS Papers 24. Basel.

Bordo, M. D., and D. C. Wheelock. 1998. "Price Stability and Financial Stability: The Historical Record." *Federal Reserve Bank of St. Louis Review* 80(4): 41–62.

Borio, C., C. Furfine and P. Lowe. 2001. "Procyclicality of the Financial System and Financial Stability: Issues and Policy Options." BIS Working Paper 1. Basel.

Borio, C., and P. Lowe. 2002. "Asset Prices, Financial and Monetary Stability: Exploring the Nexus." BIS Working Paper 114. Basel.

______. 2004. "Securing Sustainable Price Stability: Should Credit Come Back from the Wilderness?" BIS Working Paper 157. Basel.

Cayazzo, J., A. G. Pascual, E. Gutierrez and S. Heysen. 2006. "Toward an Effective Supervision of Partially Dollarized Banking Systems." IMF, Working Paper 06/32.

Chichilnisky, G., and O. Gorbachev. 2005. "Volatility and Job Creation in the Knowledge Economy." In *Essays in Dynamic General Equilibrium Theory: Festschrift for David Cass*, edited by A. Citanna et al. New York: Springer.

Choi, W. G., S. Sharma and M. Strömqvist. 2007. "Capital Flows, Financial Integration, and International Reserve Holdings: The Recent Experience of Emerging Markets and Advanced Economies." IMF Working Paper 07/151.

Cornford, A. 2005. "Basel II: The Revised Framework of June 2004." UNCTAD Discussion Paper 178.

Dailami, M. 2000. "Managing Risks of Global Financial Market Integration". In *Managing Financial and Corporate Distress: Lessons from Asia*, edited by C. Adams, R. E. Litan and M. Pomerleano. Washington, DC: Brookings Institute Press, 447–80.

Damill, M., R. Frenkel and R. Maurizio. 2007. "Macroeconomic Policy Changes in Argentina at the Turn of the Century." International Institute for Labour Studies, Research Series. Geneva.

Davis, E. P. 1992. *Debt, Financial Fragility and Systemic Risk*. Oxford: Clarendon Press.

De Antoni, E. 2006. "Minsky on Financial Instability." In *A Handbook of Alternative Monetary Economics*, edited by P. Arestis and M. Sawyer. London: Edward Elgar, 154–71.

Detken, C., K. Masuch and F. Smets. 2003. Issues Raised at the ECB Workshop on Asset Prices and Monetary Policy, 11–12 December. www.ecb.europa.eu/events/pdf/conferences/detken-masuch-smets.pdf. Accessed 1 May 2006.

Disyatat, P., and G. Galati. 2005. "The Effectiveness of Foreign Exchange Intervention in Emerging Market Economies." BIS Papers 24, May, 97–113.

Dixit, A. K., and R. S. Pindyck. 1994. *Investment Under Uncertainty*. Princeton: Princeton University Press.

ECB (European Central Bank). 2003. "Asset Prices and Monetary Policy." ECB Workshop, 11–12 December. http://www.ecb.europa.eu/events/conferences/html/assetmp.en.html. Accessed 1 May 2006.

Eichengreen, B. 2001. "Capital Account Liberalization: What Do the Cross-Country Studies Tell Us?" *The World Bank Economic Review* 15 (3): 341–65.

Epstein, G., I. Grabel and K. S. Jomo. 2003. "Capital Management Techniques in Developing Countries: An Assessment of Experiences from the 1990s and Lessons for the Future." UNCTAD, G-24 Discussion Paper 27.

Francis, S. 2006. "The Revised Basel Capital Accord: The Logic, Content and Potential Impact for Developing Countries." IDEAs Working Paper 09/2006.

Freeman, R. B., and W. M. Rodgers. 2005. "The Weak Jobs Recovery: Whatever Happened to the Great American Job Machine?" *Economic Policy Review* 11 (1). Federal Reserve Bank of New York.

Groshen, E. L., and S. Potter. 2003. "Has Structural Change Contributed to a Jobless Recovery?" *Current Issues in Economics and Finance* 9 (8): 1–7. Federal Reserve Bank of New York.

ILO (International Labour Office). 2004. *A Fair Globalization: Creating Opportunities for All*. ILO, World Commission on the Social Dimension of Globalization. Geneva.

IMF. 2007a. *Balance of Payments and International Investment Position Manual*, sixth edition, draft (BPM6). Washington, DC.

______. 2007b. *World Economic Outlook*. October. Washington, DC.

______. 2007c. *Global Financial Stability Report*. October. Washington, DC.

IMF/IEO (IMF Independent Evaluation Office). 2005. *Report on the Evaluation of the IMF's Approach to Capital Account Liberalization*. Washington, DC.

Jeanne, O., and R. Rancière. 2006. "The Optimal Level of International Reserves for Emerging Market Countries: Formulas and Applications." IMF, Working Paper 06/229.

Kansara, B. R., and Y. Kansara. 2007. "Sebi Stand on PNs Shows India Is in Driver's Seat." *Financial Express*, 9 November.

Kindleberger, C. 1995. "Asset Inflation and Monetary Policy." *Banca Nazionale del Lavoro Quarterly Review* 192: 17–37.

Kregel, J. A. 2007. "The Natural Instability of Financial Markets." The Levy Economics Institute of Bard College, Working Paper 523.

Kuttner, R. 2007. "1929 Redux: Heading for a Crash?" 8 October. http://www.alternet.org/story/64684/1929_redux%3A_heading_for_a_crash. Accessed 20 January 2008.

Maki, D. M., and M. Palumbo. 2001. "Disentangling the Wealth Effect: A Cohort Analysis of Household Saving in the 1990s." FEDS Working Paper 2001-21. Washington, DC.

Mihaljek, D. 2005. "Survey of Central Bank Views on Effectiveness of Intervention." BIS Papers 24, May: 82–96.

Miniane, J. 2004. "A New Set of Measures on Capital Account Restrictions." IMF Staff Papers 51(2): 276–308.

Minsky, H. P. 1977. "A Theory of Systemic Fragility". In *Financial Crises*, edited by E. I. Altman and A. W. Sametz. New York: Wiley.

______. 1978. "The Financial Instability Hypothesis: A Restatement." North East London Polytechnic, Thames Papers in Political Economy. Reprinted in H. P. Minsky, *Can "It" Happen Again? Essays on Instability and Finance*. Armonk, New York.

______. 1986. *Stabilizing an Unstable Economy*. New Haven and London: Yale University Press.

______. 1992. "The Financial Instability Hypothesis." The Jerome Levy Economics Institute of Bard College, Working Paper 74.

Mohanty, M. S., and P. Turner. 2006. "Foreign Exchange Reserve Accumulation in Emerging Markets: What Are the Domestic Implications?" *BIS Quarterly Review*, September: 39–52.

Papadimitriou, D. B., and L. R. Wray. 1998. "The Economic Contributions of Hyman Minsky: Varieties of Capitalism and Industrial Reform." *Review of Political Economy* 10 (2): 199–225.

Polak, J. J. and P. B. Clark. 2006. "Reducing the Costs of Holding Reserves: A New Perspective on Special Drawing Rights." In *The New Public Finance: Responding to Global Challenges*, edited by I. Kaul and P. Conceição. New York: Oxford University Press.

Prasad, E. S., K. Rogoff, S. Wei and M. A. Kose. 2003. "Effects of Financial Globalization on Developing Countries: Some Empirical Evidence." IMF, Occasional Paper 220.

Reinhart, C. 2002. "Default, Currency Crises and Sovereign Credit Ratings." NBER Working Paper 8738.

Reinhart, C., and V. Reinhart. 1998. "Some Lessons for Policymakers Who Deal with the Mixed Blessing of Capital Inflows." In *Capital Flows and Financial Crises*, edited by M. Kahler. Ithaca, NY: Cornell University Press.

Roach, S. 2007. "America's Inflated Asset Prices Must Fall." *Financial Times*, 7 January.

Rodrik, D. 2006. "The Social Cost of Foreign Exchange Reserves." NBER Working Paper 11952.

Sarno, L., and M. P. Taylor. 2001. "Official Intervention in the Foreign Exchange Market: Is It Effective and, if so, How Does It Work?" *Journal of Economic Literature* 39 (3): 839–68.

Schreft, S. L., A. Singh and A. Hodgson. 2005. "Jobless Recoveries and the Wait-and-See Hypothesis." Federal Reserve Bank of Kansas City, *Economic Review*, fourth quarter: 81–99.

Schwartz, A. J. 1995. "Why Financial Stability Depends on Price Stability." *Economic Affairs*, Autumn: 21–25.

Truman, E. M. 2007. "The Management of China's International Reserves: China and a SWF Scoreboard." Peterson Institute for International Economics. Washington, DC.

UNCTAD TDR (various issues). *Trade and Development Report*. Geneva: United Nations.

Van der Hoeven, R., and M. Lübker. 2005. "Financial Openness and Employment: The Need for Coherent International and National Policies." Paper prepared for the G24 Technical Group Meeting, 15–16 September. IMF, Washington, DC.

WB/IEG (World Bank Independent Evaluation Group). 2006. *The World Bank in Turkey: 1993–2004. An IEG Country Assistance Evaluation*. Washington, DC: World Bank.

Weisman, S. 2007. "U.S. Fears Overseas Funds Could 'Buy up America.'" *International Herald Tribune*, 21 August.

White, W. 2006. "Procyclicality in the Financial System: Do We Need a New Macrofinancial Stabilization Framework?" BIS Working Paper 193. Basel.

Williamson, J. 1995. "The Management of Capital Flows." *Pensamiento Iberoamericano*, January–June.

World Bank. 2003. *Global Economic Prospects*. Washington, DC.

______. 2007. *Global Development Finance*. Washington, DC.

Chapter III

FROM LIBERALIZATION TO INVESTMENT AND JOBS: LOST IN TRANSLATION[1]

A. Global Economic Integration and the Labor Market

> There is nothing so disastrous as a rational investment policy in an irrational world.
> John Maynard Keynes

The past two decades have seen an increased global integration of labor markets to a degree unprecedented in recent history despite continued barriers to labor mobility, particularly for low-skilled and unskilled workers. This has been driven by a rapid opening to and expansion of international trade and capital flows, and a growing spread of global production networks, outsourcing and offshoring. The total number of workers producing for international markets in goods alone rose from around 300 million in 1980 to almost 800 million at the turn of the millennium. This has been associated with a significant increase in the share of developing countries in world trade in manufactures. Accordingly, about 90 percent of the labor participating in world trade is now low-skilled and unskilled (Akyüz 2003, 100–101). Integration of labor markets has also been reinforced by increased trade in services, traditionally seen as nontraded activities, particularly through expansion of cross-border supply of certain services from the territory of one country to the territory of another, and consumption and commercial presence abroad. Services trade has expanded not only in low-skill, low-value-added activities such as call centers or transaction processing, but also in high-value-added sectors that involve skilled labor, notably in information technology, finance and health. Developing countries have become suppliers of some of these services, including in high-value added sectors.

It has been argued that China's shift to capitalism, India's turn from autarky and the collapse of communism have added to the economically active persons in the world by almost 1.5 billion workers, doubling the global labor force (Freeman 2004 and 2005). As a consequence there has been a major shift in the global balance between labor and capital because the new entrants brought little useful capital with them; it is estimated that the global capital–labor ratio has been cut by more than 50 percent. This works against labor not only because labor productivity and pay tend to increase with the capital–labor ratio, but also because it shifts the balance of power in markets toward capital as too many workers chase too few jobs or too little capital to employ them. While capital and workers from the new entrants are the main winners, the pressure is felt primarily by workers already participating in the global economy, both in developing and industrial countries.[2]

Closer integration of developing countries with large surplus labor into the trading system and their greater openness to foreign firms have no doubt increased the global reserve army of labor and created new opportunities for capital to find cheaper locations for production for world markets and to connect them within international production networks. Since labor cost absorbs a large proportion of corporate revenues, wage differentials relative to productivity (i.e., differences in unit labor costs) is one of the main factors in the decisions by transnational corporations (TNCs) for the location of production through foreign direct investment (FDI). This underlines the so-called process of "global labor arbitrage" wherein high wage jobs in the developed world are seen to be eliminated in favor of low wage jobs in the developing world (Roach 2004).

Thus, even though labor mobility remains restricted, conditions in labor markets of different countries have become increasingly interdependent as many jobs have become highly mobile, moved from one location to another through international trade and investment.[3] The distribution of jobs across countries is also influenced by rapidly growing international financial flows through their impact on exchange rates, competitiveness and trade flows. Consequently, unemployment has increasingly become a global issue and it has become more and more difficult for any country to address its labor market problems independently of what is happening elsewhere.

It should, however, be recognized that global economic integration and interdependence of labor markets have not advanced as much as it is popularly believed. The participation of many countries with large amounts of surplus labor in the expansion of international production networks, international trade and investment is still limited. Furthermore, closer external integration has not always been accompanied by greater internal integration but by the emergence of enclave economies (Wade 2003, xlviii–li). Informal labor markets continue to absorb rising numbers of workers, particularly in countries which have experienced deindustrialization as a result of rapid liberalization (UNCTAD TDR 2003, chap. 5). Despite rapid expansion of FDI in developing countries, labor employed by TNCs is only a fraction of the total work force. This is so even in China where foreign-funded enterprises employ around four million workers and in India where employment in the entire IT services is one million. More importantly, evidence shows that despite rapid expansion of trade and FDI, large intercountry differences have persisted and indeed increased in wages in similar occupations, in a large part because of differences in labor market institutions and average productivity levels (Freeman and Oostendorp 2000).

Even though growth of international trade and labor arbitrage has so far had limited impact in terms of convergence of incomes and wages, there is little doubt that differences in labor costs have become increasingly important in the determination of international trade and investment flows, and in the distribution of jobs across countries, not only between the North and the South but also among developing countries. The combination of rapid economic integration and widespread global unemployment has become the main source of insecurity among workers. Growing competition among labor located in different countries, together with increased international mobility of capital, is putting pressure on labor and creating popular backlash against economic integration almost everywhere, including in industrial countries. This combination has also become a major source of tension in international economic relations as countries are inclined to export unemployment through mercantilist, beggar-my-neighbor exchange rate, trade and investment policies, creating frictions in international economic relations reminiscent of the difficulties that pervaded the world economy during the interwar period. It is the single most important reason why trade negotiations are facing increased difficulties from one round to the next, from one ministerial to another. It is also provoking xenophobia. All in all, the fate of globalization appears to hinge very much on the resolution of the problem of global unemployment.

The labor market problems in industrial countries cannot be traced to the expansion of North–South trade, but originate primarily in macroeconomic and financial policies pursued after the 1970s (UNCTAD TDR 1995, part 3; Akyüz, Flassbeck and Kozul-Wright 2002). Similarly, massive unemployment and underemployment in developing countries have their origins in structural weaknesses rather than in liberalization and integration. However, global labor arbitrage has certainly been aggravating labor market problems in many industrial countries, particularly for low-skilled labor. Similarly, a large number of developing countries have suffered deindustrialization and serious job losses as a result of the rapid liberalization of trade and investment. Capital has become increasingly footloose everywhere, including within the developing world, shifting the location of labor-intensive production in response to profit opportunities created by the emergence of cheaper producers.

That liberalization of trade and investment flows causes displacements in labor markets should not come as a surprise. However, the key problem is that global economic integration is serving more to redistribute investment and jobs among countries than to accelerate capital accumulation and job creation. International trade has been growing faster than ever, capital flows, including FDI, have been booming, but global income growth is slower and the world economy is allocating a smaller proportion of its income to fixed capital formation. This is why globalization is increasingly seen as a zero-sum game. This problem is due to a major shortcoming in the approach to international economic integration. Rather than aiming at full employment and rapid growth as a basis for the expansion of international trade and investment, policy in recent years has emphasized liberalization and global economic integration as a remedy to high unemployment and sluggish growth. This stands in sharp contrast with the approach adopted by the architects of the postwar economic system at the Bretton Woods and Havana Conferences, which saw full employment as a necessary condition for closer economic integration[4] – an approach which produced the golden age of capitalism with gradual but continuous liberalization and expansion of trade in the context of full employment and rapid growth.

With few notable exceptions, capital accumulation and job creation have been slow and erratic in developed and developing countries alike, in large part because policy has neglected these key determinants of social welfare. Consequently, at the level of existing production capacity and skill profile, the labor force cannot all be productively employed – that is, it is not possible to provide decent jobs for all. Even though there is excess capacity in some countries that could allow expansion of employment if adequate effective demand is forthcoming, the solution to unemployment lies primarily in the acceleration of capital formation and improvements of the skill profile of labor. In this process capital formation plays a key role because it also helps develop human skills by allowing application of knowledge acquired in formal education, and through learning by doing.

This chapter focuses on capital accumulation. The following section will review the experience regarding investment and growth over the past two decades. While attention will concentrate mainly on developing countries, features of developed countries that are similar in nature will also be discussed. A main conclusion that emerges is that the performance of a large number of developing countries which have adopted a strategy of reigniting a dynamic process of capital accumulation and growth through a combination of rapid liberalization, increased reliance on foreign capital and reduced public investment and policy intervention is highly disappointing. The review of the experience is followed by an examination of the role that policies have played in accumulation and growth in three areas. Section C will focus on the link between investment and profits and discuss the experience of late industrializers in harnessing profits through industrial-cum-investment policies for faster accumulation. Sections D and E will examine the impact of macroeconomic and financial policies respectively on accumulation, employment and growth. The chapter will end with a discussion on policy priorities at the national and international levels.

B. Capital Formation, Growth and Employment

1. Issues at stake

There is broad agreement that capital accumulation holds the key to economic growth even though there is no consensus on the precise nature of the link between the two. While there is no singular relation between investment and growth, in empirical studies capital accumulation emerges as the single most important variable with a robust and independent influence on economic growth.[5] This influence arises not only because investment, as a dynamic component of effective demand, generates income, but also it expands productive capacity and carries strong complementarities with other elements of growth, notably technological progress and productivity growth.[6] Clearly the structure of investment has an important bearing on the impact of accumulation on growth. Investment in machinery and equipment, as opposed to residential and nonresidential construction, appears to have a close linkage with growth across all developing regions (De Long and Summers 1993). Since much technological change is embodied in new equipment, and application of technology to production through use of machinery and equipment is essential for learning by doing, the scope for productivity growth would be limited in the absence of capital accumulation.

The impact of accumulation on labor is shaped by the extent to which growth is associated with increases in productivity and employment. Productivity growth is essential to increase labor income. In developing countries this typically takes place through the absorption of surplus labor by industry. However, when productivity growth is strong and demand is sluggish, the impact of growth on employment would be limited. This creates a potential trade-off between employment and productivity growth. However, since investment is an important component of effective demand and there are limits to raising productivity by substituting capital for labor, rapid growth in productivity can be combined with sizeable increases in employment if the pace of accumulation is strong.

The experiences of both Japan and Korea show that there need not be a trade-off between employment and productivity growth. During the 1960s and early 1970s in Japan overall labor productivity grew at a rate of 9 percent per annum while the unemployment rate was around 1 percent, thanks to a very high rate of gross fixed capital formation (GFCF) which stood at some 32 percent of GDP.[7] Productivity and wage growth in Korea was even more impressive during its strong drive for industrialization which also generated rapid increases in employment (Amsden 1989). In the 1980s it was argued that high unemployment in Europe compared to the United States was due to its faster productivity growth, but the United States was able to combine a rapid increase in productivity with falling unemployment in the 1990s as a result of a strong investment drive and growth.[8] In the past ten years productivity growth has been slower in the euro area where unemployment is higher than in both the United States and the United Kingdom.

How much growth is needed to make a dent in unemployment and how much investment is needed to generate such a growth are matters difficult to judge a priori because of the complexities in the relations among accumulation, growth and employment. Nevertheless, on underlying trends in growth of labor force and productivity, some 3 percent is generally considered as the minimum rate needed to start reducing unemployment in advanced industrial countries.[9] In developing countries, the labor force has been growing at around 2 percent per annum, and it could even grow faster if accelerated growth increases the participation rate. Productivity growth would need to be at least 3 percent in order to narrow the income gap with the industrial world, and again with increased accumulation and capital deepening productivity could be expected to increase even faster. On current trends, therefore, developing countries appear to need an average growth rate of at least 5 percent in order to close the productivity gap with the industrial world and improve conditions in the labor market by raising wages and reducing open and disguised unemployment. For the reasons noted, such a growth rate could be generated by different rates of investment, but thresholds of 20 and 25 percent of GDP are identified for low income and middle income countries respectively as the minimum rates of accumulation needed (UNCTAD TDR 2001; ECLAC 2000).

2. *The record*

On these criteria the recent performance of the world economy is poor. The period from 1980 to 2000 witnessed a remarkable collapse of growth in many parts of the world. In industrial countries, on average, growth of output per worker slowed from an annual rate of some 3 percent in 1960–80 to 1.5 percent during 1980–2000. The slowdown was similar for developing countries taken as a whole, from 2.5 percent to 0.6 percent. Notable exceptions include China and India where growth increased by 7 and 3.5 percentage points respectively between the two periods (Bosworth and Collins 2003, tables 1 and 5).

This performance is shaped in a large part by policies pursued in response to disequilibria and instability that pervaded first the developed countries then the developing economies in the late 1970s and early 1980s. In industrial countries the wage–price spiral set off by the first oil shock and accommodating macroeconomic policies resulted in rapid inflation. As the burden was placed largely on profits, incentives for private investment were reduced, resulting in stagflation. The policy response to the second oil price shock in 1979 was different. Aggregate demand policy no longer accommodated the acceleration in inflation induced by the oil price rise. "It was considered important not only to reduce inflation in its own right, but also to moderate growth of labor costs relative to product prices, and to restore profit margins to levels sufficient to support a higher rate of investment" (OECD 1982, 9).

This medium-term financial strategy, supported also by supply-side policies including the liberalization of labor, product and financial markets, was indeed successful in bringing inflation under control. By the end of the 1980s the downward trend in profits which had set in during the 1970s was already reversed. With increased mobility of capital, there was a rapid upward convergence of profits, and as of the mid-1990s both capital income share and the rate of return on capital in the business sector in the G-7 countries reached pre-1970s levels (UNCTAD TDR 1995, part 2, chap. 3; 1997, 95–98). However, this did not generate the expected boom in investment. In industrial countries taken together, investment as a percentage of GDP was lower in the 1990s than in the 1980s, and this decline continued further in the new millennium (Table 3.1). Growth in output and employment mirrored the trends in capital accumulation. After staying at 4 percent, the average unemployment rate in the OECD rose to 7.5 percent in the 1980s. Despite subsequent recovery in the United States and the United Kingdom, it fluctuated around an average rate of 7 percent during 1990–2004 without any long-term tendency to decline, in large part because at some 2.6 percent average growth in industrial countries has remained below the 3 percent threshold needed to make a dent in unemployment (OECD 2005a, 237, table A).

Policy response to the second oil shock and ongoing stagflation by industrial countries caused serious dislocations for developing countries. The combination of the hike in interest rates and sharp declines in commodity prices brought about by the 1980–82 recession in major industrial countries caused acute balance of payments problems, notably in commodity-dependent countries. Economic difficulties were aggravated as international banks behaved procyclically and cut lending to indebted countries, notably in Latin America, forcing many of them to generate trade surpluses by cutting economic growth and imports, eventually leading to a debt crisis and a lost decade. The policy response to falling growth and rising unemployment and inflation was essentially the same as the earlier response of industrial countries to stagflation, although it was much less orderly. The predominant objective was first to stabilize prices and balance of payments through monetary and fiscal tightening, and secondly to undertake market-friendly reforms in wide areas of policy with a view to overcoming structural difficulties that had rendered these countries highly vulnerable to external shocks and balance of payment crises. Stabilization and structural reforms that constituted the so-called Washington Consensus were to prepare the ground for sustained growth based on a rapid recovery in investment.

Table 3.1: Investment and FDI flows

	Investment as percentage of GDP			FDI as percentage of GDP		
	1981–90	1991–2000	2001–2004	1981–90	1991–2000	2001–2004
World	23.8	22.7	21.4	0.67	1.73	1.91
Industrial Countries[a]	22.8	22.0	20.3	0.75	1.60	1.74
Developing Countries[b]	26.0	25.6	25.5	0.43	2.28	2.57

Source: IMF World Economic Outlook, September 2005 and UNCTAD FDI database.
a. Includes also newly industrialized Asian economies.
b. Includes also countries in Central and Eastern Europe and Commonwealth of Independent States.

Table 3.2: Investment and growth in developing countries

	1981–90	1991–2000	2001–2004
East Asia and Pacific			
Investment[a]	26.8	31.9	36.1
Growth[b]	7.3	7.7	7.2
South Asia			
Investment[a]	20.2	21.6	23.1
Growth[b]	5.6	5.2	5.9
Latin America and Caribbean			
Investment[a]	20.2	20.0	18.3
Growth[b]	1.1	3.3	1.7
Sub-Saharan Africa			
Investment[a]	19.0	17.1	19.2
Growth[b]	1.6	2.3	3.3
Middle East and North Africa			
Investment[a]	25.5	20.5	21.7
Growth[b]	3.6	3.7	4.7
Europe and Central Asia			
Investment[a]	40.6	23.9	21.0
Growth[b]	1.8	-1.4	4.9

Source: World Bank (2005a).
a. Percentage of GDP.
b. Percentage per annum.

However, this policy approach failed to deliver on its promises. In developing countries taken together investment as a proportion of GDP was not higher in the 1990s or in the new millennium than the levels reached in difficult times of the 1980s (Table 3.1). Average growth in the 1990s was somewhat faster than in the 1980s (3.2 compared to 2.7 percent), since the underutilized capacity that emerged during the times of import strangulation in the 1980s allowed output to rise without additional investment as

Table 3.3: Gross fixed capital formation, 1970–2004 (percentage of GDP)

	1970–80	1980–90	1990–2000	2000–2004
Argentina	21.5	16.4	16.5	13.9
Bolivia	15.6	11.4	16.8	14.3
Brazil	32.4	25.5	21.8	20.0
Chile	15.4	15.1	20.9	21.1
China	28.2	28.9	32.6	40.9
Colombia	18.4	18.7	18.1	15.4
Côte d'Ivoire	34.1	23.6	13.8	9.6
Ecuador	37.0	30.5	24.0	22.9
Egypt	22.5	29.2	17.5	17.5
Ghana	21.6	16.0	27.5	24.3
India	17.9	19.3	21.0	22.4
Indonesia	–	20.7	23.7	20.4
Kenya	21.1	15.9	15.9	13.2
Korea	19.7	27.5	35.4	30.0
Malaysia	19.4	24.7	32.3	23.8
Mexico	20.4	18.0	18.8	20.3
Morocco	24.9	22.1	20.8	24.7
Nigeria	24.4	17.1	19.6	22.1
Pakistan	21.6	20.5	18.6	16.0
Peru	16.4	16.8	21.1	18.6
Philippines	16.9	18.8	19.7	18.2
Taiwan	19.0	18.8	22.2	19.2
Thailand	31.9	33.6	38.3	22.7
Turkey	15.2	18.6	24.1	18.1
Uruguay	15.5	13.4	13.9	10.5
Venezuela	31.6	25.4	22.0	19.3
Latin America	**25.1**	**20.8**	**19.8**	**18.9**
Asia	**21.6**	**23.9**	**28.6**	**29.9**
Asia excluding China	**19.4**	**22.4**	**26.7**	**23.3**
Sub-Saharan Africa	**24.0**	**19.5**	**17.4**	**17.4**

Note: Figures for regions are weighted averages of the values of the countries listed, except for sub-Saharan Africa, where the average is for all countries of the region.
Source: Based on World Bank, World Development Indicators and Thomson Financial Datastream.

external constraints eased up.[10] There has also been an acceleration of growth in the new millennium as private capital flows to emerging markets recovered sharply thanks to exceptionally low international interest rates and ample global liquidity. But, even an average growth rate of 4.5 percent attained in the past few years would not make much of a dent in unemployment even if it could be sustained.

This broad picture conceals considerable diversity among developing countries. In terms of investment and growth two regions stand out: East Asia and South Asia (Tables 3.2 and 3.3).[11] Both regions have improved their investment performance since the 1980s and maintained an average growth rate above 5 percent. The performance of these regions is dominated by two large economies, China and India, which have adopted a measured and gradual approach to liberalization, but most of the remaining countries, including both the first tier newly industrializing economies (NIEs), notably Korea and Taiwan, and the second tier NIEs, Indonesia, Malaysia and Thailand, have also had strong investment and growth performance. Clearly the sheer weight of China and India implies that their performances matter a lot more than those of the other developing countries in reducing global unemployment and poverty. Indeed, the income convergence that is claimed to be taking place between the North and the South over the past two decades is due largely to rapid growth in these countries.[12]

But there are also important differences between China and India in terms of accumulation and growth. In the 1990s investment in China generated a lot more growth than in India. During the decade the average investment rate in China was 60 percent higher than in India while its growth exceeded that of India by a greater margin (10.1 percent against 5.5 percent). This relation appears to have been reversed in the more recent period as China deepened its integration into the global economy at a faster pace, and experienced a surge in inflows of FDI, an investment boom and rapid growth of exports and imports. The investment rate in China rose in the new millennium, averaging at some 41 percent of GDP, while its average growth was 8.5 percent. By contrast, in India growth accelerated compared to the 1990s, averaging at some 7 percent between 2000 and 2005, while its investment rate was only marginally higher, suggesting that since the turn of the decade investment in India has generated more growth than in China. Among the factors mentioned for apparently high overall capital—output ratio in China compared to India are excess capacity, misallocation of resources and a gross wastage of capital (Nagaraj 2005).[13]

There are only 18 developing countries with an average growth rate of 5 percent or more during 1990–2003 and eight of them are in Asia (World Bank 2005a, table 4.1). Only two of these, Chile and the Dominican Republic, are in Latin America. In that region capital accumulation fell sharply during the debt crisis of the 1980s, but the recovery that began at the end of the decade was not robust enough for it to return to earlier levels. After many years of reform along the lines of the Washington Consensus and a reasonable degree of success in restoring fiscal and monetary discipline and price stability, the region has continued to suffer from low investment and anaemic growth, failing to address deep-seated structural difficulties, including massive unemployment and underemployment. Furthermore, the more recent period saw a weakening of the link between accumulation and growth despite extensive market-oriented reforms undertaken to improve the efficiency of allocation and use of resources. In the 1960s and 1970s both GFCF and GDP rose, on average, at similar rates, around 6 percent per annum. In the 1980s GFCF stagnated and there was little growth in GDP. During the 1990s, GFCF grew on average by some 5 percent, about the same rate as in the 1960s, but GDP growth was slower, staying around 3 percent. This weakening investment–growth link is associated with a decline in the share of investment in and imports of machinery and equipment in several countries of the region (UNCTAD TDR 2003, 80–82).

The situation is much the same in sub-Saharan Africa. The region enjoyed relatively rapid accumulation and growth in the 1960s and early 1970s. However, these investment booms were often followed by slumps, rather than being translated into a virtuous growth process. During the 1980s and 1990s, even where adjustment policies were rigorously implemented, they failed to establish a sustained accumulation process, with growth lasting as long as commodity prices and/or aid flows were favorable (Akyüz and Gore 2001, 272). Even though in sub-Saharan Africa there were eight countries with growth rates of 5 percent or more during 1990–2003, GFCF in the region as a whole was below the 20 percent threshold, and at some 3 percent average growth was too weak to make a tangible improvement in the conditions of labor. Furthermore, as in Latin America, the investment–growth link is weak compared to the 1970s.

3. Public investment

The past two decades have seen a considerable retrenchment of the public sector in most countries both in the North and the South through the privatization of state-owned enterprises and cuts in public investment. In the more dogmatic version of the Washington Consensus the withdrawal of the public sector has been advocated not only from industry and commerce, but also from public utilities on the assumption that the private sector would be willing and able to invest in these areas if the investment climate was right, and downsizing the public sector is one way of improving the investment climate. Thus, many governments simultaneously divested through privatization, stopped investing in industry and commerce, and started reducing investment in physical and human infrastructure to allow the private sector a greater role. Where governments run large deficits and debt, such arguments gained additional force, and invariably the burden of fiscal adjustment fell on public investment.

This approach is based on the premise that public investment would have little or even a negative effect on economic growth. According to this view, over the short term a higher level of public investment would crowd out private spending by pushing up interest rates, and the impact would be felt primarily by private investment as the most interest-sensitive component of private demand. Secondly, it could drive out the private sector by entering activities that might otherwise offer acceptable returns to private investors. Thirdly, the public sector tends to make bad investments because state-owned enterprises operate under a soft budget constraint. Finally, since, for the same reason, public enterprises are not run efficiently, even investment of the same quality would generate higher output in the hands of the private than in the hands of the public sector.

While there are widespread inefficiencies in the public sector in many countries, the argument that state-owned enterprises are invariably inefficient and government investment is unproductive cannot stand against evidence. In many developing countries public enterprises played a strategic role in industrialization and generated significant positive externalities for the private sector while in industrial countries there is ample evidence that government capital is productive, even more so than private capital.[14] Again the evidence on crowding out does not lend support to any definite conclusions on the impact of public investment on private investment and overall capital accumulation.[15] It is often the case that even when there is a crowding out effect, a higher level of public investment is rarely associated with a lower level of aggregate investment. It has, thus, been recognized by the IMF (2004, 6) that the "possibility that a declining share of public investment in GDP could have adverse consequences for economic growth over the longer term is a legitimate concern, although the empirical evidence in this area is inconclusive."

Despite the evidence that the impact of public investment on overall capital accumulation and growth is generally positive, this indiscriminate attack on public ownership and investment gained wide acceptance, resulting in deep cuts in public investment. In most OECD countries the downward trend in public investment started already in the 1970s, on average falling from around 4.5 percent of GDP in the early 1970s to 4 percent at the end of the decade. The decline accelerated with the rise of neoliberalism in the 1980s, and by the end of the millennium the ratio of public investment to GDP was as low as 3 percent for the OECD as a whole (IMF 2004). The decline is more marked in Europe, particularly in the United Kingdom where public investment fell to 1.5 percent of GDP in recent years. In the United States there was a recovery in the early 1980s, followed by a relatively stable rate of around 3 percent of GDP. In Japan, there is no visible downward trend; on average public investment has been above 6 percent of GDP over the past two decades. With the notable exceptions of Japan, Sweden and some smaller European countries, there have been sharp declines in the public net capital stock relative to GDP (Kamps 2004).

Public investment as a proportion of GDP is typically higher in developing than in developed countries. The 1960s and 1970s saw a rapid increase in public investment which reached 10 percent of GDP at the end of the 1970s in developing countries taken together. In some regions such as South Asia and North Africa, it was even greater than private investment (Everhart and Sumlinski 2001). In Latin America the decline that started with the debt crisis in the 1980s continued in the 1990s and public investment as a proportion of GDP fell even below the levels of some industrial countries with much better human and physical infrastructure (Table 3.4). In Turkey, public investment as a proportion of GDP fell as the debt burden increased: during 2002–2004 it averaged at around 2 percent of GDP, while interest payments from the budget stood at some 16 percent (ISSA 2006, table 12). By contrast, in East Asia there has been no downward trend in public investment and currently its share in GDP is more than three times the average rate in the major Latin American countries and Turkey. In Africa, where data are limited, public investment in a selected number of countries fell from over 12 percent in the late 1970s to some 7 percent in the 1980s. There was a weak recovery beginning at the end of the 1980s, with public investment staying around 9 percent of GDP throughout the 1990s (IMF 2004, figure 2).

The retrenchment of public investment outside some Asian countries has gone to such an extent that it has become a major concern even to the Bretton Woods Institutions (BWIs). In a recent report the IMF (2004, 9–10) has expressed concern that much of the cuts in public investment were undertaken as part of fiscal adjustment rather than for allowing greater room for private initiative, noting that such cuts in the 1980s in Latin America were on average more than three times the cuts in current spending, and that half of the fiscal adjustment in several countries during the 1990s reflected compression of investment in infrastructure. It is noted that the decline in public investment reduced

Table 3.4: Public investment (percent of GDP)

	1980–90	1990–2000
Developing Countries	8.6	7.7
Latin America[a]	6.3	3.9
East Asia[b]	12.2	12.3
China	17.6	19.0

Source: UNCTAD TDR (2003).
a. Argentina, Brazil, Chile, Colombia and Mexico.
b. Indonesia, Malaysia, the Philippines, Korea and Thailand.

long-term growth by 1.5–3 percent in Latin America. There is a sizeable infrastructure gap in most developing countries. Despite increased emphasis on private–public partnerships, the private sector has not increased infrastructure investment as hoped for. It is also recognized that this not only compromises the growth prospects of these regions but also reduces the likelihood of meeting MDGs.

4. FDI and capital formation

Another important ingredient of the new development strategy has been increased reliance on FDI. In addition to the belief that it would provide resources for development and balance of payments support, FDI has been seen as a crucial factor for success in industrialization because of its role in the transfer of technology and entrepreneurial know-how, in linking developing countries to international production networks and enhancing their access to global markets for goods and finance. Many countries have thus removed impediments to FDI and provided foreign investors with incentives and security through unilateral action or bilateral investment agreements, over and above those enjoyed by national investors.[16]

These policies, together with the increased outreach of TNCs, have resulted in a rapid increase of FDI flows to developing countries, rising from some $20 billion at the end of the 1980s to $160 billion a decade later and almost $240 billion in 2005 (IMF 2005). While in absolute terms much of the increased FDI is concentrated in the larger East Asian and Latin American countries, almost all regions shared in this expansion, particularly when measured as a proportion of income. In South America FDI has been attracted primarily by privatization of public enterprises; on some estimates about two-thirds of the FDI inflows to the region were linked to privatization (UNCTAD TDR 1999, 118–19). In several countries in Central America and East Asia, including Mexico, Malaysia and China, FDI has been in the form of greenfield investment, designed to link these low-cost locations to international production networks for the production of labor-intensive manufactures for global markets. In Africa FDI has concentrated mainly in countries rich in natural resources, particularly fuel and minerals (UNCTAD TDR 2005). In East Asia efforts to promote FDI have been premised on its potential contribution to technology, know-how and market access rather than to balance of payments. By contrast in Latin America, where liberalization of regimes governing FDI have gone further, the prime objective has been the financing of public sector and external deficits and debt.

The impact of FDI on capital accumulation and growth is highly contentious.[17] Its contribution to balance of payments appears to be generally negative over the long term even though it may provide net positive transfers in the short run before profit remittances pick up. This is so not only where FDI is concentrated in nontraded activities, but also in export-oriented sectors linked to international production networks because of high import content and profit margins.[18] This appears to be the case even in China and Malaysia, two of the most successful countries in attracting export-oriented greenfield FDI (Akyüz 2005a).

When FDI is in the form of acquisition of existing public or private assets, it has no direct contribution to domestic capital formation although changes in ownership can give rise to productivity gains or stimulate investment that would not have otherwise taken place. Privatization could also add to domestic capital accumulation if the proceeds are used for investment, but not if they are used for servicing debt. When FDI is in greenfield investment, its contribution to GFCF would depend on its effect on the behavior of domestic investors. Research on whether FDI crowds in or crowds out domestic investment is not conclusive and it appears that the impact of FDI depends on other variables endogenous to the growth process, including those linked to policy (Blomstrom, Lipsey and Zejan 1994; Alfaro, Chanda, Kalemli-Ozcan and Sayek 2001; Borensztein, de Gregorio and Lee 1998).

That the recent surge in FDI flows has contributed not so much to an acceleration of capital formation and growth as to a reallocation of production facilities, jobs and ownership across different countries can be clearly seen in Table 3.1. For the world economy as a whole, in recent years the share of FDI as a proportion of GDP has almost tripled compared to the 1980s, but the proportion of world GDP allocated to investment has fallen by 2.5 percentage points. The contrast is even sharper in developing countries where the increase in total FDI inflows as a proportion of GDP is almost fivefold during the same period.

There is again considerable diversity in the relation between FDI inflows and capital formation in developing countries. Figures in Table 3.5 show that the difference between East Asia and Latin America in the policy approach to FDI is also reflected by its relation to domestic capital formation. Both regions witnessed a significant increase in FDI inflows as a proportion of GDP during the 1990s compared to the 1980s. However, in Latin America there was a widespread association of increased FDI with reduced fixed capital formation. For the region as a whole FDI as a proportion of GDP was higher in the 1990s than in the 1980s by more than 1.7 percentage points, but the share of GFCF in GDP was lower by some 0.6 percentage points. In all major Latin American economies FDI as a proportion of GDP rose strongly while GFCF either stagnated or fell between the two periods. The picture is much the same when FDI inflows are compared with private investment alone. It is also notable that the inverse association between GFCF and FDI is found not only in countries where FDI has been attracted primarily by privatization, such as Argentina and Brazil, but also in Mexico where there was considerable greenfield investment stimulated by NAFTA. Again in several countries

Table 3.5: Changes in FDI and gross fixed capital formation: 1990–2000 compared to 1980–90 (percentage of GDP)

	FDI	GFCF
Latin America and Caribbean		
Argentina	2.0	0.1
Bolivia	4.9	3.2
Brazil	1.3	–1.3
Chile	3.4	5.7
Colombia	0.9	0.5
Costa Rica	1.2	–1.4
Jamaica	3.8	6.6
Mexico	1.5	–0.8
Peru	2.6	–2.5
Uruguay	0.1	0.1
Venezuela	2.4	2.6
South Asia		
Bangladesh	0.2	5.6
India	0.4	1.7
East Asia		
China	3.5	4.8
Hong Kong	4.4	2.5
Indonesia	0.3	1.7
Korea	0.5	4.2
Malaysia	3.0	5.5
Philippines	1.1	-0.7
Singapore	-0.4	-4.8
Thailand	1.0	4.8
Taiwan	0.2	0.8
Africa		
Cameroon	0.9	–4.4
Côte d'Ivoire	1.6	–3.5
Egypt	–1.1	–7.3
Kenya	–0.1	–0.7
Mauritania	–0.6	–5.5
Mauritius	0.6	5.2
Morocco	1.2	–1.1
Senegal	1.0	3.5
South Africa	0.6	–6.7
Tunisia	0.9	–0.8
Zimbabwe	1.3	3.1

Source: UNCTAD TDR (2003).

in Africa FDI and GFCF moved in opposite directions. By contrast in none of the rapidly growing East Asian NIEs was rising FDI associated with falling domestic GFCF.[19]

Even in the presence of a crowding out effect, higher FDI tends to result in increased GFCF since domestic investment is unlikely to fall to the same extent as FDI rises.

In this respect the negative association between the two in Latin America is quite revealing. Whatever the direct impact of FDI on domestic capital formation may have been, this is a clear indication that the economic conditions that attracted foreign enterprises were not conducive to faster capital formation, and that the two sets of investment decisions can be driven by different considerations. As discussed in subsequent sections, in many economies experiencing strong surges in FDI but stagnant or declining GFCF, macroeconomic and financial policies have played an important role in creating conditions favorable to asset acquisition but not to fixed capital formation.

5. Policy failure: Omission or commission?

The evidence thus shows that investment and growth have generally been too weak to improve labor market conditions in most developing countries. The outcome of the strategy adopted for activating a dynamic process of capital accumulation, technological progress and growth based on rapid domestic and external liberalization, reduced public investment and policy intervention, and increased reliance on FDI, is disappointing. The slowdown in accumulation that emerged in the course of adjustment to the debt and balance of payments crises of the 1980s has become a more permanent feature of these economies. Weak private investment has been associated with declines in the share of public investment in GDP, and the surge in FDI encouraged by rapid opening up, privatization and special incentives has failed to ignite growth by accelerating capital formation. Furthermore the link between accumulation and growth has weakened despite measures adopted to improve the allocation and utilization of resources.

The poor outcome in terms of investment and growth has not given rise to a fundamental rethinking of Washington Consensus policies despite the rhetoric to the contrary. In fact, there has been a tendency to attribute failure to omissions and slippages in reforms rather than shortcomings in the policies recommended. Originally, it was expected that restoring macroeconomic stability through monetary and fiscal orthodoxy would prepare the ground for sustained growth based on private investment. The subsequent failure of investment to recover despite the apparent success in stabilization and structural reform was interpreted by the World Bank (1992, 34–45) as a temporary "investment pause" in the "transition to a new relative price regime." However, as the investment pause became a permanent feature for most economies and it became clear that the first generation reforms of "getting the prices right" failed to deliver on their promises, attention has turned to second generation reforms emphasizing "getting the investment climate right" by combining macroeconomic stability with good governance and policies promoting greater competition. It has been argued that richer and faster-growing countries tend to have more competition and fewer barriers to entry, and promotion of productive investment would require removing barriers to imports and foreign investment, and dismantling administrative obstacles to private business (World Bank 2003, 85–95).

Once again this is an act of faith. First, the relationship between economic openness and growth is highly controversial, both theoretically and empirically. Second, even though there are still barriers to international trade and investment, there has been considerable liberalization in these areas. Similarly while some administrative obstacles to business remain, governance has improved considerably in most developing countries. Therefore, shortcomings in these areas cannot explain why investment and growth performance has failed to improve and, in fact, has in many cases worsened. More importantly, as discussed in the following section, it is a gross exaggeration to claim that successful examples of rapid accumulation and growth in East Asia relied on competitive market forces.

C. Managing Profits and Accumulation

Despite increased international mobility of capital, a very large proportion of domestic investment continues to be supported by domestic savings in both developed and developing countries.[20] The conventional theory tells us that the savings propensity increases with income; that is, the rich save proportionately more than the poor and richer countries are capital abundant compared to less developed economies. In reality, however, some countries save and invest a lot more than the others at similar levels of per capita income, and more equitable income distribution is not always associated with lower savings and investment.

This is certainly the case in the industrial world, as exemplified by a comparison between Japan and the United States.[21] But perhaps it is even more so in the developing world. For the sample of countries in Table 3.3 there is a very weak correlation between investment rates and per capita incomes.[22] Countries such as Argentina, Brazil, Mexico, Uruguay and Venezuela with per capita incomes at least three times the levels in China, India and Indonesia have much lower savings and investment rates. Again in many Latin American countries income concentration measured as the percentage share of the richest quintile of the population in national income is much greater than the concentration ratio in high-saving and high-investing Korea and Indonesia (Table 3.6). Some second tier NIEs such as Malaysia and Thailand have concentration ratios comparable to Latin America, but considerably higher private investment ratios. Regression estimates show that no more than 36 percent of the variations in investment rates for countries in Table 3.6 for the period 1995–2000 can be explained by intercountry differences in per capita income and the concentration ratio.

Evidence shows that after the initial stages of development, when agricultural incomes provide the main source of investment, private capital accumulation in industry is financed primarily by profits in the form of corporate retentions. Indeed in the course of industrial development, dynamic interactions between profits and investment, or the profit–investment nexus, become the main driving force whereby profits constitute simultaneously an incentive for investment, a source of investment and an outcome of investment (Akyüz and Gore 1996). A high rate of profit retention is usually associated with a high rate of corporate investment since the decision of corporations to save (i.e., to retain profits rather than distribute them as dividends) is not independent of their decision on investment.

In major industrial countries up to 95 percent of corporate investment was financed by retained earnings during 1960–90, with the ratio being higher in the United States,

Table 3.6: Capital accumulation and income concentration

	I[a] (1995–2000)	IC[b] (1995–2000)	ACR[c] (1995–2000)	ACR[c] (1980–94)
Korea	27.4	39.3	69.7	52.7
Thailand	23.7	48.4	49.0	45.6
Indonesia	19.3	41.1	47.0	44.4
Malaysia	22.1	54.3	40.7	31.8
Turkey	18.8	47.7	39.4	21.6
Peru	18.4	51.2	36.0	28.7
India	15.5	46.1	33.7	28.1
Bangladesh	14.3	42.8	33.5	16.3
Morocco	14.6	46.6	31.4	28.9
Philippines	16.2	52.3	31.1	32.9
Egypt	12.1	39.0	31.0	18.7
Chile	18.3	61.0	30.1	24.6
Argentina	16.4	55.3	29.7	26.6
Mexico	16.6	57.4	28.9	22.4
Costa Rica	14.5	51.0	28.5	27.7
Tunisia	12.6	47.9	26.2	29.4
Brazil	16.1	64.1	25.1	26.0
Côte d'Ivoire	11.0	44.3	24.8	15.8
Kenya	11.8	51.2	23.0	16.6
Pakistan	9.1	41.1	22.1	18.4
Colombia	10.1	60.9	16.7	17.8
Venezuela	8.6	53.2	16.1	18.8
Ghana	4.9	46.7	10.5	0.4

Source: UNCTAD TDR (2003).
a. Private investment as a percentage of GDP.
b. Income concentration; share of the richest quintile of the population in total income.
c. Accumulation–concentration ratio; share of private investment in GDP expressed as a percentage of the share of the richest quintile of the population in total income.

United Kingdom and France than in Japan and Italy.[23] In most of these countries the contribution of gross profits to total savings and capital formation was as high as and even higher than household savings. Household gross savings did not significantly exceed household gross capital formation, and voluntary household savings were just sufficient to meet housing investment while mandatory savings in pension contributions, together with gross retained earnings, financed corporate investment.

For the more recent period there appears to be a decline in the extent to which corporate profits have been channeled into investment in the major industrial countries. As already noted aggregate capital formation as a proportion of GDP has been stagnant or falling in the G7 countries even though the rate of return on capital has been rising since the early 1980s. Indeed, there is a visible downward trend in the ratio of investment to capital income in the business sector. As seen in Chart 3.1, during 1980–2000 this ratio moved in parallel with the overall business cycle, falling at times of stagnation or recession (namely 1980–82; 1991–92 and 2001–2002) and rising subsequently. However, each recovery appears to be

Chart 3.1: Private nonresidential investment as a percentage of capital income in the business sector

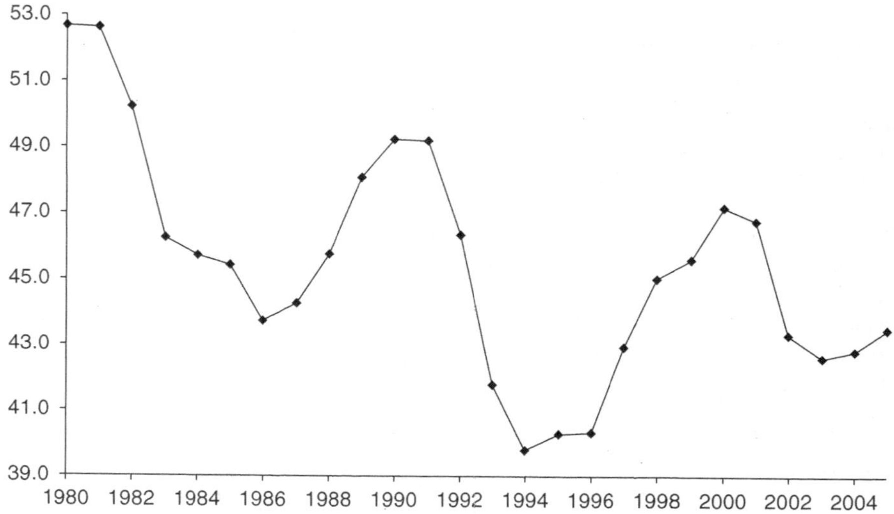

Source: OECD Economic Outlook, December 2004.

weaker than the previous one. Thus, for the G7 countries taken together, investment is now generating higher returns than before while profits are generating less investment.

Available evidence also shows that high rates of capital accumulation in more successful developing countries have been associated with high rates of corporate retention and investment. This is particularly true in East Asian countries including Korea, Taiwan, Malaysia, Thailand and China where the impressive savings–investment performance over the past decades compared to other developing countries owed a great deal to significantly higher business savings and investment rates rather than higher household savings, except in Malaysia and Singapore where household savings were particularly high due to compulsory savings schemes. During the 1980s in these countries business savings were in the order of 8–14 percent of GDP, financing between 42 percent and 65 percent of corporate investment.[24] Evidence for the more recent period also shows a strong relationship between a high savings rate, a high share of manufacturing in GDP and a high profit share in East Asia, while in Latin America savings rates were lower than expected on the basis of the share of profits in income (Ros 2000, 79–83).

The accumulation–concentration ratio in Table 3.6 provides a measure of the animal spirit of the entrepreneur class in countries for which data are available. It effectively gives the ratio of private investment to income received by the richest quintile of the population. Since private investment is undertaken primarily by the richest strata, this ratio is a reasonably good indicator of the propensity of the rich to save and invest. Successful East Asian countries again top the table. The ratio in Korea is more than twice the ratio in Argentina, Brazil and Mexico. Furthermore, all second tier NIEs have higher ratios than all Latin American and African countries. A comparison with the earlier figures in the last column shows that while East Asian NIEs and South Asian countries experienced increases in this ratio in recent years, this is not always the case for Latin America despite the recovery from the debt crisis of the 1980s.[25]

A strong profit–investment nexus does not emerge spontaneously from market forces. Market-based incentives and competition do not always translate profits into investment or ensure that investments generate adequate profits to justify undertaking them. Indeed an important element of the successful industrialization in East Asia was the willingness and ability of governments to intervene effectively to accelerate accumulation and growth by animating the investment–profits nexus, rather than relying on market forces alone.

The kind of measures used is studied extensively in the literature (Amsden 1989 and 2001; Wade 2003; Chang 1994; Rodrik 1995; Akyüz and Gore 1996; and Akyüz 1999). They fall into two broad categories. First, a number of fiscal instruments such as tax exemptions and special depreciation allowances were employed in order to raise gross profits and encourage their retention. Second, a range of selective trade, financial and competition policies were used to increase profits over and above the levels that could be attained under free market conditions, provided that protection and support were reciprocated by faster accumulation and productivity growth. Measures were introduced in all these areas to coordinate investment decisions, to direct investment to sectors with greater potential for learning and productivity growth, to prevent investment races and to control external borrowing. They were supplemented by restrictions over luxury consumption through import control and progressive taxation, and by measures designed to close unproductive channels of wealth accumulation and speculation. High retention ratios resulted in relatively equitable personal income distribution despite high share of capital income in value added, and rapid accumulation and job creation provided social justification for high profits.[26]

Such policies have not been fashionable in recent years in many parts of the developing world. The scope for managing profits and accumulation is also severely restricted by WTO rules, conditionalities attached to multilateral lending by the BWIs, and liberalization of the capital account (Chang 2005; Gallagher 2005). These, together with the neglect of accumulation and employment in macroeconomic and financial policies, explain in a large part why investments now generate more profits than previously, but profits generate less investment. Inequality within developing countries, as measured by the Gini coefficient, increased substantially between 1980 and 2000 (Freeman 2004), but this has not been associated with increases in savings or investment ratios. This is true not only collectively but also for a large majority of developing countries taken individually. For the countries in Table 3.6, there is a visible weakening of the relation between income concentration and capital accumulation in recent years. The positive correlation observed between the two during 1980–95 disappeared altogether in the second half of the 1990s.[27] This is also true for the significance of the coefficient for the concentration estimated in a cross-country regression of investment share on per capita income and the concentration ratio.[28] Although such simple statistics have their limits in revealing the underlying relations, their significance lies in confirming the general trends discussed above.

Even some countries in East Asia have not been spared from the winds of orthodoxy. It is true that many of the policies designed for support and protection in the earlier stages of industrialization are no longer needed because they have succeeded in meeting their objectives. However, in two areas the break with past practice has proved troublesome and made significant contributions to the East Asian financial crisis: policy guidance of investment and control over external borrowing. Abandoning investment coordination was an important reason for misallocation and overinvestment while capital account liberalization proved fatal when firms were allowed to raise money abroad without the traditional supervision and control, and became extremely vulnerable to an external debt run (Akyüz 2000).

D. Macroeconomic Policy: What Policy?

With few exceptions, macroeconomic policy has not been directed toward maintaining a high and stable level of employment and rapid capital accumulation either in developed or in developing countries. In the developed world there have been persistent inconsistencies in the mix and stance of monetary and fiscal policies both within and across major industrial countries, which served not only to dampen growth but also to generate global imbalances and instability. In many developing countries, the scope to use monetary and fiscal policy for macroeconomic management has largely been restricted by financial liberalization and increased public indebtedness. Policy stance has generally been procyclical, aggravating boom–bust cycles in economic activity associated with rapid surges and exits of capital, thereby contributing to instability in key relative prices that affect investment decisions such as interest rates and exchange rates.

1. Imbalances in the industrial world

Fiscal policy has generally ceased to be an instrument of macroeconomic management in industrial countries with the result that too much pressure has been placed on monetary policy for ensuring growth and stability, a task which it could not fulfil satisfactorily. In the United States monetary policy focused entirely on inflation in the early 1980s, combined with supply-side tax cuts. This combination of tight monetary policy with fiscal laxity resulted in a sharp appreciation of the dollar and provided considerable growth stimulus to Europe and Japan, allowing them to undertake fiscal adjustment without seriously affecting aggregate demand and employment. However, as the resulting United States budget and external deficits threatened global stability, an agreement was reached in 1985 for macroeconomic policy coordination to realign the dollar and reduce global imbalances without sacrificing growth or stability. But the United States failed to relax monetary policy and focused on expenditure reduction and then tax increases while Europe and Japan were unwilling to undertake expansionary macroeconomic policies. The result was a hard landing of the dollar and the 1987 global stock market crash (UNCTAD TDR 1992, part 2, chap. 2).

The depreciation of the dollar and recession led to a swift payments adjustment in the early 1990s. As inflation came down, the Federal Reserve paid more attention to economic activity than in the 1980s, while fiscal tightening and growth brought a rapid correction to budget deficits, producing a surplus in the second half of the 1990s. However, monetary policy neglected the conditions in financial markets, notably the increased fragility resulting from excessive investment in high-tech sectors, supported by a stock market (dot-com) bubble and highly inflated and leveraged asset prices. The boom was associated with large inflows of capital into the United States, resulting again in a persistent appreciation of the dollar, adding to growing trade imbalances caused by disparities in demand creation among the major industrial countries. However, the recession brought about by the bursting of the dot-com bubble and the stock market collapse at the turn of the millennium was short-lived as massive supply-side tax cuts and increased military spending, together with repeated cuts in interest rates, brought a swift recovery, before the cyclical downturn could improve the United States external balance.

Europe and Japan both relied for growth primarily on markets abroad, notably in the United States, rather than expansion of domestic demand. This, together with the inappropriate mix of policies in the United States, has been a major factor in the emergence of large trade imbalances, both in the 1980s and more recently. Europe was preoccupied throughout much of the 1980s with inflation and in the 1990s with convergence to conditions deemed to be necessary for monetary union, which consisted of arbitrary limits to inflation, government debt and deficits set first by the Maastricht Treaty and then by the Stability and Growth Pact. These arrangements in effect denied Europe countercyclical monetary and fiscal policy, and even introduced procyclical elements in the management of public finances. Even after control over inflation was firmly established, the Bundesbank and subsequently the European Central Bank continued to adhere to monetarism; they were generally unwilling to use monetary policy for anything other than disinflation. All these factors constrained the willingness of the private sector to expand production capacity and employment beyond the limits assumed by the policymakers to be compatible with stability.[29]

Japan enjoyed export-led growth in much of the 1980s. Its policy response to the appreciation of the yen was to relax monetary policy to allow an adjustment based on accelerated investment. The result was a financial bubble with a sharp escalation of prices in stock and property markets and overinvestment which eventually led to a prolonged process of debt deflation and three fully fledged recessions. The first came in 1991 when Japan moved to halt the boom in asset prices by tightening monetary policy; the second one was associated with the large appreciation of the yen and the East Asian financial crisis in 1997–98; and the third one came at the beginning of the new millennium. As deflation set in and prices started to fall, conditions reminiscent of the Keynesian liquidity trap developed and the limits of monetary policy were reached. In effect Japan is the only major industrial country which tried to respond to economic slowdown and contraction with fiscal expansion, introducing several packages throughout the 1990s in order to ignite recovery. However, fiscal stimulus has never been translated into sustained increases in private spending. As a consequence growth has been sluggish and erratic, and government debt and deficits have grown faster than output since the early 1990s.

In both continental Europe and Japan consumer spending has been generally weak, not making a significant contribution to demand expansion. This is in large part due to the behavior of wages. In the United States and the United Kingdom real wages broadly kept up with productivity growth after the mid-1990s. By contrast, in Continental Europe and Japan they stagnated for over seven years. In France real unit labor costs were flat while in Germany they actually fell between 1996 and 2002. In Japan the decline in real unit labor costs was deeper, partly due to sharp falls in profit-related earnings such as bonuses. In particular while the Japanese system of compensation based on links to enterprise profits has the advantage of providing the firms with flexibility regarding costs, it tends to accentuate economic recessions by adding to downward pressures on demand (UNCTAD TDR 2002, chap. 1; 2003, chap. 1).

Despite the aversion to Keynesian fiscal management, chronic public deficits have emerged and public debt has grown faster than output in both the United States and Europe. In the United States, Federal debt as a proportion of GDP rose from 32 percent in 1980 to 63 percent at the end of 2004 due to an inappropriate mix of monetary and fiscal policies that pushed up the cost of public borrowing throughout the 1980s and to supply-side tax cuts. In the euro area, despite efforts to bring down public debt after the Maastricht Treaty of 1991, the average ratio of public debt to GDP has remained around 72 percent because of high interest rates and low growth. Increased indebtedness, in turn, has made an important contribution to budget deficits. In the euro area, the general government budget has had a primary surplus since 1995, but the overall budget has been in deficit on account of interest payments which averaged at close to 4 percent of GDP. Interest payments from the budget in the United States was also close to 4 percent of GDP in the 1990s, coming down only in the new millennium as interest rates fell to historically low levels.

Of all the major industrial countries, the United States' economy appears to have benefited considerably more from increased global integration, enjoying faster growth in output, jobs and productivity in the past two decades. However, this performance has not been based on a judicious combination of monetary and fiscal policy, or an appropriate cross-country pattern of domestic demand growth. As a result, it has been associated with large domestic and global imbalances which pose serious threats for growth and stability over the coming years, not only for the United States itself, but also for the rest of the world, including developing countries.[30]

It is generally agreed that maintaining the recent pattern of growth in the United States would exacerbate trade imbalances and lead to an unsustainable process of debt accumulation. Adjustment based on fiscal tightening would imply a slowdown in growth unless accompanied by rapid and sustained growth in exports which would require acceleration of demand growth in its major trading partners. Faster growth in Europe is unlikely without governments ignoring the constraints placed on fiscal expansion by the Stability and Growth Pact or the ECB abandoning monetarism. Not much additional stimulus can come from Japan, where policy interest rates are effectively zero and, at some 7 percent of GDP, fiscal deficits are higher than even in the United States. Nor could one expect a swift turnaround in the savings–investment balance in the East Asian developing countries running trade surpluses with the United States, since they (notably China) are already investing at very high rates. If, on the other hand, too much pressure is put on the dollar for external adjustment, then the United States could face a dilemma in monetary policy between maintaining growth and price stability, particularly if the decline of the dollar does not generate a swift turnaround in its trade balance. All in all, the chances of an orderly adjustment to these imbalances while maintaining strong and sustained growth and exchange rate stability, and without frictions in international trade, appear to be quite slim.

2. *Fiscal constraints and procyclical policy in emerging markets*

Macroeconomic policy in developing countries has been circumscribed by global economic conditions shaped in a large part by the mix and stance of policies in industrial countries. In this respect developments in financial conditions, notably with respect to international liquidity, risk spreads and interest rates, and capital flows have exerted a much greater influence on the scope and effect of policies in the developing world than those in the world trade and commodity markets, except for the poorest countries.

There has been considerable diversity among developing countries regarding overall macroeconomic conditions and the scope to use monetary and fiscal policy for macroeconomic management. Policy constraints have generally been tighter in most middle income Latin American countries with high and volatile inflation, chronic budget and payments deficits, and higher levels of public debt than Asian countries with relatively stable prices and sustainable fiscal and external balances. In most low income countries, notably in sub-Saharan Africa, with moderate inflation but relatively high and volatile fiscal and payments deficits, the stance of policy has generally depended on external aid and the conditions attached to its availability.

Notwithstanding this diversity, evidence strongly suggests that macroeconomic policy in developing countries has generally been procyclical, and much more so for fiscal than monetary policy.[31] Stabilization programs supported by the BWIs in low income countries facing payments difficulties have almost invariably promoted fiscal and monetary austerity, emphasising adjustment rather than financing regardless of the origin of budget or external deficits. Aid has been increasingly volatile, particularly since 1990, and much more so than government revenues or GDP. It has also been procyclical, introducing a deflationary bias to macroeconomic adjustment. Unexpected declines in aid to low income countries facing payments difficulties typically necessitated sharp cuts in imports and economic activity as most of these countries have had little access to private markets, which are, in any case, even more procyclical.[32]

Following a series of failed attempts to bring inflation down under control through traditional stabilization policies relying on fiscal and monetary tightening and currency devaluations, most high inflation countries adopted exchange-rate-based stabilization programs in the 1990s with the support of the BWIs, often accompanied by rapid trade and financial liberalization, relying on capital inflows to finance fiscal and external deficits. This populist policy mix served to avoid hard policy choices and allowed price stability to be achieved without running into distributional conflicts. However, disinflation has generally been achieved at the expense of increased financial instability, leaving many of these countries in conditions as fragile as those prevailing in the 1980s.

In countries with exchange-rate-based stabilization programs, macroeconomic policy mix has generally been inconsistent, combining relatively tight money with procyclical fiscal policy.[33] An examination of the monetary conditions index, defined as a weighted average of changes in real effective exchange rate and the ratio of the real short-term interest rate to the trend growth rate, shows that monetary conditions were on average much tighter and more volatile in Latin America during the 1990s than in East Asia.[34] In Latin America the boom phase of the cycles generally combined sharp currency appreciations with high real interest rates. Declines in nominal interest rates lagged considerably behind inflation as tight monetary policy designed to attract foreign capital and high credit risks offset much of the benefits of lower inflation and exchange rate stability. When the bust came, currencies collapsed, leading to an easing of the overall monetary stance, but often this was more than offset by hikes in interest rates, recommended by the IMF to restore confidence. Overall, monetary conditions in Latin America in the 1990s were too stringent and unstable to encourage growth based on rapid and sustained capital accumulation. In East Asia where interest rates were much lower because of low and stable inflation, and currency appreciations were limited, boom in capital flows and economic expansion were associated with neutral monetary conditions while the 1997–98 crisis led to a procyclical tightening.

Fiscal policy has been procyclical in most developing countries but above all in Latin America (BIS 2003; Moreno 2003; Mohanty and Scatigna 2003; Mihaljek and Tissot 2003; Ocampo 2002; Kaminski, Reinhart and Végh 2004). In the latter region most countries started stabilization programs with large budget deficits and where there was some success in fiscal adjustment, it was based on unsustainable spending cuts rather than expansion of government revenues. Surges in capital inflows thus presented an opportunity to raise public spending and cut taxes by facilitating government borrowing and bringing some additional cyclical revenues. This reinforced the expansion fuelled by increased capital inflows and private consumption. However, increased public debt, interest rate hikes, sharp declines in currencies and economic contraction necessitated a retrenchment of public spending at times of reversal of capital flows and financial crises, thereby deepening deflation. In East Asia there does not appear to be a systematic procyclicality in fiscal policy. There was no notable fiscal expansion during the surge in capital inflows in the mid-1990s, but procyclical fiscal tightening added to deflationary pressures at the time of the 1997–98 crisis in countries following the IMF recipe. However, this policy stance was reversed soon and most East Asian countries were able to respond to the weakness of global demand after 2000 by fiscal and monetary expansion while such policy space was not available to Latin America and Africa facing stringent financial conditions (UNCTAD TDR 2003; Moreno 2003, 5–6; Mohanty and Scatigna 2003, 38–43).

As a result of boom–bust cycles in international capital inflows and recurrent financial crises, public debt has been rising in emerging market economies both in Latin America and Asia since the mid-1990s. Although external sovereign debt has declined in Latin America and stayed relatively stable in Asia, there has been a considerable increase in domestic debt in both regions (IMF 2003, chap. 3). Much of this increase is accounted for by interest and exchange rate movements and the assumption of private liabilities by the public sector, notably through recapitalization of insolvent banks, as well as excessive borrowing by some governments during surges in capital inflows. As a result the average public debt in emerging market economies now stands at around 70 percent of GDP.

An outcome of increased public indebtedness is to narrow the scope for discretionary public spending and reduce fiscal flexibility. Given that many countries with high public debt also face high real interest rates and have relatively low potential growth rates, they need to generate large amounts of primary surplus in order to avoid debt explosion.[35] With a debt/GDP ratio of 70 percent and a potential growth rate of 4 percent, debt sustainability would require a primary surplus of some 2.8 percent when the real interest rate is 8 percent. This figure would be doubled when the interest rate is 12 percent, and it would rise further to 7.2 percent when sovereign debt is 90 percent of GDP.

Given the political difficulties in sustaining a high rate of primary surplus, even a moderately high ratio of public debt to GDP is unlikely to remain stable over time. It has been argued that the threshold debt ratio above which a country becomes vulnerable to external shocks that may threaten sustainability is in the order of 25 percent of GDP even though it is generally recognized that the threshold depends on a host of other factors (Moreno 2003, 2–3; Mihaljek and Tissot 2003, 16–22; IMF 2003, chap. 3; Goldstein 2005, 54). This is far below the debt ratios in most emerging market economies.[36] At present such ratios appear to be sustainable because of highly favorable global financial conditions including exceptionally low interest rates, and exchange rate appreciations. However, many of these economies which have been enjoying a surge in capital inflows in recent years appear to be vulnerable to a hike in interest rates, a reassessment of risks and reversal of capital flows. Thus, fiscal and monetary policies in such countries could be challenged by deterioration in global financial conditions (Goldstein 2005, 57). A rise in interest rates due to changed perceptions of risk and an increase in the ratio of public debt to GDP resulting from sharp currency depreciations could necessitate much higher rates of primary surplus, thereby forcing the governments into excessively procyclical fiscal positions, and adding to deflationary forces triggered by rising interest rates.

E. Financial Instability, Investment and Employment

1. Financial boom–bust cycles

Until recent bouts of financial boom–bust cycles in industrial and developing countries, it was generally believed that price stability was both necessary and sufficient for economic and financial stability. However, in many countries in East Asia, as well as in the industrial world, asset price bubbles, excessive credit creation, and currency appreciations and gyrations all occurred under conditions of price stability. In the more extreme cases, as in Latin America, disinflation has been achieved at the cost of increased financial fragility and instability, through exchange-rate-based stabilization programs relying on unstable capital flows.

Not only have financial markets become the single most important source of instability, but the influence of financial developments over economic cycles has increased significantly. This is particularly so in the developing world where financial instability associated with greater mobility of capital has been mirrored by sharp changes in economic activity. Both theoretical and empirical literature shows that high volatility has an adverse effect on long-term economic growth and that financial liberalization tends to strengthen the trade-off between growth and volatility.[37] On the one hand, growing uncertainties created by sharp and unexpected swings in key relative prices such as interest rates, exchange rates and real wages, as well as increased fluctuations in the level of demand, increase the risks associated with irreversible investment decisions, shorten planning horizons and promote defensive strategies.[38] On the other hand, greater opportunities for quick capital gains presented by a high degree of volatility of asset prices encourage speculative behavior. These exert a significant influence on the pace and pattern of capital accumulation and the conditions in the labor market.

With rapid financial liberalization boom–bust cycles have become common features of both currency and asset markets. These reflect abrupt and unexpected changes in markets' assessment of risks which cannot always be attributed to policy shifts. A plausible explanation is provided by the theory of endogenous fragility developed by Minsky (1977), which sees financial cycles as an intrinsic feature of market economies.[39] Booms generated by improved opportunities for profitable investment lead to an underestimation of risks, overexpansion of credits and overindebtedness. Excessive risk taking eventually results in a deterioration of balance sheets and increases in nonperforming loans. Lenders respond by reassessing risks and sharply cutting credits, which in turn lead to credit crunch, debt deflation and defaults. However, while crises are almost always associated with a certain degree of financial fragility, they can also take place in the absence of serious economic weaknesses, because of the so-called self-fulfilling prophecies resulting from the existence of multiple equilibria and debt runs associated with herding behavior and collective action problems (Obstfeld 1996; Krugman 1996 and 1998).

Boom–bust cycles also involve mutually reinforcing and destabilizing feedbacks among credit, capital and currency markets. Booms in capital markets tend to increase opportunities for capital gain, attracting capital flows from foreign investors or encouraging foreign borrowing for investment in domestic asset markets. These would, in turn, appreciate the currency, thereby widening profit opportunities. In the downturn, falling asset prices reduce the attractiveness of domestic investment, leading to a rapid exit of capital and a depreciation of the currency. Similarly, credit cycles are often associated with cycles in property and equity prices. Booms in stock and property markets raise collateral values, which in turn encourage domestic credit expansion by loosening credit standards, reducing the cost of borrowing and increasing the availability of credit. Where the banking sector holds sizeable amounts of stocks (as in Japan), stock market booms can expand credit by raising bank equity relative to current exposure. Faster growth in bank lending in turn serves to increase the market valuation of these assets, setting off a mutually reinforcing process of credit expansion and asset price inflation. This process works in the opposite direction when asset prices are declining and economic conditions are deteriorating; falling asset prices reduce the value of collaterals, raise the cost of borrowing and lead to cuts in lending and credit crunch.

In a world of unstable capital flows every country with an open capital account is vulnerable to sharp and unexpected swings in the external value of its currency. However, in industrial countries currency instability rarely spills over to domestic capital and credit markets. For instance during the 1992 EMS crisis there were sharp drops in the lira and pound sterling, but these did not provoke serious financial crises in Italy and the United Kingdom. Again in recent years there have been sharp swings in the dollar vis-à-vis other reserve currencies, but these did not generate destabilizing spillovers to domestic financial markets of the countries concerned.

By contrast, in developing countries domestic financial cycles have often been associated with sharp swings in external capital flows and exchange rates. It is very rare that currency crises in developing countries are contained without having a significant impact on domestic financial conditions, economic activity and living standards. The greater vulnerability of domestic financial conditions in developing countries to currency instability is due primarily to the existence of large stocks of public and/or private debt denominated in foreign currencies; i.e. the so-called liability dollarization.

While country-specific factors no doubt influence the volume and terms of private capital flows, global financial conditions were the dominating factors in the two postwar boom–bust cycles in such flows to developing countries. The first boom started in the early 1970s and was driven by the rapid expansion of international liquidity associated with oil surpluses, and facilitated by financial deregulation in industrialized countries and the rapid growth of Eurodollar markets. Excess liquidity was recycled in the form of syndicated bank credits, and this was encouraged by the BWIs fearing a collapse of global demand. It ended with a debt crisis in the 1980s as a result of the hike in United States interest rates, global recession and a sharp cutback in bank lending. The second boom came in the early 1990s, after almost ten years of suspension in private lending to developing countries. It was encouraged by the success of the Brady Plan for sovereign debt restructuring, liberalization and stabilization in developing countries, and rapid expansion of liquidity in the United States and Japan in conditions of economic slowdown. Unlike the first boom, a large proportion of private inflows were in equity investment, rather than international lending, attracted by prospects of quick capital gains and short-term arbitrage opportunities. It again ended with a series of crises in Latin America, East Asia and elsewhere.

These cycles were thus driven by temporary and special factors beyond the control of recipient countries, including monetary and financial policies in industrial countries. Aggregate flows to developing countries have manifested a degree of instability not justified by changes in the underlying fundamentals in the recipient countries. For instance in the last cycle, total annual net private capital inflows fell from more than \$200 billion in 1996 to less than \$20 billion in 2000–2001, and after the East Asian crisis until 2002 net international private lending to developing countries was negative. These swings in the volume of private capital are also mirrored in sharp changes in their terms. Booms tend to be associated with the underestimation of risks and relatively low spreads while crises led to overpricing of risks, generalized increases in spreads and shortening of maturities (UNCTAD TDR 2003, 27; Cunningham, Dixon and Hayes 2001; Sy 2001).

A third boom now appears to be underway, driven by a combination of highly favorable conditions including historically low interest rates, abundant international liquidity, oil surpluses, strong commodity prices and buoyant international trade.

Total inflows to developing countries are currently above the peak of the previous boom, and almost all emerging markets have shared in this recovery. But as noted by the IIF (2005a, 4), "there is a risk that the pickup in flows into some emerging market assets has pushed valuations to levels that are not commensurate with underlying fundamentals." Thus, a combination of tightened liquidity, rising interest rates, slowing growth and persistent global trade imbalances can reverse the boom, hitting particularly countries with weak fundamentals and incomplete self-insurance (IIF 2005b; Goldstein, 2005).

2. *Financial and investment cycles*

Almost all financial bubbles give rise to excessive investment in certain sectors which loses its viability with the return of normal conditions, leading to prolonged underutilization and even destruction of production capacity. Such investment is concentrated not only in areas susceptible to speculative influences such as housing and commercial construction, but can also be in machinery and equipment. This is true both for industrial and developing countries. However, in the latter countries the abrupt change of economic regime, particularly in the sphere of money and finance, has made it difficult for investors to identify underlying trends and separate them from cyclical developments. Long-term decisions affecting the balance sheets of corporations through acquisition of assets and assumption of liabilities on the basis of favorable cyclical conditions have thus resulted in increased financial fragility and waste of resources.

A notable example from recent history is the Japanese experience since the early 1990s.[40] After the Louvre Agreement in 1987, Japan relaxed monetary policy in order to help reduce trade imbalances with the United States and to facilitate the adjustment of the industry to yen appreciation. The result was a rapid expansion of liquidity and a decline in the cost of capital almost to zero through a sharp escalation of prices in the stock market. The share of capital spending rose from 27 percent of GDP in 1987 to 32 percent in 1990. However, when increased concern with asset price inflation led to monetary tightening, the bubble burst, resulting in sharp declines in stock and property prices, which, in turn, threatened the solvency of banks and highly leveraged corporations. This set off a debt deflation-cum-recession process which crippled the economy for a decade, necessitating disinvestment and debt restructuring and raising unemployment to exceptionally high levels by Japanese standards.

Expansionary phases of business cycles in the United States in the 1980s and 1990s were also associated with financial excesses and investment bubbles that subsequently hampered the ability of the economy to maintain steady and robust growth. The rapid increase in lending against real estate in the second half of the 1980s led to massive overbuilding, and when the bubble burst in the early 1990s, the outcome was a sharp decline in occupancy rates, increased defaults and delinquency, and drying up of bank lending. The economy went into a double-dip recession as private investment dropped from some 17 percent of GDP to less than 13 percent. Even more remarkable was the expansion in the 1990s sustained by a boom in business investment which lasted much longer than in other major industrial countries and in previous investment cycles in the United States itself. This was driven primarily by investment designed to exploit new advances in information technology, and greatly facilitated by easy financial conditions, notably the boom in venture capital funding and the stock market bubble. These allowed the emergence of many companies that would not have been created under normal financial conditions. Thus, a sudden reversal of expectations about the future earning capacity of these companies led to a collapse in their share prices, producing a sharp drop in investment spending at the turn of the millennium.

In developing countries boom–bust financial cycles driven by capital flows have almost invariably been mirrored by sharp movements in capital accumulation.[41] Even in Latin America where surges in capital inflows were invariably associated with booms in consumption, investment tended to follow the boom–bust cycles in capital flows. This was much more evident in East Asia where surges in capital flows were more closely tied to private investment booms. In response to rapidly falling prices of many of the manufactures exported from East Asia, notably semiconductors, which accounted for more than 40 percent of exports of some countries in the region, in the mid-1990s many firms augmented investment in the hope of increasing productivity and market shares, and expanded into new areas of production, very much in the same way as the response of Japanese firms to loss of competitiveness in the late 1980s. This process was facilitated by easy access to cheap foreign credits. There was also a speculative surge in the property market supported by borrowing abroad, notably in Thailand. Some firms also invested heavily in other nontraded activities including infrastructure with the funds borrowed abroad. Excessive investment was thus a key factor in the subsequent financial difficulties and the sharp drop in accumulation and growth when cheap foreign capital was no longer available. While in the boom the investment ratio rose by 3–14 percentage points in the four countries most affected by the crisis; the decline was sharper during the bust, ranging between 15 and 18 percentage points of GDP (UNCTAD TDR 2000, chap. 4).

The recent investment boom in China too has certainly been supported by the surge in private inflows, including FDI. In 2004 fixed capital investment grew by almost 28 percent over the previous year, reaching 44 percent of GDP while net private capital inflows set a record at $101 billion.[42] As noted, there is evidence of excessive and wasteful investment in some sectors. It has indeed been argued that the current investment boom is unsustainable and will probably take several years to undo (Goldstein and Lardy 2004). However, while an unwinding of the boom may generate financial difficulties in certain sectors, it is unlikely to be coupled with the kind of currency and debt crises experienced in several other emerging markets in recent years, given China's solid payments and reserve positions.

Investment is generally the most unstable component of aggregate demand and especially vulnerable to external shocks in developing countries. Evidence shows not only that it has been more volatile than GDP almost everywhere, but volatility has increased in the 1990s compared to the turbulent years of the 1980s in both developed and developing countries (World Bank, 2003, 23–26). This is clearly associated with financial rather than trade shocks, and particularly boom–bust cycles in capital flows. Furthermore, both the level of and the increase in volatility is high in low income countries where macroeconomic and financial conditions can be easily altered by movements of small sums of money.

Increased volatility of investment resulting from financial cycles has two adverse consequences for capital accumulation and job creation. First, investment tends to fall a lot faster under financial busts than it rises during financial booms; that is, the average investment rate over the cycle tends to be lower. Secondly, financial booms distort the composition of investment, increase its speculative components and lead to excessive expansion of productive capacity in certain sectors. Clearly, these two phenomena are related: financial busts result not only in sharp declines in investment but also in the waste of existing productive capacity which becomes unviable with changed conditions.

3. Bubbles, crises and jobless recoveries

Any adverse effect of financial instability on capital accumulation and economic growth would no doubt be transmitted to the labor market. But boom–bust cycles also generate dislocations and instability in employment and wages independent of their impact on capital accumulation. Booms can temporarily lift employment and wages above their long-term levels, while crises depress them significantly on a more durable basis. In particular, in recoveries from deflation-cum-recessions, both employment and wages tend to lag considerably behind income growth. While this is also true for industrial countries, the boom–bust cycles driven by capital flows in developing countries are particularly harmful for labor, causing large adverse shifts in unemployment, wages, income distribution and poverty.

The experience of the United States in this respect is quite revealing. As noted above, the periods of expansion in the 1980s and 1990s were both characterized by excessive investments in certain sectors, asset price inflation and increased private indebtedness while the recessions that followed involved widespread financial difficulties and debt-deflation. In both episodes recoveries from recessions were commonly described as jobless. In the former cycle the recovery that started in the course of 1991 was not felt in the labor market until well after several years of growth. Although investment soon picked up, it was designed for industrial restructuring rather than capacity expansion, focusing on IT sectors. Income was soon restored to its prerecession peak, but employment started increasing only in 1993, and the unemployment rate did not return to its pre-recession low of 5.3 percent before 1996, after reaching 7.5 percent in 1992. Similarly wages did not share in the recovery of productivity until the second half of the 1990s (UNCTAD TDR 1994, 78–84; and 1995, 62–65).

In the second cycle the economy went through a short recession in spring 2001. The recovery that followed was the worst in recent United States history for employment creation. In terms of investment it was also the weakest since 1949. From the end of the recession in the third quarter of 2001 until the end of 2003, job losses outside the farm sector amounted to over two million, with employment falling particularly steeply in overexpanded IT sectors, but GDP rising by 2–3 percent per annum. As of the end of 2005, real weekly and hourly wages were still below what they were at the start of the recovery in November 2001, and jobs in the private sector were up only by 0.8 percent, compared to an average 8.8 percent increase at the same stages of previous business cycles. The combination of falling wages and employment with surging profits not only worsened income distribution but also increased poverty (Freeman and Rodgers 2005; UNCTAD TDR 2003, 7; Mishel and Eisenbrey 2005).

Financial excesses at times of expansion were an important reason for jobless recoveries in both cycles, but above all after the more recent downturn following one of the strongest postwar expansions in the United States driven by the dot-com bubble. In both cases deflation-cum-recessions exposed financial fragility and overindebtedness, and the efforts of corporations during recoveries focused on restoring the health of their balance sheets. Increased profits were used either for industrial restructuring or for reducing debt rather than the expansion of production capacity and employment, and downsizing and labor shedding resulted in a combination of falling employment with rising labor productivity and profits (UNCTAD TDR 1994, 80–84; 2003, 6–9).[43]

Jobless recoveries from recessions triggered by crises are even more marked in emerging market economies. The impact of financial crises on the labor market and social conditions lasts much longer in these economies because of financial difficulties created by liability dollarization and the external constraint. Even after income recovers to levels prevailing before the crisis, both employment and wages tend to lag, remaining well below not only their precrisis (boom) levels, but also their preboom levels.

At times of surges in capital flows, real wages generally rise alongside the appreciation of the currency, but what happens to employment depends on a host of factors. If the boom is driven by consumption and productivity, growth is sluggish, employment tends to fall in traded goods sectors due to loss of competitiveness while rising in services. High wages and cheap imports of capital goods, together with easy access to credit, can also lead to higher investment and capital deepening in an effort to restructure industry and raise productivity to meet foreign competition. When investment is strong and currency appreciation is limited, industrial employment can remain relatively stable or even rise despite loss of competitiveness. Under such circumstances financial booms would be associated with falling unemployment rates.

Available evidence suggests that in almost all emerging market economies which went through boom–bust cycles in the 1990s, real wages rose rapidly at times of surges in capital inflows and financial booms, but employment changed in different ways in different episodes.[44] In Korea, Malaysia, Indonesia and Thailand where the boom was driven by investment, productivity growth kept up with wages. In all these countries except Indonesia, the unemployment rate fell during the boom and full employment was secured. By contrast, in Latin America productivity growth lagged behind real wages and the rate of unemployment was either stable or higher at times of the boom. Unemployment hit manufacturing industries particularly hard because of loss of competitiveness brought about by currency appreciations.

At times of crisis wages fell almost everywhere. The decline was particularly sharp in Indonesia, Mexico and Turkey, between 11 and 25 percent per annum. In East Asia unemployment went up rapidly, exceeding the levels prevailing not only during the boom but also the preboom period. The impact in Korea and Indonesia was particularly strong, raising the unemployment rate to 6.5 percent. The only exception was Malaysia where rising unemployment mostly affected migrant workers and was reflected in the statistics of their countries of origin including Indonesia and the Philippines. In Latin

America, where unemployment was already on the rise, the crisis took it to exceptionally high levels. The Mexican crisis in 1995 led to a doubling of open unemployment within a year, pushing several workers to the informal labor market. In Argentina, where the currency board and the fixed exchange rate were maintained despite worsening external conditions, unemployment shot up in the wake of the Mexican crisis, reaching almost 20 percent in 1995. In Brazil open unemployment rose to almost 10 percent in 1999, up from 6 percent in the mid-1990s. A similar increase was registered in Turkey during the 2001 crisis.

The pace of recovery again differed among countries, being more robust in East Asia, except Indonesia, than in Latin America. At the time when GDP was restored to its precrisis level, real wages regained their precrisis levels only in Korea while they remained depressed elsewhere in the region. In Latin America, during recovery phases real wages were lower than the peaks reached during the booms. In all countries in both Latin America and East Asia, employment lagged considerably behind output growth. Postcrisis open unemployment rates were higher than precrisis rates by 1 percentage point in Brazil and Mexico, 5.5 points in Argentina and 4 percentage points in Korea and Indonesia. In Turkey the 2001 crisis was followed by a strong recovery driven again by a surge in capital inflows, leading to a rapid appreciation of the currency and a worsening of the current account. But growth averaging over 7 percent during 2002–2005 did not make any dent in unemployment while real wages barely recovered after a sharp decline during the 2001 crisis.[45] The deterioration in the conditions of labor, particularly among the unskilled, is a major reason why poverty levels have stayed high despite economic recovery not only in Turkey and Latin America, but also in East Asia.

Thus, in emerging market economies, as in industrial countries, during recovery, productivity and profits tend to rise while wages and employment remain depressed compared to their long-term sustainable levels. Dislocations created by crises in the balance sheets of banks and nonbank corporations in developing countries are much greater than those generated by asset price deflations in industrial countries because of the impact of currency collapses and procyclical monetary and fiscal policies. This is a major reason why recessions are deeper, and recoveries are slower in generating jobs. An additional factor accounting for the failure of employment to follow recovery in GDP is changes in the composition of output. The collapse of the currency eventually leads to a recovery in exports, particularly in countries with a robust industrial base. The shift in economic activity from nontradable services toward tradable industries lowers the employment content of aggregate GDP since average productivity in industry is typically higher than that in services.

F. Policy Priorities

A number of conclusions can be drawn from the recent experience of developed and developing countries with respect to economic stability and growth. First, while macroeconomic stability may be necessary to sustain rapid accumulation and growth, it is certainly not sufficient. Secondly, price stability on its own cannot secure stability in key macroeconomic aggregates and relative prices, since it is not sufficient to secure financial stability. Accordingly, the source of macroeconomic instability now is not instability in product markets but asset markets, and the main challenge for policymakers is not inflation but unemployment and financial instability.

At the national level a reorientation of policy would need to focus on three areas in developing countries. First, fiscal policy would need to be employed in a countercyclical way, with a view to combining stability with a high level of economic activity. Second, a whole array of policy instruments would need to be redeployed in order to reduce financial instability and prevent boom–bust cycles in capital flows. Third, in most countries at intermediate stages of industrialization, action needs to be taken at the sectoral level in order to directly influence the volume and composition of investment.

Bringing back fiscal policy as an instrument for macroeconomic management calls for restoring fiscal autonomy which, in turn, requires elimination of chronic, structural deficits. In many cases this should be possible through a reform of taxation and primary spending. However, in some countries it would be necessary to act directly on the stock of public debt, notably the domestic debt, as the single most important determinant of fiscal sustainability. As pointed out by Keynes long ago in his analysis of what he called "progressive and catastrophic inflations" in Central and Eastern Europe during the early 1920s, there are three ways of dealing with a debt overhang: repudiation, inflation and capital levy. He argued that of these, "the capital levy [...] is the rational, the deliberate method. But it is difficult to explain, and it provokes violent prejudice by coming into conflict with the deep instincts by which the love of money protects itself. [...] But if it has become clear that the claims of the bond-holder are more than the taxpayer can support, and if there is still time to choose between the policies of a levy and of further depreciation [inflation], the levy must surely be preferred on grounds both of expediency and of justice" (Keynes 1971, 53–55). Clearly, inflation is an even less viable option today given the short maturities of debt in many countries and open capital accounts. A once-and-for-all capital levy on the holders of government debt (or other equivalent measures such as swapping old debt with new debt at a discount) may indeed be the only option to eliminate the debt overhang in countries facing unsustainable debt stocks.

Using fiscal policy in the Keynesian tradition for macroeconomic management implies that governments should run deficits at times of contraction but generate surpluses during upturns so that over the full cycle the budget should be balanced or in a small surplus. If the revenue and expenditure structures are appropriately designed, much of the task would be done by automatic stabilizers. But there would often be a need for discretionary fiscal action according to the strength of underlying contractionary and expansionary impulses. It is particularly important to pursue countercyclical fiscal policy in the boom in order to have adequate fiscal space during contractions. This should be undertaken mainly by adjustments in spending on public works which is, inter alia, politically easier to control than current spending. There may also be adjustments on the revenues side including value added taxes or financial transaction taxes, which can also be particularly effective in checking consumption and credit booms while providing additional revenues.[46]

In what way the budget should be balanced is a contentious matter. According to one view, over the cycle total expenditures including both current and capital spending should be balanced by revenues from taxes and charges for public services. This implies that any debt incurred during recessions should be repaid by surpluses generated during expansions. However, there may be a sound rationale for the public sector to incur debt across the cycle provided that it is used to finance productive investment. An alternative way of conducting fiscal policy is thus by making a distinction between current and capital spending and using the Golden Rule of public finance; that is, governments should be able to borrow to invest, but not to finance current spending – an old idea which has recently been revived in the debate over fiscal constraints imposed by IMF conditionalities and the European Stability and Growth Pact. Such an approach would have the advantage of preventing the burden of adjustment falling disproportionately on public investment. It would also imply that analysis of fiscal sustainability should not focus on gross public debt alone but also consider assets built up on the other side of the balance sheet of the public sector.

In some industrial countries such as the United Kingdom and Japan fiscal policy is conducted on the basis of the Golden Rule.[47] A number of reasons have been given against using such an approach in developing countries, including financing constraint, lack of fiscal discipline and debt overhang.[48] These may be valid for many countries, particularly in Latin America, but without resolving these problems in the first place, it would not be possible to use fiscal policy as an effective countercyclical device, whether one targets the overall fiscal balance or current balance alone.

Just as countercyclical fiscal policy should start in the boom, prevention of unsustainable booms in capital inflows and currency appreciations holds the key to greater financial stability in developing countries. In this respect monetary policy on its own is quite ineffective. Avoiding currency appreciations and overheating would require sterilization, but this would lead to higher interest rates and increase the international arbitrage opportunities. It would also entail large carry costs since interest on government paper used for sterilization typically exceeds the rate that could be earned on reserves. Higher reserve requirements for banks may be used for this purpose, but these would raise intermediation costs and could push the borrowers toward foreign creditors, and/or encourage foreign banks to seek regulatory arbitrage by lending through their affiliates abroad.

To a certain extent traditional prudential regulations can help prevent excessive risk taking, credit creation and borrowing at times of economic expansion. Rules governing provisions, capital requirements, collateral valuation and other measures affecting conditions in credit and asset markets, such as margin requirements, could be employed in a countercyclical manner, tightened at times of boom and loosened during contractions.[49] However, there are limits to what such measures can do in checking excessive risk taking and the build-up of fragility in developing countries particularly when arbitrage opportunities are large and market perceptions are highly favorable. They thus need to be supplemented by direct and indirect controls over capital inflows of the kind extensively used in industrial countries in the postwar era until as recently as the 1980s. Taxes on capital inflows would be effective not only because they would reduce or eliminate arbitrage margins but also because they would facilitate countercyclical fiscal policy.

None of these may guarantee prevention of financial crises even in economies with good track records in macroeconomics and development. The policy response by most emerging market economies facing such situations has generally involved procyclical fiscal and monetary tightening designed to restore market confidence, combined with IMF interventions to bail out international creditors and investors. However, this often failed to prevent financial meltdown, and in fact deepened crises. A more viable and equitable alternative, which would also facilitate countercyclical macroeconomic policies, would be to impose temporary debt standstills and suspension of capital account convertibility, as implemented successfully by Malaysia during the 1997–98 crisis.[50]

A third key area of policy intervention concerns measures affecting the volume and composition of investment since macroeconomic stability as such would not be enough to secure a rapid pace of accumulation of productive capital. The kind of policies used for this purpose in more successful examples of industrial development has already been discussed. The space to use some of these policy measures has no doubt been narrowed down by global economic integration and multilateral rules and practices in trade and finance. Nevertheless, there is considerable space to influence the pace and pattern of capital accumulation. In particular, taxes and certain financial instruments could still be effectively used to ensure that allocation of profits and credits favor productive investment rather than luxury consumption or unproductive forms of wealth accumulation. Furthermore, policies at sectoral levels may need to be so designed as to lessen the uncertainties associated with investment decisions.

There can be little doubt that such policies at the national level would need to be supported by international policies. In this respect the task falls on multilateral financial arrangements and institutions, notably the IMF. So far the intensive policy surveillance by the Fund has not succeeded in preventing boom–bust cycles in capital flows in developing countries. The standard policy measures recommended by the IMF to prevent unsustainable surges in capital inflows and exchange rate appreciations are not only ineffective but they also entail large costs.[51] Since there is now increased consensus that crisis prevention calls for the prevention of unsustainable booms and that full capital account convertibility is not an appropriate objective for most developing countries, a major task for the Fund is to help these countries to manage capital inflows. For this purpose it is necessary to specify circumstances in which the IMF should actually recommend the imposition or strengthening of capital controls over inflows. The IMF should also develop techniques and mechanisms designed to separate, to the greatest extent possible, capital account from current account transactions, to distinguish among different types of capital flows from the point of view of their sustainability and economic impact, and to provide policy advice and technical assistance to countries at times when such measures are needed.

In the same vein the IMF should stop promoting procyclical policies in countries facing payments difficulties as a result of trade and financial shocks. For poorer developing countries facing export shortfalls, this would mean providing more current account financing and demanding less adjustment. Many of these countries would also need considerably increased amounts of development finance, but this task should be undertaken by multilateral development banks rather than the IMF. For emerging market economies facing rapid exit of capital, the policy of combining procyclical macroeconomic tightening with bailouts is counterproductive, not only because it deepens crises but also it creates a moral hazard and leads to an inequitable distribution of costs of crises between debtors and creditors. Instead, the IMF should develop orderly debt workout mechanisms for crisis management and resolution, including temporary standstills and capital account restrictions, and provide international liquidity not to bailout creditors but to support imports and economic activity in the countries concerned.

While global economic and financial conditions affecting developing countries are shaped primarily by policies in the major industrial countries, the IMF surveillance over these countries has lost its meaning with their graduation from the Fund and the breakdown of the Bretton Woods arrangements for exchange rates. Initiatives taken at various occasions to achieve greater coordination and coherence of macroeconomic policies among the United States, the European Union and Japan have not been successful in removing trade imbalances and bringing about a more stable system of payments and exchange rates. There are serious political difficulties in strengthening the IMF surveillance over the policies of these countries and making the Fund a symmetrical organization between its creditors and debtors, because of political leverage exercised by its major shareholders. Therefore, any reform seeking to secure greater international economic and financial stability would need to address not only the policies and operational modalities of the Fund, but also the shortcomings in its governance structure.

Notes

1 First published as an ILO working paper in July 2006. An earlier version was presented at a conference "Help Wanted: More and Better Jobs in a Globalised Economy," held on 14–15 April 2005 at the Carnegie Endowment for International Peace, Washington. I am grateful to Detlef Kotte and Juan Pizarro of UNCTAD for their assistance with the data used in this paper.

2 It seems that these arguments draw on elements of both the neoclassical theory of distribution and growth where return on capital is inversely related to capital intensity, and bargaining models where wage–profit distribution is linked to balance of power between labor and capital influenced not only by the scarcity of capital vis-à-vis labor but also by sociopolitical factors including labor market institutions.

3 Labor was much more mobile in the previous episode of globalization, typically dated from the 1870s until the First World War, than the recent period of deepened economic integration (Nayyar 2002; O'Rourke and Williamson 2000, chap. 7).

4 This was most clearly stated in the charter of the stillborn International Trade Organization (chap 2, article II): "The Members recognize that the avoidance of unemployment or underemployment, through the achievement and maintenance in each country of useful employment opportunities for those able and willing to work and of a large and steadily growing volume of production and effective demand for goods and services, is not of domestic concern alone, but is also a necessary condition for the achievement of [...] the expansion of international trade, and thus for the well-being of all other countries." See Akyüz (2002).

5 On the significance of capital accumulation in growth accounting and regressions see Kenny and Williams (2001) and Bosworth and Collins (2003).

6 While Easterly and Levine (2001) argue that there is no strong support for the contention that factor accumulation ignites faster growth in labor productivity, a recent study by Bond, Leblebicioglu and Schiantarelli (2004) of 98 countries found that an increase in investment as a share of GDP predicts a higher growth rate of output per worker.

7 Figures on Japan are from OECD (1986).
8 For an earlier critique of the trade-off argument see Gordon (1995).
9 For OECD as a whole average labor force growth is around 1 percent and productivity growth 2 percent per annum (OECD 2005b, annex tables).
10 Growth figures in this section are from World Bank (2005a, table A.8).
11 Investment figures in Table 3.2 include inventory changes as well as GFCF. This difference notwithstanding, investment will be used throughout this chapter for fixed capital formation.
12 Fischer (2003) and Freeman (2004). However this does not mean that more people converge globally in terms of income since income distribution is generally worsening, including particularly in China (UNDP 2005).
13 See also Kuijs and Wang (2005), who argue that continuing with the current growth pattern in China would lower employment growth in industry from 2.9 percent achieved over 1993–2004 to 1.7 percent in the coming years, and the task of absorbing agricultural surplus labor would fall on services.
14 On developing countries see UNCTAD TDR (1992, part 3, chap. 2) and Chang (2003, chap. 6). A recent study using comparable data on industrial countries confirms that the elasticity of output with respect to public capital is positive and quite large for some countries (Kamps 2004). For a review of the literature on the effect of public investment on output, productivity and growth, see IMF (2004, appendix I). For a restatement of orthodoxy on the inefficiency of state-owned enterprises see World Bank (2003, 95–96).
15 For a review of the literature see Everhart and Sumlinski (2001), where five of the twenty studies reviewed find crowding out. A more recent study finds that a 10 percent increase in public investment is associated with a 2 percent increase in private investment in developing countries while crowding out occurs in developed countries (Erden and Holcombe 2005).
16 On tax concessions see Hanson (2001) and World Bank (2003, 80–82).
17 For the issues involved and the evidence see UNCTAD TDR (1999, chap. 5), Milberg (1999), Agosin and Mayer (2000), Hanson (2001), Ghose (2004) and Gallagher and Zarsky (2005). One of the problems in research on the impact of FDI on GFCF is that no distinction is made between acquisition of existing assets and greenfield investment. This problem is partly due to the absence of such a distinction in FDI statistics.
18 Most TNCs apply hurdle rates of return in the order of 20 to 25 percent (Kregel 1996, 58).
19 These observations are consistent with the findings from empirical studies testing the impact of FDI on capital formation and growth by Agosin and Mayer (2000) and Kumar and Pradhan (2002).
20 This is to say that over the long term investment rates do not correlate with current account deficits. This observation was first claimed by Feldstein and Horioka (1980).
21 In Japan the savings ratio in the past ten years has averaged at around 28 percent while the investment ratio around 24 percent. The corresponding figures for the United States, where income is less evenly distributed, are 16 and 19 percent respectively (IMF 2005, table 43).
22 Simple correlation coefficient for 1990–2004 between average investment rates and per capita incomes of the countries in Table 3.3 is 0.09.
23 For corporate savings and investment in developed countries see UNCTAD TDR (1997, table 42). In Japan the retention rate was very high, but exceptionally high corporate investment necessitated greater reliance on household savings. In general households in Japan generated a much greater surplus to support public and corporate investment than in other countries – see Horioka (1995). In Italy the inclusion of unincorporated enterprises in the household sector in the national accounts is an important reason for a lower corporate savings/investment ratio.
24 For the evidence on corporate savings and investment in East Asia compared to other countries see Akyüz and Gore (1996) and UNCTAD TDR (1997, table 44). Despite high retentions of profits, corporate leverage in East Asian NIEs was also high because of very high rates of accumulation, as in Japan in the earlier period (Wade and Veneroso 1998).

25 The high propensity to consume of property-owning classes in Latin America is not of recent origin. Kaldor noted that in the 1940s and 1950s the capitalist class in Chile spent on personal consumption three-quarters of their net income, absorbing more than 20 percent of national resources as opposed to less than 8 percent in the United Kingdom, and suggested that part of this income could be released for investment if "effective measures were taken to encourage retention of profits by enterprises" (Kaldor 1964, 266).

26 Corporate retentions do not appear among personal incomes. If these are added to the top quintile, differences in income inequality between East Asia and other regions narrow down considerably. For the relation between functional and personal distribution see UNCTAD TDR (1997, 172–73).

27 The correlation (Pearson) coefficient is 0.26 for 1980–94 and -0.01 for 1995–2000. The rank correlation coefficient fell from 0.31 to 0.09 between the two periods.

28 In the estimates for 1980–94, the coefficient for the concentration ratio was positive but statistically insignificant while in those for 1995–2000 it turned out to be negative and significant at the margin.

29 These limits are often expressed in terms of potential growth rate and NAIRU (nonaccelerating inflation rate of unemployment), which are both subject to hysteresis; if policymakers act on the assumption that a sustained growth rate faster than, say, 2.5 percent, or an unemployment rate lower than 7 percent, would lead to an acceleration of inflation, the private sector would unlikely expand production capacity and employment faster so that these assumptions would become self-fulfilling prophecies.

30 The risks entailed by these imbalances have been analysed by several economists belonging to different schools of thought: see, e.g., Godley and Izurieta (2004), Goldstein (2005), Izurieta (2005), Mussa (2005) and Cline (2005).

31 For evidence and a brief review of the literature see Kaminski, Reinhart and Végh (2004). Talvi and Végh (2000) find that government spending rises and taxes fall during expansions, while the reverse is true in recessions. They argue that procyclical fiscal policy can be optimal since surpluses create political pressure to increase spending.

32 For a discussion of aid volatility and procyclicality see World Bank (2005a, 104–106), and for the procyclicality of private capital flows Kaminski, Reinhart and Végh (2004).

33 The evidence on monetary policy is inconclusive. Kaminski, Reinhart and Végh (2004) find some evidence that policy rates are lowered in goods times (when output is above trend) while recognizing the difficulties in empirically identifying the policy component of monetary aggregates. According to Mohanty and Scatigna (2003, 52–55 and table 7) in some countries monetary policy was expansionary at times of fiscal expansion, suggesting the accommodating nature of monetary policy. But they also point out that there were various episodes of an inconsistent mix of monetary and fiscal policy during the 1990s. In general, recent years have seen both excessive tightening of monetary policy to bring inflation under control and several episodes of credit boom associated with surges in capital inflows.

34 In Latin America the index fluctuated between 70 percent and -8 percent during 1990–99 with an average value of 22 percent while in East Asia the range of fluctuations was much narrower, between 4 and –8 percent, with an average index value of -1.8 percent (an index number of zero indicates neutrality of monetary conditions, a positive index indicates restrictive monetary policy) (UNCTAD TDR 2003, 136).

35 More specifically, since $\Delta D = rD - P$ where D is the stock of public debt, r the real interest rate and P the primary surplus, and since sustainability of debt requires that the growth rate of debt stock should be equal to or smaller than the growth rate of real income (g), the primary surplus as a proportion of income (Y) needed to sustain debt is given by $P/Y \geq (r-g)(D/Y)$.

36 As of 2004 the sovereign debt ratio was around 90 percent in the Philippines and Turkey, 75 percent in India and Brazil, 60 percent in Malaysia, Hungary and Indonesia, 50 percent in Colombia, Poland and Thailand, and 40 percent in South Africa and Venezuela. The ratio in

Argentina was 121 percent, not accounting for the default. Notable exceptions with sovereign debt ratios below 30 percent include Mexico, Russia, China and Korea (Goldstein 2005, table 8).

37 See Aizenman and Pinto (2005) for a review. See also Kose, Prasad and Terrones (2005, 59) who find that "financial integration [...] seems to strengthen the negative relationship between growth and volatility," but de-emphasise this finding.

38 For a discussion of investment under uncertainty see Dixit and Pindyck (1994).

39 The approach goes back to Fisher's analysis of the Great Depression (Davis 1992, chap. 5).

40 For financial and investment cycles in industrial countries see UNCTAD TDR (1991, chap. 2; 1992, chap. 2; and 2001, chap. 1).

41 See UNCTAD TDR (2000, chap. 4; and 2003, chap. 4) and World Bank (2003, 23–26).

42 For investment figures see Qin, Cagas, Quising and He (2005), and for capital inflows IIF (2005c).

43 For corporate debt in the United States see Arestis and Karakitsos (2003). Many other explanations have also been advanced for the recent jobless recovery; see Bernanke (2003), Groshen and Potter (2003), and Freeman and Rodgers (2005).

44 For evidence cited in this section on the evolution of employment and wages in boom–bust recovery cycles in emerging markets see UNCTAD TDR (2000, chap. 4), ILO (2004), and van der Hoeven and Lübker (2005).

45 The unemployment rate rose to 8.2 percent during the 2001 crisis, from 6.3 percent in 2000. It continued to rise afterwards, staying over 10 percent in each year between 2002 and 2005; OECD (2005b, annex tables). Real wages in manufacturing dropped by more than 20 percent during the 2001 crisis and the decline continued in 2002–2003 despite economic recovery. They rose around 2 percent per annum during 2004–2005, but in mid-2005 they were some 25 percent below their precrisis levels (CBRT 2005).

46 For a discussion of these issues see Ocampo (2002, 29–31).

47 In the United Kingdom the government combines the Golden Rule with a sustainable investment rule of keeping the national debt below 40 percent of GDP (HM Treasury 2003, 6). In Japan there is a second budget alongside the central budget which provides for financing public investment programs, and only the spending financed by bonds issued to cover the central deficits is considered as deficit financing (UNCTAD TDR 1993, 78).

48 See IMF (2004) which also gives arguments in favor of using such an approach, and tries to find a middle way.

49 For a discussion of these measures see BIS (2001, chap. 7), Ocampo (2003), and Akyüz (2004).

50 There is a large literature on crisis management and resolution. For an overview of the issues see Akyüz (2005b).

51 For a detailed discussion of the issues taken up in this section see Akyüz (2005b).

References

Agosin, Manuel R., and Ricardo Mayer. 2000. "Foreign Investment in Developing Countries: Does it Crowd in Domestic Investment?" UNCTAD Discussion Paper 146.

Aizenman, Joshua, and Brian Pinto, eds. 2005. *Managing Volatility and Crises: A Practitioner's Guide.* Cambridge: Cambridge University Press.

Akyüz, Y., ed. 1999. *East Asian Development: New Perspectives.* London Frank Cass.

______. 2000. *Causes and Sources of the Asian Financial Crisis.* Paper presented to the Symposium on Economic and Financial Recovery in Asia at the Tenth Session of UNCTAD, Bangkok, 17 February. *TWN Series on the Global Economy* 1. Penang, Malaysia.

______. 2002. "The Effects of Financial Instability and Commodity Price Volatility on Trade, Finance and Development." Presentation made to the WTO Working Party on Trade, Debt and Finance, Geneva, 23 June.

______, ed. 2003. *Developing Countries and World Trade: Performance and Prospects.* London: Zed Books.

______. 2004. "Managing Financial Instability and Shocks in a Globalizing World." Paper presented at a public lecture sponsored by Bank Negara and the University of Malaya, Kuala Lumpur, 6 February.

______. 2005a. *Trade, Growth and Industrialization: Issues, Experience and Policy Challenges. TWN Trade and Development Series* 28. Penang, Malaysia.

______. 2005b. "Reforming the IMF: Back to the Drawing Board." UNCTAD, G-24 Discussion Paper 38. Geneva.

Akyüz, Y., and Charles Gore. 1996. "The Investment–Profits Nexus in East Asian Industrialization." *World Development* 24 (3).

______. 2001. "African Economic Development in a Comparative Perspective." *Cambridge Journal of Economics* 25 (3).

Akyüz, Y., Heiner Flassbeck and Richard Kozul-Wright. 2002. "Globalization, Inequality and the Labour Market." Paper Prepared for ILO, UNCTAD, Geneva.

Alfaro, Laura, Areendam Chanda, Sebnem Kalemli-Ozcan and Selin Sayek. 2001. "FDI and Economic Growth: The Role of Local Financial Markets." Harvard Business School, Working Paper 01-083. Boston, MA.

Amsden, Alice. 1989. *Asia's Next Giant: South Korea and Late Industrialization*. Oxford: Oxford University Press.

______. 2001. *The Rise of "the Rest": Challenges to the West from Late-Industrializing Economies*. Oxford: Oxford University Press.

Arestis, Philip, and Elias Karakitsos. 2003. "The Conditions for Sustainable U.S. Recovery: The Role of Investment." The Levy Economic Institute, Bard College, Working Paper 378.

Bernanke, Ben S. 2003. "The Jobless Recovery." Remarks made at the Global Economic and Investment Outlook Conference, Carnegie Mellon University, Pittsburgh, PA, 6 November.

BIS (Bank for International Settlements). 2001. *Annual Report*. Basel.

______. 2003. "Fiscal Issues and Central Banking in Emerging Markets." BIS Papers 20. Basel.

Bond, Steve, Asli Leblebicioglu and Fabio Schiantarelli. 2004. "Capital Accumulation and Growth: A New Look at the Empirical Evidence." IZA Discussion Paper 1174.

Blomstrom, Magnus, Robert E. Lipsey and Mario Zejan. 1994. "What Explains Growth in Developing Countries?" In *Convergence and Productivity: Cross-National Studies and Historical Evidence*, edited by William Baumol, Richard Nelson and Edward Wolff. Oxford: Oxford University Press.

Borensztein, E., J. de Gregorio and J.-W. Lee. 1998. "How Does Foreign Direct Investment Affect Economic Growth?" *Journal of International Economics* 45.

Bosworth, Barry, and Susan M. Collins. 2003. "The Empirics of Growth: An Update." Brookings Papers on Economic Activity 2.

CBRT (Central Bank of Republic of Turkey). 2005. *Monetary Policy Report 2005 I–III*. Ankara: TCMB.

Chang, Ha-Joon. 1994. *The Political Economy of Industrial Policy*. London: St. Martin's Press.

______. 2003. *Globalization, Economic Development and the Role of the State*. Penang: Zed Books.

______. 2005. "Policy Space in Historical Perspective – with special reference to Trade and Industrial Policies." Paper presented at the Queen Elizabeth House 50th Anniversary Conference, the Development Threats and Promises, University of Oxford, 4–5 July.

Cline, William. 2005. *The United States as a Debtor Nation*. Washington: Institute of International Economics.

Cunningham, Alastair, Liz Dixon and Simon Hayes. 2001. "Analysing Yield Spreads on Emerging Market Sovereign Bonds." Bank of England, Financial Stability Review 11. London.

Davis, E. P. 1992. *Debt, Financial Fragility and Systemic Risk*. Oxford: Clarendon Press.

DeLong, B., and L. Summers. 1993. "How Strongly Do Developing Countries Benefit from Equipment Investment?" *Journal of Monetary Economics* 32 (3).

Dixit, Avinash K., and Robert S. Pindyck. 1994. *Investment under Uncertainty*. Princeton: Princeton University Press.

Easterly, W., and R. Levine. 2001. "It's Not Factor Accumulation: Stylized Facts and Growth Models." *The World Bank Economic Review* 15 (2).

ECLAC (Economic Commission for Latin America and the Caribbean). 2000. *Equity, Development and Citizenship*. Santiago, Chile.

Erden, Lutfi, and Randall G. Holcombe. 2005. "The Effects of Public Investment on Private Investment in Developing Economies." *Public Finance Review* 33 (5).

Everhart, S., and M. Sumlinski. 2001. "Trends in Private Investment in Developing Countries. Statistics for 1970–2000 and the Impact on Private Investment of Corruption and the Quality of Public Investment." International Finance Corporation, Discussion Paper 44. Washington, DC.

Feldstein, Martin, and Charles Horioka. 1980. "Domestic Savings and International Capital Flows." *Economic Journal* 90 (2).

Fischer, Stanley. 2003. "Globalization and Its Challenges." *American Economic Review Papers and Proceedings* 93 (2).

Freeman, Richard B. 2004. "Doubling the Global Workforce: The Challenge of Integrating China, India, and the Former Soviet Block into the World Economy." Paper presented to the conference, Doubling the Global Work Force, Institute of International Economics, Washington, DC, 8 November.

______. 2005. "What Really Ails Europe (and America): The Doubling of the Global Workforce." *Globalist*, 3 June .

Freeman, Richard B., and Remco Oostendorp. 2000. "Wages around the World: Pay across Occupations and Countries." NBER Working Paper 8058.

Freeman, Richard B., and William M. Rodgers. 2005. "The Weak Jobs Recovery: Whatever Happened to the Great American Job Machine?" New York Federal Reserve, *Economic Policy Review* 11 (1).

Gallagher, Kevin, ed. 2005. *Putting Development First: The Importance of Policy Space in the WTO and International Financial Institutions*. London: Zed Books.

Gallagher, Kevin, and Lyuba Zarsky. 2005. "No Miracle Drug: Foreign Direct Investment and Sustainable Development." In *International Investment for Sustainable Development* edited by Lyuba Zarsky. London: Earthscan.

Ghose, Ajit K. 2004. "Capital Inflows and Investment in Developing Countries." ILO, Employment Strategy Paper 2004/11. Geneva.

Godley, Wynne, and Alex Izurieta. 2004. "The US Economy: Weaknesses of the 'Strong' Recovery." *Banco Nazionale del Lavaro Quarterly Review* 57 (229).

Goldstein, Morris. 2005. "What Might the Next Emerging-Market Financial Crisis Look Like?" Institute for International Economics, Working Paper 05-7. Washington, DC.

Goldstein, Morris, and Nicholas R. Lardy. 2004. "What Kind of Landing for the Chinese Economy?" Institute for International Economics, Policy Brief 04-7. Washington, DC.

Gordon, Robert J. 1995. "Is There a Tradeoff Between Unemployment and Growth?" NBER Working Paper 5081.

Groshen, Erica L., and Simon Potter. 2003. "Has Structural Change Contributed to a Jobless Recovery?" Federal Reserve Bank of New York, *Current Issues in Economics and Finance* 9 (8).

Hanson, Gordon H. 2001. "Should Countries Promote Foreign Direct Investment?" UNCTAD, G-24 Discussion Paper 9.

HM Treasury. 2003. End of Year Fiscal Report. December. London: HM Stationery Office.

Horioka, C. Y. 1995. "Is Japan's Household Saving Rate Really High?" *Review of Income and Wealth* 41 (4).

IIF (Institute of International Finance). 2005a. *Update on Capital Flows to Emerging Market Economies*, 31 March. Washington, DC.

______. 2005b. "Tightened Monetary Conditions, Slowing Growth, Global Economic Imbalances Pose Challenges for Emerging Markets." Press Release. 26 May. Washington, DC.

______. 2005c. *Capital Flows to Emerging Market Economies*. 24 September. Washington, DC.

ILO (International Labour Office). 2004. *A Fair Globalization: Creating Opportunities for All.* World Commission on the Social Dimension of Globalization. Geneva: ILO.

IMF. 2003. *World Economic Outlook.* September. Washington, DC.

______. 2004. *Public Investment and Fiscal Policy.* Washington, DC.

______. 2005. *World Economic Outlook.* September. Washington, DC.

ISSA (Independent Social Scientists Alliance). 2006. *Turkey and the IMF Macroeconomic Policy: Patterns of Growth and Persistent Fragilities.* Penang, Malaysia: Third World Network.

Izurieta, Alex. 2005. "Hazardous Inertia of Imbalances in the US and World Economy." *Economic and Political Weekly.* August.

Kaldor, Nicholas. 1964. "Economic Problems in Chile." In *Essays on Economic Policy.* London: Duckworth.

Kaminski, Graciela L., Carmen M. Reinhart and Carlos A. Végh. 2004. "When It Rains, It Pours: Procyclical Capital Flows and Macroeconomic Policies." In *NBER Macroeconomics Annual,* edited by M. Gertler and K. Rogoff. National Bureau of Economic Research, Cambridge, MA: MIT Press.

Kamps, Christophe. 2004. "New Estimates of Government Net Capital Stock for 22 OECD Countries. 1960–2001." IMF, Working Paper. 04/67. Washington, DC.

Kenny, C., and D. Williams. 2001. "What Do We Know About Economic Growth or Why Don't We Know Very Much?" *World Development* 29 (1).

Keynes, J. M. 1971. "Public Finance and Changes in the Value of Money." In *A Tract on Monetary Reform,* in *The Collective Writings of John Maynard Keynes,* vol. 4. Cambridge: Cambridge University Press.

Kose, Ayhan M., Eswar S. Prasad and Marco E. Terrones. 2005. "Growth and Volatility in an Era of Globalization." IMF Staff Papers 52. Special issue.

Kregel, Jan. 1996. "Some Risks and Implications of Financial Globalization for National Policy Autonomy," UNCTAD Review. Geneva.

Krugman, Paul. 1996. "Are Currency Crises Self-Fulfilling?" In *NBER Macroeconomics Annual,* edited by Ben S. Bernanke and Julio J. Rotemberg. Cambridge, MA: MIT Press.

______. 1998. "Currency Crises". Unpublished paper, MIT, Cambridge, MA.

Kuijs, Louis, and Tao Wang. 2005. "China's Pattern of Growth: Moving to Sustainability and Reducing Inequality." World Bank, Policy Research Working Paper 3767.

Kumar, Nagesh, and Jaya Prakash Pradhan. 2002. "Foreign Direct Investment, Externalities and Economic Growth in Developing Countries: Some Empirical Explorations and Implications for WTO Negotiations on Investment." RIS Discussion Paper, 27. New Delhi.

Mihaljek, Dubravko, and Bruno Tissot. 2003. "Fiscal Positions in Emerging Economies: Central Bank Perspective." In *Fiscal Issues and Central Banking in Emerging Markets.* BIS Papers 20. Basel.

Milberg, William. 1999. "Foreign Direct Investment and Development: Balancing Costs and Benefits." *International Monetary and Financial Issues for the 1990s,* XI, UNCTAD. Geneva.

Minsky, Hyman. 1977. "A Theory of Systemic Fragility". In *Financial Crises,* edited by E. I Altman and A. W. Sametz. Wiley: New York.

Mishel, Lawrence, and Ross Eisenbrey. 2005. "What's Wrong with the Economy?" Economic Policy Institute. 21 December.

Mohanty, M. S., and Michela Scatigna. 2003. "Countercyclical Fiscal Policy and Central Banks." In *Fiscal Issues and Central Banking in Emerging Markets.* BIS Papers, 20. Basel.

Moreno, Ramon. 2003. "Fiscal Issues and Central Banking in Emerging Economies: An Overview." In *Fiscal Issues and Central Banking in Emerging Markets.* BIS Papers, 20. Basel.

Mussa, Michael. 2005. "Sustaining Global Growth While Reducing External Imbalances." In *The United States and the World Economy: Foreign Economic Policy for the Next Decade,* edited by C. Fred Bergsten. Institute for International Economics, Washington, DC.

Nagaraj, R. 2005. "Industrial Growth in China and India: A Preliminary Comparison." *Economic and Political Weekly.* 21 May.

Nayyar, Deepak. 2002. "Cross-Border Movements of People". In *Governing Globalization.* New York: Oxford University Press.

Obstfeld, Maurice. 1996. "Models of Currency Crises with Self-Fulfilling Features." *European Economic Review* 40.

Ocampo, Jose Antonio. 2002. "Developing Countries' Anti-Cyclical Policies in a Globalized World." *Informes y Estudios Especiales* 4. Santiago: CEPAL.

______. 2003. "Capital Account and Counter-Cyclical Prudential Regulations in Developing Countries." *Informes y Estudios Especiales* 6. Santiago, CEPAL.

OECD. 1982. *Economic Outlook*. 31, July. Paris.

______. 1986. *Historical Statistics: 1960–1984*. Paris.

______. 2005a. *Employment Outlook*. Paris.

______. 2005b. *Economic Outlook*. 78, December. Paris.

O'Rourke, Kevin, and Jeffrey G. Williamson. 2000. *Globalization and Economic History: The Evolution of Nineteenth Century Atlantic Economy*. Cambridge, MA: MIT Press.

Qin, Duo, Marie Anne Cagas, Pilipinas Quising and Xin-Hua He. 2005. "How Much Does Investment Drive Economic Growth in China?" Queen Mary, Working Paper 545. London.

Roach, Stephen. 2004. "How Global Labour Arbitrage Will Shape the World Economy." *Global Agenda*. World Economic Forum.

Rodrik, Dani. 1995. "Getting Intervention Right: How South Korea and Taiwan Grew Rich." *Economic Policy* 20.

Ros J. 2000. *Development Theory and the Economics of Growth*. Ann Arbor: University of Michigan Press.

Sy, Amadou N. R. 2001. "Emerging Market Bond Spreads and Sovereign Credit Ratings: Reconciling Market View with Economic Fundamentals." IMF Working Paper 01/165. Washington, DC.

Talvi, Ernesto, and Carlos A. Végh. 2000. "Tax Base Variability and Procyclical Fiscal Policy." NBER Working Paper 7499.

UNCTAD. 2005. *Economic Development in Africa: Rethinking the Role of Foreign Direct Investment*. United Nations: Geneva.

UNCTAD TDR (various issues). *Trade and Development Report*. Geneva: United Nations.

UNDP. 2005. *China's Human Development Report*. New York.

Van der Hoeven, Rolph and Malte Lübker. 2005. "Financial Openness and Employment: The Need for Coherent International and National Policies." Paper prepared for the G24 Technical Group Meeting, IMF, Washington, DC, September 15–16.

Wade, Robert. 2003. *Governing the Market*, second edition. Princeton: Princeton University Press.

Wade, Robert, and Frank Veneroso. 1998. "The Asian Crisis: The High Debt Model Versus the Wall Street-Treasury-IMF Complex." *New Left Review* 228: 3–23.

World Bank. 1992. *Adjustment Lending and Mobilization of Private and Public Resources for Growth*. Washington, DC.

______. 2003. *Global Economic Prospects*. Washington, DC.

______. 2005a. *Global Development Finance*. Washington, DC.

______. 2005b. *World Development Indicators*. Washington, DC.

Chapter IV

EXCHANGE RATE MANAGEMENT, GROWTH AND STABILITY: NATIONAL AND REGIONAL POLICY OPTIONS IN ASIA[1]

A. Introduction

The exchange rate has become a growing focus of attention in the recent policy debate in developing countries. This is due mainly to two reasons. First, with increased emphasis placed on export-led growth and the dismantling of tariff and nontariff barriers, the role of the exchange rate in growth and development has gained added importance. Drawing on the experience of late industrializers in East Asia, competitive and stable exchange rates have come to be seen as a key ingredient of successful industrialization

Second, with rapid liberalization of the capital account in developing countries and the growing size and speed of international capital flows, the impact of exchange rate swings on economic activity has undergone a fundamental transformation. Currency movements no longer affect economic activity simply by leading to expenditure switching between domestic and foreign goods, as assumed in the traditional analysis. Their impact on the economy operates mainly through private balance sheets because of growing dollarization of assets and liabilities.[2] Since dollarization is almost always associated with widespread currency and maturity mismatches, exchange rate swings tend to generate windfall losses or gains, thereby exerting significant influence on spending decisions and the viability of firms and financial institutions. For this reason, swings in exchange rates now tend to generate much greater variations in economic activity than in the past, when the dollarization of private balance sheets was limited.

While these developments have made the management of the exchange rate all the more important, they have also made its control more difficult. This is because exchange rates are no longer determined as a by-product of the international flow of goods and services, or trade balances, but in asset markets where expectations of future changes and risk assessments play a central role. For this reason, it has now become increasingly evident that the management of exchange rates would call for action to influence the demand for and supply of foreign exchange as an asset, including currency market interventions as well as market-based and direct (administrative) regulations and control over capital flows and the extent of dollarization. These measures are needed not only to stabilize the exchange rate but also to reduce the vulnerability of domestic asset markets to external financial shocks, such as those transmitted from the current global financial turmoil, triggered by widespread speculative lending and investment in major international financial centers.

These are the issues to be taken up in this chapter. The following section examines the link between the exchange rate and economic growth in developing countries. Since this operates mainly through trade, the analysis will start with a discussion of the effects of exports on capital accumulation and technical progress, followed by an analysis of the short- and long-term impact of the real exchange rate on economic activity, jobs and capital accumulation. Limits to what the exchange rate can achieve on its own are discussed, and it is argued that, important as it may be, exchange rate policy is no substitute for trade and industrial policy. Past historical experience and more recent cross-country evidence on the link between the exchange rate and economic growth are reviewed. The main conclusion of this section is that stable and competitively valued real exchange rates may be necessary, but not sufficient, for directing resources to traded goods sectors and reaping the dynamic benefits associated with manufacturing exports. However, a weak currency is not always preferable to a strong currency because of a weaker currency's ramifications for intracountry and intercountry distribution of income. These imply that, in practice, considerable judgment and discretion are required for a judicious management of the exchange rate.

Section C examines the links among international capital flows, exchange rates, and the real economy. It is argued that the boom–bust cycles in capital flows due to global factors have come to dominate exchange rate movements of most developing countries, capable of generating gyrations independent of their underlying fundamentals and macroeconomic conditions. Sharp devaluations caused by sudden stops and reversals of capital flows are severely contractionary—not because of supply rigidities emphasized by the structuralists in the 1970s and 1980s, but because of their impact on credit conditions and balance sheets. More importantly, these cycles tend to produce durable adverse effects on jobs and investment. Not only can losses of jobs and wages during crises exceed the gains that may have been reaped during boom periods, but recoveries from finance-driven recessions are often jobless and without strong increases in investment.

This is followed in Section D by an analysis of national policy options in managing exchange rates. It is argued that free floating is not a viable choice for developing countries. But under an open capital account regime, currency stability cannot be guaranteed even if monetary policy is fully assigned to this task. Monetary policy is often powerless in checking massive outflows triggered by sudden and widespread loss of confidence. At times of strong inflows currency market interventions and reserve accumulation could be reasonably effective in preventing unsustainable appreciations and current account positions, but they can also lead to credit, asset and investment bubbles. Nor can they prevent currency and maturity mismatches in private balance sheets. Reserves accumulated from capital flows – *borrowed reserves* – are highly costly because they are invested in low yielding foreign assets. For these reasons regulation and control over capital inflows need to be an integral part of exchange rate management.

Section E examines the post-1997 crisis experience of Asian countries in the light of the above considerations. It is shown that the region's response to the surge in capital inflows after the early years of the current decade has been to relax restrictions over resident outflows and to absorb excess supply of foreign exchange by intervention and reserve accumulation. While this approach has enabled countries in the region to avoid unsustainable currency appreciations and payments positions, it has not prevented rapid credit expansion or asset and investment bubbles which now render these countries vulnerable to shocks and contagion from the current global financial turmoil.

Section F turns to regional cooperation for greater monetary and financial stability in East Asia, including exchange rate arrangements and supporting such regional institutions and mechanisms as a common regional capital account regime, regional funds, and rules and guidelines for policy coordination and adjustment. It is argued that, given increased regional integration and the absence of multilateral arrangements for exchange rate cooperation, there is a strong economic rationale for regional monetary integration in Asia. Various options are discussed, drawing on the lessons from the European experience. The concluding section gives a summary of the main propositions, including national and regional policy recommendations for managing exchange rates and international capital flows.

B. Exchange Rate, Trade and Growth

1. The export–investment nexus

The role of the exchange rate in the process of economic growth derives mainly from its impact on trade, aggregate demand, capital accumulation and productivity growth. However, this issue is barely addressed in the mainstream trade theory based on Ricardian comparative advantages, whereby cost differences that govern trade, specialization, and resource allocation are determined solely by differences in resource endowments or technology, and the impact of the exchange rate on trade and production is ignored.[3] On the other hand, the theory of comparative advantages focuses on the allocation of existing resources and the resulting one-off static gains, leaving aside dynamic interactions among trade, accumulation, and productivity growth that determine the evolution of comparative advantages over time.[4]

Nor is trade properly integrated into mainstream growth theories. Both neoclassical and Keynesian growth theories are designed primarily for closed economies, without paying attention to possible impact of trade on key parameters determining the long-term growth path – that is, savings, investment and technological progress. Although there is a host of ad hoc models designed to show the benefits of trade for growth, there is no accepted theory where growth is rigorously linked to international trade.[5]

There are supply-side and demand-side linkages between trade and growth. Neoclassical thinking emphasizes the former. According to this view, free trade improves efficiency not only because of better allocation of resources based on comparative advantages (allocative efficiency) but also better use of resources (cost or X-efficiency) resulting from increased competitive pressures (Bhagwati 1994). However, for such one-off increases in efficiency and income to lift the growth path, they would need to translate into a permanently higher rate of investment.

A more dynamic supply-side impact of trade emphasizes technical progress and productivity growth. This depends not so much on import liberalization as expansion in foreign markets. Since Adam Smith's dictum that the division of labor is limited by the extent of the market, it has been recognized that exports can provide dynamic productivity gains by reducing the dependence of production on a domestic market and helping achieve economies of scale.[6] These gains assume particular importance for industrialization and growth not only in small economies where the population size cannot accommodate optimum scale in most lines of industry, but also for larger developing countries where income levels are not high enough for certain industries to become viable without exports.

In its most rudimentary form, exports provide a vent for surplus for countries with large amounts of underutilized land and labor, allowing them to increase production of primary products for foreign markets. Further progress depends crucially on industrialization, except for very small economies that could attain a relatively high level of income by specializing in offshore financial services and tourism or by providing trade-related services to a vast industrial hinterland, such as Hong Kong.[7] This is true also for most resource-rich economies.[8] There is ample evidence that rapid expansion of manufacturing production and exports is a common feature of rapidly growing developing countries (UNCTAD TDR 2003, chap. 5).

With progress in industrialization, expansion in markets abroad helps firms to overcome high entry costs and to benefit from specialization and exploitation of scale economies, which can, in turn, accelerate learning by doing and productivity growth. These can also generate a range of externalities at the industry level and positive productivity-enhancing spillovers for the economy as a whole, including nonexport sectors. However, the productivity-enhancing effects of exports are not automatic and depend on a number of complementary factors, including public support (Keesing and Lall 1992; Lall 2004). This is the main reason why empirical evidence on the link between exports and productivity growth and positive spillovers from exporting is not conclusive.[9]

While recognizing that expansion to markets abroad could provide dynamic gains, the Keynesian and Structuralist schools emphasize the demand-side linkages between exports and growth, and focus on the balance of payments constraint – issues that have been underplayed in the orthodox theory by virtue of its assumptions of balanced trade and sustained full employment.[10] Not only are exports a component of aggregate demand but sustained export growth is essential for growth of components of domestic demand, since most developing countries are heavily dependent on imported intermediate inputs, capital goods, energy, and food for investment, production, and consumption. In particular, the imports of capital goods and technology needed to overcome the constraint that domestic production capabilities places on accumulation, growth, and industrialization requires generation of adequate foreign exchange through exports.

The dependence on imported capital goods and technologies embodied therein is generally greater during the initial stages of development, when such industries are lacking. Indeed, in the absence of foreign borrowing, an economy without a significant capital goods industry cannot really save and invest without exporting. It would need to put aside (save) part of its current production of consumables for exports in order to be able to expand its existing production capacity or invest in new lines of production by importing the capital equipment needed.[11]

Despite the hype about the benefits of removing barriers to imports in the mainstream literature, the trade–growth linkages are often discussed around the so-called export-led growth – a concept that is not always rigorously defined. Since sustained growth – as opposed to one-off increases in the degree of utilization of existing capacity – depends on capital accumulation and productivity growth, the concept of export-led growth should imply that growth of exports, rather than domestic demand, is the principal driving force behind investment and technological progress. However, the empirical literature on the link between growth and exports often relies on demand-side-growth-accounting based on ex post national income identities.[12] This not only ignores the supply-side effects, but also the linkages between external and domestic components of demand, notably manufactured exports and investment. This linkage can be particularly strong in economies where an important part of manufactured value added finds outlet in foreign markets, as in most East Asian countries. It also implies that an adverse export shock could impinge on income not only by reducing the foreign component of aggregate demand but through its direct impact on investment in traded goods sectors.[13]

A virtuous interaction and cumulative causation between manufactured exports and investment in the growth and industrialization process involves, in effect, both supply-side and demand-side linkages.[14] Exports broaden the size of the market and thus allow scale economies to be exploited. They encourage investment over and above what can be done on the basis of domestic demand, and provide the foreign exchange needed for capital goods imports and investment. Investment, in turn, improves export potential by adding to productive capacity and raising industrial competitiveness through productivity growth.

As demonstrated by successful late industrialization in East Asia, such a process of growth and industrialization is typically characterized by rising investment, exports, and manufacturing value added, both absolutely and as a proportion of GDP. In the early stages of East Asian industrialization, imports generally exceeded exports, and domestic savings fell short of investment, necessitating external financing. But over time both foreign exchange and savings gaps were closed as exports and domestic savings began to grow faster than investment. Growing profits supported by exports and investment have been the main factor behind rapid growth of savings. Thus, the *export–investment nexus* is complemented by an *investment–profit nexus* – a process of dynamic interaction between profits and investment wherein profits are simultaneously an incentive for investment, a source of investment, and an outcome of investment (Akyüz and Gore 1996). By contrast, most other developing countries in Latin America and Africa have been unable to sustain a virtuous interaction among exports, investment and savings. Although they experienced occasional investment booms supported by strong commodity export earnings and/or capital inflows, these could not be translated into a solid manufacturing export base and rising savings rates, with the result that these investment booms often came to an end when global trading and financial conditions deteriorated.[15]

2. Exchange rate, employment and investment

What is the role of the exchange rate in animating and sustaining a virtuous investment–export nexus and stimulating growth? Since the real exchange rate is the relative price between nontradeable and tradeable goods, changes in the real exchange rate exert a strong influence on the distribution of resources between these two sectors.[16] However, from the point of view of dynamic linkages between exports and economic growth, what matters is not the effect of the real exchange rate on the use and allocation of existing resources, but on investment decisions, accumulation, and structural change. The role of the real exchange rate in the growth process runs through its effects on the relative profitability of investment in sectors with significant potential for increasing returns and productivity growth.

In many developing countries there are often limits to what currency changes can achieve in the short term in reallocating resources from nontraded goods toward traded goods sectors, including both exports and domestic substitutes for imports. In the conventional analysis these limits are formulated in terms of demand for traded goods or, more specifically, the impact of exchange rate changes on the distribution of aggregate spending between domestic and foreign goods – that is, expenditure switching. According to this analysis, a devaluation of the exchange rate reduces the prices of exports for foreign buyers and increases the prices of imports in domestic markets, and these changes raise the volume of exports and lower the volume of imports, respectively. The overall effect depends on price elasticities of demand. According to the Marshall–Lerner condition, if the sum of the elasticities of demand for exports and imports is greater than unity, the trade balance will improve. It is, however, recognized that there can be a J-curve effect; that is, the immediate impact of a devaluation on the trade balance can be adverse, because it takes time for expenditure patterns to adjust to changed relative prices. Thus, initially, quantity response tends to be sluggish. Over time, however, as export volumes increase and import volumes decline, the trade balance will improve and economic activity and employment will expand.

This analysis makes no reference to supply conditions, either for exportables or for domestic substitutes for imports. It assumes, in effect, that supply is fully flexible. However, supply rigidities are an inherent feature of many developing countries, as constantly pointed out by the structuralists during the 1970s and 1980s in the debate over the impact of devaluations on income and employment. The structuralist theory of contractionary devaluations was founded on the inelasticity of supply in economies where exports and the consumption basket of wage earners were supplied by the primary sector.[17] On this analysis, the reduction in real wages brought about by a devaluation would reduce the demand for domestic manufactures, but increased domestic prices of exportables would fail to raise output and employment in the primary sector because of supply rigidities. The increase in exports would also be limited because of low price elasticity of domestic demand for food while imports would fall alongside declining employment in industry.[18] On the other hand, higher prices of imports would not stimulate production of domestic substitutes because of complementarity of imports with domestic manufactures – an outcome often attributed by the mainstream to import substitution industrialization.

In other words, devaluation would fail to switch resources from nontradeables to tradeables and raise production for exports and import substitution. It would reduce the trade gap primarily through a contraction in economic activity.

There can be little doubt that supply rigidities can arise even in more diversified exporters of manufactures. Where exports are specific to foreign markets and consumed little at home (such as Barbie dolls or golf clubs), there would be a limited scope for switching goods from domestic absorption to exports. This is the case for many developing country exporters of manufactured consumer goods closely linked to international production networks. There are also limits to reallocation of resources so as to increase the supply of exportables. Unlike in the neoclassical theory of production where "factors of production" can be shifted freely among different lines of production, in reality skills, capital equipment, and organizational structures are often industry-specific and even product-specific, and cannot easily be reshuffled and deployed from one sector to another as the incentive structure is altered by changes in the exchange rate. Under these conditions the immediate impact of devaluations on exports and import substitution would depend largely on spare capacity in these sectors. Resources released from nontraded sectors may remain unemployed, skills may be eroded, and equipment may become obsolete until the production capacity is restructured and expanded through investment in skills and equipment according to changed incentives. Indeed, one can even talk about the supply-side J-curve effect of devaluations, whereby quantity response is delayed because existing resources cannot be rapidly redeployed to traded goods sectors.

That such supply-side rigidities can create "adjustment costs" in the case of changes in the incentive structure due to import liberalization is recognized in the mainstream literature even though they are almost never explicitly quantified and incorporated in estimated benefits from trade liberalization (Akyüz 2009). Like big bang trade liberalization, such costs tend to be much higher and more persistent when exchange rate changes are sharp and unexpected.

Whether or not devaluations are contractionary in the short term, the main conduit of a shift in relative prices to resource allocation is investment. But for real exchange rates to have a significant influence on investment, they need to remain relatively stable and predictable over time. Uncertainties created by large and unexpected swings in exchange rates and the consequent fluctuations in demand increase the risks of investment in traded goods sectors. Even when the average level of the real exchange rate over an extended period is favorable to traded goods sectors, if it is subject to gyrations, it will not provide a reliable basis for directing investment to export and imports substitution industries. In this sense the stability of the real exchange rate may be more important for growth than its average level over the medium term.

3. Limits and costs of reliance on the exchange rate

While competitive and stable real exchange rates play an important role in growth and industrialization, there are some caveats that need to be kept in mind. First, there are limits to what the exchange rate can do on its own in promoting industrialization and growth. Second, a weak currency is not always beneficial to stability and growth.

Finally, there is a need to strike an appropriate balance between exchange rate stability and flexibility since under certain conditions efforts to maintain stable nominal and/or real exchange rates could prove to be highly damaging.

In no area of development policy can success be explained by the behavior of a single variable, and this is certainly the case for the role of the exchange rate in growth and industrialization. While it is usually very difficult to maintain rapid growth for an extended period under overvalued and unstable real exchange rates, a weak and stable currency alone is not sufficient for sustained growth. Its impact on resource allocation, investment, and productivity growth depends very much on how it is combined with a host of other factors, including trade-related industrial policy measures, notably import tariffs and export subsidies.

Like the exchange rate, tariffs and subsidies can no doubt be used to shift resources to tradeable goods sectors. It has long been established that if exports are subsidized to the same extent as imports are taxed, the price ratio between exportables and importables would not be affected, but their prices will rise relative to nontradeables, having the same effect as real devaluations.[19] As industrial policy tools, however, tariffs and subsidies are useful only when they differentiate among different categories of imports and exports, respectively, and this is how they were used by successful late industrializers in East Asia.

While the exchange rate could be used to protect import competing and export industries, it would do so uniformly.[20] However, in the course of industrialization the effective use of tariffs for infant industry protection would require the coexistence of low and high tariffs. Since at any point in time different industries would need different degrees of infant industry protection, an effective system of tariffs tends to be highly dispersed rather than uniform. Furthermore, over time tariffs need to be raised on some products but lowered on others, and dispersion may be rising or falling according to the stage of industrial development reached (Akyüz 2009). Much the same is true for subsidies; a country should not need to subsidize exports of products in which it has static comparative advantages, but would need to do so for industries that are yet to achieve maturity and benefit from scale economies.

These considerations suggest that, important as it may be in the allocation of resources between traded and nontraded goods industries and in reaping the dynamic benefits of exporting, the exchange rate policy is no substitute for trade and industrial policy interventions. However, since these instruments are no longer available to most developing countries because of their commitments in the World Trade Organization (WTO), it is now absolutely essential to sustain stable and competitive real exchange rates in order to avoid payments crises and interruption to growth and development.[21]

The concept of equilibrium real exchange rate (ERER) is the standard reference in judging whether a currency is misaligned vis-à-vis underlying fundamentals. It is the rate that simultaneously secures internal and external equilibrium. Internal equilibrium refers to full employment or the attainment of potential output. External equilibrium is used synonymously with external sustainability and means that the intertemporal budget constraint for the economy is met.[22] Defined in this way, ERER depends on a host of factors, both external and internal, including technology and productivity, tariffs and subsidies, capital account regimes, interest rates, and world prices for traded goods.

There are several and repeated attempts in the literature to operationalize this theoretical concept and to measure the extent to which currencies are misaligned. However, since there are considerable uncertainties over how the key determinants of the ERER would move over time, such measures are not always a reliable guide to policymaking.

It has been argued that neutrality of incentives between traded and nontraded goods sectors, as advocated in the mainstream literature, would not be sufficient to secure their balanced growth because traded goods sectors suffer disproportionately from institutional and market failures that pervade poor countries (Rodrik 2008). According to this view, the costs entailed by these failures need to be compensated by sustained real exchange rate depreciations to increase the relative profitability of investment in traded goods sectors.[23] However, since in principle the ERER should allow for any distortions that impinge on productivity and costs in traded and nontraded goods sectors, this argument boils down to the proposition that the impact of institutional and market failures on costs in the traded goods sectors is not properly accounted for in measured/estimated ERERs.[24]

While overvaluation is generally considered as undesirable on the grounds of its negative consequences for trade, industrialization and growth, there is much less emphasis on the problems that could be posed by a policy of weak currency. Two types of difficulties are often mentioned, one internal, another external, and these will be discussed in some detail in the subsequent sections. On the internal side, currency interventions needed at times of large current account surpluses and/or capital inflows to prevent appreciations entail costs because reserves are invested in low yielding foreign assets. Moreover, since it is not always possible to achieve full sterilization (that is, to offset the impact of the currency intervention on the monetary base), such a policy could also lead to domestic credit expansion, creating inflationary pressures in asset and/or products markets.[25] Externally, a policy of cheap currency could create frictions with trading partners and trigger competitive devaluations or hostile trade actions.

Perhaps more important from the viewpoint of social welfare is the impact of an aggressive export push through an undervalued currency on income distribution within and across countries. This raises the old issues of fallacy of composition and immiserizing growth, which have been largely sidelined in the more recent discussion of the link between growth and the real exchange rate. Given labor productivity, real devaluations imply declines in real wages. To put it differently, for a nominal depreciation to produce a decline in the real exchange rate, nominal wages should lag behind traded goods prices. If dollar prices of exports remain unchanged, profit margins in export sectors will increase – that is, real devaluations would redistribute income from wages to profits (Diaz-Alejandro 1963). Of course, if productivity increases over time, a weaker currency can be associated with rising real wages, as often happened in East Asia. But to the extent that real devaluations result in lower export prices in dollars, part of the productivity gains would be captured by consumers abroad at the expense of wages. With dollar prices of imports remaining unchanged, this would also be reflected in a decline in net barter terms of trade.

This outcome depends crucially on whether or not developing country exporters are "price takers" in world markets for manufactures. It is generally recognized that a small economy may be able to increase its exports of manufactures without putting any significant downward pressure on world (dollar) prices, but this would not be true for developing countries as a whole or for large economies such as China. However, even a small economy may need to lower the dollar prices of its exports if it supplies nonstandard, differentiated products – which is more often the case in manufactures than in commodity exports. In such cases the benefits of any increased volume of exports may be more than offset by losses due to lower export prices, giving rise to immiserizing growth (Bhagwati 1958). Even when rising quantities more than offset the impact of the decline in prices on export earnings, and the purchasing power of exports (income terms of trade) improves, falling export prices and net barter terms of trade can still entail resource losses. Evidence suggests that the purchasing power of manufacturing exports of developing countries have been rising rapidly, but prices of their manufactured exports have been weakening vis-à-vis those exported by advanced industrialized countries.[26]

This is also true for China, the most prominent developing economy pursuing an aggressive export-led growth policy based on cheap labor and cheap currency.[27] An important part of the benefits of productivity growth in China is shared between profit earners, including transnational companies, and Western consumers, even though absolute living conditions of workers have been improving rapidly. Since the early years of the decade labor productivity in the manufacturing industry has grown by some 20 percent per annum, while nominal wage increases have been under 15 percent and real wage increases even lower. The share of labor cost in total gross output in mining, manufacturing, and utilities fell from 11.5 percent in 2002 to 7.1 percent in 2006; for the economy as a whole, the share of wages in GDP fell to about 40 percent after fluctuating between 50 and 55 percent in the 1990s. While average labor productivity in China is just under 20 percent of that in the United States, the Chinese manufacturing hourly wage rate is about 3 percent of that in the United States. At the same level of average industrial productivity and income, Japanese and Korean wages in dollar terms were much higher than those in China today.[28]

The extent to which Chinese productivity growth has been passed onto Western consumers in the form of lower export prices rather than to workers in the form of higher wages is not very clear and further research is needed. However, there is no doubt that the United States consumers are one of the main beneficiaries of productivity growth in Asian exporters of manufactures. For instance, prices of products imported from the first tier NIEs (Korea, Taiwan, Singapore and Hong Kong) fell by 2.4 percent per year from 1993 to 2006, compared with a 0.3 percent rise in average prices of total non-oil imports into the United States (Amiti and Stiroh 2007). Available statistics for more recent years show a similar trend for prices of imports from China, which registered a decline of 3 percent between 2003 and 2006. There was some increase in prices of products imported from China after 2006; but much of this was due, in the case of industrial supplies, to increases of prices that China paid for commodity inputs and, in the case of consumer and capital goods, to the sharp appreciation of the renminbi against the dollar, rather than domestic wage pressures (Amiti and Davis 2009).

The decline in the share of wages in China is mirrored by the decline in the share of consumption in GDP. During 2002–2007, the average growth rate of consumer spending was around 8 percent per annum, while gross fixed capital formation grew at a rate of

15 percent and exports 25 percent. Consequently, the share of consumption fell below 40 percent of GDP – almost half of the figure in the United States and considerably less than the share of investment. The imbalance between the two key components of domestic demand has meant increased dependence of Chinese industry on foreign markets (Akyüz 2008a).

This experience stands in sharp contrast to that of late industrializers in Asia, particularly Japan and Korea, where wages and household consumption grew in tandem with productivity and underpinned the expansion of capacity by providing a growing internal market. There is the risk that a cheap currency, cheap labor policy can weaken the efforts for upgrading and productivity growth while increasing the dependence of growth on expansion in foreign markets. This is indeed one of the conclusions reached by the Commission on Growth and Development (CGD):

> As with other forms of export promotion, exchange rate policies can outlive their usefulness. If the currency is suppressed by too much or for too long, it will distort the evolution of the economy by removing the natural market pressure for change. The cheap currency will tend to lock activity into labor-intensive export sectors, reduce the return to upgrading skills, and eventually harm productivity as a result. Like other industrial policies, a keenly priced currency is supposed to solve a specific, transitory problem. Eventually, as an economy grows more prosperous, domestic demand should and usually does play an increasingly important role in generating and sustaining growth. Exchange rate policy should not stand in the way of this natural evolution (CGD 2008, 51).

Late industrializers in East Asia did not rely on cheap currency for industrial development. By contrast, they occasionally tolerated moderate appreciations which, in some instances, provided incentives for upgrading and productivity growth. In Taiwan, for instance, the real exchange rate was allowed to appreciate almost continuously after the late 1960s. This, together with the rise in real wages, put considerable pressure on business to remain competitive in international markets, forcing them to achieve productivity gains that made it possible for the economy to continue to be one of the fastest growing in the world (Jenkins and Kuo 1997).

Finally, a rigid, immovable exchange rate can be as damaging as a highly volatile currency. Recurrent currency and balance of payments crises in emerging markets since the mid-1990s show that, under capital account liberalization, efforts to maintain a fixed nominal exchange rate can be disastrous even where monetary and fiscal disciplines are secured – often a recipe for boom–bust cycles in capital flows and exchange rates with serious repercussions for the real economy. There is now a growing consensus that a reasonable degree of flexibility is needed in order to prevent such gyrations.

This consensus also extends to the real exchange rate in view of increased susceptibility of developing countries to external trade and financial shocks as a result of their greater openness. Clearly a permanent shift in the variables affecting the ERER, including terms of trade and international interest rates, would call for an adjustment in the real exchange rate in order to avoid unsustainable current account positions. Similarly, temporary trade and financial shocks may call for changes in the real exchange rate in order to prevent the burden of adjustment from falling on domestic absorption, economic activity, and employment.

4. Cross-country evidence

Historically, real exchange rates have been more competitive and stable in late industrializers in East Asia than in most other developing countries, including those in South Asia, Africa and Latin America. This is an important, though not the only, reason why Asian NIEs were more successful in agricultural transformation in their initial stages of development and, subsequently, in building dynamic and competitive manufacturing industries. In Africa, where real exchange rates were relatively stable (Table 4.1), persistent overvaluation appears to have been a deliberate policy for extracting resources from agriculture, whereas in Latin America the extreme degree of instability is a reflection of the inability of countries to maintain competitive rates despite occasional devaluations in response to recurrent payments crises.

In most developing countries in the early stages of industrialization the evolution of exports and capital accumulation depends crucially on the performance of the agricultural sector. A major difficulty facing policymakers at this stage is how to sustain agricultural growth while extracting a surplus from agriculture for industrial development. In this respect the contrast between East Asia and sub-Saharan Africa is quite striking. Evidence shows that in both regions agriculture was taxed in the early stages of industrialization through pricing policies. Comparative analysis of the ratio of producer prices to border prices show that the implicit rate of taxation was not always higher in Africa, but the overall rate of taxation was much higher because exchange rate policies were not favorable to export crops. Rather, they were designed primarily for providing cheap imports to heavily protected industries (UNCTAD TDR 1998, part 2, chap. 3; and Boratav 2001). However, the Asian success in agricultural development depended not only on favorable exchange rates for agricultural producers but also on complementary policies, including investment in agricultural infrastructure and provision of various productivity-enhancing services (Karshenas 2001).

In Latin America the dominant approach to exchange rate policy during the 1960s and 1970s was to maintain fixed nominal exchange rates (often vis-à-vis the dollar), sometimes for as long as ten years or even more, against a background of relatively rapid inflation, followed by sharp devaluations as real appreciations led to balance of payments crises. Real devaluations following nominal adjustments could not be sustained because inflation often continued unabated and even accelerated after currency adjustments. Many of these adjustments were stepwise, but even where devaluations were followed by crawling pegs whereby **the peg was shifted over time,** subsequent nominal adjustments were not sufficient to maintain real exchange rates at levels favorable to traded goods sectors. In other words, devaluations were not effective in bringing about real exchange rate adjustments needed to reduce structural external deficits and avoid recurrent payments crises.[29]

Table 4.1: Stability of the real exchange rate[a] (quarterly data 1965–85)

Asia		Latin America		Africa	
Singapore	6.32	Colombia	11.87	Zambia	16.48
Malaysia	7.59	Mexico	13.21	Ethiopia	14.84
Korea	8.80	Paraguay	16.50	Tunisia	11.18
Thailand	8.14	Bolivia	18.35	South Africa	10.79
Philippines	14.62	Peru	21.51	Mauritius	8.00
India	18.09	Brazil	22.44	Kenya	7.86
Pakistan	27.53	Chile	28.29		

Source: Edwards (1989).
a. Measured by the coefficient of variation of quarterly changes in the multilateral real exchange rate index.

While nominal pegs were also used in some Asian countries such as Korea – which maintained a regime of de facto dollar peg until the end of the 1970s – in such cases not only were real appreciations generally more moderate but devaluations were not followed by rapid erosion of the real exchange rate.[30] Most Asian countries avoided gyrations in nominal and real exchange rates – until they liberalized the capital account in the 1990s and left their currencies to the whims of international capital flows.[31] Large devaluations, such as that in 1980 in Korea, were responses to external trade shocks, notably a sharp deterioration in the terms of trade, rather than to the erosion of the real exchange rate through rapid inflation. They were followed by a regime of crawling pegs, preventing appreciation of the real exchange rate. The Asian countries, too, no doubt experienced occasional misalignments and appreciations, but various other measures, including industry policy instruments, were used to maintain export momentum and avoid recurrent payments crises.

Recent studies on cross-country regressions to account for growth differences have increasingly included the level and volatility of the real exchange rate among the explanatory variables.[32] Evidence based on such regressions for Latin America suggests that overvaluations tend to slow growth of industrial employment and output. According to a cross-country study of 18 Latin American and Caribbean countries for 1970–96, trade liberalizations had a small negative effect on employment growth, but the impact was greatly amplified by the appreciation of the real exchange rate, underlying the importance of proper exchange rate management at times of trade reforms (Marquez and Pagés 1998).

As already noted, most studies trying to estimate the impact of exchange rate misalignments on growth use purchasing power parity (PPP) measures, often adjusted for the Balassa–Samuelson effect. Studies by Cavallo, Cottani and Kahn (1990) and by Dollar (1992) on developing countries report inverse correlations between real exchange rate overvaluations and economic growth. Similar results are found by Gala (2007) for 58 developing countries for the period 1960–99. Razin and Collins (1999) lump together a large number of developing and developed countries and find that overvaluations harm growth, but this is not the case for undervaluation. Hausman, Pritchett, and Rodrik

(2004) and Rodrik (2008) find that growth accelerations are usually associated with real depreciations.[33]

By contrast, a study of 60 countries over the period 1965–2003 finds that both real overvaluations and undervaluations hinder growth, although in the former case the effect is stronger (Aguirre and Calderón 2005). Moreover, the effect is nonlinear: growth declines are larger, the larger the size of the misalignments. Thus, while small to moderate undervaluations enhance growth, large undervaluations hurt growth. Furthermore, in this study the impact of a movement of the real exchange rate would depend on the underlying circumstances. An increase in the real exchange rate at a time of significant and sustained improvements in terms of trade implies, in effect, a movement toward the ERER. The study shows that exchange rate changes in response to shifts in key determinants of the ERER help promote growth. Most other studies on the effect of exchange rate variability on employment, investment and growth focus on the observed behavior of the real exchange rate without considering whether its movements are warranted by shifts in the underlying fundamentals.[34] Results are mixed, varying according to country samples, measures of volatility and the specifications used.

It is sometimes argued that, while provoking instability, financial and currency markets also provide the means to hedge against instability so as to minimize its impact on the real economy. According to the findings of a cross-country study of 83 countries over the period 1960–2000, in countries with relatively low levels of financial development, exchange rate volatility generally reduces growth, whereas in financially advanced countries there is no significant effect (Aghion et al. 2006).

It is true that in developing countries the absence or underdevelopment of relevant derivatives markets limits the ability of individual agents to hedge against instability.[35] But it is not evident that in a country with liability dollarization it would be possible for the agents to hedge collectively, since this would require, in effect, pushing the currency risk abroad.[36] Moreover, quite apart from transaction costs, there are limits to hedging: "while forward contracts and currency options have proved to be effective means of reducing risk in managing financial portfolios, they cannot cushion companies engaged in international trade against the risk of exchange rate fluctuations" and "even the most sophisticated hedges are no substitute for stable exchange rates."[37] There is evidence that forwards, swaps and options markets often develop faster when the currency is allowed to fluctuate. However, this is not only because these markets provide hedges against volatility, but also because currency volatility creates profit opportunities. In other words, it is not only that volatility is conducive to the development of hedging markets and instruments but the development of these markets and instruments can breed in greater volatility.[38]

The obvious conclusion from this maze of empirical work and theoretical considerations is that the influence of the exchange rate on growth is circumscribed by the overall economic environment and that there is no symmetry between the economic impact of overvaluation and undervaluation, and of gyrations and stability. First, there is no single and sure way of determining whether a currency is properly aligned with the underlying economic fundamentals, that is, to what extent it is overvalued or undervalued. This is largely because what constitutes the equilibrium exchange rates depends, inter alia, on long-term, sustained capital inflows, and passing a judgment on the latter has become almost an impossible undertaking. Second, while it may be very difficult to sustain rapid growth under sustained appreciations, whether or not depreciations would accelerate growth depends on a host of other factors. Finally, an economy is unlikely to maintain rapid growth for an extended period under highly unstable real exchange rates, but a stable currency may not necessarily promote growth; it may even hinder it when shifts in underlying fundamentals call for currency adjustments.

These considerations suggest that in practice a judicious management of the exchange rate would call for considerable judgment and discretion. Attention would need to be paid not only to the trade and growth performance of the economy and the evolution of its current account position but also to financial vulnerabilities that may result from capital flows and currency movements – an issue to be taken up presently.

C. Capital Flows, Exchange Rates and the Real Economy

1. Boom–bust cycles in capital flows and exchange rate gyrations

A common feature of the cross-country studies on the link between the exchange rate and economic growth is that they do not specify the forces driving the currency and the nature and causes of instability. Many of them lump together earlier episodes of appreciation and instability caused by domestic policy inconsistencies with those arising from boom–bust cycles in capital flows driven by global forces in the more recent periods. These episodes differ not only with respect to the causes of appreciations and instability but also their impact on employment, investment and growth and, hence, the appropriate policy response. Indeed, the failure of the IMF to diagnose the nature of these crises and distinguish them from traditional currency appreciations and payments difficulties caused by domestic demand expansion and inflation led to serious errors in policy response, notably in East Asia where procyclical monetary and fiscal tightening adopted in response to the 1997 crisis served to deepen the economic contraction caused by the reversal of capital flows.

Exchange rate misalignments and instability caused by boom–bust cycles in private capital flows is not a recent phenomenon. Perhaps the first most significant postwar episode was the experience of the Southern Cone countries in Latin America, notably Chile, during the late 1970s and early 1980s. The combination of financial liberalization, tight monetary policy and fixed nominal exchange rates attracted large amounts of foreign capital to the region, leading to debt accumulation by the private sector and a consumption boom. Massive inflows of capital allowed the currencies to appreciate in real terms despite mounting trade deficits. The experiment ended with a currency and financial crisis, bringing down many banks and causing a sharp contraction in economic activity (Diaz-Alejandro 1985).

With rapid liberalization of the capital account in the 1990s, international private capital flows have become the driving force behind business cycles and exchange rates in many developing countries, capable of producing unsustainable economic expansions and currency appreciations followed by financial crises and recessions. While country-specific (pull) and global (push) factors both play important roles in determining the direction, size, and nature of capital flows, evidence shows that the most damaging episodes of such crises are those associated with boom–bust cycles in capital flows driven by global factors beyond the control of the recipient countries.[39]

Indeed, since the early 1990s currency and balance of payments crises have occurred under varying macroeconomic and financial conditions in Latin America, East Asia, and elsewhere (UNCTAD TDR 1995, chap. 2; 1997, chap. 3; 1999, chap. 3; and 2003, chap. 4). They were seen not only in countries with large and widening current account deficits (e.g., Mexico and Thailand), but also where deficits were relatively small and presumed sustainable (Indonesia and Russia). A significant currency appreciation is often a feature of countries experiencing currency turmoil (Brazil, Mexico, Russia and Turkey), but this has not always been the case; appreciations in most East Asian countries hit by the 1997 crisis were moderate or negligible. In some cases crises were associated with large budget deficits, as in Brazil, Russia and Turkey, but in others (Mexico and East Asia) the budget was either balanced or in surplus. Crises occurred not only where capital flows supported a boom in private consumption, as in Latin America, but also in private investment, as in East Asia. Again, in some episodes of crises external liabilities were largely public (Brazil and Russia) while in others they were private (East Asia). Finally, most countries hit by balance of payments and financial crises are said to have been lacking effective regulation and supervision of the financial system, but Argentina could not avoid a currency and payments crisis and default despite having one of the best systems of prudential regulations in the developing world and a financial system dominated by foreign banks.

Recurrent currency and financial crises under varying macroeconomic conditions have raised serious questions about the mainstream thinking that currency and balance of payments crises result primarily from macroeconomic policy inconsistencies, notably lack of fiscal and monetary discipline, and that price stability is both necessary and sufficient for financial and exchange rate stability. In reality, in most countries financial boom–bust cycles, asset price and exchange rate gyrations, and credit surges and crunches, have all occurred under conditions of low and stable inflation – the most recent example being the global financial crisis triggered by the subprime débacle.[40] In the more extreme cases, as in Latin America, where price instability has traditionally been regarded as structural and chronic, single digit and stable inflation rates have been attained at the expense of increased financial fragility and instability through exchange-rate-based stabilization programs relying on short-term, unstable capital inflows.

The pattern of exchange rate movements over the boom–bust cycles in capital flows is well known. If the currency is allowed to float freely, both nominal and real exchange rates would appreciate when capital inflows exceed the current account deficit; but the deficit itself would be widened by real exchange rate appreciations, requiring growing amounts of inflows to finance it. Under a nominal peg currency, market interventions would be necessary when inflows exceed the current account deficit. Still, the real exchange rate could appreciate depending on the rate of inflation. Here, too, real appreciations could widen the current account deficit so that increased amounts of capital inflows would be needed to support a nominal peg. This was the case in exchange-rate-based stabilization programs implemented in Latin America and Europe in the 1990s. In East Asia, too, in the run-up to the 1997 crisis nominal exchange rates were broadly stable, but this had nothing to do with disinflation; rather, it reflected the long-standing emphasis on stable exchange rates in export-led industrialization and growth. Moreover, central banks in Asian countries hit by the 1997 crisis had occasionally intervened in order to prevent appreciation.[41]

With a sharp reversal of capital flows, nominal rates tend to collapse, overshooting their longer-term levels. Thus, over the boom–bust cycle, nominal rates first appreciate or remain relatively stable during the surge in capital flows depending on the regime adopted, resulting in moderate-to-sharp real appreciations. The rapid exit of capital then leads to a collapse in the nominal rate. Even though this often leads to an increase in inflation, currency-cum-financial crises generally result in large real devaluations.[42] This is often followed by a recovery in the nominal exchange rate – a correction to downward overshooting seen at times of capital flight – but real exchange rates remain below the levels attained during the surge in capital flows. This pattern is observed even where the sudden stop or reversal of capital flows do not trigger a balance of payments crisis, as was the case in Singapore and Taiwan during the 1997 crisis and, as discussed below, in the current episode of sharp declines in capital flows triggered by the subprime crisis.

2. *Wages, employment and investment over the cycle*

In almost all emerging market economies that experienced boom–bust cycles in capital flows in the 1990s, real wages rose rapidly at times of surges in capital inflows, but employment behaved differently in different countries.[43] Where the boom was driven by investment, unemployment fell during the expansion phase. This was the case in all the countries hit by the 1997 Asian crisis except Indonesia. By contrast, in Latin America, where booms were driven by consumption, unemployment was either stable or higher despite expansion of employment in services sectors, because of loss of competitiveness and jobs in industry.

During a surge in capital inflows, high real wages and cheap imports of capital goods, together with easy access to credit, tend to encourage investment and lead to capital deepening in an effort to restructure industry and raise productivity to meet foreign competition. This happened even in Latin America, where booms were driven primarily by private consumption. Investment growth was much stronger in East Asia, where firms augmented investment in the hope of increasing productivity and market shares, and expanded into new areas of production in response to rapidly falling prices of many of the electronic products exported, notably semiconductors. Again, most episodes of strong capital inflows produce booms in property markets and increased investment in residential and commercial construction.

Currency and maturity mismatches in balance sheets create serious problems for firms and financial institutions at times of rapid exit of capital and the collapse of the currency. These set off a process of debt deflation whereby attempts to escape from the squeeze on balance sheets of rising domestic cash needs to service foreign debt simply increase their financial difficulties by driving down exchange rates and asset values even further. Credit is cut as collateral values fall and banks try to consolidate their balance sheets (UNCTAD TDR 1998, chap. 3; and Krugman 1999). Credit conditions are often aggravated by

Table 4.2: Precrisis and postcrisis unemployment in Asia (percentage of labor force)

	1994–96	1998–99	2003	2007
Indonesia	4.0[a]	6.0	9.7	9.1
Korea	2.1	6.6	3.6	3.2
Malaysia	2.8[b]	3.3	3.6	3.3
Thailand	1.1	3.2	1.5	1.2

Source: ILO LABORSTA.
a. 1996.
b. 1995–96.

monetary tightening and interest rate hikes aiming to check capital flight, producing sharp declines in employment and real wages alongside a deep contraction in output.

The decline in real wages was particularly steep in Indonesia, Mexico and Turkey at times of crises – between 11 and 25 percent per annum. In East Asia unemployment went up rapidly, particularly in Korea and Indonesia (Table 4.2). In Latin America, where booms failed to produce a significant growth in jobs, the subsequent crises took unemployment to exceptionally high levels: in Mexico open unemployment doubled within a year; in Argentina, where the currency board and the fixed exchange rate were maintained despite worsening external conditions, unemployment shot up in the wake of the Mexican crisis, reaching almost 20 percent in 1995; in Brazil open unemployment rose from 6 percent in the mid-1990s to almost 10 percent in 1999. A similar increase was registered in Turkey during the 2001 crisis.

Almost all episodes of crisis-induced currency declines in emerging markets produced sharp declines in output, reviving the debate over if and why devaluations are contractionary. Even in countries with highly diversified production and exports such as Korea, real depreciations were not immediately translated into larger export volumes. One possible reason given is contagion: that is, if currencies of all countries competing in the same export markets fall, none of them would gain competitive advantage.[44] However, this is not very plausible since most Asian countries hit by the crisis achieved rapid export growth subsequently. A much more important factor in delaying the response of exports to real depreciations was credit crunch; that is, with the breakdown of the credit system, firms became unable to raise operating capital needed to increase production and exports. Indeed, in Asia currency declines appear to have inflicted less damage on firms than cutbacks in domestic credit lines and rise in interest rates because many firms with large foreign debt were export-oriented.

During crises not only do exports fail to rise quickly in response to the decline in the currency but domestic demand shrinks because of the impact of the collapse of the currency on private balance sheets. Indeed, there is now a growing agreement that the balance sheet impact of currency declines, rather than supply-side rigidities or demand inelasticities, is the main reason why crisis-induced devaluations in emerging markets are contractionary (Krugman, 1999; Frankel, 2005). There is also some support from empirical studies, including a study of nine Latin American countries by Galindo,

Izquierdo, and Montero (2006), that finds that real exchange rate depreciations can have a positive impact on employment growth, but this effect is reversed as liability dollarization increases.[45]

In expansion–recession–recovery cycles in emerging markets governed by international capital flows, losses of real wages, employment and investment incurred at times of downturn are not fully recovered when the economy regains its precrisis level of GDP. In Asia during the recovery phase, real wages regained their precrisis levels only in Korea while they remained depressed elsewhere in the region. In Latin America, real wages were all lower than the peaks reached before the crises. More importantly, everywhere employment lagged considerably behind output growth, giving rise to the phenomenon of jobless recovery. Post-crisis open unemployment rates were higher than precrisis rates by 1.0 percentage point in Brazil and Mexico, 5.5 points in Argentina, and 4 points in Korea and Indonesia. In Turkey growth averaging over 7 percent for four years after the 2001 crisis did not make any dent in unemployment, and real wages barely recovered. The deterioration in the conditions of labor, particularly among the unskilled, is a major reason why poverty levels in most of these countries stayed high despite economic recovery. In all four Asian countries hit by the 1997 crisis, unemployment levels in 2007 stood above those observed before the crisis, particularly in Indonesia. Much the same is true for investment: investment rates in all Asian countries hit by the 1997 crisis are still below their precrisis levels (Table 4.3).

Recoveries from economic downturns caused by the bursting of financial bubbles have also been weak in job creation and investment in some advanced countries. This was the case in the United States' recovery from the recession caused by the bursting of the dot-com bubble in 2001. Several explanations have been offered for this phenomenon (Akyüz 2008b, 184–86), but there is a growing consensus that the damage inflicted by financial crises on industry tends to be much deeper and longer lasting than difficulties resulting from economic contractions that occur in the context of traditional business cycles wherein finance takes a more passive and accommodative role.

D. Managing Capital Flows and Exchange Rates

1. Policy trade-offs and exchange rate regimes

According to conventional economic theory, it is not possible simultaneously to pursue an independent monetary policy, control the exchange rate and maintain an open capital account. All three are *potentially* feasible, but only two of them could be chosen as *actual* policy – thus, the dilemma known as impossible trinity or trilemma. Once the capital account is opened, a choice has to be made between controlling the exchange rate and preserving an independent monetary policy. Using monetary policy as a countercyclical tool to stabilize economic activity could result in large cyclical swings in the exchange rate and the balance of payments. Conversely, if monetary policy is used to stabilize the exchange rate, it cannot act as a countercyclical macroeconomic tool and prevent large cyclical swings in economic activity.

Table 4.3: Precrisis and postcrisis investment in Asia (percentage of GDP)

	1994–97	2003–2007
Indonesia	31.4	24.4
Korea	36.5	30.0
Malaysia	42.3	21.7
Thailand	39.1	27.7
Philippines	23.2	15.4
Singapore	35.9	20.0
Taipei	23.8	21.0

Source: ADB Asian Development Outlook (April 2000 and April 2008).

The orthodoxy takes financial openness for granted and argues that only one of the two corner solutions is feasible. At the one corner lies independent floating whereby the currency is left to market forces without intervention. At the other corner there are the so-called hard pegs based on legally mandated, credible commitments to a fixed exchange rate by locking into a reserve currency through currency boards or adopting a reserve currency as a national currency (full dollarization) or by joining a monetary union – arrangements that would effectively eliminate monetary policy autonomy, and even the central bank as it is traditionally known with the function of lender of last resort.

This trilemma, however, is not absolute. In principle it is possible to choose from a variety of intermediate exchange rate regimes and secure a reasonable degree of currency stability by judiciously combining different degrees of monetary policy independence, financial integration, and currency market interventions.[46] Even under floating rates it may be possible for a central bank without an explicit exchange rate target to retain a relatively high degree of monetary policy autonomy and, at the same time, try to influence the exchange rate by currency market interventions in order to curb excessive volatility.

Intermediate regimes between corner or bipolar solutions include soft pegs, defined as "exchange rates that are currently fixed in value (or a narrow range of values) to some other currency or basket of currencies, with some commitment by the authorities to defend the peg, but with the value likely to change if the exchange rate comes under significant pressure" (Fischer 2001, 3). They also include crawling pegs, where the peg is shifted over time; fixed exchange rate bands, where the currency is allowed to float within a specified range; or crawling bands, where the band itself is allowed to move over time.[47] Among examples of intermediate regimes are the Bretton Woods system of adjustable pegs, the Exchange Rate Mechanism (ERM) of the European Monetary System (EMS), the fixed nominal pegs used in exchange rate based stabilization programs in Latin America to pin down inflation expectations, and the regime known as BBC – a basket parity, a band and a crawl of the exchange rate – successfully implemented by Singapore and adopted in different versions by some other countries, including, since 2005, China and Malaysia.[48] The BBC regime combines flexibility with stability; it allows the currency to fluctuate within a relatively narrow range and for the central parity to be shifted in response to changes in the underlying fundamentals and to large and durable shocks.

These intermediate regimes call for the use of monetary policy, currency market interventions, and rules over capital flows in appropriate combinations. Otherwise, instability and crises can be unavoidable. For instance, the Bretton Woods system of adjustable pegs operated under widespread controls over international capital movements but broke down with increased mobility of capital, which resulted from and exposed the inconsistencies between the pattern of exchange rates and domestic policy stances. Similarly, adjustable pegs in the ERM worked successfully under conditions of free capital movements as long as macroeconomic fundamentals were consistent with exchange rate targets, but broke down during 1992–93 when high inflation countries such as Italy and the United Kingdom failed to make the necessary currency and/or policy adjustments (Akyüz and Flassbeck 2002). Again, the combination of soft pegs, free capital flows, and high inflation and interest rates proved to be damaging in countries pursuing exchange-rate-based stabilization programs, creating not only currency gyrations but also costly financial crises.

After recurrent crises in emerging markets with soft pegs in the 1990s, developing countries were advised to go for corner solutions. However, with the collapse of the Argentine currency board (convertibility), hard pegs fell from favor. The orthodox policy advice has increasingly emphasized assigning monetary policy to the task of inflation control (inflation targeting) and leaving the currency to float under a reasonably open capital account.

The problems with corner solutions are well established.[49] It is now widely recognized that hard pegs are not a viable option for a large majority of developing countries. Free floating, on the other hand, does not prevent boom–bust cycles in capital flows, unsustainable current account positions, and currency gyrations since exchange rate uncertainty cannot always curb herd behavior in financial markets. Experience shows that crises are as likely to occur under floating rates as under soft pegs. The latest example is Iceland – an economy practising inflation targeting and independent floating. It saw its currency strengthen during the surge in capital inflows after 2002; and its current account deficit grow to reach 18 percent of GDP in 2008, when its currency and economy collapsed with the global turmoil triggered by the subprime crisis (Table 4.4).

Most emerging-market economies with independent floating currency regimes have been affected more severely by the current global instability than those with intermediate regimes of managed floating. In independent floaters, exchange rates appreciated sharply during the surge in capital inflows, and many of these countries ran large and growing current account deficits despite a favorable global trading environment (Table 4.4). With the deepening of the subprime crisis and reversal of capital flows after mid-2008, currencies in all these countries fell sharply from their peaks. In countries with managed floating, appreciations during the earlier boom were moderate and most of these countries succeeded in generating sizeable current account surpluses in the preceding expansion. Even though they too have been hit by the global crisis, declines in their currencies have been moderate compared to independent floaters.

Table 4.4: Effective exchange rates and current accounts in emerging markets (percentage change)

	Nominal		Real		Ca/GDP
	Boom	Bust	Boom	Bust	2008
Independent Floating					
Brazil	81.8	–24.3	44.0	–21.9	–1.8
Chile	29.0	–20.1	28.8	–15.8	–1.1
Mexico	–4.6	–24.1	0.5	–20.0	–1.4
Korea	15.7	–34.6	18.7	–33.5	–1.3
Iceland	6.7	–47.3	18.2	–38.3	–18.2
Poland	29.3	–21.6	29.3	–21.7	–4.7
SAR	6.5	–27.2	14.9	–20.1	–8.0
Turkey	9.6	–18.1	40.2	–7.1	–6.5
Managed Floating					
Argentina[a]	–16.4	–6.2	2.6	–2.3	0.8
China	9.8	0.3	12.4	1.3	9.5
India	2.7	–14.0	16.8	–11.2	–2.8
Malaysia	1.3	–5.9	1.2	–4.1	14.8
Singapore	7.5	–2.2	3.2	0.8	19.1
Thailand	12.9	–4.6	20.3	–7.4	3.1

Source: Exchange rate regimes from IMF (2008) based on members' actual, de facto arrangements. Effective exchange rates from BIS; current account balances from IMF WEO (October 2008).
Boom: January 2003 to peak 2007/2008.
Bust: Peak 2007/2008 to end of January 2009.
a. Classified as managed peg in IMF (2005) but fixed peg in IMF (2008).

There is ample evidence against the bipolar view that with increased financial integration countries will move to the polar extremes of free float or hard pegs. It is true that with financial development and openness countries tend to move away from rigid exchange rate regimes, but instead of adopting free floating they seem to prefer intermediate regimes. A large majority of developing countries were using intermediate regimes until the second half of the 1990s. Moreover, many countries that claimed to have allowed their exchange rates to float were actually managing them by using interest rates and currency market interventions because of "fear of floating" (Calvo and Rheinhart 2002). Following recurrent emerging market crises in the 1990s, there was a shift toward independent floating. After recovery, however, many countries shifted back toward intermediate regimes: "The persistent popularity of intermediate regimes [...] suggests that such regimes may provide important advantages. Indeed, the absence of a general bipolar tendency may be indicative of the possibility that intermediate regimes are able to capture some of the benefits of both extremes while avoiding many of the costs."[50]

2. Capital flows, monetary policy and the exchange rate

A key question for countries adopting intermediate regimes is, therefore, how best to combine monetary policy action, currency market interventions, and regulation of capital flows in order to sustain stable and competitive exchange rates without giving up the objectives of price stability, full employment and rapid growth. This is not an easy task, since for developing countries global financial integration brings much greater erosion of monetary independence than is typically portrayed in economic theory. Monetary policy cannot always secure financial and macroeconomic stability whether it is geared toward a stable exchange rate or conducted independently as a countercyclical tool to pursue domestic objectives.

Because of exchange rate pass-through and extensive liability dollarization, there are strong spillovers from exchange rates to domestic economic and financial conditions. Thus, using monetary policy as a domestic countercyclical tool, with the benign neglect of external conditions, does not guarantee price and financial stability when there are large swings in capital flows and exchange rates. On the other hand, the effect of monetary policy on exchange rates is much more uncertain and unstable than is typically assumed in the theory of the impossible trinity because of the volatility of risk assessments and herd behavior. During financial turmoil hikes in interest rates are often unable to check currency collapses, while at times of favorable risk assessment a much smaller arbitrage margin can attract large inflows of private capital and cause significant appreciations.

Even when authorities are prepared to use greater discretion in monetary policy, they may face serious trade-offs because domestic conditions may call for one sort of intervention and external conditions another. This is most clearly seen at times of rapid exit of capital when liquidity expansion and cuts in interest rates needed to prevent financial meltdown and stimulate economic activity could simply accelerate flight from the currency. As a result, monetary authorities are often compelled to pursue a procyclical policy in an effort to restore confidence. However, this is rarely effective since, under crisis conditions, the link assumed in the conventional theory between the interest rate and the exchange rate also breaks down. When market sentiment turns sour, higher interest rates aiming to retain capital tend to be perceived as increased risk of default. As a result, the risk-adjusted rate of return could actually fall as interest rates are raised. This is the main reason why procyclical interest rate hikes implemented as part of IMF support during several episodes of financial crises were unable to prevent the collapse of the currency, instead serving to deepen economic contraction. Under such conditions, unilateral temporary debt standstills and exchange restrictions present themselves as the only viable options to prevent financial meltdown and a deep recession.

Monetary policy also faces hurdles at times of economic expansion associated with surges in capital inflows, asset bubbles and currency appreciations. Tightening to check overheating could encourage external borrowing and short-term arbitrage flows. Lower interest rates could discourage such flows, but they fuel domestic credit expansion and overheating.

Countercyclical fiscal policy can no doubt help manage expansions. When the economy is overheating due to a boom in private spending supported by capital inflows, fiscal tightening would obviate the need for tighter monetary policy and higher interest rates and, hence, prevent further arbitrage inflows and appreciations. If budget revenues and expenditure structures are appropriately designed, this task could partly be done by automatic stabilizers. However, most developing countries lack either the policy space or the political will needed for the kind of fiscal tightening necessary to check strong economic expansions supported by a surge in capital flows. In reality, governments in many emerging markets tend to run procyclical fiscal policy, notably those with chronic fiscal deficits and large public debt (Akyüz 2006).

3. Currency market interventions and reserves

i. Interventions and sterilization

A policy of resisting appreciations and accumulating reserves through interventions in currency markets at times of strong capital inflows and economic expansion and using such reserves to prevent sharp depreciations during sudden stops and reversals appears to be a sensible countercyclical response to instability in international capital flows. However, this is not always neutral in its consequences for monetary policy. If interventions are not fully sterilized, they would result in credit expansion, thereby generating inflationary pressures in asset and/or product markets. If they are sterilized by issuing government debt, they could lead to higher interest rates, which could, in turn, attract more arbitrage capital.

Whether or not interventions in emerging markets are successful in stabilizing exchange rates and preventing credit expansion and inflation is highly contentious. Examining several episodes of surges in capital inflows since the early 1990s, the IMF World Economic Outlook (October 2007, 122–24) concludes that sterilized intervention is likely to be ineffective and inflationary when the influx of capital is persistent: "a policy of resistance to exchange rate pressures does not seem to be associated with lower real appreciation while countercyclical fiscal policies have had the desired effect" and "the policy of sterilized intervention [...] often tends to be associated with higher inflation." By contrast, work done in the Bank for International Settlements (BIS) suggests that sterilized intervention has generally been more successful in emerging markets than in advanced countries, particularly where the banking sector is closely scrutinized.[51] Evidence from Asian emerging markets discussed below suggests that currency market interventions have been quite effective in checking appreciations in the recent surge in capital flows, but they have been only partially successful in sterilization.

The impact of sterilization on interest rates and arbitrage capital depends on the size and composition of capital flows. When capital inflows are moderate in size and concentrated in the market for fixed income assets, sterilization by issuing government debt would not raise the interest rate. However, when they are broad based and concentrated in direct and portfolio equity, as in most emerging markets in recent years, sterilizing them by issuing government debt can raise the interest rate and attract arbitrage flows, particularly when inflows are large compared to the size of the debt market.[52]

Sterilization by issuing government (or central bank) debt is also costly because interest earned on reserves is usually much lower than interest paid on such debt. This fiscal – or quasi-fiscal – cost of reserves has two components: in part due to the difference between external borrowing rate and the rate earned on reserves, which constitutes a net transfer of resources abroad, and in part due to the difference between the interest rate on government debt and the external borrowing rate, which is an internal transfer to the private sector.[53]

Sterilization by raising non-interest-bearing reserve requirements of banks could address some of these problems; it could help reduce the fiscal cost of intervention and check credit expansion. However, by increasing the cost of credit, it could also encourage firms to go to foreign creditors. Banks may also shift business to offshore centers and lend through their affiliates abroad, particularly where foreign presence in the banking sector is important. A relatively tight supervision over the banking system would be needed to impose high reserve requirements and prevent regulatory arbitrage.

ii. Reserve accumulation as self-insurance

Traditionally, reserves covering three months of imports were considered adequate for addressing the liquidity problems arising from time lags between payments for imports and receipts from exports. The need for reserves was also expected to lessen as countries gained access to international financial markets and became more willing to respond to balance of payments shocks by adjustments in exchange rates. However, capital account liberalization in developing countries and their greater access to private finance has produced exactly the opposite result. Private capital flows have allowed running larger and more persistent current account deficits beyond the levels that could be attained by relying on international reserves or borrowing from the IMF. But this has also resulted in an accumulation of large stocks of external liabilities. Consequently, debtor countries have become increasingly vulnerable to sudden stops and reversals in capital flows, and this has increased the need to accumulate reserves to safeguard against currency turmoil and speculative attacks. Indeed, evidence shows a strong correlation between capital account liberalization and reserve holding, and a growing tendency to absorb capital inflows into reserves rather than using them for current payments (Aizenman and Lee 2005; Choi, Sharma and Strömqvist 2007).

Vulnerability to a sudden stop and reversal of capital flows is often assessed on the basis of short-term external liabilities in relation to reserves. Foreign investment in equity and local currency debt is not considered a serious potential threat to stability because the exchange rate risk is assumed by investors. Indeed, according to the so-called Greenspan–Guidotti rule formulated after the Asian crisis, in order to avoid a liquidity crisis, international reserves in emerging markets should meet short-term external foreign currency denominated liabilities, defined as debt with a remaining maturity of up to one year.[54]

A problem with such rules is that vulnerability is not restricted to short-term foreign currency debt; what matters in this respect is liquidity of liabilities, including those denominated in domestic currencies. A move by nonresidents from domestic equity and bond markets could create significant turbulence in currency and asset markets with broader macroeconomic consequences, even though losses from asset price declines and currency collapses fall on foreign investors. This potential source of instability naturally depends on the relative importance of foreign participation in local financial markets. The degree of vulnerability in this sense can be measured in terms of stock of foreign portfolio investment as a percentage of reserves.

iii. Cost of reserve holding

Even when the fiscal cost of interventions is reduced by control over interest rates or higher reserve requirements, there could be a large transfer of resources abroad since the return earned on international reserves is less than the cost of foreign capital, including the cost of foreign borrowing and the foregone return on assets sold. In fact, it is more so for equity flows for the acquisition of ownership rights of existing assets, since rates earned by transnational companies exceed the cost of international borrowing by a very large margin (UNCTAD TDR 1999, chap. 5).

Reserve accumulation in developing countries accelerated after the Asian crisis, particularly with the strong recovery of capital inflows in the early years of the 2000s. It has gained further momentum as developing countries taken together started to run twin surpluses in their balance of payments, that is, on both current and capital accounts.[55] Since 2001 reserves have increased at an average rate of $600 billion per year, exceeding $5.5 trillion, or 7 months of imports, at the end of 2008.[56]

Of the $4.6 trillion additional reserves accumulated by developing countries after 2001, less than two-thirds were earned from current account surpluses. The rest was accumulated from capital inflows; that is, they are "borrowed" in the sense that they accompany increased claims by nonresidents in one form or another, including direct and portfolio equity investment, which entail outward income transfers. Other than China and Fuel Exporters, reserves in developing countries are entirely borrowed since, taken together, their current account has been in deficit.

Since in previous decades the current account of developing countries was in deficit, the entire stock of reserves held at the beginning of this decade was borrowed reserves. This means that almost half of the current stock of reserves in developing countries – that is, some $2.6 trillion – are borrowed reserves. This is more than twice their short-term debt and over 65 percent of their total debt to private creditors. Assuming a moderate 500 basis points margin between the borrowing rate and return on reserves, the annual carry cost of these reserves would reach some $130 billion.[57] This constitutes a net transfer of resources to major reserve currency countries and exceeds total official development assistance to developing countries.[58]

4. Regulation and control of capital flows

While interventions in currency markets and reserve accumulation can prevent unsustainable currency appreciations and current account positions and provide self-insurance against sudden stops and reversals, it is not necessarily the best way to deal with volatile capital flows. In fact, this strategy lacks a strong rationale since it implies that a country should borrow only if the funds thus acquired are not used to finance investment and imports, but held in short-term, low yielding foreign assets, resulting in large fiscal and social costs.

Furthermore, currency market interventions are not neutral in their impact on domestic monetary conditions. Failure to sterilize them fully would lead to domestic credit expansion, fuelling inflation in asset and/or product markets while debt financed sterilization can attract further destabilizing capital flows. Finally, such a strategy does not prevent currency and maturity mismatches in private balance sheets, or increased presence of foreigners in domestic financial markets, which often increases vulnerability to external shocks and contagion. Thus, regulation and control over capital flows would often be necessary to address the problems caused by volatile capital flows and the costs and difficulties encountered in dealing with them through monetary policy actions and/or currency market interventions.

There are several ways of influencing unstable capital flows, including market-based and administrative measures, widely used in industrial countries before the breakdown of the Bretton Woods system in the early 1970s and in many European countries until the late 1980s.[59] Since a large proportion of cross-border and cross-currency operations are intermediated by domestic financial institutions, notably banks, prudential rules such as capital and liquidity requirements and provisions for nonperforming portfolios no doubt have implications for international capital flows. Similarly, market-based (indirect) measures of control over capital flows, such as unremunerated reserve requirements used in Chile and elsewhere, can be considered as part of prudential regulations insofar as they contribute to the solvency of these institutions. This means that measures to control capital flows cannot always be distinguished from prudential rules, and several measures that normally come under prudential policies can in fact be used for managing capital flows.

The risks associated with capital flows through the banking system could be addressed by applying more stringent rules for capital charges, loan loss provisions and liquidity and reserve requirements for transactions involving foreign currencies. In this respect, banking regulations need to address three fundamental sources of fragility: maturity mismatches, currency mismatches and exchange-rate-related credit risks.

Maturity transformation is a traditional function of the banking system, but this should not be encouraged in the intermediation between international financial markets and domestic borrowers, particularly since national monetary authorities cannot act as lenders of last resort in foreign currency. Banks tend to rely on central banks for the provision of international liquidity, trying to shift the cost of carrying a large stock of reserves onto them. This exposes them to exchange rate and interest rate risks since, in the event of a sudden stop in capital inflows and inadequate central bank reserves, they may not have access to international liquidity or can do so only at very high costs.

To reduce the liquidity risk, restrictions can be applied to maturity mismatches between foreign exchange assets and liabilities of banks with a view to preventing borrowing short in international markets and lending long at home, through stricter liquidity and reserve requirements and even direct limits.

Similarly, it is important to restrict currency mismatches between bank assets and liabilities and to discourage banks from assuming the exchange rate risk. Banks with short foreign exchange positions (that is, where forex liabilities exceed assets) run the risk of losses from depreciations while those with long positions lose from appreciations. Furthermore, maturity mismatches between forex assets and liabilities imply exposure to exchange rate risks even when assets are matched by liabilities in the aggregate. Currency mismatches can be restricted through quantitative limits on short and long positions (e.g., as a proportion of equity or total portfolios) or high capital charges on foreign exchange exposures. In most cases it may be more appropriate to prohibit currency mismatches altogether.

The third important risk associated with foreign exchange borrowing and lending by banks is the exchange-rate-related credit risk. Banks can eliminate currency and maturity mismatches by lending in foreign currency, but unless their borrowers have foreign exchange earning capacity, this simply implies migration of the exchange rate risk which, in turn, results in greater credit risk. This kind of lending is particularly common in economies where an important part of bank deposits are in foreign currencies. It also proved problematic in some countries in East Asia in the run-up to the 1997 crisis, where banks lent heavily in foreign currency for investment in property as well as to firms with little foreign exchange earning capacity. Such practices could be discouraged by applying higher risk weights and capital charges for foreign assets and more stringent standards of provision for foreign currency loans, or by prohibiting altogether. However, evidence suggests that only a few emerging markets have addressed the vulnerabilities arising from currency-induced credits risks even though many of them appear to have taken measures to reduce exposure to foreign exchange risks (Cayazzo et al. 2006).

External financial fragility can no doubt be contained if prudential regulations could be appropriately extended to address specific risks associated with capital flows. Contrary to a widely held view, however, this does not imply that capital account liberalization should not be a cause for concern if it is accompanied by more comprehensive prudential regulations and supervision. First of all, conventional risk assessment methods and prudential rules tend to aggravate the cyclicality of the financial system. They need to be designed in a countercyclical fashion, tightened particularly at times of strong surges in capital inflows.[60] Second, regulatory safeguards are pretty ineffectual in the face of macroeconomic shocks that can drastically alter the quality of bank assets, and this is more so when the capital account is open. Finally, capital flows are not always intermediated by the domestic financial system. Indeed, the proportion of bank-related capital flows has been falling rapidly in recent years, with portfolio and direct equity flows now accounting for a large proportion of total inflows.[61] Therefore, direct restrictions over foreign borrowing and investment as well as market access may have to play a key role in managing the risks associated with capital flows.

When capital inflows are excessive, liberalization of resident outflows is sometimes seen as an option to relieve the upward pressure on the currency. This is, in fact, an alternative to sterilized intervention and it avoids the cost of carrying large stocks of international reserves. But, like interventions, it effectively does nothing to prevent currency and maturity mismatches in private balance sheets, or instability and vulnerability to shocks associated with greater presence of foreigners in domestic asset markets. It may encourage inflows, particularly the return of flight capital of residents (Reinhart and Reinhart 1998). In countries with weak property rights, it could also facilitate asset stripping and money laundering (Yu 2009). Its rationale as a longer-term strategy for closer integration of developing countries into global financial markets is highly contentious. As a countercyclical measure, it can be even more problematic: once introduced for cyclical reasons, it may not be easily rolled back when conditions change. Thus, unlike official reserves, these do not provide self-insurance against payments and currency instability and may even aggravate them when market sentiments change.

E. Recent Experience in Asia

Capital account and exchange rate policies in many Asian countries in recent years have been shaped by a determination never to allow a repeat of the 1997 crisis. A key lesson drawn from that experience is that if capital inflows are allowed to create large currency and maturity mismatches in private sector balance sheets and unsustainable bubbles in asset markets under conditions of weak payments and reserve positions, there is not much that governments can do at times of a sudden stop and reversal of these flows. There is, thus, an increased awareness that vulnerability to financial contagion and shocks depends in large part on how capital inflows are managed.

After a brief interruption, capital flows to emerging markets recovered strongly in the earlier years of this decade, and Asia has been among the main recipients. These flows were greatly influenced by the very same factors that led to a surge in speculative lending in the United States and elsewhere in the developed world – notably, ample global liquidity resulting from a policy of easy money and search for yield. Rather than applying tighter countercyclical restrictions over capital inflows, most Asian countries chose to relax restrictions over resident outflows and to absorb excess supply of foreign exchange in reserves while building strong payments positions by maintaining competitive exchange rates. In this way they have successfully avoided unsustainable currency appreciations and payments positions, and accumulated more than adequate international reserves to counter any potential current and capital account shocks without recourse to the IMF. However, they have not always been able to prevent capital inflows from generating asset, credit and investment bubbles and reduce the vulnerability of domestic financial markets to adverse shocks and contagion from financial instability abroad. These policies are now exposing them to certain risks due to spillovers from the global financial turbulence, but not always of the kind that hit the region in the 1990s.

Table 4.5: Private capital flows, current account balances, and changes in reserves in emerging markets (billions of US dollars)

	Total			Asia		
	2004	2007	2008[e]	2004	2007	2008[e]
Capital Flows	348.8	928.6	465.8	165.6	314.8	96.2
Current Account	150.2	434.0	387.4	115.2	420.2	386.4
Reserve Increases	398.2	948.7	444.3	296.1	587.8	373.1

Source: IIF (January 2006; October 2007; January 2009).
e. estimate.

1. The surge in capital inflows

After falling to some $100 billion at the beginning of the millennium, private flows to emerging markets picked up rapidly, reaching an estimated level of $929 billion in 2007 before falling drastically to an estimated $465 billion in 2008 (Table 4.5).[62] Recovery in capital flows to Asia was also strong, exceeding $300 billion at their peak in 2007. In gross terms capital inflows to Asia as a proportion of GDP have been close to historical highs, but in net terms they have been around the long-term average because of increased resident outflows (IMF REOAP April 2007; IIF, October 2007).

During 2003–2007, about 60 percent of private capital inflows to Asia were in equity investment, of which two-thirds were in direct equity and one-third in portfolio equity.[63] Equity flows were particularly strong in China where a relatively large proportion of financial inflows appear to have been motivated by expectations of appreciation of the yuan (Setser 2008; Yu 2008). Some of these are reported to have entered the country through over-invoicing of exports. According to some estimates, the so-called "hot money" amounted to $5–10 billion a month during 2007 (Anderlini 2007).

India also received large amounts of equity capital, but much of this was in portfolio equity rather than foreign direct investment (FDI). This is also true for Malaysia where cumulative equity portfolio inflows during 2002–2007 were nine times cumulative inflows of FDI (Khor 2009). Hedge funds from the United States and the United Kingdom have been very active in equity markets in the region, with assets managed by them being estimated to have grown sevenfold between 2001 and 2007.

Following the cutback after the 1997 crisis, international bank lending in Asia started to exceed repayments in the early years of this decade. There was a visible growth in syndicated loans privately placed by corporations in several countries. Private financial and nonfinancial corporations also engaged in carry-trade-style short-term external borrowing in India, Korea and the Philippines, particularly through low-interest yen-linked loans. Highly leveraged hedge funds are also known to have been very active in carry trades in Asia. While restrictions on foreign entry to domestic bond markets were generally maintained, in countries such as Malaysia and Indonesia there have been marked increases in foreign holding of local-currency debt instruments. In the region as a whole, local claims of foreign banks, including local bond holdings, as a percentage of all foreign banks' claims, more than doubled since the beginning of the decade, suggesting a growing preference for international banks to lend in local currencies at higher rates.

2. Policy response: Currency market interventions and reserve accumulation

As noted above, after the Asian crisis several countries in the region moved toward more flexible exchange rate arrangements. But they have followed various shades of managed floating rather than leaving their currencies entirely to the whims of international capital flows. In order to build a strong payments position, most countries in the region successfully intervened heavily in foreign exchange markets to prevent appreciations.

Asian developing countries taken together had a current account surplus of 7 percent of GDP in 2007 and over 5 percent in 2008, up from 1.5 percent in 2001. Although this is largely due to China's strong export performance, a number of other countries have also been enjoying surpluses, in some cases in double digit figures, as a percentage of GDP. India has been running current account deficits, but at moderate levels. Among large countries, only in Pakistan and Vietnam have deficits reached high levels: 8.7 and 11.7 percent of GDP in 2008, respectively. Most Asian currencies were kept relatively stable in real terms, despite excess supply of foreign exchange generated by capital inflows and current account surpluses, thanks to extensive interventions in currency markets (Table 4.4).

To keep liquidity expansion and inflation under control, governments tried to sterilize interventions by issuing debt and raising reserve requirements in the banking system. In China, government control over the financial system allowed it to keep the fiscal cost of intervention down. Reserve requirements of banks were continuously raised from 7 percent in 2003 to 17.5 percent in 2008, and banks have come to hold over 80 percent of central bank securities issued for that purpose, with their share in total bank assets exceeding 20 percent (Yu 2008; BIS 2009, box D4). In India the cash reserve ratio was also increased in several steps to reach 7.5 percent in 2008, but because of higher interest rates the cost of intervention is reported to have reached 2 percent of GDP in 2007 – more than half of the central government deficits.[64]

As in some mature economies, monetary policy in many countries in Asia has been expansionary and real interest rates have been considerably lower than those in other regions. After 2003 private credit growth in real terms reached nearly 9 percent per annum in China and 5 percent in many other East Asian countries.[65] The surge in capital flows was an important reason for the rapid expansion of liquidity since interventions in foreign exchange markets could not always be fully sterilized.

As of the end of 2008 total reserves in developing Asia (excluding NIEs) exceeded \$2.2 trillion, and 86 percent of this figure was generated after 2001 (Table 4.6).[66] Asian reserves now account for more than half of total reserves of the developing world. The twin surpluses that the region as a whole has been running on its balance of payments have been fully converted into reserves. Of the \$2.4 trillion reserves accumulated after 2001, 60 percent is earned and the rest is borrowed. However, excluding China, almost three-quarters of Asian reserves in recent years were from capital inflows. In countries

Table 4.6: Current account and reserves[a] (billions of US dollars)

	Asia	China
Reserves		
2008	2830.4	2201.3
2001	379.5	216.3
Increase	2450.9	1985.0
Current account[b]		
2002–2008	1458.9	1331.8
Borrowed reserves[c]		
2002–2008	992.0	652.3
Import coverage[d]		
2001	4.9	6.6
2008	9.4	13.8

Source: IMF WEO (October 2008).
a. 2008 figures are estimates.
b. Cumulative current account balance over 2002–2008.
c. Difference between increases in reserves and cumulative current account balance over 2002–2008.
d. Months of imports covered by reserves.

running current account deficits, such as India, Pakistan, and Vietnam, reserves are 100 percent borrowed.

Asian reserves exceed the level needed to prevent a currency and balance of payments crisis under the Greenspan–Guidotti rule noted above. They are several times the total short-term external debt of the region, which stood at around $400 billion at the end of 2008, and more than twice the total external debt of some $1,160 billion. They now cover more than nine months of imports. However, in many countries reserves are not large in comparison with the stock of foreign portfolio investment. In 2008 the ratio of the latter to total reserves was greater than unity in Korea, Indonesia and the Philippines and exceeded 80 percent in Singapore and Malaysia (ESCAP 2008). About half of the total stock of reserves in Asia is borrowed. This is a little more than the existing stock of external debt of the region. Again assuming a 500 basis point spread, this would give an annual carry cost of some $60 billion for the region as a whole – that is, this is how much the region as a whole could save per year by paying up its external debt by drawing on reserves.[67]

3. Policy response: liberalization of resident outflows

Many Asian emerging markets have been incurring high reserve costs and facing macroeconomic policy dilemmas mainly because they have chosen to keep their economies open to the surge in capital inflows rather than imposing tighter countercyclical measures of control. Capital accounts in the region are more open today than they were during the 1997 crisis.[68] In China, for instance, one of the countries with the tightest restrictions, calculations based on an IMF formula are said to show that 80 percent of the capital account has been liberalized.[69]

In several cases the opening to inflows has been selective, such as raising the limits on the QFII (qualified foreign institutional investors) in China. Some countries, including India, have liberalized sectoral caps on FDI. Foreign banks have generally been allowed greater freedom to operate, with many domestic borrowers receiving funding from such banks directly from abroad or through their local offices.

There have been, to be sure, some efforts to curb excessive inflows in order to ease the upward pressure on currencies. In 2006 China extended to foreign banks the restriction over borrowing abroad to fund domestic dollar assets. In 2007 its foreign exchange regulators took action against ten international banks for breaching capital account regulations by "assisting speculative foreign capital to enter the country disguised as trade and investment" (Anderlini 2007). Exporters have been required to park their export revenues in temporary accounts in order to enable officials to check and verify that invoices are backed by genuine trade transactions.

In December 2006 Thailand imposed a 30 percent unremunerated reserve requirement on capital inflows held less than one year, including investment in portfolio equity, in order to halt continued appreciation of the currency. This provoked a strong reaction from the stock market, forcing the government to exempt investment in stocks from the requirements. The remaining restrictions were removed in March 2008. With a continued surge in capital inflows, India reversed the liberalization of the limits on external commercial borrowing, tightening them in 2007. Similarly, Korea restricted external funding of domestic lending by foreign banks and reintroduced limits on lending in foreign currency to domestic firms.

However, the main response to the surge in capital inflows has been to liberalize outward investment by residents. This is partly motivated by a desire to allow national firms to expand abroad and become important players in world markets. This has particularly been the case in China and India. However, while in China assets acquired abroad are financed from trade surpluses, in India these are, in effect, funded by capital inflows. As remarked by an observer, "the global flood of money (and attendant hubris) has enabled Indian companies like Tata to buy themselves a place on the world stage rather than earning it through export success or technological advance" (Bowring 2008a).

There has also been considerable liberalization of portfolio outflows. China took a decision to permit investment by its residents in approved overseas markets and raised the limits on corporate and individual purchases of foreign currency for mitigating the pressure for appreciation through the so-called QDII (qualified domestic institutional investor) scheme. The share of portfolio investment in the total international assets of China in 2006 was three times that of FDI abroad. In Malaysia, where limits on foreign assets held by some institutional investors were increased significantly, cumulative portfolio outflows during 2004–2007 were slightly below cumulative portfolio inflows and nine times direct investment abroad. In 2007 there was a net outflow of capital (excluding reserve accumulation), which absorbed as much as half of the current account surplus (Khor 2009). India, Korea and Thailand have all liberalized rules limiting portfolio investment abroad, and Thailand abolished the surrender requirement for exporters.

4. Credit, asset and investment bubbles

Recent capital inflows have resulted in a rapid increase in foreign presence in Asian equity markets. Figures for net equity inflows understate this because, as noted, there has also been a rapid increase in resident outflows. Nonresident holding of Korean equities reached almost half of market capitalization (McCauley 2008). In China foreign share as a percentage of market capitalization rose from 2.5 percent in 2001 to 23.2 percent in 2006, and in India from 6.6 percent to 10 percent in the same period (BIS 2009, table E1). The share of foreigner transactions in 2005 in average daily turnover was around 20 percent in Korea, 30 percent in Thailand and 70 percent in Taiwan (Chai-Anant and Ho 2008).

There is also strong evidence that foreign investors tend to move in and out of some of the different Asian markets simultaneously. The IMF Global Financial Stability Report (IMF GFSR, October 2007) finds evidence on herd behavior among institutional investors. BIS (2009, 69) notes that increased market liquidity resulting from greater participation of foreigners in equity markets tends to reduce day-to-day volatility, but also argues that "even highly liquid markets do not insulate EME [emerging market economy] equity markets from a global retrenchment in risk appetite or a withdrawal of foreign investors."

Large investment by foreigners in equity markets, together with the consequent expansion of liquidity associated with the surge in capital inflows, have both been the cause and effect of sharp increases in stock prices in several Asian markets.[70] This is also suggested by a strong correlation between changes in net portfolio equity flows and stock prices in Asia – much stronger than that observed in Latin America (IIF October 2007, chart 13). For the region as a whole equity prices tripled between 2002 and 2008, with increases exceeding 500 percent in China and India. The price–earnings ratios also rose rapidly, resulting in a sharp drop in equity costs.[71] That such increases more likely reflected bubbles than improvements in underlining fundamentals was cautioned by the Institute of International Finance (IIF March 2005, 4): "there is a risk that the pickup in flows into some emerging market assets has pushed valuations to levels that are not commensurate with underlying fundamentals."

The two largest countries, China and India, that saw the strongest surge in capital inflows and stock markets also experienced a boom in property markets. During 2002–2006 residential property prices rose in real terms by over 8 percent per annum in China and 10 percent in India, and the price-to-rent ratio rose by more than 20 percent.[72] There was also acceleration of property price increases in Korea (15 percent), Singapore and Vietnam during 2006–2007. While these were not as dramatic as increases in the United States – where the price-to-rent ratio rose by 30 percent over the same period – there are large pockets in China, India, Korea and the Philippines where increases were comparable and even greater.[73] Housing loans expanded faster than other types of lending and have been a major factor in sharp increases in household indebtedness. In Korea where bank lending to households grew rapidly after 2005, household debt reached 140 percent of disposable income – above the level of household indebtedness in the United States (ADB 2007).

Such booms in equity and property markets are often a potential source of macroeconomic instability. There is evidence, not only from industrial countries but also from a number of Asian emerging markets, including Hong Kong (China), Indonesia, Japan, Korea, Malaysia, the Philippines, Singapore and Thailand, that asset booms (defined as periods in which asset prices exceed their trend by more than 10 percent) significantly raise the probability of output being eventually pushed below its potential level, and the price level above its trend (Gochoco-Bautista 2008).

In China and India ample liquidity, low equity costs and low loan rates together have also created an investment boom, which may not be sustained with the return of normal financial conditions. In China where the share of investment in GDP reached 46 percent, the increase appears to have been associated with considerable excess capacity and wastage of capital.[74] Similarly, in India growth in investment has been faster than GDP by more than 5 percentage points per annum, with the investment ratio rising to over 30 percent of GDP from less than 24 percent in the early years of the decade.

5. *Shocks and contagion from the global financial crisis*

As a result of closer global financial integration, notably the increased presence of foreigners in domestic financial markets and liberalization of resident investment abroad, Asia has become highly susceptible to external financial influences. The region has indeed been receiving severe shocks and contagion from the global financial turbulence triggered by the subprime debacle through various channels, and facing the risk of asset deflation, a high degree of currency instability, and a sharp economic slowdown.

The increased holding of foreign assets has no doubt resulted in greater exposure to instability in their market valuations as well as exchange rate swings. Asian economies do not have large direct exposure to securitized assets linked to subprime lending, even though some losses have been reported in the region.[75] However, they appear to have invested large amounts in debt issued by United States Government–sponsored enterprises, including mortgage firms Fannie Mae and Freddie Mac, with combined liabilities of around $5.5 trillion. Holding by central banks outside the United States of such debt is estimated to be in the order of $1 trillion, and large amounts are also known to be held in private portfolios. China's holding of US agency debt is estimated to be at least 10 percent of its GDP, mostly in Fannie and Freddie assets (Pesek 2008). Had the United States government not bailed out these institutions, losses would have been severe. Moreover, should the dollar come under pressure, countries with a large stock of dollar reserves stand to incur considerable exchange rate losses.

There is considerable variation among Asian emerging markets in their vulnerability to sharp swings in the risk appetite and capital flows. Capital flows to emerging markets, including bank-related flows, initially kept up after the outbreak of the subprime crisis, but with the deepening of the credit crunch there is now a sharp decline that is more marked in Asia than in other regions (Table 4.5). FDI remained relatively resilient, but with the widespread credit crunch in the United States and Europe there has been a sharp drop in commercial bank credits, from $156 billion to an estimated $30 billion, and this is expected to turn negative in 2009. Net portfolio equity flows to Asia, including outflows by residents, were already negative in 2007, and they are expected to have become even bigger in 2008, reaching $55 billion.[76] Redemption by highly-leveraged hedge funds from the United States and the United Kingdom is an important factor. These institutions, which had been very active in Asian equity markets in earlier years, are now hard hit by the crisis, and deleveraging by them appears to be a main reason for the exit of equity portfolio investment not only from Asia but also from emerging markets as a whole.[77]

With the rapid exit of foreign capital and global retrenchment of risk appetite, asset bubbles in Asia have come to an end. Equity markets lost almost half of their values in 2008 in China and India. Booms in property markets too are now bust. In China house prices declined in December 2008 for the first time since the government started releasing the data in 2005, and urban fixed asset investment has been falling since September 2008. The government is now taking measures to revive the property market.[78] In Korea the slump that started in 2008 is now threatening to set off a process of debt deflation, reminiscent of the 1997 crisis when housing prices fell by some 13 percent (Citigroup 2009).

This cycle in Asian asset markets has many features reminiscent of the cycle in the 1990s, but is different in an important respect. In the current cycle asset deflation is not associated with currency crises and interest rate hikes, but severe trade shocks. The combination of asset deflation with sharp drops in exports and consequent retrenchment in investment can no doubt wreak havoc in the real economy.[79] This explains why in Asia "the slump in industrial production has been more significant and more rapid than in 1997–98."[80]

It is important to avoid destabilizing feedbacks between the real and financial sectors, particularly in China because of its wider regional ramifications. A sharp drop in growth can threaten the solvency of the banking system given the high degree of leverage of many firms, which can in turn lower growth further.[81] Whether or not the massive fiscal package introduced by the government would prevent such an outcome remains to be seen. In any event, the challenge faced by China is not only to overcome the deflationary impulses from the global financial crisis but to shift to a growth trajectory led by the expansion of domestic consumption.

Because of the sharp slowdown in total capital flows and reversal of portfolio flows, several currencies that had faced strong upward pressure against the dollar and the yuan after 2003, particularly the Indian rupee, Korean won and Thai baht, have been falling sharply against both currencies since summer 2008 (Table 4.7). Given strong deflationary impulses from the crisis, this may be viewed as a welcome development; and unlike in 1997, governments now seem to be wary of throwing all their reserves into stabilizing their currencies. However, in some of these countries, notably India and Korea, reserves have declined rapidly as a result of exit of capital and growing current account deficits.[82]

F. Regional Monetary Cooperation for Stability

1. Global instability and the search for regional solutions

The main objective of the planners of the postwar economic architecture was to avoid the repetition of the breakdown of international trade and payments that had devastated the world economy during the interwar years. Exchange rate stability was believed to

Table 4.7: Exchange rate swings in Asia during subprime bubble and bust (percentage change in nominal bilateral rates)

	Dollar rates		Yuan rates	
	Boom	Bust	Boom	Bust
Chinese Yuan	9.3	10.7	–	–
Indian Rupee	19.2	−16.6	9.0	−26.2
Indonesian Rupiah	−2.7	−20.0	−1.0	−27.7
Malaysian Ringgit	10.0	−4.5	0.6	−13.8
Philippine Peso	7.9	−3.0	7.9	−12.4
Singapore Dollar	14.7	0.3	4.9	−9.5
S. Korean Won	28.8	−33.5	7.8	−40.0
Taiwan Dollar	5.9	−2.7	−3.2	−12.1
Thai Baht	43.4	−14.3	30.9	−22.6

Source: OANDA
Boom: From January 2003 to July 2007.
Bust: From August 2007 to February 2009.

hold the key to the realization of this objective. This was most emphatically expressed by Keynes (1980, 5) during the Bretton Woods negotiations: "Tariffs and currency depreciations are in many alternatives. Without currency agreements you have no firm ground on which to discuss tariffs [...] It is very difficult while you have monetary chaos to have order of any kind in other directions." The Bretton Woods architecture was based on three legs: multilateral discipline over exchange rate policies, restrictions over destabilizing capital flows, and provision of adequate international liquidity to countries facing temporary payments imbalances.

The convertibility of the dollar vis-à-vis gold at a fixed rate was designed to exert multilateral discipline over policies of the main reserve currency country, the United States. Other countries undertook obligation to maintain their exchange rates within a narrow range of their par values and were allowed to change their par values under fundamental disequilibrium only with the consent of the Fund. Restriction over short-term capital flows, which had proved highly destabilizing during the interwar years, was seen as a key to stability of exchange rates. The IMF was to provide short-term financing to countries facing temporary shortfalls in international liquidity in order to avoid destabilizing currency adjustments, retrenchment in domestic absorption, and contraction in economic activity.

All three building blocks of the Bretton Woods system disappeared in the early 1970s with the default of the United States on gold convertibility and adoption of floating with incongruous commitments to exchange rate stability. Free movement of capital became the norm. And the IMF started to impose exactly the kind of procyclical policies that the postwar planners wanted to avoid in countries facing temporary payments difficulties.

Europe sought to maintain a certain degree of multilateral discipline over exchange rate policies among the countries in the region, having suffered most from political fallouts from instability and the collapse of world trade and payments in the interwar years. It agreed to float against the dollar but decided to try to stabilize intraregional exchange rates, since a move to free floating among the European countries would pose a serious threat of instability and disruption to intraregional trade, given a high degree of regional integration. Initial efforts to stabilize intra-European exchange rates through ad hoc arrangements led to the creation of the European Monetary System (EMS) in 1979, which culminated in the European Monetary Union (EMU) three decades later.[83]

Instability among reserve currencies after the breakdown of the Bretton Woods system had a relatively limited impact on developing countries that were pursuing intermediate exchange rate regimes under relatively tight control over capital flows. But shortcomings of the third leg of the Bretton Woods arrangements – the provision of adequate international liquidity by the IMF – became highly visible with the increased volatility of the global economic environment, particularly in the early 1980s when a combination of hikes in interest rates and recession in industrial countries produced severe payments difficulties in several indebted countries, culminating in a debt crisis in Latin America. These shortcomings became even more visible with the 1997 Asian crisis. Realizing that developing countries could no longer rely on international financial institutions to address their liquidity problems during such times, an attempt was made to bring a regional solution by establishing an Asian Monetary Fund. After this was abandoned because of opposition from the United States and the IMF, the "ASEAN+3" (the ten members of the Association of Southeast Asian Nations plus China, Japan and Korea) went ahead with swap arrangements with the so-called Chiang Mai initiative, building on the existing ASEAN Swap Arrangement (ASA) established in 1977.[84] However, the initiative was largely symbolic, since the swap lines agreed would have been inadequate in the face of a strong region-wide attack on currencies. Thus, countries went for a more reliable solution by accumulating large stocks of international reserves.

Again, with the spread of shocks and contagion from the global financial crisis in 2008, ASEAN+3 decided to establish an $80 billion fund to safeguard regional stability, replacing the existing bilateral currency swaps under the Chiang Mai Initiative with a reserve pooling mechanism (called the Chiang Mai Initiative Multilateralization) and coming closer to a regional monetary fund. Subsequently, the amount was raised in February 2009 to $120 billion as pressure mounted on currencies and reserves of several countries, to be accompanied by an independent regional surveillance mechanism to help determine the conditions for activation of and access to the Fund.[85] There have also been further bilateral swap agreements among some countries in the region, e.g., between China and Korea, Japan and Indonesia, and Korea and Japan.

These initiatives no doubt reflect a shared concern over currency instability, against a background of rapidly deepening regional integration through trade and investment. However, the region lacks effective arrangements for the coordination of exchange rate policies. It is true that recent sharp swings in intraregional exchange rates (Table 4.7) have been greatly influenced by differences in capital flows, current account balances, and macroeconomic conditions in different countries. Nevertheless, their origin also lies in differences in currency regimes pursued by the countries in the region, which now span the entire spectrum between the two corners, compared to widespread de facto dollar pegs before the crisis. At one corner there are economies with independent floating – Japan, Korea and the Philippines; at another there is Hong Kong with a currency board. The intermediate regimes adopted in the region also show significant variations, with China and Malaysia using very tightly managed pegs against Thailand's and Singapore's more flexible regimes.[86]

The coexistence of a variety of regimes in East Asia implies that the intraregional exchange rates tend to manifest a high degree of instability in periods of large swings in the dollar. Lack of regional cooperation in exchange rate policies is of particular concern in the current juncture not only because the ongoing instability evokes the memories of contagion that led to a severe crisis about a decade ago but also because contraction in export markets often raises the temptation of beggar-my-neighbor exchange rate adjustments.

2. *Rationale for exchange rate cooperation in East Asia*

Significant changes in policy and institutions often follow severe economic shocks and disruptions. The Bretton Woods system was established after the world went through one of the bloodiest armed conflicts in the history of mankind following the breakdown of international trade and payments in the interwar period. The European process of monetary integration was triggered by the collapse of the Bretton Woods system, and the Asian monetary cooperation was sparked off by the 1997 crisis. Now, the global spread of financial crisis is giving rise to several initiatives for tighter regulation of international financial markets. Likewise, current difficulties provide considerable food for thought for deeper monetary integration in East Asia, including a common currency regime and, eventually, a monetary union.

It is generally recognized that Asia lacks a culture of regionalism, that is, the political will and regional institutions needed for such a drastic change. To date regional economic integration in Asia has been driven by markets, notably by transnational corporations, rather than by governments. By contrast, the European integration was a politically driven process based on postwar transnational reconciliation in Franco-German relations, and on a shared vision by political left and right alike that regional political stability depended crucially on economic integration and stability. Such a reconciliation is lacking in East Asia where some countries have still failed to come to terms with their past. This is no doubt a major impediment to regional monetary integration even though there appears to be a strong economic rationale for it. Nevertheless, exploring various options can still help prepare the ground for the time when political realities become favorable, even though at present such efforts may appear to be no more than academic exercises. After all, history teaches that big changes almost always look implausible until they happen.[87]

East Asia has been undergoing rapid economic integration associated with fast and broad-based growth. Intraregional trade among ASEAN+3 has been growing faster than trade with the rest of the world.[88] Intraregional exchange rates no doubt play an increasingly important role in determining the division of labor in the region. Maintaining stable and properly aligned currencies is essential for this process to be driven by underlying economic fundamentals, and for preventing financial instability and trade tensions in the region. It is quite unlikely that these objectives could be achieved with each country acting alone. They require closer monetary and financial cooperation to underpin the ongoing regional economic integration.

The main benefit of a regional monetary integration comes from greater currency, payments and financial stability. This depends, of course, on how integration is designed, including supporting institutions and mechanisms. The European experience in this respect is quite encouraging. Despite the temporary setbacks in 1992–93 and shortcomings in the design of policies and institutional arrangements (to be discussed below), the EMS was very successful in securing stability in intraregional exchange rates, containing financial contagion, and dealing with fluctuations vis-à-vis the dollar and the yen. The main beneficiaries were smaller economies. Although they had lost monetary policy autonomy vis-à-vis Germany as the anchor currency country, they gained considerable strength vis-à-vis international financial markets. Besides, none of these countries, including Greece, Ireland and Portugal, had to go to the IMF after the establishment of the EMS in 1979, even though economically they were less advanced than Korea when it had to resort to IMF support in 1997. In the absence of the EMS, open and smaller European countries would have had little option but to peg their currencies to the deutschmark and follow German monetary policy without enjoying the protection and support provided by the EMS.

The cost of giving up autonomy in exchange rate policy depends on the difficulties this would cause in maintaining stable and high levels of employment and economic activity. This issue is often examined in terms of whether the countries concerned could form an optimal currency area (OCA). According to the OCA theory, a monetary union would bring benefits if the economies concerned are sufficiently closely integrated, the shocks they are expected to receive are symmetrical, and their labor markets are flexible enough to absorb such shocks without causing unemployment.

Several studies examined empirically whether East Asia (ASEAN and/or ASEAN+3) adequately meets the conditions for a monetary union so as to generate benefits to all its potential members, often taking the European Union as a reference point. As in most empirical studies of this kind, the findings are inconclusive. According to some, Asia is too diverse to meet the criteria for an OCA: intraregional trade and financial integration are limited, and regional shocks are not always symmetrical. According to others, however, it comes very close to meeting OCA conditions: income gaps of Asian countries have been closing not only with the rest of the world but also with each other, business cycles are closely correlated, and the shocks they receive are sufficiently symmetrical because of similarities in their trade patterns and integration into the global financial system.

A study by Goto and Hamada (1994) found that in some areas East Asia was more closely integrated than Europe. Similarly, an analysis conducted at the beginning of this decade showed that, in terms of various economic criteria, the region was no less ready for a regional monetary arrangement than Europe was before the EMU (Kawai and Takagi 2000). Bayoumi and Eichengreen (1999) came to the conclusion that East Asian countries satisfied the standard OCA conditions almost as well as Europe and that a common currency peg would be particularly beneficial for smaller and more open economies, while pointing out that because of the lack of an institutional framework such an arrangement would be risky. A subsequent study by Kawai and Motonishi (2005) reached a similar conclusion. According to Bayoumi and Mauro (1999) and Bayoumi, Eichengreen and Mauro (2000), ASEAN is less suited for a regional currency arrangement than Europe was before the Maastricht Treaty, although the difference is not large. Plummer and Wignaraja (2007) argue, on the basis of increased correlation of business cycles, that the economic potential for monetary integration is strong, while Zhang, Sato, and McAleer (2004) maintain that labor markets in East Asia are no less flexible than in Europe. By contrast, Nicolas (1999) contends that similarity in ASEAN countries are exaggerated because of high levels of aggregation, and Chow and Kim (2003) and Kim (2007) find that macroeconomic shocks are quite asymmetric and heterogeneous not only in East Asia but also within ASEAN. More recently, Shirono (2008) has followed a different approach, focusing on the trade aspects of monetary integration, and found that a currency union could double bilateral trade in the region and bring welfare benefits, particularly if Japan were included.

While the OCA theory provides insight into understanding the factors affecting the costs and benefits of a monetary integration, it cannot be relied on to draw practical guidelines to decisions over monetary union. First, it pays little attention to costs of potential conflicts that may arise from beggar-my-neighbor trade, FDI, and exchange rate policies. Second, the theory does not provide thresholds on the degree of integration, symmetry in shocks, or labor market flexibility by which to judge whether conditions for the OCA are reasonably met. There are indeed studies that show that neither Europe nor the United States forms an OCA, with the costs of using a single currency exceeding the benefits in both cases; and that for Germany it would not be economically advantageous to join a monetary union (Ghosh and Wolf 1994).

More importantly, the theory of OCA ignores that trade patterns and income levels are endogenous; that is, joining a monetary union is likely to move countries closer to each other and hence to the conditions for an OCA. This has clearly been the case in Europe where considerable convergence of income and macroeconomic conditions occurred throughout the process of integration culminating in the EMU.[89] However, it is also important to recognize that endogenous convergence depends very much on institutional and behavioral changes that would be required to manage integration and to compensate for the loss of the exchange rate instrument – issues to which the theory of OCA pays little attention (Buiter 1995).

Intraregional trade was no doubt much higher in Europe than it is in East Asia today, reaching almost 70 percent of total trade of the former, compared to less than 50 percent in the latter. But in East Asia, too, it is likely to reach similar magnitudes if recent trends are maintained, and if initiatives such as the ASEAN Economic Community can be put into practice and extended to include China and Korea. Besides, intraregional trade and monetary integration can constitute mutually reinforcing processes in East Asia in the same way as they have in Europe: stable exchange rates help to expand trade and deepen regional economic integration, which can, in turn, achieve greater convergence to conditions needed to increase the benefits from common currency arrangements.

The contagion which spread the currency attacks during the 1997 crisis from Thailand to several other countries was partly caused by the belief that regional integration was deep enough to trigger competitive devaluations. In reality there is both competition and complementarity in East Asian trade. An important part of trade among the countries of the region is complementary intra-industry trade in intermediate goods linked to international production networks, with China at the center.[90] In these networks based on vertical intra-industry trade specialization, China imports components and parts (mostly from the NIEs) and capital goods (mainly from Japan and Korea) as inputs into consumer goods exported largely to industrial countries, but also partly to other developing countries, including in the region.[91] Clearly, this is different from western-European-type intra-industry trade, where countries both import and export final products produced by the same industries and compete in these markets. In vertical production networks competition is largely among countries supplying intermediate goods (e.g., computer chips) rather than in markets for final consumer products.

Although intra-industry trade in final consumables has also been developing rapidly in East Asia, the increase in intraregional trade over the past decade is largely due to the growth of trade between China and other East Asian countries within industry-specific production networks, mirroring the rapid growth of Chinese exports to the United States and the European Union. Thus, trade shocks from advanced economies tend to generate symmetrical effects across the region. Because of a high degree of import content of Chinese assembly industries, a one dollar decline in China's exports to the United States and Europe tends to reduce its imports from the rest of East Asia by more than a one dollar decline in its domestic consumption. This is clearly seen in the current crisis, during which declines in China's exports to the United States and Europe are mirrored by sharp contractions in its imports from the region and intraregional trade, with all major Asian economies experiencing double digit drops in exports.

Competition among East Asian countries in the United States and European markets for final products appears to be more intense than competition in intraregional trade in these products. Not only did the countries hit by the 1997 crisis export to the same destinations but they also exported the same products. Their exports to the United States were concentrated in two groups, namely, (i) semiconductors and capital goods industries, and (ii) apparel, footwear and household goods (Kochhar, Loungani and Stone 1998, 18–19). Competition among Asian producers in third markets has certainly intensified since the 1997 crisis with growing penetration of China in the United States and European markets in areas of export interest to other Asian NIEs.

In finance, Asian regional integration is much more limited than in trade (MAS 2007, chap. 5; Kawai 2007). In fact Asia is integrated more closely with global financial markets than regionally. A very large proportion of portfolio investment in Asia comes from the United States and Europe, which also constitute the main destinations for Asian portfolio investment abroad. This provides a strong rationale for closer regional monetary cooperation because it implies, in effect, that Asian emerging markets are exposed to similar external financial shocks and contagion, and require similar policy responses. As already discussed, this has indeed been the case in the current global turmoil where such shocks have caused sharp declines in asset markets across the region. Such common financial shocks and contagion are generally neglected in the literature on OCA, which tends to focus on real supply and demand shocks.

3. Options for regional currency arrangements

As noted above, the main objective of European monetary cooperation after the collapse of the Bretton Woods system was to secure intraregional stability while floating collectively vis-à-vis the dollar and other reserve currencies. After the initial and barely successful experiments with "snake" and "snake in the tunnel," parity grids were established for each member currency vis-à-vis all other ERM currencies in two tier bands of ± 2.25 percent, with the Italian lira enjoying a wider band of ± 6 percent, widened further to ±15 percent when it came under attack in the early 1990s.[92] The ERM was anchored to the deutschmark not only because it was the main reserve currency in the region but also because Germany was a large economy with a good track record in price stability. France was also big but not stable, while Holland was stable but not big enough (Bofinger and Flassbeck 2000). Joint intervention and unlimited short-term bilateral credits to weak currency countries were the main instruments for maintaining currencies in parity grids. Parity adjustments were allowed to prevent build-up of fundamental disequilibria, at least until the 1987 Basel–Nyborg agreement, which sought to avoid further parity changes by liberalizing intramarginal interventions in order to strengthen the credibility of the EMS.[93]

Could and should East Asia try to replicate the European experience by aiming at intraregional stability while adopting a benign neglect toward the values of their currencies vis-à-vis the rest of the world? Or should they go for a common mechanism designed to attain both internal and external stability, with provisions for appropriate adjustments if and when needed? What are the options in common exchange rate arrangements?

Replicating the ERM in East Asia can pose serious problems. First of all, there would be practical difficulties in pegging bilaterally and floating collectively without an independently floating reserve currency as an anchor. The yen is the only such currency at present, but there are political impediments to forming intraregional currency arrangements around the yen. More importantly, floating collectively – with or without an anchor reserve currency – would mean a significant degree of instability vis-à-vis third currencies. This would not have mattered much if East Asian developing countries traded mainly with each other and/or competed among themselves in third markets. But for the region as a whole and for most countries, the share of non–East Asian trade as a proportion of GDP is still very high and competition from third countries is quite intense. This means that fluctuations vis-à-vis third currencies could generate considerable swings in economic activity and undermine export-led growth strategies.[94] Adopting managed floating vis-à-vis the rest of the world would also be difficult without an internal reserve currency as an anchor. Thus, an AMS modelled on the EMS, with or without management of external parities, may have to wait until the Chinese yuan becomes a fully convertible world currency.

If the main objective is simply to maintain a stable pattern of intraregional exchange rates, a solution would be to move collectively to the other corner and fix all regional currencies to a reserve currency, notably the dollar.[95] This was advocated by McKinnon (2001) for most East Asian countries on grounds that soon after the 1997 crisis they had all gone back to some form of de facto dollar peg, but lack of any formal agreement left the door open to beggar-my-neighbor exchange rate policies, instability and contagion. By this view, such threats could be avoided by a collective formal dollar peg, which would also insulate the intraregional exchange rates against fluctuations in the dollar. In order to avoid instability, it is argued, it would be necessary to strengthen prudential regulations limiting banks' foreign exchange exposures.

As noted above, since the beginning of the decade, Asian developing countries have moved away from dollar pegs toward intermediate regimes of managed floating. Indeed, as indicated by wildly disparate fluctuations of regional currencies against the dollar since 2003 (Table 4.7), the region is not a de facto dollar block. Returning to the dollar peg could defeat the central objective of improving the ability of the countries to collectively manage their exchange rates in the service of stability and growth. Unilateral pegging to the dollar is not the same thing as going into a monetary union with the United States, since it would not entail any commitment on the part of the latter country in the conduct of its monetary and exchange rate policies, or for financial support. The consequences of loss of monetary autonomy could be particularly severe given that the United States and East Asia do not come close to forming an OCA. Moreover, fixing to the dollar would not eliminate instability vis-à-vis third currencies and, hence, of effective exchange rates. Nor can the vulnerability of such a regime to instability and crises be easily eliminated through standard prudential regulations for reasons discussed in Section D, above. Such a solution may be appropriate for countries looking for a credible external anchor to stabilize the domestic price level, but not for East Asia, where the record in monetary and fiscal discipline is as good as, and even better than, the United States.[96]

An alternative proposal is to collectively target a basket of three reserve currencies, rather than the dollar alone, with a common set of weights determined on the basis of regional trade shares.[97] Each country would announce a central parity vis-à-vis the basket and commit to keep it within a unilaterally chosen band. There would be no restrictions over the choice of the exchange rate regime by individual countries; that is, each country would be free to choose its own regime with respect to the common basket, including hard pegs and managed floating, provided that its exchange rate action is disciplined by the central basket rate. Thus, Hong Kong could stick to its currency board, except that it would now fix its currency to the common basket rather than the dollar, and China, Malaysia and Singapore could all continue with their own variants of the BBC regime provided that they were willing to have their intervention disciplined by the central basket rate.[98] A restoration clause is proposed whereby countries would be allowed to temporarily suspend the peg when confronted with a massive speculative attack, with a credible commitment to return to the original parity as soon as practical. However, central parity and the band would also be allowed to crawl in response to changes in economic fundamentals and large and durable shocks.

Here, too, as in the dollar peg, changes among reserve currencies would not affect intraregional exchange rates: in other words, if each economy stabilizes its currency vis-à-vis a common basket of reserve currencies, they would also stabilize against each other. Moreover, the common basket peg would have the advantage of securing greater stability of effective exchange rates. However, these can still show considerable instability since weights used in the common basket would diverge from the optimal weights in unilateral country baskets. The compromise needed regarding the weights to be used in the common basket may face political hurdles when the trade of countries with the three reserve currency countries differs widely. However, instability in effective exchange rates caused by pegging to a common basket (rather than their own optimal baskets) is expected to diminish over time as countries move closer to each other and, hence, toward the conditions for an OCA.

The proposed system is more flexible and less formal than the EMS. It does not call for a drastic change in the existing exchange rate regimes except for changing the target currency to a basket of three reserve currencies with common weights. Moreover, its implementation would not depend on the existence of an anchor reserve currency in the region. An argument advanced against a common East Asian basket system is that, in the absence of support by the three reserve currency countries, it would not be able to stand a determined speculation even under the Chiang Mai Initiative.[99] However, this would not be a problem if East Asia could collectively maintain a current account surplus and large amounts of reserves, and establish adequate intraregional credit lines.

The major problem, however, is that such an informal and flexible arrangement would not secure adequate discipline and commitment. Here, unlike in the EMS, central parities and bands would be unilaterally determined. Since any band width with a central parity in the common basket is permissible, there can be considerable intraregional instability unrelated to shifts among the reserve currencies. Although changes in exchange rates unwarranted by changes in the basket currencies can be challenged by other members, this might not be very effective if there is no commitment to defend a particular rate.[100] On the other hand, despite the restoration rule, the proposed arrangement would not have effective safeguards against arbitrary changes in the central parity and even bands, and would not eliminate the scope for beggar-my-neighbor parity adjustments. Thus, it can only be an initial step until there is an economic and political convergence toward conditions needed for a formal and more tightly regulated system.[101]

Given the difficulties posed by soft regimes, and the lack of political will and solidarity to put in place more robust institutions and currency arrangements, it is sometimes suggested that Asia should make an even slower start by replicating the European Currency Unit (ECU) rather than the EMS by establishing an Asian Currency Unit (ACU) and promoting its use as a parallel currency alongside national currencies.[102] This is also seen as fitting better to the Asian approach to integration as a market-based rather than politically driven process. However, the ECU never played an important role in the European monetary integration. The use of an ACU alongside national currencies would lead to currency mismatches, and these could be quite damaging when intraregional exchange rates are highly unstable. This could in fact deter its widespread use in the absence of mechanisms to stabilize intraregional exchange rates. More importantly, the success of the ACU would depend in large part on strong government support, giving it legal tender status by using it in bond issues, settlements among central banks, and even pricing of public services. Thus, successful development of an ACU is politically no less untenable than effective intraregional currency arrangements.[103] One may then try to go all the way to introduce arrangements that would secure a reasonable degree of extraregional and intraregional exchange rate stability, instead of selecting a half-way house that would turn out to be neither one thing nor the other.

4. Supporting mechanisms: Lessons from Europe

A regional arrangement designed to maintain stable intraregional and effective exchange rates needs to be supported by several mechanisms and institutions. The list of areas of cooperation needed is quite long, and includes macroeconomic policy coordination, market regulation and surveillance, but here attention is focused on two areas that hold the key for the viability of any arrangement for collective management of exchange rates: i) the management of capital flows, and ii) intraregional lending and policy adjustment. In both respects, the European experience holds a number of useful lessons, by both its successes and its shortcomings.

i. A regional capital account regime

Regional currency arrangements require a common set of principles regarding rules to be applied to international capital flows. This was indeed the case in Europe. The Treaty of Rome stipulated gradual removal of restrictions among the member states, but it also permitted the introduction of controls in response to disturbances in the functioning of financial markets due to international capital movements, and authorized the use of protective measures by countries experiencing balance of payments difficulties. Until 1988 when the council adopted a new directive calling for the liberalization of capital movements within the community by 1990, the EEC regime for capital movements was governed by guidelines established by various directives issued from the early 1960s onwards. These divided capital flows into four different categories, with different rules for liberalization and regulation to be applied to each. They provided considerable leeway for restricting capital movements, particularly toward third parties. In fact, governments were required to have available and be able to use certain policy instruments for the control of international capital movements and for the sterilization of their impact on domestic liquidity, and to have rules governing investment in money markets by nonresidents, loans and credits unrelated to current transactions, net external positions of credit institutions, and reserve requirements for holdings by nonresidents.

In effect, until liberalization in the late 1980s, the EMS operated under capital controls. The 1988 directive prohibited restrictions among member countries and recommended that they should endeavour to attain the same degree of liberalization of capital movements with third countries. But recognizing that short-term international capital movements were capable of seriously disrupting the conduct of monetary and exchange rate policies even when there was no appreciable divergence among countries in economic fundamentals, the directive retained provisos concerning control over such capital movements during periods of financial strain. This was subject to authorization by the commission, but the right to unilateral action was recognized in urgent cases. It was indeed exercised during the 1992–93 turmoil by a number of countries, including Ireland, Portugal and Spain.

It is often argued that the main reason for the acceleration of the process of integration in Europe in the early 1990s toward full monetary union was because volatile capital flows made it very difficult to maintain parities (e.g., Park and Wyplosz 2007). Since this is not yet an option in Asia, any regional arrangement to stabilize intraregional and extraregional parities should be built on a common and effective capital account regime in the region.

Even though the overall trend in East Asia has been toward greater capital account openness, there is still considerable disparity among countries regarding the regimes for nonresident and resident flows. Harmonization of these should seek considerable tightening of rules and regulations to be applied to capital flows with third countries, along the lines discussed in Section D, above. By contrast, the East Asian countries, notably the ASEAN 5 countries plus China and Korea, can afford a greater degree of capital account openness among themselves than was the case in Europe during the first decade of the EMS. In this respect China could play a special role by making the yuan fully convertible within the region and hence promoting it as a regional reserve currency. The recent move by China to allow the yuan to be used as settlement currency with neighboring countries (including ASEAN and Russia), partly triggered by problems caused by dollar instability for China's exporters, and a number of bilateral swaps that China's Central Bank has signed with countries inside and outside the region are important steps in the internationalization of the yuan (Asia News 2009). Such moves could be supplemented by opening Chinese financial markets to residents in other member countries, including those with weaker savings and payments positions, to tap its high savings through the so-called Panda bonds – a step that could also help develop regional bond markets for closer financial integration and reduce the dollar-denominated external claims of China.[104]

ii. Intraregional lending and policy adjustment

Maintaining currencies within agreed bands would call for, inter alia, occasional interventions in foreign exchange markets in both directions. Countries would be constrained in doing this when markets push down a currency toward the lower edge of the band. In the case where currencies are pegged to a common basket of three reserve currencies, intervention and stabilization would require adequate holding of or access to these currencies.

The EMS did not incorporate a regional fund to support countries having to intervene to keep their currencies within the grids. Rather, it relied on bilateral lending and borrowing between strong currency countries (often Germany) and weak currency countries. There were two types of intervention: intramarginal and marginal. Intramarginal interventions were carried out, often in dollars, by the country concerned at its own discretion, when its currency was within intervention points. But interventions had to be done jointly by both weak and strong currency countries when a currency reached its bilateral intervention points, or by the strong currency country making available unlimited amounts of a very short-term financing (VSTF) to the weak currency country.[105] Lending and intervention by a strong currency country were formally equivalent since reserves used in interventions were added to VSTF claims on the weak currency country, and such claims had to be settled within 45 days. In the case of extension, the amount available was limited.

This VSTF did not have sufficient flexibility to provide breathing space for a country suffering from contagion. This was the case of France during the 1992–93 turmoil when its macroeconomic fundamentals did not justify the attack on its currency alongside the lira and pound sterling; indeed, tight German monetary policy was a main factor in the speculative attack on the French franc. Provisions for suspension of asset settlement obligations for countries satisfying certain macroeconomic criteria linked to payments and fiscal positions and inflation would have certainly facilitated the stabilization of the French franc and prevented interest rate hikes and loss of jobs and incomes (UNCTAD TDR 1993, part 2, chap. 1). By contrast, the system left considerable discretion to strong currency countries to opt out of their obligations to provide unlimited VSTF. This is what Germany eventually did in 1992 for fear of inflationary consequences of its lending to countries under distress, thereby deepening the crisis.

The EMS lacked symmetry in policy formulation and distribution of the burden of macroeconomic adjustment between weak and strong currency countries. In fact, there were no clear guidelines for their respective responsibilities for policy adjustment in the face of market pressures on parities. Hegemony by Germany was not always balanced by its responsibilities vis-à-vis other members. Its policies did not always pay enough attention to the overall macroeconomic conditions of the region and their possible adverse impact on other members. This, together with lack of effective intraregional financing and lender-of-last-resort facilities, often pushed the burden onto weak currency countries. This was the price paid for the stabilization influence that Germany provided to countries lacking a similar degree of fiscal and monetary discipline and credibility. Moreover, German monetary policy had a deflationary bias, and was mainly responsible for sluggish growth and persistently high unemployment in the region as a whole – an approach now inherited by the European Central Bank.

Multilateralization of regional credit lines would be necessary to avoid asymmetry. In this respect the move from Chiang Mai bilateral credit lines toward a regional monetary fund is a positive step in Asia. Furthermore, possible arrangements for guidelines for policy adjustment and conditions of access to an Asian fund should pay attention to shortcomings of the EMS as well as IMF lending practices to emerging markets in order to avoid deflationary and procyclical biases.

This brings us to a final point about relative positions and responsibilities of members of a possible AMS among the developing countries of the region. It is sometimes argued that China is far too big for other developing countries to join in partnership – far bigger than Germany was relative to other European countries. This means that the terms of any agreement for regional monetary integration could be dictated by the needs of the Chinese economy, which may not always coincide with those of smaller and more advanced countries in the region.

That China is likely to be more dominant than Germany ever was in Europe in shaping policies and practices in an AMS is probably correct. But this is a matter of relative economic power, not existence or otherwise of formal agreements for monetary integration. China will wield considerable influence on policies in the region with or without an AMS. Under current trends, it can soon consolidate its global position as an industrial powerhouse by becoming a major actor in the global financial system by moving to full convertibility and independent floating, making the yuan challenge the US dollar as the international reserve currency – possibly sooner than Chinese politicians are willing to accept and most observers expect.[106] This is likely to go through two stages: increasing the use of the yuan first in pricing and settlement of trade and financial transactions, and second in denomination of financial assets for lending and investment. As noted, China has already taken steps in both directions.

As the yuan becomes an international reserve currency, smaller and open Asian economies with close trade and investment links to China would not have much autonomy in monetary and exchange rate policies, but would have to follow it in very much the same way as the Swiss policy mimicked that of the Bundesbank and is now doing so with the ECB. For smaller and open East Asian economies, entering into monetary cooperation with China now under carefully defined and properly balanced reciprocal responsibilities could bring them more benefits than unilaterally pegging to the yuan and following China's monetary policy. In this bargain they are in a better position than were weak currency countries of Europe in that most of them have a good record of monetary and fiscal discipline and do not depend on the stabilizing influence of another central bank.

G. Conclusions

With the increased integration of developing countries into the global trading system and international production networks, the exchange rate has gained additional importance in growth and development. The need to maintain stable and competitive exchange rates is further enhanced by loss of space in trade and industrial policies as a result of multilateral commitments in the WTO. However, the ability of developing countries to achieve this has been greatly compromised by their closer integration into international financial markets and increased openness to inherently unstable capital flows.

Maintaining stable and competitive exchange rates in most developing countries depends, inter alia, on how boom–bust cycles in capital flows are managed. An effective management should start in good times since options are quite limited under sudden stops and reversals. Failure to prevent surges in capital inflows and unsustainable currency appreciations do not simply lead to instability in exchange rates and balance of payments but also to virulent financial and economic crises with durable and severe consequences for jobs, incomes and investment. However, the task has become particularly daunting since the most damaging swings in capital flows are caused by global factors beyond the control of developing countries, notably by macroeconomic and financial conditions in major industrial countries, and there are no effective multilateral arrangements to discipline either policies in countries with disproportionately large impacts on global financial conditions or financial markets.

Management of exchange rates under the free flow of capital faces serious dilemmas – even beyond those predicted by the conventional impossible trinity. Monetary policy on its own is often quite powerless to influence capital flows so as to stabilize the exchange rate even when all available instruments are used, particularly at times of sudden shifts in market sentiments. Currency market interventions designed to absorb a surge in capital inflows to avoid appreciations and to build self-defense against sudden stops and reversals by accumulating reserves are second best policies because they are costly and their impact on domestic liquidity cannot always be fully neutralized. Nor can they prevent asset market bubbles and currency and maturity mismatches in private balance sheets.

Under most circumstances regulation and control over capital flows would be necessary to prevent build-up of fragility. Standard prudential rules regarding capital charges, loan loss provisions and reserve and liquidity requirements can be extended and applied more rigorously and in a countercyclical fashion to foreign currency positions and transactions in the financial system with a view to reducing maturity and currency mismatches and exchange-rate-related credit risks. While useful and necessary, in most developing countries such measures would not be sufficient to prevent build-up of external fragility since not all foreign investment and borrowing are intermediated by financial institutions. Direct tools may need to be applied to prevent currency and maturity mismatches in private sector balance sheets. Easing or removing restrictions on resident outflows at a time of a surge in inflows to relieve the pressure on the currency carries the risk of opening the way to one-way traffic.

Monetary policy would be quite ineffective at times of rapid exit of capital resulting from a sudden change of market sentiment for reasons beyond the control of the country concerned, such as the shocks and contagion caused by the current global financial turmoil triggered by widespread speculative lending and investment in major international financial centers. Attempts to stem outflows by interest rate hikes and fiscal retrenchment simply add to deflationary and destabilizing impulses. In the absence of voluntary agreements by international creditors and investors to roll over their claims, unilateral temporary debt standstills and exchange restrictions may be the only viable option to check financial meltdown and economic contraction.

For most developing countries intermediate exchange rate regimes, and particularly the BBC regime, provide the most viable option for combining a relatively high degree of stability with the flexibility needed for occasional adjustments in order to maintain competitive exchange rates. A successful pursuit of such a regime calls for a judicious combination of monetary policy adjustments, currency market interventions, and control over capital flows. Indeed, well aware of the risks of leaving the exchange rate to the whims of cross-border capital flows, most Asian developing countries have opted for intermediate regimes in an effort to combine stability with flexibility against the orthodox advice to float independently and spare monetary policy for inflation targeting. They have been successful in maintaining relatively stable and competitive exchange rates and strong payments positions, even though lack of adequate control over capital inflows exposed their asset markets to adverse shifts in global financial conditions. By contrast, countries that chose free floating have been hit harder by the current international financial turmoil both because of unsustainable appreciations and current account deficits, and the bursting of asset bubbles resulting from the earlier surge in capital inflows.

In the absence of effective global arrangements to secure international monetary stability and difficulties in finding unilateral solutions, regional mechanisms present themselves as viable alternatives. This is particularly true for countries with close trade and investment links as in East Asia. Despite large stocks of international reserves and strong payments positions, intraregional and extraregional exchange rates have been highly unstable in the region. This carries not only the risk of contagion but also the seeds of conflicts, particularly when global markets are shrinking. There is a strong economic case for establishing common currency arrangements with supporting institutions and mechanisms, including rules for policy coordination and adjustment, guidelines for capital account policies, and regional funds and lender-of-last-resort facilities. What is missing is not the need or the scope but the political will and solidarity. Perhaps current difficulties will provide an occasion for a common reflection for change before ever-growing international monetary and financial instability inflicts irreparable damages.

Notes

1 First published in September 2009 by UNDP Regional Centre for Asia Pacific, Colombo Office. An earlier version was presented in a UNDP Regional Conference, "Promoting Human Development in Trade Regionalism: Scope for South–South Cooperation in the Asia Pacific," Bali, 24–26 November 2008. I am grateful to the participants of the conference, particularly to Manuel Montes and Martin Khor, as well as to C. P. Chandrasekhar, Mehdi Shafaeddin and staff members of the Asia–Pacific Trade and Investment Initiative of the UNDP Regional Centre, Colombo and the UNDP editor John Tessitore for comments and suggestions. As usual, the opinions expressed here are those of the author, and may not reflect those of UNDP.

2 Here dollarization is used to express denomination of assets and liabilities in foreign currencies generally, not just in dollars.

3 See Palley (2003) on the neglect of the impact of the exchange rate on the pattern of trade and production in the mainstream trade models.

4 For further discussion of the shortcomings of the mainstream trade theory and its application through the so-called computable general equilibrium models, see Akyüz (2009).

5 See the exchange between Srinivasan and Bhagwati (1999) and Rodrik (1999) on the link between trade and growth theories. That there is nothing new in these respects in the "new" or the endogenous growth theory, see Thirlwall and Sanna (1996) and Thirlwall (2003b).

6 A main reason for increasing returns to scale is the existence of firm- or industry-specific fixed costs (Krugman 1979).

7 Hong Kong is industrially less developed than other first tier newly industrialized economies (NIEs), including not only Korea and Taiwan but also Singapore – an economy with a smaller population but much stronger industry. For a comparison, see UNCTAD TDR (1996, 130–32).

8 A good example is Sweden where large-scale modern manufacturing in a number of sectors played a key role in breaking its reliance on traditional commodity exports and rapidly upgrading its industrial capacity; see UNCTAD TDR (1997, box 5).

9 See various country studies in Helleiner (1994) and the discussion in Eichengreen (2008, 17–19).

10 For a lucid analysis, see Thirlwall (2003a), who emphasizes payments constraints and develops a model combining supply and demand linkages between exports and growth. The foreign exchange constraint also plays a key role in income determination and growth in gap models (Taylor 1994). For an emphasis on the role of exports and the exchange rate as a driver of aggregate demand, see Frenkel (2008).

11 If such an economy does not export, it can save only by storing consumables, which does not add to its production capacity. This also means that in such an economy investment cannot precede savings (exports).

12 Growth is said to be led by exports if exports (or net exports) are growing faster than domestic demand, including public and private consumption and investment. For a recent attempt to quantify the contribution of exports to growth in some Asian countries, see ADB (2005).

13 On this link in China, see Akyüz (2008a).

14 The notion of a virtuous circle linked to export of manufactures is closely associated with the work of Kaldor (1989).

15 On a comparison of phases of investment transition, exports, and savings between sub-Saharan Africa and East Asia, see Akyüz and Gore (2001); on the weakness of the links among investment, manufacturing value added, and exports in Latin America, see UNCTAD TDR (2003; chap. 5); on weak savings from profits and the high propensity to consume of property-owning classes in Latin America, see Akyüz (2006).

16 For a succinct account of the impact of the real exchange rate on resource allocation and employment, see Frenkel and Taylor (2006). It should be noted that this theoretical notion of the real exchange rate does not have a single empirical counterpart. For alternative definitions and measurement, see Edwards (1989) and Harberger (2004).

17 For a detailed analysis of the structuralist contractionary devaluation hypothesis, see Edwards (1989, chap. 8); for a more recent account, see Keifman (2007).

18 It should be noted that exportables are not always wage goods in all commodity-dependent economies; for instance "basic food staples behave essentially as nontradeables in much of sub-Saharan Africa" (Delgado 1995, 231), while most exported primary commodities have limited domestic markets. In such a case, too, devaluations would not lead to a significant expenditure switching and release goods for exports.

19 See Edwards (1989, 81–82). According to orthodox views, when tariffs and subsidies differentiate among sectors they are "distortionary" and harmful. When they are "nondistortionary" they would not be needed since one can dispense with them and use the exchange rate to shift resources to tradeables; this would also have the advantage of avoiding rent seeking behavior associated with such interventions.

20 For exchange rate protection, see Corden (1985).

21 In Korea in the early 1980s "proper management of the exchange rate was considered all the more important [...] since the government began to expand trade liberalization, phasing out various exports subsidies and import protection measures" (Nam and Kim, 1999, 235). But the very same country faced, 15 years later, the most serious balance of payments crisis and recession in its history because of its failure to manage capital flows and its currency.

22 For the external debt–income ratio not to explode, today's external liabilities should be matched by the present value of future current account surpluses; for a discussion, see Akyüz (2007).

23 Frenkel and Rapetti (2008) rightly ask why these failures should affect tradeable activities more than nontradeable goods sectors.

24 Most empirical measures of misalignments are based not on the ERER; but on purchasing power parity (PPP) deviations, often adjusted for the Balassa–Samuelson effect, allowing for appreciations as a result of increases in productivity or per capita income. For alternative measures, see Aguirre and Calderón (2005) and Gala (2007). As noted by Aguirre and Calderón (2005, 3–4), a shortcoming of using PPP-based measures is that "PPP only accounts for monetary sources of exchange rate fluctuations and does not capture exchange rate fluctuations attributed to real factors," of which distortions due to institutional or market failures are a part.

25 Corden (2008) focuses on reserve costs while Eichengreen (2008) emphasizes that a policy of weak currency sustained by interventions runs the risk that the currency adjustment may eventually come through a costly and financially disruptive inflation.

26 For a discussion, see UNCTAD TDR (2002, chap. 4) and Mayer (2003).

27 See Zeng and Yumin (2002) for the earlier trend in China's terms of trade, and Yu (2007) for the more recent period.

28 For productivity, wages, and profits, see Akyüz (2008a). Labor productivity figures refer to the whole economy and are taken from ILO (2007; Labor productivity and unit labor costs indicator, KILM 18). For hourly compensation in manufacturing in China in relation to those in the United States and other developing countries, see Banister (2005) and Roach (2007).

29 Edwards (1989, part 2) provides an empirically rich account of the evolution of real exchange rates in Latin America and elsewhere over 1965–85. Sachs (1985) attributes the superior adjustment of East Asia to shocks leading to the debt crisis in Latin America to better exchange rate and trade regimes; see also Gala (2007) for a similar view. In a study of 80 developing countries Shafaeddin (1992) found that in low income countries, each 10 percent nominal devaluation led to a real devaluation of 3 percent after a year.

30 For Korean exchange rate policy, see Nam and Kim (1999) and Eichengreen (2008, 8–9).

31 For the evolution of exchange rates in a number of South and East Asian economies throughout the past three decades, see Chowdhury (2005).

32 For a critical assessment of empirical studies on the growth–exchange rate link, see Frenkel and Rapetti (2008). It should be kept in mind that cross-country growth regressions suffer from several methodological problems, including the failure to identify whether or not the explanatory variables are truly exogenous. The founder of the neoclassical growth theory, Solow (2001), criticises cross-country growth accounting exercises on the grounds that the same specification applies to countries with different institutional histories so that differences in growth rates can only be explained by differences across countries in the values of the regressors used. Srinivasan and Bhagwati (1999) also criticise cross-country regressions, at least insofar as the benefits of trade openness are concerned, because of their weak theoretical foundations, poor quality of their data base, and their inappropriate econometric methodology; see also Rodrik (2005).

33 The explanation given by Rodrik (2008) is already discussed above. A country making a rapid switch from an import substitution strategy to an aggressive export push would need substantial incentive for producers in traded goods industries since there are important entry costs to foreign markets. In such cases sharp depreciations and other export incentives can lead to a surge in exports and accelerate growth by easing the payments constraint. This happened in Turkey during the 1980s, as shown by several papers in Aricanli and Rodrik (1990). However, not all growth accelerations are associated with shifts in trade strategy.

34 For a recent survey of these studies, see Eichengreen (2008), which also provides empirical, cross-country evidence on the link between volatility and growth.

35 For the development of hedge markets in emerging-market economies in recent years, see Saxena and Villar (2008). In Asia, over-the-counter (OTC) derivatives for foreign exchange barely exist outside Hong Kong and Singapore, which together account for over 50 percent of total turnover in foreign exchange spot markets in all emerging markets and 70 percent in OTC derivatives markets.

36 Several Bank for International Settlements (BIS) studies find that the presence of foreigners helps in the development of derivatives markets in foreign exchange, and the demand for hedging is driven mainly by international investors in emerging market bonds and equities. The banking sector is the biggest user of OTC forex derivatives and keeps the largest open position in most emerging markets; see Saxena and Villar (2008) and Turner (2008) and the studies cited therein.

37 See CEPR (2000), summary of a talk by Bernard Dumas based on Dumas (1994).

38 On the evidence that these markets develop faster where the currency is allowed to fluctuate freely, see Eichengreen (2008, 3), who cautions that "there are limits to this argument that price variability is conducive to the development of hedging markets and instruments; high levels of volatility will be subversive to financial development [...] insofar as it induces capital flights and leads the authorities to resort to policies of financial repression."

39 This is also recognized by the World Bank (2003, 26): "dynamics of net capital inflows and the changes of official reserves over the cycle do indeed indicate that the push factor is more important for middle income countries, while the pull factor dominates in high income countries." On postwar cycles in capital flows, see UNCTAD TDR (2003, chap. 2); for more recent episodes, see IMF WEO (October 2007, chap. 3).

40 See Borio and Lowe (2002) on the emergence of exchange rate and financial instability in a low inflation environment.

41 For instance, in the run-up to the 1995 Mexican crisis the peso remained pegged to the dollar while in Korea the won fell against the dollar from 1996 until the contagion from the Thai crisis in 1997. For the exchange rate regimes in Asia before the 1997 crisis, see UNCTAD TDR (1998, chap. 3, box 2).

42 It should be noted that several countries, including Argentina, Brazil, Mexico, Russia and Turkey, have succeeded in overcoming their chronic price instability and avoiding a return of rapid inflation despite the collapse of their currencies and the external adjustment necessitated by the crisis.

43 For the evidence cited in this section on the evolution of wages, employment, and investment in boom–bust-recovery cycles in emerging markets, see UNCTAD TDR (2000, chap. 4; TDR 2003, chap. 4), ILO (2004), Van der Hoeven and Lübker (2005), and World Bank (2003, 23–26). In the more recent boom–bust cycle after 2002, the boom phase was not associated with faster wage growth in several Asian countries, notably India and China. On the Indian experience, see Chandrasekhar (2008).

44 See Rajan and Shen (2006), which also discusses other possible explanations and reviews studies on the income effect of crisis-induced devaluations in Latin America and Asia.

45 See, however, Tovar (2006), which contends in an econometric analysis for Korea that devaluations are expansionary despite the balance sheet effect.

46 For an attempt to quantify these configurations and to link them to exchange rate stability, see Aizenman, Chinn, and Ito (2008), which measures the degree of monetary independence by correlation between home and international interest rates, and uses an index of financial openness and the ratio of reserves to GDP, and links them to exchange rate stability measured as annual standard deviations of monthly exchange rates.

47 On various regimes, see Edwards and Savastano (1999) and Williamson (2000).

48 In Singapore monetary policy is focused on the management of the exchange rate, rather than money supply or interest rates, which is seen as the most effective tool in maintaining price stability and competitiveness in a small and highly open economy. The system also relies on a large positive net foreign asset position and tightly regulated financial system (Parrado 2004; and Burton 2005).

49 For a discussion, see Williamson (2000) and Akyüz and Flassbeck (2002) and the references therein.

50 Rogoff et al. (2004, 14). For the evolution of exchange rate regimes in emerging markets, see also Edwards and Savastano (1999), Fischer (2001), and Stone, Anderson, and Veyrune (2008). On the basis of quantitative measures of degrees of exchange rate flexibility, monetary independence and capital account openness, it has been shown that, since the beginning of this decade, emerging markets have moved toward managed exchange rate flexibility, using international reserves as a buffer and retaining some degree of monetary independence (Aizenman, Chinn and Ito 2008). On "the return of the middle way" in Asia, see MAS (2007, chap. 5) and Kawai (2007).

51 See various studies in BIS (2005), notably Disyatat and Galati (2005) and Mihaljek (2005). See also Mohanty and Turner (2006).

52 Damill, Frenkel, and Maurizio (2007) argue that sterilized intervention would not interfere with monetary policy, focusing on the Argentine experience after 2002. Indeed, in Argentina where capital inflows were relatively moderate, sterilization seems to have been successful in keeping the real exchange rate within range and absorbing the resulting excess liquidity

through emission of central bank paper despite opposition from the IMF. However, in a subsequent paper Frenkel (2008) recognizes that when foreigners invest in a wider range of local assets, sterilization could raise short-term rates.

53 Rodrik (2006) calls the first component the social cost of foreign exchange reserves. For the distinction between the two types of transfers, see UNCTAD TDR (1999, chap. 5); for a formal description, see Akyüz (2008b).

54 For a discussion of the underlying theory, see Furman and Stiglitz (1998) and UNCTAD TDR (1999, chap. 5); for an attempt to empirically determine the optimum level of reserves, see Jeanne and Rancière (2006).

55 Here capital account refers to nonreserve financial account as defined in IMF (2007).

56 These figures, derived from the IMF *World Economic Outlook Database*, exclude the NIEs.

57 The spread exceeded 700 basis points during the 1990s and never fell below 400 basis points. In the early years of this decade it fell toward 200 basis points but climbed up sharply after the subprime crisis, exceeding 400 basis points. As noted, foregone return on assets sold is generally much higher.

58 The method used here to estimate reserve costs differs from that in the literature (e.g. Rodrik, 2006) in that a distinction is made here between borrowed and earned reserves. Polak and Clark (2006) also refer to borrowed reserves in their estimation of the cost to poorest developing countries.

59 For various measures of control used during the 1960s and 1970s see Swoboda (1976); for international regimes applied to cross-border capital, see Akyüz and Cornford (2002); for the experience in developing countries, see Epstein, Grabel and Jomo (2003); for more recently introduced capital account measures, see IMF WEO (October 2007) and IMF GFSR (October 2007).

60 Countercyclical design of prudential regulations is finding growing support after several boom–bust cycles in industrial countries, including the subprime expansion and crisis in the United States. For such measures, see BIS (2001); Borio, Furfine, and Lowe (2001); and White (2006).

61 According to the Institute of International Finance (IIF, January 2009), net flows from commercial banks never reached 50 percent of total private flows during the past several years. Since the IIF gives equity flows on a net–net basis (that is, net outflows of equity by residents are deducted from net inflows by nonresidents) and debt flows on gross basis, the share of net inflows from banks in total net inflows from nonresidents is even lower.

62 The underlying figures in Table 4.5 are on net–net basis for equity flows and gross basis for debt flows; that is, net outflows of foreign direct investment (FDI) and portfolio equity by residents are deducted from net inflows by nonresidents. Thus, the current account balance plus private capital flows minus net lending by residents (and errors and omissions) would give changes in reserves – see IIF (October 2007, box 3).

63 For further discussion of components of capital flows to Asian emerging markets, see BIS (2007), IMF REO (October 2007), IMF GFSR (October 2007), and McCauley (2008).

64 Fiscal cost from ESCAP (2007, 21) and government deficits from IMF REOAP (October 2007, 20).

65 For credit conditions and interest rates in Asia, see BIS (2007, 39–41), Mohanty and Turner (2006, 43), and IMF WEO (October 2007, 5).

66 It should be noted that reserve figures are subject to a valuation effect, which can be large because of sharp changes in cross rates among reserve currencies.

67 Since "borrowed" reserves of some countries fall short of their total external debt, realization of this aggregate benefit would require lending by countries with excess reserves to those with deficits, at rates earned on reserves.

68 For recent measures in Asia, see BIS (2007), IMF REOAP (April 2007), IMF GFSR (October 2007), and McCauley (2008).

69 See Yu (2008 and 2009). It has been argued that China's capital controls remained substantially binding during the period of a de facto dollar peg until July 2005, as suggested by sustained and significant gaps between onshore and offshore renminbi yields. It is also found that since July 2005 there has been a partial convergence between onshore and offshore yields (Ma and McCauley 2007).

70 In China the equity market is segmented between residents and nonresidents in A-share and B-share markets, with the former being reserved exclusively for residents. Both residents and nonresidents are allowed to use foreign exchange to invest in B shares. Large inflows of capital, together with growing current account surpluses, affect A-share equity prices mainly through liquidity expansion.

71 Data on equity prices and price–earnings ratios are from IMF GFSR (October 2007).

72 For an analysis of developments in Asian housing markets, see IMF REOAP (April 2007), which somewhat underplays the extent of the bubble and the risks involved, but nevertheless points out that speculative dynamics cannot be ruled out, notably in China, India, and Korea.

73 Korean and United States data from OECD (2007, annex table 60). For others, see BIS (2007, 50).

74 On the excess capacity, waste and sustainability of the investment boom in China, see BIS (2007), Goldstein and Lardy (2004), Nagaraj (2005), and Branstetter and Lardy (2006).

75 The Bank of China is reported to have lost some $2 billion on its holdings of collateralized securities, including those backed by US mortgages (Pearlstein 2008). Standard Chartered, in which Singapore's sovereign wealth fund, Temasek, owns a 19 percent stake, is reported to have been walking away from its $7.5 billion special investment vehicles (SIVs) sold in Asia and the Middle East (Bowring 2008b).

76 Net portfolio investment outflows in 2008 from emerging markets as a whole are estimated to have been $89 billion (IIF January 2009). It appears that all the money that came into emerging markets funds in 2007 came out again in 2008.

77 *Wall Street Journal*, 17 October 2008. The tendency of investors to liquidate their holdings in emerging markets in order to cover mounting losses and margin calls means that, as suggested by McCauley (2008, 1), emerging markets are providing "liquidity under stressed conditions to portfolios managed in the major markets."

78 See Xinhuanet (2009a) and Forbes (2008). In earlier years, concerned with the growing speculative spree, China had adopted measures to stem increases in property prices (ESCAP 2007, 10).

79 On some accounts, on its own the bursting of asset bubbles in China would lower growth only by a couple of percentage points (Chancellor 2008).

80 IIF (January 2009, 11). According to preliminary estimates, as of January 2009 some Asian countries, notably Korea and Singapore, experienced severe contraction in output during the last quarter of 2008. In China, where manufacturing output also dropped and loss of employment reached some 20 million, more recent indicators seem to be more encouraging (Xinhuanet 2009b).

81 BIS (2007, 56) notes that in China the bulk of recorded profits are earned by relatively few enterprises while the rest have high leverage, so that if growth slows significantly a substantial proportion of bank loans can become nonperforming.

82 For the behavior of reserves in India and Korea during 2008, see Obstfeld, Shambaugh and Taylor (2009).

83 The first major political initiative for a European monetary union was taken in 1969 with the Werner Report, which proposed: for the first stage, a reduction of the fluctuation margins between the currencies of the members of the European Community (EC); for the second stage, complete freedom of capital movements; and for the final stage, an irrevocable fixing of exchange rates. For a critical account of the EMS and its applicability to other regions, see Bofinger and Flassbeck (2000) and UNCTAD TDR (2007).

84 For ASA and Chiang Mai, see Henning (2002). These are not the first initiatives for regional monetary cooperation among developing countries. The Andean Reserve Fund and the Arab Monetary Fund were among the earlier examples, both going back to 1976 (Akyüz and Flassbeck 2002 and UNCTAD TDR 2007, chap. 5).

85 Thailand proposed to go even further, using 10 percent of reserves of ASEAN+3 to establish a reserve fund of some $350 billion (Kate and Adam 2008). For more recent developments regarding the Chiang Mai Initiative, see Henning (2009).

86 This classification is from IMF (2008) based on members' actual, de facto arrangements as identified by IMF staff, not officially announced arrangements.

87 This was expressed with some foresight by Rogoff (1999, 28) during the debate on the reform of the international financial architecture after the Asian crisis: "It is easy to fall into the trap of thinking that big institutional changes are unrealistic or infeasible [...] Not so long ago, the prospects for a single European currency seemed no more likely than those for the breakup of the Soviet empire or the reunification of Germany. Perhaps large institutional changes only seem impossible until they happen – at which point they seem foreordained. Even if none of the large-scale plans is feasible in the present world political environment, after another crisis or two, the impossible may start seeming realistic."

88 For the evolution of East Asian trade in comparison with other blocks, see MAS (2007, chap. 5).

89 The pioneering study in this area is Frankel and Rose (1996), which empirically shows, using the intensity of intra-union trade and correlation of business cycles, that countries are more likely to satisfy the criteria for entry into a currency union after taking steps toward economic integration than before. The OCA indices developed by Bayoumi and Eichengreen (1997) also show considerable convergence in Europe toward criteria for monetary union after 1987.

90 For the nature and extent of intraregional trade in East Asia, see MAS (2007, chap. 5) and Shafaeddin (2008, section 5). For variations among countries' participation, see Rana (2006, table 1).

91 According to an estimate based on 1995 input–output tables, only 20 percent of non-Japan intra-Asian exports in 2002 were for domestic demand – including consumption and capital formation – and the rest were in intermediate goods. Half of the latter was used in production for domestic markets and half for exports; see MAS (2003). Since 1995 there has been a rapid expansion of industry-specific production networks, notably in electronics. Therefore, more up-to-date input–output tables are likely to show a higher share of intermediate imports in production for exports. The same study also finds that about 68 percent of China's imports from East Asia are used, directly or indirectly, for domestic demand in China, including investment. However, no account is taken that an important part of investment in Chinese manufacturing is directly linked to exports.

92 After the suspension of gold convertibility by the United States, the 1971 Smithsonian agreement established a 4.5 percent margin (*the tunnel*) for other currencies against the dollar (that is, ± 2.25 percent relative to the central rate). This effectively meant that European currencies could move by up to 9 percent against each other. Soon after the European Community established the *snake*, that is, bilateral margins of 2.5 percent, which effectively limited such movements among members of the EC to 4.5 percent. The *snake in the tunnel* came to an end in 1973 when the dollar started to float freely.

93 This, in effect, helped create one-way bets against fundamentally misaligned lira and pound sterling, leading to the 1992–93 turmoil (Akyüz and Flassbeck 2002).

94 Park and Wyplosz (2007, 14), who otherwise favor the replication of the EMS by establishing an Asian Monetary System (AMS) in the way suggested by Wyplosz (2004) over other regional alternatives, recognize that should a significant number of Asian countries adopt the European strategy, "they would be unlikely to sustain the export-led strategy. Either the exchange rates would jointly float, both up and down, or, given the economic weight of the AMS countries,

attempts to manage the external parities would quickly meet strong resistance from the G7 and the IMF. This would likely signal the end of the export-led strategy for the region."

95 According to Calvo and Reinhart (2002) dollar pegging is a rational response to the problem of original sin, that is, the inability of developing countries to borrow in their own currencies. This is not relevant for most East Asian countries, which do not need to borrow in any currency. It has also become less relevant in Latin America where domestic currency debt held by nonresidents has been increasing rapidly, with international investors assuming the exchange rate risk in return for high yields. Some countries have also been able to issue local-currency-denominated global bonds at rates below those in domestic markets to benefit from lower jurisdiction spreads (Akyüz 2007).

96 These considerations are equally and even more valid for establishing a yen block in East Asia (Kwan 1998), which would face, in addition, political difficulties.

97 For the original proposal, see Williamson (1999). See also Kawai and Takagi (2000), Ogawa and Ito (2000), and Williamson (2000 and 2005). A similar proposal was made by the staff of the French and Japanese Ministries of Finance in a joint paper: a "possible solution for many emerging market economies could be a managed floating exchange-rate regime whereby the currency moves within a given implicit or explicit band with its center targeted to a basket of currencies" and "a group of countries with close trade and financial links should adopt a mechanism that automatically moves the region's exchange rates in the same direction by similar percentages" (MOF Japan 2001, 3–4).

98 However, both Williamson (2000) and Kawai and Takagi (2000) consider a BBC regime combining a band and crawl with the basket as the norm for most countries.

99 See Park and Wyplosz (2007, 13), which reiterates that an AMS modelled on the EMS would be as effective as pegging to a common basket in stabilizing the regional bilateral exchange rates.

100 If, as Williamson (2005, 11) points out, a country accepts only an obligation not to intervene in a way that would tend to push the market rate away from the reference rate, but no obligation to defend a particular rate, it can adopt a behavior of benign neglect when markets push the rate away from the central parity, and this could generate considerable instability when the band is very wide.

101 For instance, Kawai (2007) sees a common basket system as a step toward a more rigid intraregional exchange rate stabilization scheme such as an Asian snake or an Asian ERM.

102 This idea of ACU was pioneered by the Asian Development Bank. Eichengreen (2007) gives support to it as a parallel currency, while recognizing some of the difficulties noted below.

103 Whether an ACU should be introduced and used alongside a common basket is contentious. According to Williamson (2005, 1) there is nothing to preclude the introduction and use of an ACU in the common basket system, but Eichengreen (2007) sees a major contradiction since a common basket in three reserve currencies would encourage use of these outside currencies in the region instead of the ACU.

104 The ADB and the World Bank IFC issued Panda bonds in 2005. China has recently given permission to two foreign banks to issue yuan-denominated bonds in Hong Kong for sale to overseas investors (Areddy 2009). Currently there are suggestions in China that the United States government and the World Bank consider issuing yuan-denominated bonds in Hong Kong and Shanghai markets. This would mean China lending foreigners in its own currency rather than in dollars, passing the exchange rate risk onto borrowers.

105 With the 1987 Basel–Nyborg agreement the VSTF was extended to intramarginal interventions.

106 Empirical evidence indicates that the renminbi has been exerting significant impact on the exchange rates of the Asian currencies. It is also estimated, on the basis of a reserve currency model and counterfactual simulations, that the renminbi's potential as a reserve currency would be comparable to that of the Japanese yen and the British pound if it were to become fully convertible today (Chen, Peng and Shu 2009).

References

ADB (Asian Development Bank). ADO (various issues). *Asian Development Outlook*. www.adb.org. Accessed 1 July 2008.

Aghion, P., P. Bacchetta, R. Ranciere and K. Rogoff. 2006. "Exchange Rate Volatility and Productivity Growth: The Role of Financial Development." NBER Working Paper 12117.

Aguirre, A., and C. Calderón. 2005. "Real Exchange Rate Misalignments and Economic Performance." Central Bank of Chile Working Paper 315.

Aizenman, J., and J. Lee. 2005. "International Reserves: Precautionary vs. Mercantilist Views, Theory, and Evidence." IMF Working Paper 05/198.

Aizenman, J., M. D. Chinn and H. Ito. 2008. "Assessing the Emerging Global Financial Architecture: Measuring the Trilemma's Configurations over Time." NBER Working Paper 14533.

Akyüz, Y. 2006. "From Liberalization to Investment and Jobs: Lost in Translation." ILO Working Paper 74. Geneva.

______. 2007. "Debt Sustainability in Emerging Markets: A Critical Appraisal." DESA Working Paper 61.

______. 2008a. "The Current Global Financial Turmoil and Asian Developing Countries." *TWN Global Economy Series* 11.

______. 2008b. "Managing Financial Instability in Emerging Markets: A Keynesian Perspective." *METU Studies in Development* 35 (10).

______. 2009. "Industrial Tariffs, International Trade and Development." In *Industrial Policy and Development: The Political Economy of Capabilities Accumulation*, edited by G. Dosi, M. Cimoli and J. E. Stiglitz. New York: Oxford University Press.

Akyüz, Y., and A. Cornford. 2002. "Capital Flows to Developing Countries and the Reform of the International Financial System." In *Governing Globalization: Issues and Institutions*, edited by D. Nayyar, WIDER Studies in Development Economics. New York: Oxford University Press.

Akyüz, Y., and H. Flassbeck 2002. "Exchange Rate Regimes and the Scope for Regional Cooperation." In *Reforming the Global Financial Architecture*, edited by Y. Akyüz London: Zed Books.

Akyüz, Y., and C. Gore. 1996. "The Investment–Profits Nexus in East Asian Industrialisation." *World Development* 24 (3): 461–70.

______. 2001. African Economic Development in a Comparative Perspective. *Cambridge Journal of Economics* 25 (3): 265–88.

Amiti, M., and K. Stiroh. 2007. "Is the United States Losing Its Productivity Advantage?" *Current Issues in Economics and Finance* 13 (8). Federal Reserve Bank of New York.

Amiti, M., and D. R. Davis. 2009. "What's Behind Volatile Import Prices from China?" *Current Issues in Economics and Finance* 15 (1). Federal Reserve Bank of New York.

Anderlini, J. 2007. "China Hits Out over 'Hot Money.'" *Financial Times*, 27 June.

Areddy, J. T. 2009. "China Loosens Yuan-Bond Market." *Wall Street Journal*, 20 May.

Aricanli, T., and D. Rodrik, eds. 1990. *The Political Economy of Turkey*. London: Macmillan.

AsiaNews. 2009. "Chinese Yuan Set to Replace Dollar." 1 March. http://www.asianews.it/index.php?l=en&art=14131. Accessed 15 March 2009.

Banister, J. 2005. "Manufacturing Earnings and Compensation in China." *Monthly Labor Review*, August.

Bayoumi, T., and B. Eichengreen. 1997. "Ever Closer to Heaven. An Optimum Currency Area Index for European Countries." *European Economic Review* 41 (3–5): 761–70.

______. 1999. "Is Asia an Optimal Currency Area? Can It Become One? Regional, Global, and Historical Perspectives on Monetary Relations." In *Exchange Rate Policies in Emerging Asian Countries*, edited by S. Collignon, J. Pisani-Ferry, and Y. C. Park. London: Routledge, 347–367.

Bayoumi, T., B. Eichengreen and P. Mauro. 2000. "On Regional Monetary Arrangements for ASEAN." *Journal of the Japanese and International Economies* 14 (2): 121–48.

Bayoumi, T., and P. Mauro. 1999. "The Suitability of ASEAN for a Regional Currency Arrangement." IMF Working Paper WP/99/162. Washington, DC.

Bhagwati, J. 1958. "Immiserizing Growth: A Geometrical Note." *The Review of Economic Studies* 25 (3), June.

______. 1994. "Free Trade: Old and New Challenges." *The Economic Journal* 104, March: 231–246.

BIS (Bank for International Settlements). 2001. *Annual Report.* Basel.

______. 2005. "Foreign Exchange Market Intervention in Emerging Markets: Motives, Techniques and Implications." BIS Papers 24. Basel.

______. 2007. *Annual Report.* Basel.

______. 2009. "Capital Flows and Emerging Market Economies." CGFS Paper 33. Basel.

Bofinger, P., and H. Flassbeck. 2000. "The European Monetary System (1979–88): Achievements, Flaws and Applicability to Other Regions of the World." Paper prepared for United Nations Commission for Europe, Geneva.

Boratav, K. 2001. "Movements of Relative Agricultural Prices in Sub-Saharan Africa," *Cambridge Journal of Economics* 25 (3): 395–416.

Borio, C., C. Furfine and P. Lowe. 2001. "Procyclicality of the Financial System and Financial Stability: Issues and Policy Options." BIS Working Paper 1. Basel.

Borio, C., and P. Lowe. 2002. "Assets Prices, Financial and Monetary Stability: Exploring the Nexus." BIS Working Paper 114. Basel.

Bowring, P. 2008a. "Asia Won't Get Away Clean." *Asia Sentinel*, 25 January.

______. 2008b. "StanChart Leaves Investors Out in the Cold." *Asia Sentinel*. 12 February.

Branstetter, L., and N. Lardy. 2006. "China's Embrace of Globalization." NBER Working Paper 12373.

Buiter, W. H. 1995. "Macroeconomic Policy During a Transition to Monetary Union." CEPR Discussion Paper 1222.

Burton, J. 2005. "Singapore Sees 'Basket, Band and Crawl' System as Template for E. Asia." *Financial Times*, 23 July.

Calvo, G., and C. Reinhart. 2002. Fear of Floating. *Quarterly Journal of Economics* 117, May: 379–408.

Cavallo, D. F., J. A. Cottani and M. S. Kahn. 1990. "Real Exchange Rate Behavior and Economic Performance in LDCs." *Economic Development and Cultural Change* 39: 61–76.

Cayazzo, J., A. G. Pascual, E. Gutierez and S. Heysen. 2006. "Toward an Effective Supervision of Partially Dollarized Banking Systems." IMF Working Paper 06/32.

CEPR (Centre for Economic Policy Research). 2000. "Exchange Rate Risk: The Limits of Hedging." http://dev3.cepr.org/pubs/bulletin/meets/516.htm. Accessed 3 September 2008.

CGD (Commission on Growth and Development). 2008. *The Growth Report: Strategies for Sustained Growth and Inclusive Development.* The International Bank for Reconstruction and Development. Washington, DC.

Chai-Anant, C., and C. Ho. 2008. "Understanding Asian Equity Flows, Market Returns and Exchange Rates." BIS Working Paper 245.

Chancellor, E. 2008. "Bursting Chinese Bubble Could Hurt." *Independent Investor* 18, January.

Chandrasekhar, C. P. 2008. "Financial Liberalization and the New Dynamics of Growth in India." *TWN Global Economy Series* 13.

Chen, H., W. Peng and C. Shu. 2009. "Renminbi as an International Currency: Potential and Policy Considerations." Hong Kong Institute of Monetary Research Working Paper 18/2009.

Choi, W. G, S. Sharma and M. Strömqvist. 2007. "Capital Flows, Financial Integration, and International Reserve Holdings: The Recent Experience of Emerging Markets and Advanced Economies." IMF Working Paper 07/151.

Chow, H. K., and Y. Kim. 2003. "A Common Currency Peg in East Asia? Perspectives from Western Europe." *Journal of Macroeconomics* 25 (3): 33–50

Chowdhury, A. 2005. "Exchange Rate Policy and Poverty Reduction: Thematic Report on the Macroeconomics of Poverty Reduction." UNDP Regional Centre, Colombo.

______. 2009. "Korea: Asset Deflation Impact on Construction and Banking." *The Asia Investigator.* 19 January. http://www.theiafm.org/publications/370_SAP23775.pdf. Accessed 14 March 2010.

Citigroup. 2009. "Korea: Asset Deflation Impact on Construction and Banking." *The Asia Investigator.* 19 January. http://www.theiafm.org/publications/370_SAP23775.pdf. Accessed 14 March 2009.

Corden, W. M. 1985. "Exchange Rate Protection." In *Protection, Growth and Trade: Essays in International Economics.* Oxford: Basil Blackwell.

______. 2008. Reflections on the Indian Exchange Rate Regime. Unpublished paper, University of Melbourne. www.ncaer.org/downloads/IPF2008/MaxCordenPaper.pdf.

Damill, M., R. Frenkel and R. Maurizio. 2007. "Macroeconomic Policy Changes in Argentina at the Turn of the Century." International Institute for Labour Studies, Research Series. Geneva.

Delgado, C. 1995. "Agricultural Diversification and Export Promotion in Sub-Saharan Africa." *Food Policy* 20 (3): 225–43.

Diaz-Alejandro, C. F. 1963. "A Note on the Impact of Devaluation and the Redistributive Effect." *Journal of Political Economy* 71: 577–80.

______. 1985. "Good-bye Financial Repression, Hello Financial Crash." *Journal of Development Economics* 19 (1–2).

Disyatat, P., and G. Galati. 2005. "The Effectiveness of Foreign Exchange Intervention in Emerging Market Economies." BIS Papers 24, May: 97–113.

Dollar, D. 1992. "Outward-Oriented Developing Economies Really Do Grow More Rapidly: Evidence from 95 LDCs, 1976–1985." *Economic Development and Cultural Change* 40: 523–44.

Dumas, B. 1994. "Short- and Long-Term Hedging for the Corporation." CEPR Discussion Paper 1083.

Edwards, S. 1989. *Real Exchange Rates, Devaluation, and Adjustment: Exchange Rate Policy in Developing Countries.* Cambridge, MA: MIT Press.

Edwards, S., and M. A. Savastano. 1999. "Exchange Rates in Emerging Economies: What Do We Know? What Do We Need To Know?" NBER Working Paper 7228.

Eichengreen, B. 2007. "The Parallel Currency Approach to Asian Monetary Integration." In *Asian Financial and Monetary Integration.* Singapore Monetary Authority.

______. 2008. "The Real Exchange Rate and Economic Growth." Commission on Growth and Development Working Paper 4.

ESCAP (Economic and Social Commission for Asia and the Pacific). 2007. *Key Economic Developments in the Asia–Pacific Region 2008.* Bangkok: United Nations.

______. 2008. *Macroeconomic Policy Brief,* vol. 1: *Financial Crisis* 1, December.

Epstein, G., I. Grabel and K. S. Jomo. 2003. "Capital Management Techniques in Developing Countries: An Assessment of Experiences from the 1990s and Lessons for the Future." UNCTAD, G-24 Discussion Paper 27.

Fischer, S. 2001. "Exchange Rate Regimes: Is the Bipolar View Correct?" *Journal of Economic Perspectives* 15 (2): 3–24.

Forbes. 2008. "China Seeks to Revive Property Market." 30 December. http://www.forbes.com/2008/12/29/china-cisis-property-cx_1230oxford.html. Accessed 2 February 2010.

Frankel, J. A. 2005. Mundell-Fleming Lecture: "Contractionary Currency Crashes in Developing Countries." IMF Staff Papers 52 (2): 149–92.

Frankel, J. A., and A. K. Rose. 1996. "The Endogeneity of the Optimum Currency Area Criteria." NBER Working Paper 5700.

Frenkel, R. 2008. "The Competitive Real Exchange-Rate Regime, Inflation and Monetary Policy." CEPAL Review 96: 191–201.

Frenkel, R., and M. Rapetti. 2008. "Economic Development and the New Order in the International Financial System." Paper presented at the Initiative for Policy Dialogue Meeting of the Task Force on Financial Markets Regulation at the University of Manchester's Brooks World Poverty Institute, 1–2 July.

Frenkel, R., and L. Taylor. 2006. "Real Exchange Rate, Monetary Policy and Employment." DESA Working Paper 19. New York: United Nations.

Furman, J., and J. Stiglitz. 1998. "Economic Crises: Evidence and Insights from East Asia." *Brookings Papers on Economic Activity* 2: 115–35.

Gala, P. 2007. "Real Exchange Rate Levels and Economic Development: Theoretical Analysis and Econometric Evidence." *Cambridge Journal of Economics* 32 (2): 273–88.

Galindo, A., A. Izquierdo and J. M. Montero. 2006. "Real Exchange Rates, Dollarization and Industrial Employment in Latin America." Inter-American Development Bank, Working Paper 575.

Ghosh, A. R. and H. C. Wolf. 1994. "How Many Monies? A Genetic Approach to Finding Optimum Currency Areas." NBER Working Paper 4805.

Gochoco-Bautista, M. S. 2008. "Asset Prices and Monetary Policy: Booms and Fat Tails in East Asia." BIS Working Paper 243.

Goldstein, M., and N. R. Lardy. 2004. "What Kind of Landing for the Chinese Economy?" Institute for International Economics, Washington, DC, Policy Brief 04-7.

Goto, J., and K. Hamada. 1994. "Economic Preconditions for Asian Regional Integration." In *Macroeconomic Linkages, Savings, Exchange Rates, and Capital Flows*, edited by T. Ito and A. Krueger. Chicago: University of Chicago Press.

Harberger, A. C. 2004. "The Real Exchange Rate: Issues of Concept and Measurement." Paper prepared for a conference in honor of Michael Mussa, University of California, Los Angeles. www.imf.org/external/np/res/seminars/2004/mussa/pdf/haberg.pdf. Accessed 15 December 2008.

Hausman, R., L. Pritchett and D. Rodrik. 2004. "Growth Accelerations." NBER Working Paper 10566.

Henning, C. R. 2002. *East Asian Financial Cooperation*. Policy Analyses in International Economics 68. Institute for International Economics, Washington, DC.

______. 2009. "Moment of Truth." *Emerging Markets*. 3 May.

Helleiner, G., ed. 1994. *Trade Policy and Industrialization in Turbulent Times*. London: Routledge.

IIF (Institute of International Finance) (various issues). *Capital Flows to Emerging Markets*. www.iif.com.

ILO (International Labour Organization). 2004. *A Fair Globalization: Creating Opportunities for All*. World Commission on the Social Dimension of Globalization, ILO, Geneva.

______. 2007. *Key Indicators of the Labour Market*, fifth edition. www.ilo.org/public/english/employment/strat/kilm/index.htm. Accessed 21 September 2008.

IMF. 2005. "De Facto Classification of Exchange Rate Regimes and Monetary Policy Framework." 30 June. Washington, DC.

______. 2007. *Balance of Payments and International Investment Position Manual*, sixth edition, draft BPM6. Washington, DC.

______. 2008. "De Facto Classification of Exchange Rate Regimes and Monetary Policy Framework." 31 April. Washington, DC.

IMF GFSR (various issues). *Global Financial Stability Report*. Washington, DC.

IMF REOAP (various issues). *Regional Economic Outlook: Asia and Pacific*. October. Washington, DC.

IMF WEO (various issues). *World Economic Outlook*. Washington, DC.

Jeanne, O., and R. Rancière. 2006. "The Optimal Level of International Reserves for Emerging Market Countries: Formulas and Applications." Working Paper 06/229.

Jenkins, G. P. and C-Y Kuo. 1997. "Which Policies Are Important for Industrialization: The Case of Taiwan." Development Discussion Paper 594, Harvard Institute for International Development.

Kaldor, N. 1989. "The Role of Increasing Returns, Technical Progress and Cumulative Causation in the Theory of International Trade and Economic Growth." In *The Essential Kaldor*, edited by F. Targetti and A. P. Thirlwall. London: Duckworth.

Karshenas, M. 2001. "Industrial and Economic Development in Sub-Saharan Africa and Asia." *Cambridge Journal of Economics* 25 (3): 315–342.

Kate, D. T. and S. Adam. 2008. "Thailand Proposes Asia Pool of $350 Billion for Crisis." Bloomberg.com. 22 October. http://www.bloomberg.com/apps/news?pid=newsarchive&sid=aUnG8ywDK._E. Accessed 20 December 2008.

Kawai, M. 2007. "Toward a Regional Exchange Rate Regime in East Asia." ADBI Discussion Paper 68.

Kawai, M., and T. Motonishi. 2005. "Macroeconomic Interdependence in East Asia: Empirical Evidence and Issues." In *Asian Economic Cooperation and Integration: Progress, Prospects and Challenges*. Manila: ADB, 213–68.

Kawai, M., and S. Takagi. 2000. "Proposed Strategy for a Regional Exchange Rate Arrangement in Post Crisis East Asia." World Bank Policy Research Working Paper 2503. Washington, DC.

Keesing, D., and S. Lall. 1992. "Marketing Manufactured Exports from Developing Countries: Learning Sequence and Public Support." In *Trade Policy, Industrialization and Development: New Perspectives*, edited by G. Helleiner. Oxford: Clarendon Press.

Keifman, S. 2007. "Le rapport entre taux de change et niveau d'emploi en Argentine: une revision de l'explication structuraliste." *Revue Tiers Monde* 189 (1).

Keynes, J. M. 1980. John Maynard Keynes at the House of Lords, 23 May 1944. In *The Collected Writings of John Maynard Keynes*, edited by Donald Moggridge, vol. 26: *Activities 1941–1946, Shaping the Post-War World: Bretton Woods and Reparations*. Cambridge: Cambridge University Press.

Khor, M. 2009. "Financial Policy and the Management of Capital Flows: The Case of Malaysia." *TWN Global Economy Series* 16.

Kim, D. 2007. "An East Asian Currency Union? The Empirical Nature of Macroeconomic Shocks in East Asia." *Journal of Asian Economies* 18 (6): 847–66.

Kochhar, K., P. Loungani and M. R. Stone. 1998. "The East Asian Crisis: Macroeconomic Developments and Policy Lessons." IMF Working Paper 98/128. Washington, DC.

Krugman, P. 1979. "Increasing Returns, Monopolistic Competition and International Trade." *Journal of International Economics* 9, November: 469–79.

_______. 1999. "Balance Sheets Effects, the Transfer Problem, and Financial Crises. In *International Finance and Financial Crises: Essays in Honor of Robert Flood*, edited by P. Isarc, A. Razin and A. Rose. New York: Kluwer Academic Publishers: 31–44.

Kwan, C. H. 1998. "The Possibility of Forming a Yen Bloc in Asia." *Journal of Asian Economics* 9 (4): 555–80.

Lall, S. 2004. "Reinventing Industrial Strategy: The Role of Government Policy in Building Industrial Competitiveness." UNCTAD, G-24 Discussion Paper 28. Geneva.

Ma, G., and R. N. McCauley. 2007. "Do China's Capital Controls Still Bind? Implications for Monetary Autonomy and Capital Liberalisation." BIS Working Paper 233.

Marquez, G., and C. Pagés. 1998. "Trade, Employment: Evidence from Latin America and Caribbean." Inter-American Development Bank, Research Department Working Paper 336. Washington, DC.

MAS (Monetary Authority of Singapore). 2003. *Macroeconomic Review*, 2 (1), January.

_______. 2007. *Asian Financial and Monetary Integration*. Singapore.

Mayer, J. 2003. "The Fallacy of Composition: A Review of the Literature." UNCTAD Discussion Paper 166.

McCauley, R. 2008. "Managing Recent Hot Money Flows in Asia." ADBI Discussion Paper 99. Tokyo.

McKinnon, R. I. 2001. "After the Crisis, the East Asian Dollar Standard Resurrected: An Interpretation of High Frequency Exchange Rate Pegging." Hong Kong Institute for Monetary Research Working Paper 4/2001.

Mihaljek, D. 2005. "Survey of Central Bank Views on Effectiveness of Intervention." BIS Working Papers 24, May: 82–96.

MOF, Japan (Ministry of Finance). 2001. "Exchange Rate Regimes for Emerging Market Economies." Discussion Paper prepared by staff of the French and Japanese Ministries of Finance, Ministry of Finance, Tokyo. 16 January.

Mohanty, M. S., and P. Turner. 2006. "Foreign Exchange Reserve Accumulation in Emerging Markets: What are the Domestic Implications?" *BIS Quarterly Review*, September: 39–52.

Nagaraj, R. 2005. "Industrial Growth in China and India: A Preliminary Comparison." *Economic and Political Weekly*, 21 May.

Nam, S. W. and S. J. Kim. 1999. "Evaluation of Korea's Exchange Rate Policy." In *Changes in Exchange Rate Polices in Rapidly Developing Countries: Theory, Practice, and Policy Issues*, edited by T. Ito and A. Krueger. NBER East Asia Seminar on Economics Series; Chicago: University of Chicago Press.

Nicolas, F. 1999. "Is There a Case for a Single Currency within ASEAN?" *Singapore Economic Review* 44 (1): 1–25.

Obstfeld, Maurice, Jay C. Shambaugh and Alan M Taylor. 2009. "Financial Instability, Reserves, and Central Bank Swap Lines in the Panic of 2008." *American Economic Review* 99 (2): 480–86.

OECD (Organization for Economic Cooperation and Development). 2007. *Economic Outlook* 82. Paris.

Ogawa, E., and T. Ito. 2000. "On the Desirability of a Regional Basket Currency Arrangement." NBER Working Paper 8002.

Palley, T. 2003. "International Trade, Macroeconomics, and Exchange Rates: Re-examining the Foundations of Trade Policy." Paper presented at conference on Globalization and the Myths of Free Trade, New School for Social Research, New York, 18 April.

Park, Y. C. and C. Wyplosz. 2007. "Exchange Rate Arrangements in Asia: Do they Matter?" HEI Working Paper 04/2007. Graduate Institute of International Studies, Geneva.

Parrado, E. 2004. "Singapore's Unique Monetary Policy: How Does It Work?" IMF Working Paper 04/10.

Pearlstein, S. 2008. "More Room to Fall. *Washington Post*, 22 January.

Pesek, W. 2008. "Asia is About to Give U.S. a Kick in the Fannie." Bloomberg.com. http://www.bloomberg.com/apps/news?pid=newsarchive&sid=aqu59cnYfsFY. Accessed 1 September 2008.

Plummer, M. G. and G. Wignaraja. 2007. "The Post-Crisis Sequencing of Economic Integration in Asia: Trade as a Complement to a Monetary Future." ADB Working Paper on Regional Economic Integration 9.

Polak, J. J. and P. B. Clark. 2006. "Reducing the Costs of Holding Reserves: A New Perspective on Special Drawing Rights." In *The New Public Finance: Responding to Global Challenges*, edited by I. Kaul and P. Conceição. New York: Oxford University Press.

Rajan, R. S. and C-H. Shen. 2006. "Are Crisis-Induced Devaluations Contractionary? Pacific Basin Working Paper BP02-06. Federal Reserve Bank of San Francisco.

Rana, P. B. 2006. Economic Integration in East Asia: Trends, Prospects, and a Possible Road Map." ADB, Working Paper Regional Economic Integration Series 2.

Razin, O. and S. M. Collins. 1999. "Real Exchange Rate Misalignments and Growth." NBER Working Paper 6174.

Reinhart, C., and V. Reinhart. 1998. "Some Lessons for Policymakers Who Deal With the Mixed Blessing of Capital Inflows." In *Capital Flows and Financial Crises*, edited by M. Kahler. Ithaca, New York: Cornel University Press.

Roach, S. S. 2007. "Protectionist Threats: Then and Now." Morgan Stanley Global Economic Forum, 26 January.

Rodrik, D. 1999. "Response to Srinivasan and Bhagwati: Outward Orientation and Development: Are Revisionists Right?" Unpublished paper, Harvard University.

______. 2005. "Why We Learn Nothing from Regressing Economic Growth on Policies." Unpublished paper, Harvard University.

______. 2006. "The Social Cost of Foreign Exchange Reserves." NBER Working Paper 11952.

______. 2008. "The Real Exchange Rate and Economic Growth." John F. Kennedy School of Government, Harvard University, September.

Rogoff, K. 1999. "International Institutions for Reducing Global Financial Instability." *The Journal of Economic Perspectives* 13 (4). Fall.

Rogoff, K. S., A. M. Husain, A. Mody, R. Brooks, and N. Ooomes. 2004. "Evolution and Performance of Exchange Rate Regimes." IMF Occasional Paper 229, Washington, DC.

Sachs, J. 1985. "External Debt and Macroeconomic Performance in Latin America and East Asia." Brooking Papers on Economic Activity 2: 523–73.

Saxena, S., and A. Villar. 2008. "Hedging Instruments in Emerging Market Economies." BIS Working Paper 44, *Financial Globalization and Emerging Market Capital Flows*, December.

Setser, B. 2008. "The Debate over the Pace of Hot Money Flows into China." 20 February. http://blogs.cfr.org/setser/2008/02/20/the-debate-over-the-pace-of-hot-money-flows-into/. Accessed 15 March 2008.

Shafaeddin, M. 1992. "Import Shortages and Inflationary Impact of Devaluation." *Industry and Development* 32: 19–37.

______. 2008. "South–South Regionalism and Trade Cooperation in the Asia–Pacific Region, Policy Paper." UNDP Regional Centre, Colombo.

Shirono. K. 2008. "Real Effects of Common Currencies in East Asia." *Journal of Asian Economics* 19 (3): 199–212.

Solow, R. M. 2001. "Applying Growth Theory across Countries. *The World Bank Economic Review* 15 (2): 283–88.

Srinivasan, T. N., and J. Bhagwati. 1999. "Outward-Orientation and Development: Are Revisionists Right?" Yale University, Economic Growth Center, Center Discussion Paper 806

Stone, M., H. Anderson and R. Veyrune. 2008. "Exchange Rate Regimes: Fix or Float?" *Finance and Development* 45 (1): 42–43

Swoboda, A. K. 1976. *Capital Movements and their Control.* Geneva: Sijthoff Leiden, Institute, Universitaire de Hautes Etudes Internationales.

Taylor, L. 1994. "Gap Models". *Journal of Development Economics* 45:17–34.

Thirlwall, A. P. 2003a. *Trade, Balance of Payments and Exchange Rate Policy in Developing Countries.* Cheltenham: Edward Elgar.

______. 2003b. "'Old' Thoughts on 'New' Growth Theory." In *Old and New Growth Theories: An Assessment,* edited by N. Salvatori. Cheltenham: Edward Elgar.

Thirlwall, A. P. and G. Sanna. 1996. "'New' Growth Theory and Macro-economic Determinants of Growth: An Evaluation and Further Evidence." In *Employment, Economic Growth and the Tyranny of the Market,* edited by P. Arestis. Cheltenham: Edward Elgar.

Tovar, C. E. 2006. "Devaluations, Output, and the Balance Sheet Effect: A Structural Econometric Analysis." BIS Working Paper 215.

Turner, P. 2008. "Financial Globalisation and Emerging Market Capital Flows, BIS Paper 44, *Financial Globalization and Emerging Market Capital Flows*, December.

UNCTAD TDR (various issues). *Trade and Development Report.* Geneva: United Nations.

Van der Hoeven, R. and M. Lübker. 2005. "Financial Openness and Employment: The Need for Coherent International and National Policies." Paper prepared for the G24 Technical Group Meeting. 15–16 September. IMF, Washington, DC.

White, W. 2006. "Procyclicality in the Financial System: Do We Need a New Macrofinancial Stabilization Framework?" BIS Working Paper 193. Basel.

Williamson, J. 1999. "The Case for a Common Basket Peg for East Asian Currencies." In *Exchange Rate Policies in Emerging Asian Countries*, edited by S. Collignon, J. Pisani-Ferry, and Y. Park. London: Routledge.

______. 2000. "*Exchange Rate Regimes for Emerging Markets: Reviving the Intermediate Option.*" Peterson Institute for International Economics, Policy Analysis in International Economics 60. Washington, DC.

______. 2005. "A Currency Basket for East Asia, Not Just China." Policy Brief PB-05-1. Peterson Institute for International Economics, Washington DC.

World Bank. 2003. *Global Economic Prospects.* Washington, DC.

Wyplosz, C. 2004. "Regional Exchange Rate Arrangements: Lessons from Europe for East Asia." In *Monetary and Financial Integration in East Asia: The Way Ahead* 2. Asian Development Bank. Basingstoke: Palgrave Macmillan.

Xinhuanet. 2009a. "Chinese Housing Prices Decline for the First Time Since 2005." 10 January. http://news.xinhuanet.com/english/2009-01/10/content_10634712.htm. Accessed 20 January 2009.

______. 2009b. "Chinese Policymakers Need Caution to Counter Financial Crisis." 6 February. http://news.xinhuanet.com/english/2009-02/06/content_10773167.htm. Accessed 15 February 2009.

Yu, Y. D. 2007. "Global Imbalances and China." *The Australian Economic Review* 40 (1): 3–23.

______. 2008. "Managing Capital Flows: The Case of the People's Republic of China." ADBI Discussion Paper, 96. Tokyo.

______. 2009. "The Management of Cross-Border Capital Flows and Macroeconomic Stability in China." *TWN Global Economy Series* 14.

Zhang, Z., K. Sato and M McAleer. 2004. "Is a Monetary Union Feasible in East Asia?" *Applied Economics* 36(10): 1031–43.

Zeng, Z., and Z. Yumin. 2002. "China's Terms of Trade in Manufactures: 1993–2000." UNCTAD Discussion Paper 161.

Chapter V

REFORMING THE IMF: BACK TO THE DRAWING BOARD[1]

A. Introduction

> The best reformers the world has ever seen are those who commence on themselves.
> George Bernard Shaw

There have been widespread misgivings about international economic cooperation in recent years even as the need for global collective action has grown because of recurrent financial crises in emerging markets, the increased gap between the rich and the poor, and the persistence of extreme poverty in many countries in the developing world. Perhaps more than any other international organization the International Monetary Fund (IMF) has been the focus of these misgivings.

Several observers including former treasury secretaries of the United States, a Nobel Prize–winning economist and many NGOs have called for its abolition on the grounds that it is no longer needed, or that its interventions in emerging market crises are not only wasteful but also harmful for international economic stability, or that its programs in the Third World serve to aggravate rather than alleviate poverty.[2] Others want the IMF to be merged into the World Bank because they see them as doing pretty much the same thing with the same clientele.[3]

Many who still wish to keep the IMF as an independent institution with a distinct mission call for reform of both what it has been doing and how it has been doing it.[4] All these groups include individuals across a wide spectrum of political opinion, ranging from conservative free marketers to antiglobalisers.

The principal rationale for global collective action in financial matters and for institutions needed to facilitate such action is market failure. More specifically, international financial markets fail to provide adequate liquidity and development financing for a large number of countries, and they are the main source of global economic instability. These have repercussions not only for the countries directly concerned but also for the international community as a whole because of the existence of international externalities. Furthermore, due to cross-border interdependence, the pursuit of national interests by individual countries in macroeconomic and financial policies can result in negative global externalities, and preventing conflicts and collective damage calls for a certain degree of multilateral discipline over national policymaking as well as economic cooperation.[5]

Such concerns in fact provided the original rationale for the creation of the IMF and the World Bank with a clear division of labor between the two. However, these institutions have gone through considerable transformation in response to changes that have taken place in the world economic and political landscape in the past 60 years. In particular, the IMF is no longer performing the functions it was originally designed for, namely, securing multilateral discipline in exchange rate policies and providing liquidity for current account financing. Rather, it has been focusing on development finance and policy and poverty alleviation in poor countries, and the management and resolution of capital account crises in emerging markets.

This chapter argues that there is no sound rationale for the Fund to be involved in development matters, including long-term lending. This is also true for several areas of policy closely connected to development, most notably trade policy which is a matter for multilateral negotiations elsewhere in the global system. On the other hand, while the management and resolution of financial crises in emerging markets constitute a key area of interest to the IMF in the context of its broader objective of securing international monetary and financial stability, there is little rationale for financial bailout operations that have so far been the main instrument of the Fund's interventions in such crises. The original considerations that precluded IMF lending to finance capital outflows continue to be equally valid today since such operations do not correct but aggravate market failures. There are other institutions and mechanisms that can serve better the objectives that may be sought by such lending.

By contrast the IMF should pay much greater attention to two areas in which its existence carries a stronger rationale, namely, short-term, countercyclical current account financing and effective surveillance over national macroeconomic and financial policies, particularly of countries which have a disproportionately large impact on international monetary and financial stability. In other words, a genuine reform of the Fund would require as much a redirection of its activities as improvements in its policies and operational modalities. However, none of these would be possible without addressing shortcomings in its governance structure.

The purpose of this chapter is not to provide a blueprint for the reform of the IMF, but to discuss and elaborate a number of broad issues that would need to be taken into account in any serious attempt to make the Fund a genuinely multilateral institution with equal rights and obligations for all its members, in practice as well as in theory. The next section will give a brief description of the original rationale for the Fund, its evolution over the past sixty years and current focus. This is followed by a discussion of what the IMF is but should not be doing; that is, development policy and financing, and trade policy. Section E makes a critical assessment of the Fund's role in crisis management and resolution while Section F turns to issues related to the reform of its lending policy and resources. This is followed by a section on the Fund's surveillance function. Section H focuses on governance issues, notably the prerequisites for a genuinely symmetrical and multilateral financial institution. The chapter ends with a summary of the main proposals.

B. The Original Rationale and the Postwar Evolution of the IMF

The main objective pursued by the architects of the postwar economic system with the creation of the IMF was to avoid the recurrence of a number of difficulties that had led to the breakdown of international trade and payments in the interwar period. These difficulties arose in large part because of the lack of multilateral arrangements to facilitate an orderly payments adjustment in countries facing large external debt and deficits. Under conditions of excessively volatile short-term capital flows and in the absence of any obligation on the side of the surplus countries to share the burden of adjustment, deficit countries had been forced to undertake deflationary measures, or resort to trade and exchange restrictions and competitive devaluations in order to protect economic activity and employment, thereby generating negative externalities and frictions in international economic relations.

Arrangements for multilateral discipline over exchange rate policies, provision of adequate international liquidity, and restrictions over destabilizing capital flows were thus seen as essential for international monetary stability and the prevention of tensions and disruptions in international trade and payments. The IMF was designed to ensure an orderly system of international payments at stable but multilaterally negotiated, adjustable exchange rates under conditions of strictly limited international capital flows.

A key task of the Fund was to provide international liquidity in order to avoid deflationary and destabilizing adjustments and trade and exchange restrictions in countries facing temporary balance of payments deficits. Although the responsibility for addressing the problems associated with fluctuations in export earnings of developing countries effectively fell under the IMF's role for the provision of liquidity, the Fund was created primarily for securing the stability of external payments and exchange rates of the major industrial countries, rather than for the stabilization of balance of payments of developing countries.

There was a certain degree of creative ambiguity in the way the Fund's articles were drafted in order to reach consensus. This was the case for exchange rate arrangements which sought to reconcile multilateral discipline with national autonomy. Countries undertook obligations to maintain their exchange rates within a narrow range of their par values and were allowed to change their par values under fundamental disequilibrium, but the latter was never defined in the Articles of Agreement. An unauthorized change in par value was not a violation of the articles, but would enable the Fund to withhold the member's access to its resources and even to force the member to withdraw (Dam 1982, 90–93).

This was also the case with arrangements regarding the modalities for the provision of liquidity, one of the most controversial issues during the negotiations. Keynes strongly argued that members should have unconditional access to the Fund within the limits of their quotas and that "it would be very unwise to try to make an untried institution too grandmotherly" (IMF 1969, vol. 1, 72). However, the United States resisted unconditional drawings on the grounds that it would be the only source of net credit in the immediate postwar era since the dollar was then the only convertible currency. The compromise agreed to in Article V entitling members "to purchase the currencies of other members from the Fund," together with the absence of the language of credit from the articles, had the connotation that members would have the right to determine how much they would draw within the limits of their quotas, treating their subscriptions as their own reserves (Dam 1982, 106; and Dell 1981, 4–5). Most countries believed that this formulation gave members unconditional drawing rights, though there was considerable room for other interpretation.

Access to the Fund was restricted to current account financing. The Fund was prohibited to lend to meet sustained outflow of capital and empowered to compel a member to exercise capital controls as a condition for access to its resources. In effect, these arrangements discouraged reliance on private flows for balance of payment financing. During the negotiations for the Bank there was considerable debate on whether the task could be effectively performed by private lenders, but this was not the case for IMF financing. Although there were some instances of currency stabilization in the interwar years supported by officially arranged private lending (Oliver 1975, 12–15), it was almost taken for granted that commercial banks could not be relied on for such a task, particularly given the high degree of volatility of short-term capital flows during interwar years and procyclical behavior of private lending.

The members' contributions to the Fund, their drawing rights and voting rights were all linked to a single concept of quotas, determined through a highly politicized exercise so as to give an effective veto power to the United States over key decisions.[6] This has been an important factor in the evolution of the Fund over subsequent years, particularly with respect to conditions governing the members' drawings and the operational procedures followed.[7]

The process of legitimizing and ratcheting conditionality started soon after the Bretton Woods Conference. A key decision in 1952 formally adopted conditionality and introduced standby arrangements as the central operational modality (IMF 1969, vol. 3, 228–30). This was followed by a 1956 decision on the phased drawings in order to better enforce conditionality with loans disbursed in tranches, contingent on the satisfactory achievement of agreed targets, and the proliferation of performance criteria.[8] Although the board decided in 1968 to limit the number of performance criteria after developing countries argued that the minimum conditionality applied to the drawing by the United Kingdom in 1967 should become the norm, in practice there was no easing of conditionality, particularly after it was given legal sanction in 1969 through an amendment of the articles.[9]

As a result of these changes, automatic drawing has been confined to the reserve tranche with higher tranches bringing tighter conditionality. Thus, the Fund has moved away from provision of liquidity; that is, finance available on short notice and virtually unconditionally, toward finance supplied on the basis of negotiated conditions and made available through successive tranches.[10] And since the IMF quotas have considerably lagged behind the growth of world trade, countries' access to balance of payments financing has come increasingly under IMF policy oversight.

But perhaps one of the biggest divergences from the Bretton Woods objectives has been in the content of conditionality rather than the principle. Through conditionality the Fund has effectively sought to impose exactly the kind of policies that the postwar planners wanted to avoid in countries facing payments difficulties – austerity and destabilizing currency adjustments. Austerity has been promoted not only when balance of payments difficulties were due to excessive domestic spending or distortions in the price structure, but also when they resulted from external disturbances such as adverse terms of trade movements, hikes in international interest rates or trade measures introduced by another country. Furthermore, the distinction between temporary and structural disequilibria has become blurred, often implying that a developing country should interpret every positive shock as temporary and thus refrain from using it as an opportunity for expansion, and every negative shock as permanent, thus adjusting to it by cutting growth and/or altering the domestic price structure.

The evolution of IMF conditionality has been shaped by shifts in economic and political conditions and interests of its major shareholders. Initially the United States had insisted on some form of conditionality to stem excessive reliance on dollar credits. Subsequently, it used conditionality to pursue its national interests. Europe, notably the United Kingdom, initially resisted conditionality because of its need to draw on the Fund's resources. Subsequently, when they no longer relied on the Fund, conditionality ceased to be a problem for the European countries, including for the smaller ones which took refuge in the European Monetary System, losing monetary autonomy vis-à-vis Germany but gaining considerable protection from Fund conditionality.[11]

A major transformation of the Fund took place with the breakdown of the Bretton Woods exchange rate system brought about in large part by inconsistencies of policies among major industrial countries and rapid growth of international financial markets and capital movements. While floating was adopted with the understanding that its stability depended upon orderly underlying conditions, the obligations undertaken by countries were, as pointed out by Triffin (1976, 47–48), "so general and obvious as to appear rather superfluous" and the system "essentially proposed to legalise [...] the widespread and illegal repudiation of Bretton Woods commitments, without putting any other binding commitments in their place." This in effect meant that currency stability ceased to be a key objective of international economic cooperation. It also meant that there would no longer be any mechanism to ensure effective multilateral discipline over the policies of non-borrowing members of the IMF.

In its operations in developing countries the focus of the Fund was initially on short-term current account financing. The Compensatory Financing Facility (CFF) introduced in the early 1960s as a result of a UN initiative enabled countries facing temporary shortfalls in primary export earnings to draw on the Fund beyond their normal drawing rights without the performance criteria normally required for upper credit tranches (Dam 1982, 127–28). However, automaticity was effectively removed by a subsequent decision of the Fund (Dell 1985, 245), and the "reforms" introduced in 2000 tightened further the circumstances for unconditional access to CFF (IMF 2004b, 10).

A number of other similar ad hoc facilities have also been discontinued, including the buffer stock financing facility introduced in the late 1960s. This is also true for the two oil facilities of the 1970s which constituted exceptional steps in IMF lending practices as they had been introduced as deliberate countercyclical devices to prevent oil price hikes from triggering a global recession.[12] They also allowed the kind of automaticity of drawings advocated by Keynes during the Bretton Woods negotiations (Dell 1986, 1207).

The breakdown of the Bretton Woods exchange rate system together with the graduation of the European countries from the Fund pushed it closer to development issues.

In this respect the creation of the Extended Fund Facility (EFF) in 1974 marks a turning point. It was established as a nonconcessional lending facility to address persistent and structural balance of payments problems.[13] This was followed by the Structural Adjustment Facility and the Enhanced Structural Adjustment Facility, which provided concessional lending to low income countries for structural change. As a result of increased emphasis on poverty reduction, the latter was replaced in 1999 by a Poverty Reduction and Growth Facility (PRGF), a concessional window for low income countries.

In perhaps an even more important shift, the Fund has become a crisis lender and manager for emerging markets. This role effectively started with the outbreak of the debt crisis in the 1980s when many developing countries borrowed heavily from multilateral sources to finance debt servicing to private creditors (Sachs 1998, 53). And with the recurrent financial crises in emerging markets in the 1990s, crisis lending has become the dominant financial activity of the Fund. The Supplemental Reserve Facility (SRF) was created in response to the deepening of the East Asian crisis in December 1997 in order to provide financing above normal access limits to countries experiencing exceptional payments difficulties, notably in servicing their external debt to private creditors and maintaining capital account convertibility, under a highly conditional standby or extended arrangement.

Thus sixty years after its inception, the IMF is now quite a different institution from the one created by the architects of the postwar international economic system. It "has adjusted to the changing economic conditions by sponsoring amendments to its Charter, by liberal interpretations of the Charter's provisions, and in some cases by ignoring limitations imposed by the Charter."[14] It is now deeply involved in development issues, providing long-term financing on concessional terms as well as assistance on HIPC: currently the number of low income countries which are covered under financial arrangements for PRGF and HIPC assistance exceeds the number of countries with standby arrangements by a factor of four (IMF 2005a).

It started out as an institution designed to promote global growth and stability through multilateral discipline over exchange rate policies, control over capital flows and provision of liquidity for current account financing. It has ended up focusing on the management and resolution of capital account crises in emerging markets associated with excessive instability of capital flows and exchange rates, allocating a large proportion of its lending for financing capital outflows: during the financial year ending on 30 April 2004, over 85 percent of total purchases and loans were accounted for by crisis lending to Argentina, Brazil and Turkey (IMF 2004a, table 2.6).

More importantly, originally all members of the Fund had equal de jure and de facto obligations for maintaining stable exchange rates and orderly macroeconomic conditions. With the breakdown of the Bretton Woods exchange rate arrangements, the establishment of universal convertibility of the currencies of major industrial countries, and the emergence of international financial markets as a main source of liquidity for advanced economies, the Fund's policy oversight has been confined primarily to its poorest members who need to draw on its resources because of their lack of access to private sources of finance.

C. Mission Creep into Development Finance and Policy

Much of the recent debate on the role of the IMF in development has focused on three issues. First, there has been widespread criticism of rapid deregulation and liberalization promoted by the Fund in developing countries because of their adverse repercussions for economic growth and poverty. Second, the conditions attached to Fund lending have been under constant fire on the grounds that, inter alia, they interfere with the proper jurisdiction of a sovereign government and leave little room for manoeuvre to national policymakers. Finally, there is a broad consensus that financing provided in support of such programs, including in the form of debt relief, is highly inadequate.

There has been less emphasis on whether the Fund should really be involved in development finance and policy, and poverty alleviation, particularly given that there are other multilateral institutions exclusively focusing on these issues, including multilateral development banks and various UN technical assistance agencies. Nevertheless, there are some notable exceptions. For instance the Meltzer Commission (2000) unanimously recommended that the IMF should restrict its financing to provision of liquidity, and stop lending to countries for long-term development assistance and structural transformation. Accordingly, the PRGF should be eliminated and long-term institutional assistance to foster development and encourage sound economic policies should be the exclusive responsibility of the World Bank and regional development banks. Similarly, according to the former World Bank chief economist Joseph Stiglitz (2002, 232) "a broad consensus – outside the IMF – has developed that the IMF should limit itself to its core area, managing crises; that it should no longer be involved (outside crises) in development or the economies of transition."

There are indeed no compelling reasons why the IMF should deal with structural problems in developing countries. As noted, the Fund moved toward developing countries in large part because it was no longer needed by industrial countries as a source of liquidity and it lost leverage over exchange rate and macroeconomic policies of these countries. Sticking to its original mandate for facilitating payments adjustment through provision of liquidity to meet temporary current account deficits would not have generated much business for the Fund in developing countries given that their balance of payments difficulties were structural and durable, rather than cyclical and temporary. This, together with the expansion of IMF membership in Africa, was the main reason why the Fund introduced long-term facilities and concessional lending. In doing so, however, it has gone right into the domain of development since overcoming structural payments deficits calls for reducing both savings and foreign exchange gaps, including chronic public sector deficits, which, in turn, depends on structural and institutional changes and economic growth, rather than demand management. But these are exactly the kind of issues dealt with by multilateral development banks, and involve action in wide areas of policy including agriculture, industry, trade, investment, technology, finance, the labor market and the public sector.[15]

That external disequilibrium in developing countries is structural does not justify the Fund going into long-term balance of payments support because this is exactly what the World Bank has been doing since the early 1980s when it shifted its lending from project financing to structural adjustment and development policy loans which now constitute about half of total Bank lending. Furthermore, the Bank is doing this for all developing countries while such long-term balance of payments support in the Fund is limited to low income countries eligible to PRGF. This is an ad hoc arrangement without a sound rationale, since there are many middle income countries with chronic payments deficits and excessive dependence on foreign capital, notably in Latin America, in need of long-term support to strengthen domestic savings and export capacity. This inconsistency should be addressed not by bringing them under the IMF, but taking the others out to the Bank.

As part of its work on development and poverty alleviation, the Fund's programs and structural conditionality have addressed almost all areas of development policy. This is problematic for several reasons. First of all it is not clear that the Fund has the necessary competence and experience in such complex issues. Certainly, the kind of expertise in development policy resulting from research and practical experience, and access to a significant amount of information on institutions and policy environment expected from the Bank do not define the existing capabilities of the Fund.[16] Nor are they needed for the Fund to function effectively in its areas of core competence. Furthermore, there are serious risks in entrusting development matters to an organization preoccupied with short-term financial outcomes and susceptible to strong influences from sudden shifts in market sentiments about the economies of its borrowers. Finally, there is no doubt that what the IMF does or should be doing for promoting monetary and financial stability has consequences for poverty and development, but this does not provide a rationale for the Fund to work in these areas. Such interdependencies exist in many areas of policy affecting poverty and development, including trade, labor, health, environment and security, both at the national and international level. What is needed is close cooperation and coordination with the institutions specialized in these matters with a view to attaining coherence and consistency, not duplication.

The Bank and the Fund have taken great pains to show that they are closely coordinating in order to minimize overlap and duplication (IMF/WB 2004), but in reality much of what is being done in development by the Fund could easily be transferred to the Bank. This overlap has in fact given rise to calls to merge the Fund with the World Bank, including by George Shultz (1998), former secretary of the treasury and secretary of state of the United States, arguing that their activities are becoming increasingly duplicative even though basically uncoordinated.[17] More recently a former German executive director for the World Bank Group and executive secretary of the Development Committee (Fischer 2004) argued that while complete fusion of the BWIs under a new charter would be the optimal solution, politically and practically a more feasible step would be to combine the administration and the boards of the two institutions, and to reshape the single board in such a way as to give greater voice to developing countries. This would reduce extensive duplication at the administrative level, bring greater consistency in policy advice and alleviate the pressure on poor countries with limited administrative capacities in coordinating measures promoted by the Fund and the Bank in overlapping areas of policy. According to one estimate a combined administration with a single board would reduce the personnel and other costs in the administrative budget by at least 25 percent

(Burnham 1999) – costs which are now effectively paid by debtor developing countries through charges and commission.

While it is often argued that the Fund and the Bank should be merged because they are effectively doing the same thing, what is argued here is that they should remain separate institutions doing different things. In fact there are many areas in which their activities do not and should not overlap. Crisis management and resolution, surveillance over macroeconomic and exchange rate policies, and provision of international liquidity are areas where the Fund should have a distinct role and competence. By contrast, the Fund should transfer development-related activities and facilities to the Bank. This would not lead to a significant retrenchment of Fund lending; at the end of 2004 outstanding PRGF credits were less than SDR 7,000 billion or 10 percent of total outstanding credits (IMF 2004a, table 2.8). Nor would it entail a major expansion in outstanding IDA credits which currently are around $90 billion. The legal difficulties that might be involved in transferring the resources currently located in the Fund could be overcome once the principle is accepted (Ahluwalia 1999, 22).

In a recent statement the managing director has argued in favor of deepening the Fund's work on low income countries and expressed his disagreement with the view that the "Fund ought to get out of the business of supporting low income countries" on the grounds that they "need macroeconomic policy advice from the Fund and they often need financial support from us" (De Rato 2005, 4). However, the issue is not about whether or not the Fund should be involved in policy design in and provision of finance to low income countries, but the context in which such activities should be undertaken. As discussed in subsequent sections, a major task of the Fund should be to provide countercyclical current account financing to low income countries facing excessive instability in export earnings. Again, macroeconomic conditions that may need to be attached to short-term lending and Article IV consultations would give the Fund ample opportunity to provide macroeconomic policy advice to low income countries. None of these would require the Fund to be involved in development matters

D. Trespassing in Trade Policy

The Fund, as a monetary institution, was not to be involved in trade issues even though its articles, in effect, authorized, through the scarce currency clause, trade measures against surplus countries unwilling to undertake expansionary measures by allowing discriminatory exchange restrictions (Dam 1982, 233). In the event, however, the Fund has gone in the opposite direction, putting pressure on deficit developing countries to undertake payments adjustment despite mounting protectionism in industrial countries against their exports, forcing them to resort to import compression and sacrifice growth (Akyüz and Dell 1987, 54).

More importantly, as the Fund became deeply involved in development issues, it increasingly saw trade liberalization as an important component of structural adjustment to trade imbalances. As noted in a report by a group of independent experts, IMF surveillance has expanded into trade liberalization, partly as a result of pressure from the United States as part of conditions for its agreement to quota increases

(IMF/GIE 1999, 61). Trade liberalization has also been promoted in certain emerging market economies in response to surges in capital inflows as a way of absorbing excess reserves and preventing currency appreciation (IMF/IEO 2005, 8–9, 59, table 3.2).

Although greater openness to foreign competition has also been one of the pillars of the adjustment programs supported by the Bank, the Fund is known to have played a more important role in this area. Low income countries and LDCs working under Fund programs have been encouraged and even compelled to undertake unilateral trade liberalization, putting them at a disadvantage in multilateral trade negotiations. Indeed the consequences of unilateral trade liberalization by developing countries outside the WTO framework are often discussed in relation to Fund programs (see, e.g., WTO 2004a, section II.A).

An implication of unilateral liberalization is that the industrial countries would not need to lower their tariffs in areas of export interest to developing countries in order to secure better access to the markets of these countries in the WTO where trade concessions are based on some form of reciprocity. Liberalization without improved market access in the North creates the risk of deterioration in their trade balances, hence leading either to a tighter external constraint and income losses, or to increased external debt. Indeed there is an asymmetry in the multilateral consequences of trade policy actions taken by developing countries in the context of Fund-supported programs. A country liberalising unilaterally acquires no automatic rights in the WTO vis-à-vis other countries, but it could become liable if it needs to take measures in breach of its obligations in the WTO.[18]

Although this is generally recognized to be a problem and discussed during the Uruguay Round, no mechanism has so far been introduced in the WTO for crediting developing countries for their unilateral liberalization in the context of Fund-supported programs. Furthermore, arguments are advanced that this should not affect the position of developing countries regarding their obligations in the WTO since what matters there is not applied but bound tariffs. However, for a number of reasons, including pressures from financial markets and major trading partners, developing countries find it difficult to raise their tariffs once they are lowered.

More importantly, applied tariffs are now providing a benchmark in binding and reducing tariffs in the current negotiations on industrial tariffs in the WTO. For instance, paragraph five of Annex B of the so-called July package which provides a framework for these negotiations based on proposals made by industrial countries takes the applied rates as the basis for commencing reductions for unbound tariffs in developing countries (WTO, 2004b). It also proposes to give credit for autonomous liberalization by developing countries provided that the tariff lines were bound on an MFN basis. However, it is not clear that a line-by-line commitment is necessarily in the best interest of these countries, or that the kind of unilateral liberalization agreed under IMF pressure would be consistent with their bargaining positions in multilateral negotiations (Akyüz 2005b).

Despite the difficulties confronting developing countries in trade negotiations, the Fund staff have been advancing arguments in favor of unilateral liberalization in these countries that go even beyond the positions advocated by major developed countries in the current negotiations on industrial tariffs. For instance a recent Fund paper argues that Africa's interest in the Doha Round would best be served by its own liberalization, and that African countries, including the LDCs, should bind and reduce all tariffs, even though the July package exempts LDCs from tariff reductions and recognizes the need for less than full reciprocity.[19] The first deputy managing director of the IMF has encouraged developing countries to undertake unilateral liberalization on several occasions, arguing that "countries that press ahead with unilateral liberalization will enjoy enormous benefits and they will not be penalized by further multilateral liberalization – quite the opposite. Countries that open up unilaterally help themselves" (Krueger 2005, 5).

The Fund has recently introduced a Trade Integration Mechanism to mitigate concerns among some developing countries that their balance of payments position could suffer as a result of multilateral liberalization in the current round of negotiations, insisting that such shortfalls would be small and temporary (IMF 2005b), despite mounting evidence that rapid liberalization in poor countries can raise imports much faster than exports and that the external financing needed can add significantly to the debt burden.[20]

The Fund staff have been advocating binding tariffs closer to their applied levels on grounds that this would increase trade by reducing uncertainty of trade policy and hence transaction costs (see, e.g., Yang 2005, 9). This may well be the case, but it is not a matter that should be of primary concern to the Fund. The international trading system no doubt needs greater predictability and stability, but discretion over tariffs by developing country governments is not the most serious source of disruption. As the recent experience regarding the movement of the dollar shows once again, exchange rate instability and misalignments are an equal and even more important source of uncertainty and friction in the international trading system.

This was recognized by the architects of the postwar international economic system, including Lord Keynes: "Tariffs and currency depreciations are in many alternatives. Without currency agreements you have no firm ground on which to discuss tariffs [...] It is very difficult while you have monetary chaos to have order of any kind in other directions."[21] It is thus advisable for the Fund to focus on its core responsibility of ensuring stability and better alignment of exchange rates, rather than narrowing the policy space for developing countries in matters related to trade and pushing trade liberalization as if a consistent international monetary order existed.

As the Fund transfers its work on development to the Bank, it should also stop being involved in trade policy issues or undertake activities that interfere with multilateral trade negotiations. Its relation to the WTO should be confined to areas explicitly stated in the General Agreement on Tariffs and Trade (GATT), notably in Article XV on exchange arrangements. These include consultations and supplying information on monetary reserves, balance of payments and foreign exchange arrangements in order to help in matters such as the determination of whether balance of payments and reserve conditions of countries would entitle them to apply the provisions of Articles XII and XVIIIB of GATT and Article XII of GATS in order to avoid sacrificing growth and development as a result of temporary payments difficulties (see Das 1999, chap. 3.3; and Akyüz 2002, 124–25).

E. Crisis Management and Resolution: Bailouts or Workouts?

There is a consensus that crises in emerging markets will continue to occur because of financial market failures as well as shortcomings in national policies and international surveillance mechanisms. There is also a wide agreement that the IMF should be involved in the management and resolution of such crises in order to limit the damage to the economies concerned, prevent contagion and reduce systemic risks. However, there is considerable controversy over how the Fund should intervene.

Until recently the Fund's intervention in financial crises in emerging markets involved ad hoc financial bailout operations designed to keep countries current on their debt payments to private creditors, to maintain capital account convertibility and to prevent default. IMF rescue packages amounted to several times the accepted quota limits (an annual limit of 100 percent of a member's quota and a cumulative limit of 300 percent), and were in certain instances combined with funds from development banks and bilateral contributions from major industrial countries.

IMF rescue packages for six emerging markets (Mexico, Thailand, Indonesia, Korea, Russia and Brazil) between 1995 and 1998 reached $231 billion, of which 44 percent came from bilateral donors, 38 percent from the IMF, and the rest from development banks (Ahluwalia 1999, 55, table 1). From 1995 until the end of 2003 IMF exceptional financing for 9 emerging markets (the above six plus Argentina, Turkey and Uruguay) amounted to SDR 174 billion, with an average of 637 percent of quota (IMF 2005c, table 10). Such lending is the main source of income for the Fund to support its operational expenses, which stood at some SDR 1.5 billion at the end of FY2004. Thus, ironically, in the absence of financial crises and bailout operations in emerging markets, the Fund can cease to be a financially viable institution.

Crisis lending was combined with monetary and fiscal tightening in order to restore confidence, but this often failed to prevent sharp drops in the currency and hikes in interest rates, thereby deepening debt deflation, credit crunch and economic contraction. Such interventions took place not only when the country concerned was facing a liquidity problem, as in Korea, but also when there were signs of a problem of insolvency. Originally rescue packages involved short-term, temporary financing but more recently the Fund has provided medium-term financing, including to governments facing domestic debt problems such as in Turkey (Akyüz and Boratav 2003).

In addition to the SRF noted above, the Contingency Credit Line (CCL) was created in Spring 1999 in order to provide a precautionary line of defense in the form of short-term financing which would be available to meet future balance of payments problems arising from contagion.[22] Countries would prequalify for the CCL if they complied with conditions related to macroeconomic and external financial indicators and with international standards in areas such as transparency and banking supervision. However, this facility discontinued in November 2003 as countries avoided recourse to it owing to fears that it would give the wrong signal and impair their access to financial markets.[23]

There have also been suggestions to turn the Fund into an international lender of last resort with a view to helping prevent crises (Fischer 1999). It is argued that if the

IMF stands ready to provide liquidity to countries with sound policies, they would be protected from contagion and financial panic so that a lender of last resort facility would have a preventive role. Clearly, such a step would involve a fundamental departure from the underlying premises of the Bretton Woods system. The report of the Meltzer Commission (2000) virtually proposes the elimination of all other forms of IMF lending, including those for current account financing which should, in their view, be provided by private markets.[24] Such a shift in IMF lending would imply that only a small number of more prosperous emerging economies would be eligible for IMF financing (Summers 2000, 14). More importantly there are difficulties in transforming the IMF into a genuine international lender of last resort, and proposed arrangements could compound rather than resolve certain problems encountered in IMF bailouts.

The effective functioning of such a lender would require discretion to create its own liquidity in order to be able to provide an unlimited amount of financing. This problem could, in principle, be resolved by assigning a new role to the SDR, which could also help promote it as a true fiduciary asset.[25] Proposals have indeed been made to allow the Fund to issue reversible SDRs to itself for use in lender-of-last-resort operations, that is to say the allocated SDRs would be repurchased when the crisis was over.[26]

However, the real problem relates to the terms of access to such a facility. Genuine lender-of-last-resort financing (namely lending in unlimited amounts and without conditions except for penalty rates) would need to be accompanied by tightened global supervision of debtor countries to ensure their solvency, and this would encounter not only technical but also political difficulties. Pre-qualification, that is allowing countries meeting certain ex ante conditions to be eligible to lender-of-last-resort financing, as in the case of ill-fated CCL, involves several problems. First, the IMF would have to act like a credit rating agency. Second, it would be necessary to constantly monitor the fulfilment of the terms of the financing to ensure that the pressures on the capital account of a qualifying country have resulted from a sudden loss of confidence amongst investors triggered largely by external factors rather than macroeconomic and financial mismanagement. In these respects difficulties are likely to emerge in relations between the Fund and the member concerned.

Perhaps the most serious problem with rescue packages is that they tend to aggravate market failures and financial instability by creating moral hazard. This is more of a problem on the side of creditors than debtors since access to lender of last resort financing does not come free or prevent fully the adverse repercussions of financial panics and runs for debtor countries. The main difficulty is that bailouts undermine market discipline and encourage imprudent lending since private creditors are not made to bear the consequences of the risks they take.[27] A dose of constructive ambiguity by allowing lender discretion might help in reducing moral hazard, but at the expense of undermining the objective sought by establishing such a facility.

There has been growing agreement that orderly debt workout procedures drawing on certain principles of national bankruptcy laws, notably Chapters 9 and 11 of the United States law provide a viable alternative to official bailout operations.[28] These should be designed to meet two interrelated objectives. On the one hand, they should help prevent financial meltdown and economic crises in developing countries facing difficulties in servicing their external obligations – a situation which often results in a loss of confidence of markets, collapse of currencies and hikes in interest rates, inflicting serious damage on both public and private balance sheets and leading to large losses in output and employment and sharp increases in poverty, all of these being part of actual experience in East Asia, Latin America and elsewhere during the past ten years. On the other hand, they should provide mechanisms to facilitate an equitable restructuring of debt which can no longer be serviced according to the original provisions of contracts. Attaining these two objectives does not require fully fledged international bankruptcy procedures but the application of a few key principles:[29]

- A temporary debt standstill, whether debt is owed by public or private sector, and whether debt servicing difficulties are due to solvency or liquidity problems – a distinction which is not always clear-cut. The decision for a standstill should be taken unilaterally by the debtor country and sanctioned by an independent panel rather than by the IMF because the countries affected are among the shareholders of the Fund which is itself also a creditor. This sanction would provide an automatic stay on creditor litigation. Such a procedure would be similar to WTO safeguard provisions allowing countries to take emergency actions to suspend their obligations when faced with balance of payments difficulties (Akyüz 2002, 124–25). Standstills would need to be accompanied by exchange controls, including suspension of convertibility for foreign currency deposits and other foreign exchange assets domestically held by residents.
- Provision of debtor-in-possession financing automatically granting seniority status to debt contracted after the imposition of the standstill. IMF should lend into arrears for financing imports and other vital current account transactions.
- Debt restructuring including rollovers and write-offs, based on negotiations between the debtor and creditors, and facilitated by the introduction of automatic rollover and collective action clauses (CACs) in debt contracts. The IMF should not be involved in the negotiations between sovereign debtors and private creditors.

These principles still leave open several issues of detail, but they nonetheless could serve as the basis for a coherent and comprehensive approach to crisis intervention and resolution. The Fund appeared to be moving in this direction at the end of the last decade with rising opposition to bailout operations from European and other governments and the increased frequency of crises in emerging markets. The IMF Board first recognized that "in extreme circumstances, if it is not possible to reach agreement on a voluntary standstill, members may find it necessary, as a last resort, to impose one unilaterally," and that since "there could be a risk that this action would trigger capital outflows [...] a member would need to consider whether it might be necessary to resort to the introduction of a more comprehensive exchange or capital controls."[30]

Although the board was unwilling to provide statutory protection to debtors in the form of a stay on litigation, preferring instead "signalling the Fund's acceptance of a standstill imposed by a member [...] through a decision [...] to lend into arrears to private creditors," the Fund secretariat moved toward establishing a formal mechanism for sovereign debt restructuring to "allow a country to come to the Fund and request a temporary standstill on the repayment of its debts, during which time it would negotiate a rescheduling with its creditors, given the Fund's consent to that line of attack. During this limited period, probably some months in duration, the country would have to provide assurances to its creditors that money was not fleeing the country, which would presumably mean the imposition of exchange controls for a temporary period of time." (Krueger 2001, 7)

However, the provision for statutory protection to debtors in the form of a stay on litigation is not included in the proposal for Sovereign Debt Restructuring Mechanism (SDRM) prepared by the Fund management because of the opposition from financial markets and the United States government. The proposed mechanism also provides considerable leverage to creditors in seeking their permission in granting seniority to new debt needed to prevent disruption to economic activity. It gives considerable power to the Fund vis-à-vis the proposed Sovereign Debt Dispute Resolution Forum in determining debt sustainability.[31]

The SDRM proposal contains innovative mechanisms to facilitate sovereign bond restructuring for countries whose debt is deemed unsustainable in bringing debtors and bondholders together whether or not bond contracts contain CACs, in securing greater transparency, and in providing a mechanism for dispute resolution. It could thus constitute an important step in the move toward generalized CACs in international bonds. However, it only addresses part of the problem associated with financial crises. First, it would not apply to countries with sustainable debt but facing liquidity shortages. Secondly, it focuses exclusively on international bonds as a source of financial fragility even though vulnerabilities associated with international bank debt, currency risks assumed by the domestic banking system, and public domestic debt played key roles in most recent crises in emerging markets. In the presence of such vulnerabilities bond clauses alone cannot stem currency attacks or prevent financial turmoil. While the SDRM includes a provision to discourage litigation by bondholders (through the application of the so-called hotchpot rule), such a rule cannot address the problem of how to stop financial meltdown, since in a country whose debt is judged unsustainable, currency runs could take place whether or not bondholders opt for litigation.

More importantly, the SDRM proposal does not fundamentally address the problems associated with IMF bailouts. It is based on the premise that countries facing liquidity problems would continue to receive IMF support and the SDRM will apply only to those with unsustainable debt. As part of its promotion of the SDRM the IMF has argued that unsustainable debt situations are rare. That means in most cases business as usual. In any case, it can reasonably be expected that countries with unsustainable debt would generally be unwilling to declare themselves insolvent and activate the SDRM. Instead, they would be inclined to ask the Fund to provide financing.

But in most cases it would be difficult for the Fund to decline such requests on the grounds that the country is facing a solvency problem. Here lies the rationale for limits on IMF crisis lending whether the problem is one of liquidity or insolvency: with strict access limits creditors cannot count on an IMF bailout, and debtors will be less averse to activating the SDRM and standstills when faced with serious difficulties in meeting their external obligations and maintaining convertibility. This means that to encourage countries to move quickly to debt restructuring, the SDRM should be combined with limits on crisis lending. But this could be problematic unless private sector involvement is secured through a statutory standstill and stay on litigation.

Even this watered-down version of the SDRM proposal could not elicit adequate political support and has, at the time of writing, been put on the backburner. Indeed, the impetus for reform has generally been lost since the turn of the millennium because of widespread complacency associated with the recovery of capital flows to emerging markets. This recovery has been driven by a combination of highly favorable conditions including historically low interest rates, high levels of liquidity, strong commodity prices and buoyant international trade. Private capital flows to emerging markets appear to be in the boom phase of their third postwar cycle: the first began in the 1970s and ended with the debt crisis in the early 1980s, and the second began in the early 1990s and ended with the East Asian and Russian crises.[32] Total inflows in the current boom appear to have exceeded the peak observed in the previous boom, and almost all emerging markets have shared in this recovery. However, as noted by the Institute of International Finance, the system is becoming more fragile once again: "there is a risk that the pickup in flows into some emerging market assets has pushed valuations to levels that are not commensurate with underlying fundamentals" (IIF 2005a, 4). Thus, a combination of tightened liquidity, rising interest rates, slowing growth and global trade imbalances can reverse the boom, hitting particularly countries with weak fundamentals and incomplete self-insurance (IIF 2005b; Goldstein 2005b).[33] Under these conditions if the recent consensus against large-scale bailout operations is adhered to, countries that may be facing rapid exit of capital and unsustainable debt burdens could be forced to undertake action for unilateral standstill, creating considerable uncertainties and confusion in the international financial system. If not, we will be back to square one.

F. Restructuring IMF Lending and Supplementing Resources

The arguments developed above imply that the Fund should return to its original mandate for the provision of short-term current account financing and should no longer be engaged in the development finance or financial bailout operations. This means abolishing the facilities designed for these purposes including the EFF, SRF and PRGF. Despite the rapid development and integration of international banking and credit markets, there is still a strong rationale for the Fund to have a role in providing liquidity because of the procyclical behavior of financial markets and increased volatility of the global economic environment. Such financing should be made available in order to support economic activity, employment and trade when countries face sharp declines or reversals of private capital flows, or temporary shortfalls in external payments as a result of trade shocks which cannot be met by private financing. In both cases access to credit tranches through standby agreements should be the main instrument for the provision of liquidity. Greater delineation of Bank–Fund activities requires that such financing should be the sole responsibility of the Fund, and the Bank should stay out of provision of short-term finance.[34]

While it has to be recognized that money is fungible and in practice it is not always possible to identify the need catered for by a particular loan, it is important to ensure that IMF lending to counter volatility in private capital flows should aim at maintaining imports and the level of economic activity rather than debt repayment to private creditors and capital account convertibility. Such lending should be available to countries facing cutback in credit lines due to contagion as well as those facing currency and debt crises. To ensure that such lending does not amount to bailouts for private creditors, there should be strict limits to IMF crisis lending since otherwise it would be difficult to ensure private sector involvement.

This approach of constraining IMF lending to encourage private sector involvement in the resolution of international financial crises has been supported by some G-7 countries including Canada and England.[35] It has also been supported in a report to the Council on Foreign Relations which argued that the IMF should adhere consistently to normal access limits and that only "in the unusual case in which there appears to be a systemic crisis (that is a multicountry crisis where failure to intervene threatens the performance of the world economy and where there is widespread failure in the ability of private capital markets to distinguish creditworthy from less creditworthy borrowers), the IMF would return to its 'systemic' backup facilities" (CFRTF 1999, 63). However, exceptions to normal access limits could leave considerable room for large-scale bailout operations and excessive IMF discretion in assessing the conditions under which exceptional access in capital account crises are to be granted.[36] It would also allow room for considerable political leverage in IMF lending decisions by its major shareholders, as was seen in the differential treatment of Argentina and Turkey after the attacks of September 2001. Requiring supermajority for access to exceptional finance, as recommended by CFRTF (1999, 63) and Goldstein (2005a, 299–300) would certainly be an important step, but it may not always prevent large-scale bailouts driven by political motivations. In any case, the Fund should provide liquidity to countries facing cutback in private lending in order to support production, employment and trade, and should not be expected to help float imprudent international investors and lenders – a task that should fall on national authorities in creditor countries. On the other hand, the problem of inadequacy of normal lending limits for current account financing should be addressed by reforming quotas and access policy, not by making exceptions to access limits.

Exceptional current account financing may be needed in times of a contraction in world trade and growth, and/or sharp declines in capital flows to developing countries, as was the case in the early 1980s and after the East Asian and Russian crises. The Fund's regular resources may not be adequate for dealing with such cases because they are not large or flexible enough. This can be handled by a global countercyclical facility based on reversible SDR allocations, which could be triggered by a decision of the board on the basis of certain predetermined criteria regarding global trade and output and private capital flows to developing countries. Again countries could be permitted to have access to such a facility on a temporary basis within predetermined limits.

Fund lending in response to trade shocks is needed when financial markets are not willing to provide countercyclical finance. As noted the CFF was established in 1963 as an additional low-conditionality facility to help developing countries experiencing temporary shortfalls in export earnings due to external shocks in order to avoid undue retrenchment. Modifications made over the years have tightened conditions attached to the CFF, and the facility has not been used since the last review in 2000 despite two recognized temporary shocks including the attacks of September 2001 which affected earnings from tourism in the Caribbean region (IMF 2004b). A major problem is that in order to have low conditionality financing under CFF (the so-called standalone CFF purchases) a country would need to have a viable payments position except for the effects of the shocks, but such a country would normally have access to alternative sources of finance. On the other hand, countries with structurally weak payments usually have other forms of high-conditionality Fund financing including the PRGF or emergency assistance (IMF 2004b). Under current arrangements the facility serves no useful purpose and many executive directors called for its discontinuation during the recent review, arguing that the CFF is not an attractive option for low income countries given its nonconcessional nature (IMF 2004c).

It is generally recognized that IMF quotas have considerably lagged behind the growth of global output and trade. According to one estimate, in 2000 they stood at 4 percent of world imports compared to 58 percent in 1944 (Buira 2003b, 9). It is, however, often argued that this does not imply that the size of the Fund would need to be raised considerably in order to keep up with growth in world trade because closely integrated and rapidly expanding financial markets now provide alternative sources of liquidity, and the move to floating together with the universal convertibility of several currencies have reduced the need for international reserves. While this may well be so for more advanced countries, many developing countries continue to depend on multilateral financing since market liquidity tends to disappear at the time when it is most needed. These countries are also more vulnerable to external shocks, be it in trade or finance.

An across the board increase in the size of the Fund may not address the problems faced by many developing countries because of the small size of their quotas. It is known that the current distribution of quotas does not reflect the relative size of the economies of the countries member to the IMF, and a redistribution of quotas based on actual shares of countries in aggregate world output would raise the proportion of IMF quotas allocated to developing countries, particularly if incomes are valued at purchasing power parities (PPP) rather than market exchange rates (Buira 2003b). However, this would only address a small part of the problem: according to the IMF World Economic Outlook, the share of advanced countries in aggregate GDP at PPP is close to 58 percent while their share in IMF quotas is just over 60 percent. For developing countries these numbers stand at around 38 and 30 percent respectively. Moreover, a redistribution of quotas would not produce a tangible increase in the share of low income developing countries which do not have adequate access to international financial markets.

One way to tackle the problem would be to adopt differential treatment of poorer countries in the determination of their drawing rights. Under existing arrangements quotas determine simultaneously countries' contributions to the Fund, voting rights and drawing rights. But this is not the best possible arrangement and the use of a single quota to serve three purposes was rightly criticized as "both illogical and unnecessary" (Mikesell 1994, 37). Putting a large wedge between countries' contributions and voting rights by subjecting them to totally different rules may be problematic, but there is no reason why drawing rights should not be based on different quotas from contributions.[37] After all nonreciprocity between rights and obligations for poorer countries has been an agreed principle in multilateral arrangements in other spheres of economic activity, notably trade, and such an approach would also be consistent with concessionality applied to lending to such countries by the Bretton Woods Institutions. This may be arranged by setting different access limits to different groups of countries according to their vulnerability to external shocks and access to financial markets, which in effect implies that, under current arrangements, countries would have different quotas for their contributions and drawing rights. Income shares can be taken as the basis for contributions while export earning volatility and access to private finance could be used as criteria for determining drawing limits. Such a needs-based approach to access to IMF resources would make even greater sense if, as proposed in Section I, the IMF ceases to be funded by its members, relying instead on SDRs for the resources needed.

An overall expansion of Fund quotas, together with its redistribution in favor of developing countries, would increase unconditional access through reserve tranche purchases. However, automatic access would also be expanded beyond the reserve tranche for the poorer countries if quotas for drawings are differentiated from those for contributions. On the other hand, once the Fund stops dealing with development and poverty, structural conditionality should no longer be applied for access to upper credit tranches. Conditionality would then be restricted to fiscal, monetary and exchange rate policies – the Fund's core areas of competence.

Increased resources at the IMF should be expected to help strike a better balance between financing and macroeconomic adjustment. In any case, the kind of conditions to be attached to lending should depend on the nature of payment imbalances. If the shortfall is due to temporary trade and financial shocks, then it is important to ensure that the Fund do not act procyclically and impose policy tightening. In such cases the balance between policy adjustment and financing should be tilted toward the latter. If expansionary macroeconomic policies and excessive domestic absorption are at the root of the problem, then financing would need to be accompanied by realignment of monetary, fiscal and exchange rate policies. However, if it turns out that payments equilibrium can only be sustained at permanently depressed rates of economic growth, this is a matter that should be addressed by multilateral development banks through provision of development finance and promotion of structural policies, including in areas affecting government revenues and spending, rather than by IMF lending or macroeconomic policy prescriptions for demand management.

An issue here is whether it would be possible to distinguish between temporary and permanent shocks or between structural and cyclical deficits (see, e.g., IMF 2004b, 10). There are no doubt difficulties in making judgments in these areas, which call for prudence. However, such judgments are also necessary under current arrangements in order to strike a balance between adjustment and financing, and between structural and macroeconomic conditionality. Moreover, the Fund is engaged in making judgments in areas that involve even higher degrees of uncertainty such as debt sustainability and prospects of the country regaining access to private finance as part of the criteria to be met for exceptional access in capital account crises (IMF 2005c, 4). Placing macroeconomic and structural aspects of payments adjustment in different institutions is no more problematic than combining them under the same roof. It would also have the additional advantage of reducing the imbalance between adjustment and financing since structural adjustment needs to be supported by a lot more financing than macroeconomic adjustment, and the IMF programs tend to rely heavily on macroeconomic tightening to reduce payments imbalances even when they are structural in nature.

G. Ineffectiveness and Asymmetry of Fund Surveillance

The architects of the Bretton Woods system recognized the role of surveillance over national policies for international economic stability. But it was only after the collapse of the fixed exchange rate system and the expansion of capital markets that IMF surveillance gained critical importance. With the second amendment of the Articles of Agreement the Fund was charged with exercising firm surveillance over members' policies at the same time as members were allowed the right to choose their own exchange rate arrangements. Its objective, as formally adopted, was limited to surveillance over exchange rate policies, focusing primarily on the sustainability of exchange rates and external payments positions, and on the appropriateness of the associated economic policies, particularly monetary and fiscal policies, of individual countries. However, its scope and coverage have expanded over time into structural policies, the financial sector and a number of other areas (IMF/GIE 1999, 21; Mohammed 2000). The guidelines established in 1977 made an explicit reference to the obligations of members to avoid manipulating exchange rates or the international monetary system to gain an unfair competitive advantage over other members.[38] In the 1980s the major members of the Fund came to favor a broader interpretation and recognized that "to be effective surveillance over exchange rates must concern itself with the assessment of all the policies that affect trade, capital movements, external adjustment, and the effective functioning of the international monetary system."[39] After a series of emerging market crises the Interim Committee agreed in April 1998 that the Fund should intensify its surveillance of financial sector issues and capital flows, giving particular attention to policy interdependence and risks of contagion, and ensure that it is fully aware of market views and perspectives.[40] Various codes and standards established on the basis of benchmarks appropriate to major industrial countries for macroeconomic policy, institutional and market structure, and financial regulation and supervision have become important components of the surveillance process (Cornford 2002, 31–33).

However, the Fund's intensive bilateral surveillance of developing countries' policies has not been effective in crisis prevention in large part because it has failed to diagnose and act on the root causes of the problem. Indeed, according to an independent assessment of Fund surveillance, policymakers interviewed had important reservations regarding the quality of the Fund's analysis of capital account issues (IMF/GIE 1999, 13).

Experience since the early 1990s shows that preventing unsustainable surges in private capital inflows, currency appreciations and trade deficits holds the key to preventing financial crises in emerging markets. However, as recognized by the IMF's Independent Evaluation Office (IEO), there is a consensus that none of the standard policy measures recommended by the Fund for this purpose, including countercyclical monetary and fiscal policy and exchange rate flexibility, is a panacea, and each involves significant costs or otherwise brings about other policy dilemmas (IMF/IEO 2005, 60). Sterilization through issuing government paper, raising reserve requirements or generating fiscal surpluses runs up against a host of problems. While fixed or adjustable peg regimes tend to encourage short-term inflows by reducing perceived currency risks, the floating regime, which has come to be favored by the Fund after recurrent crises in emerging markets, does not provide a viable alternative. As shown by the post–Bretton Woods experience of advanced industrial countries and the more recent experience of several emerging market economies, floating does not prevent excessive inflows of capital, misalignments in exchange rates and unsustainable trade deficits; nor does it always secure an orderly currency and payments adjustment.[41] Similarly, prudential regulations can help contain the damage caused by a rapid exit of capital, but they are not always effective in checking the build-up of external fragility even when countercyclical adjustments are made to rules governing loan loss provisions, capital requirements, collateral valuation and other measures affecting conditions in credit and asset markets in order to limit the cyclicality of the financial system.

All these imply that direct measures of control over capital inflows that go beyond prudential regulations may become necessary to prevent build-up of financial fragility and vulnerability to external shocks.[42] Developing country governments have generally been unwilling to slow down excessive capital inflows, using, instead, the opportunity to pursue procyclical fiscal policies. Taiwan is a notable exception with effective restrictions over arbitrage flows which protected the economy from the East Asian crisis in 1997–98.[43] Again Chile and Colombia employed unremunerated reserve requirements in a countercyclical manner, imposed at times of strong inflows in the 1990s and phased out when capital dried up at the end of the decade. This was a price-based, nondiscriminative measure which effectively taxed arbitrage inflows with the implicit tax rate varying inversely with maturity. These measures were effective in improving the maturity profile of external borrowing but not in checking aggregate capital inflows. The Fund has been ambivalent even toward these market-based measures, questioning their rationale and effectiveness (IMF/IEO 2005, 46, box 2.3). This is largely because, as noted in an independent report on surveillance, the Fund has generally been optimistic regarding the sustainability of capital inflows to emerging markets (IMF/GIE 1999, 44, box 3.2). It has been averse to temporary control measures even when there were clear signs that surges in short-term capital inflows were leading to persistent currency appreciations and growing trade deficits, advocating, instead, fiscal tightening and greater exchange rate flexibility (IMF/IEO 2005, 8–9, 59, table 3.2).

The Fund has little leverage over policies in emerging market economies enjoying surges in capital flows, since they rarely need the Fund at such times of bliss. It cannot act as a rating agency and issue strong public warnings about the sustainability of economic conditions in its member countries because of their possible adverse financial consequences. But it is also notable that the Fund refrains from requesting policy changes and effective capital account measures to slow down speculative capital inflows, check sharp currency appreciations and growing current account deficits even in countries with standby agreements. This was certainly the case in the 1990s when it supported exchange-based stabilization programs relying on short-term capital inflows. More recently Turkey has also been going through a similar process of continued appreciation and growing current account deficits under a floating regime, brought about, in large part, by a surge in arbitrage flows encouraged by high interest rates. Although its external conditions appear to be highly fragile and unsustainable, the Fund has done little to check this process; it has actually given a further momentum by constantly praising the policies pursued under its supervision.[44] Ironically, the Fund also seems to be aware of the risks and vulnerabilities created by the current boom in capital inflows to emerging markets; as noted, it has been simulating scenarios for a group of "21 vulnerable emerging market countries" to predict the financial gap that could emerge in the event of "financial drought and poor economic conditions" (IMF 2005c, 8).

According to the recent report by the IEO "the IMF has learned over time on capital account issues" and "the new paradigm [...] acknowledges the usefulness of capital controls under certain conditions, particularly controls over inflows," but this not yet reflected in policy advice because of "the lack of a clear position by the institution" (IMF/IEO, 2005, 11). The report goes on to make recommendations to bring about greater clarity in policy advice and the role of capital account issues in IMF surveillance, but it is not clear if these would lead to the kind of fundamental changes needed in the Fund's approach to capital account regimes.

The articles allow the Fund to request members to exercise control on capital outflows and recognize the right of members to regulate international capital flows. The 1977 surveillance decision mentions, among the developments that might indicate the need for discussion with a member, the behavior of the exchange rate that appears to be unrelated to underlying economic and financial conditions including factors affecting competitiveness and long-term capital movements while the 1995 amendment explicitly refers to "unsustainable flows of private capital" as an event triggering such discussion. In other words surveillance should include sustainability of a country's external balance sheet and hence effective management of external liabilities.[45]

However, none of these give the Fund clear and effective jurisdiction over capital account issues or allow it to include capital account measures as conditionality in its financial arrangements with a member (IMF/IEO 2005, 50). Despite that the Fund has played an important role in promoting capital account liberalization in developing countries. After many years of turmoil in emerging markets, the issue now faced is how to include capital account measures in the arsenal of policy tools for effective management of international capital flows. As already argued, restrictions over capital outflows should become legitimate tools of policy in the context of orderly debt workout procedures at times of rapid exit of capital. In the same vein, guidelines for IMF surveillance should specify circumstances in which the Fund should actually recommend the imposition or strengthening of capital controls over inflows, and the Fund should be able to request exercise of control over inflows as well as outflows. It should also develop new techniques and mechanisms designed to separate, to the extent possible, capital account from current account transactions, to distinguish among different types of capital flows from the point of view of their sustainability and economic impact, and to provide policy advice and technical assistance to countries at times when such measures are needed.

How far should IMF surveillance cover subjects such as financial regulation and standards for financial reporting and accounting? This is clearly a delicate question involving not only technical competence but also powers and responsibilities in areas where there already exist other multilateral bodies. It is much more important for the Fund to focus on the analysis of capital flows including their nature and sustainability with a view to reducing the likelihood of crises than on the observance of international standards in developing countries in order to limit the damage that may be caused by their reversals, leaving these matters to institutions with the necessary expertise. This was indeed one of the recommendations of the report by independent experts on surveillance (IMF/IGE 1999, 15).

The failure of IMF surveillance in preventing international financial crises also reflects the unbalanced nature of the procedures which give too little recognition to shortcomings in the institutions and policies in major industrial countries with large impact on global economic conditions. For its borrowers the policy advice given by the IMF in Article IV consultations often provide the framework for the conditionality to be attached to any future Fund program (IMF/GIE 1999, 20), while its surveillance of the policies of the most important players in the global system has lost any real meaning with the graduation of the industrial countries from the Fund and the breakdown of the Bretton Woods arrangements for exchange rates. This asymmetry in surveillance between the creditors and debtors of the Fund has increased further after recurrent emerging market crises throughout the 1990s. Standards and codes have been designed primarily to discipline debtor developing countries on the presumption that the cause of crises rests primarily with policy and institutional weaknesses in these countries. By contrast very little attention has been given to the role played by policies and institutions in major industrial countries in triggering international financial crises. For instance while it is widely recognized that noncompliance with standards and codes is a global problem, the incentive structure for compliance is highly ineffectual for the developed country members of the Fund (Schneider and Silva 2002, 4). Again, the Fund has paid very little attention to how instability of capital flows on the supply side could be reduced through regulatory measures targeted at institutional investors in major industrial countries (IMF/IEO 2005, 7), or how transparency could be increased for institutions engaged in destabilizing financial transactions such as the hedge funds.

IMF multilateral surveillance has not paid adequate attention to systemic interrelation among countries – an area of improvement identified by a former managing director.[46] More importantly, the modalities of IMF surveillance do not include ways of responding to and dealing with unidirectional impulses emanating from changes in the monetary and exchange rate policies of the United States and a few other G-7 countries. Indeed, boom–bust cycles in capital flows to developing countries and major international financial crises are typically connected to large shifts in macroeconomic and financial conditions in the major industrial countries. The sharp rise in the United States interest rates and the appreciation of the dollar was a main factor in the debt crisis of the 1980s. Likewise, the boom–bust cycle of capital flows in the 1990s which devastated many countries in Latin America and East Asia were strongly influenced by shifts in monetary conditions in the United States and the exchange rates among the major reserve currencies (UNCTAD TDR 1998, part 2, chap. 4; and 2003, chap. 2). Again much of the current surge in capital flows to emerging markets is driven by financial market conditions in industrial countries, including historically low interest rates and ample liquidity, rather than by fundamentals in recipient countries, and a reversal of these conditions could trigger serious instability in several emerging markets.

It has often been argued that the problems regarding the quality, effectiveness and even-handedness of surveillance could be addressed by overhauling and downsizing the board to make it more representative and effective, and giving greater independence to executive directors vis-à-vis their capitals and to the IMF secretariat vis-à-vis its governing bodies.[47] This view has been taken further by a senior British Treasury official who argued in favor of a formal separation of surveillance from decisions about program lending and the use of IMF resources so as to establish the Fund as independent from political influence in its surveillance of economies as an independent central bank is in the operation of monetary policy (Balls 2003). It is argued that the current structure of the IMF treats program design as an extension of surveillance, but the lack of a clear distinction between lending and surveillance activities creates the wrong incentives and diminishes the effectiveness of surveillance. Moreover, there is currently no formal regular mechanism for assessing whether the Fund is providing objective, rigorous and consistent standards of surveillance across all member countries – program and nonprogram countries. While responsible for ensuring the effectiveness of the Fund's activities, executive directors also have responsibilities to their authorities. This creates a conflict of interest where executive directors tend to collude in surveillance in defense of the countries they represent, turning peer pressure into peer protection. Surveillance should thus rest with authorities who are independent of their governments and who are not involved in lending decisions, making it impartial, legitimate, authoritative, transparent and accountable. This would also have the advantage of protecting the board and IMF management from being dragged into decisions, which – on the basis of objective evidence – they would not want to take or publicly justify.

Such a step could indeed help improve the quality of surveillance for both program and nonprogram countries in identifying risks and fragilities and the policy measures needed. However, it is not clear if it could really secure evenhandedness between program and nonprogram countries. For program countries, it would not be possible to delink lending decisions from surveillance. Indeed, if the proposed arrangements are to improve the quality, authority and credibility, results of surveillance should provide a sound and legitimate basis for lending decisions by the board. But for nonprogram countries there would be no such mechanism to encourage governments to heed the policy advice emerging from the surveillance process. Publication of surveillance reports and a wider debate over policy could help prevent build-up of fragilities and vulnerabilities by providing signals to market participants and creating public pressure on governments in need of corrective action, but even an independent body responsible for surveillance cannot be expected to issue public warnings since they can become self-fulfilling prophecies. For G-1 or G-3 countries whose policies set the terms and conditions in global financial markets, even such warnings may be of little use in encouraging policy reorientation or coordination.

Therefore, while independent surveillance may improve its quality, credibility and impact for nonprogram countries, it cannot be relied on for bringing greater symmetry between creditor and debtor countries. Such a step may need to be supplemented by reforms in many areas of governance to be taken up in the following section. However, given the limits on improving significantly the leverage of the Fund over nonborrowing countries, evenhandedness may only be possible by minimising conditionality for program countries and increasing the degree of automaticity of their access to the Fund in the ways discussed above.

H. Governance: Making the Fund a Genuinely Multilateral Institution

The debate over governance of the IMF has focused mainly on issues raised by exercise of power by its major shareholders, particularly the United States. The most frequently debated areas of reform include the procedures for the choice of the managing director and, more importantly, the distribution of voting rights. Shortcomings in transparency and accountability are also closely related to "democratic deficit" within the governance structure of the Fund resulting from the quota regime.

The postwar bargain struck between the United States and Western Europe for the distribution of the heads of the Bretton Woods institutions between the two shores of the Atlantic has survived widespread public criticism and initiatives taken by developing countries. The latest selection of the managing director was again business as usual despite the apparent consensus reached during the previous round by the board that the decision for selection would be based on a wide and open discussion involving all members of the Fund.[48]

There is a consensus among independent observers that the present distribution of voting rights lacks legitimacy not only because it does not meet the minimum standards for equity due to erosion of "basic votes," but also because it no longer reflects the relative economic importance of the members of the Fund.[49] The existing distribution of voting rights, together with the special majority requirements for key decisions, effectively gives a veto power to the United States in matters such as adjustment of quotas, the sale of IMF gold reserves, balance of payments assistance to developing countries, and allocation of SDRs. Such a degree of control by the United States may have had some rationale during the immediate postwar years when it was the single most important creditor to the rest of the world and effectively the only creditor of the Fund. However, now not only is the United States the single largest debtor country in the world, but it is only one of the 45 creditor countries at the IMF.[50]

In theory the Fund appears to be a consensus builder since decisions by the board are taken without formal voting.[51] But there has been hardly any consensus on proposals for change favored by developing countries in areas such as quotas, voting rights or SDR allocation. In reality the consensual process of decision making on the executive board does not constitute a democratizing feature of Fund governance, but a way of exerting pressure on dissenting countries to go along with its major shareholders. The influence of developing countries is further weakened by the practice of arriving at decisions through consensus among executive directors, rather than direct exercise of voting rights by each and every member, since many developing countries are represented by executive directors from industrial countries.[52]

The procedures followed for the preparation and approval of country programs also diminish the impact of developing countries. Typically agreement is reached between the country concerned and the Fund staff before a program is presented to the board, and it is not always clear to what extent the agreement reached reflects what the country really wants to do as opposed to what it has been compelled to accept. This tends to discourage developing country executive directors to oppose potentially damaging stabilization and adjustment programs even though in theory they have collectively the required number of votes to block them. Clearly an alternative procedure allowing the country concerned to make a presentation to the board about its policy intentions and to back it up, when needed, with expert witnesses before entering into any discussion with the management could provide for a broader debate over country programs and greater say for developing countries in the board.

The current distribution of voting rights and the manner in which they are exercised effectively enable the major industrial countries to use the Fund as a multilateral seal of approval to legitimize decisions already taken elsewhere by this small number of countries. Lack of broad participation in the decision making process is also a main reason why the Fund does not meet the minimum standards of transparency or accountability. There is an increased agreement that despite certain measures recently taken, lack of transparency goes well beyond that justified by the confidential nature of the issues dealt with by the Fund. The record on accountability is even less encouraging: the Fund is protected against bearing the consequences of the decisions taken, and the burden of inappropriate policy choices invariably falls on countries following its advice.

The proposals for reform for reducing the democratic deficit fall into two categories. First, changes could be made to special majority requirements in order to remove the veto power of the Fund's major shareholders over key decisions. Second, and more importantly, voting rights could be reallocated so as to increase the voice of developing countries. This could be done by increasing the share of the basic votes in total voting rights and/or by reallocating quotas on the basis of PPP. The main loser would be the European Union, which collectively holds almost twice as many votes as the United States, far above the level justified by the share of the region in the world economy. According to a proposal for restoring basic votes to its original share of around 11 percent of total votes and allocating quota-based votes on the basis of PPP, the share of industrial countries would fall from over 62 percent to 51 percent while that of developing countries would rise from around 30 percent to 42 percent (Kelkar, Yadav and Chaudhry 2004, appendix 1).

There can be little doubt that a reform along these lines would constitute an important step in improving the Fund's governance. It would rectify anomalies such as Canada holding the same number of votes as China or smaller European countries including Belgium and the Netherlands holding more votes than India, Brazil or Mexico, making the Fund look a more participatory and democratic institution. Nevertheless, it is unlikely to make a significant impact on the political leverage of its major shareholders or reduce the imbalance between its creditor and debtors.

The problems of governance and lack of uniformity of treatment across members cannot be resolved as long as Fund resources depend on the discretion of a small number of its shareholders. Reserve currency countries are the principal creditors to the Fund and their quota subscription payments provide the only usable international assets since there is no demand for national currencies paid in by developing countries. Moreover, the Fund borrows not from international financial markets, but from a minority of its members under two standing arrangements, GAB and NAB. It is true that the distinction between creditor and debtor countries is not the same as that between industrial and developing countries, and at the end of 2004 of the 45 creditor countries to the Fund nine were developing countries. However, unlike industrial countries, developing countries' net financial position in the Fund has been highly volatile. Almost all of the 44 countries which have switched, at least once, over 1980–2004 between being net financial contributors to the Fund and being debtors, and back, are developing countries (Boughton 2005, 4). With increased frequency of financial crises in emerging markets, this classification, like international credit ratings, has become highly unstable. For instance Korea, Malaysia, Mexico and Thailand now are among the creditors of the IMF while they were heavily indebted a few years ago. Again there is no guarantee that countries such as Chile and China which have been IMF creditors for some time will remain so in the years ahead.[53]

In trade, bilateralism is often seen as a threat to multilateralism because of the preferential treatment it accords to some countries at the expense of the others in violation of the MFN principle, and the role played by political considerations in bilateral and regional trade arrangements. In the sphere of finance, by contrast, bilateral and multilateral arrangements are often seen as complementary. As already noted, in several instances the Fund's interventions in emerging market crises were combined with bilateral contributions from major industrial countries, notably but not solely the United States, particularly where political, economic and military interests were involved. Again, official debt reduction initiatives combine bilateral and multilateral debt, as in HIPC, and bilateral lenders often insist that any talks in the Paris club should be preceded by a formal IMF program. Since bilateral lending is driven largely by political considerations (Gilbert, Powell and Vines 1999; Kapur and Webb 1994; and Rodrik 1995) and bilateral debt negotiations rarely satisfy uniformity of treatment of debtors, such arrangements serve to subvert the governance of the Fund further, thereby enhancing the scope to make it an instrument for major industrial countries to pursue their national interests.

A reform that would translate the Fund into a truly multilateral institution responsible for international monetary and financial stability with equal rights and obligations of all its members, de facto as well as de jure, would call for, inter alia an international agreement on sources of finance that do not depend on the discretion of a handful of countries as well as a clear separation of multilateral financial arrangements from bilateral creditor–debtor relations. The potential sources of genuinely multilateral finance are twofold. First, an agreement could be reached on international taxes, including the currency transaction tax (the so-called Tobin tax), environmental taxes and various other taxes such as those on arms trade, to be applied by all parties to the agreement on the transactions and activities concerned (Atkinson 2003; Wahl 2005). A common feature of these is that they are all sin taxes which would provide revenues while discouraging certain global public bads such as currency speculation, environmental damage or armed conflict and violence. However, these sources of revenue are more appropriate for development grants to poorest countries or for the provision of global public goods rather than provision of liquidity for temporary payments imbalances.

A more appropriate source of funding for the provision of international liquidity is the SDR. Under present arrangements the IMF may allocate SDRs to members in proportion to their quotas, but not to itself. Members obtain or use SDRs through voluntary exchanges or by the Fund designating members with strong external positions to purchase SDRs from members with weak external position. When members' holdings rise above or fall below their allocation they earn or pay interest respectively. These arrangements would need to be changed to allow the SDR to replace quotas and GAB and NAB as the source of funding for the IMF. The Fund should be allowed to issue SDR to itself up to a certain limit which should increase over time with growth in world trade. The SDR could become a universally accepted means of payments, held privately as well as by public institutions. Countries' access would be subject to predetermined limits which should also grow over time with world trade. The demand for SDRs can be expected to be inversely related to buoyancy in global trade and production and the availability of private financing for external payments. Thus, it would help counter deflationary forces in the world economy and provide an offset to fluctuations in private balance of payments financing.

Several issues of detail would still need to be worked out, but once an agreement is reached to replace traditional sources of funding with the SDR, the IMF could in fact be translated into a technocratic institution of the kind advocated by Keynes during the Bretton Woods negotiations.[54] Its funding would no longer be subjected to arduous and politically charged negotiations dominated by major industrial countries. The case for creating SDRs to provide funding for the IMF for current account financing is much stronger than the case for using them to back up financial bailouts associated with a potential lender of last resort function advocated by some observers (Fischer 1999) in so far as it could help improve the governance of the Fund and reduce the imbalance between its creditors and debtors. Such a step, if supplemented by the kind of reforms regarding its mandate, operational modalities and governance structure discussed earlier, would give the Fund a chance to operate as an institution for all countries, rather than as an instrument of some.

I. Summary and Conclusions

A genuine reform of the international financial system generally and the Fund particularly depends on developing countries forming a coherent view on a broad range of issues which, in turn, calls for greater understanding of various options as well as extensive deliberations and consultations. This chapter aims at contributing to this process.

A main conclusion that emerges from the discussions above is that the original rationale of the Fund, namely to safeguard international monetary and financial stability, is now even stronger than in the immediate postwar era given the size and speed of international capital flows and their capacity to inflict damage on the real economy. Thus the Fund needs to go back to its core objectives and focus on preventing market and policy failures in order to attain greater international economic stability and facilitate expansion of employment, trade and income. Realization of this objective calls for reforms on several fronts:

- The Fund needs a greater focus. It should stay out of development finance and policy and poverty alleviation. This is an unjustified diversion and an area that belongs to multilateral development banks. All facilities created for this purpose should be transferred to the World Bank as the Fund terminates its activities in development and long-term lending.
- A major task of the Fund is to promote a stable system of exchange rates and payments to ensure a predictable trading environment. In this task the Fund should focus on macroeconomic and exchange rate policies and stay away from trade policies. The attempts by the Fund to promote unilateral liberalization in developing countries drawing on its resources undermine the bargaining power of these countries in multilateral trade negotiations.
- Crisis management and resolution is an increasingly important area of responsibility of the Fund. However, the Fund should not be allowed to bail out lenders and investors since such operations prevent market discipline and create lenders' moral hazard. Accordingly, there should be strict limits to the Fund's crisis lending. Instead, the Fund should help develop orderly workout mechanisms for sovereign debt both to prevent financial meltdown and to restructure debt which cannot be serviced according to its original terms and conditions. Temporary debt standstills and exchange restrictions should thus become legitimate ingredients of multilateral financial arrangements.
- The Fund should focus on lending to finance temporary current account imbalances resulting from external trade and financial shocks as well as from domestic policy imbalances. There should be greater automaticity in meeting payments imbalances resulting from external shocks and less emphasis on policy adjustment. Conditionality should not be extended to structural issues but confined to macroeconomic and exchange rate policies.
- The Fund's resources need to be increased to keep up with growth in international trade. Access of countries to Fund resources should be based on the principle of need, not on countries' contribution to the Fund or their relative importance in the world economy.
- Fund surveillance has been ineffective in preventing emerging market crises. While the primary responsibility for avoiding crises lies with individual countries' own policy choices, the Fund has contributed to increased vulnerability and fragility of emerging markets by promoting premature capital account liberalization and failing to alert

countries against unsustainable surges in capital inflows, currency appreciations and current account imbalances. Progress on this front depends on a fundamental change in the approach of the Fund to capital market issues. The Fund should improve its ability to identify risks and fragilities, and develop policy tools to prevent unsustainable capital flows to emerging markets, including direct and indirect control mechanisms, and provide policy advice.

- The Fund surveillance has also been unable to prevent destabilizing impulses originating from persistent trade imbalances and exchange rate misalignments in major industrial countries. This too is partly due to the poor quality of policy analysis and assessment of market conditions. Separating surveillance from lending decisions and assigning it to an authority independent of the board could improve its quality, legitimacy and impact. However, such a reform alone is unlikely to increase significantly the leverage of the Fund over nonprogram countries and eliminate the imbalance between the Fund's debtors and creditors.
- Any reform designed to bring greater authority and legitimacy would need to address shortcomings in the Fund's governance in several areas including the selection of its head, the distribution of voting rights, transparency and accountability. However the Fund is unlikely to become a genuinely multilateral institution with equal rights and obligations for all its members, in practice as well as in theory, as long as it depends for resources on a handful of industrial countries and its financial activities are intimately linked to bilateral debtor–creditor relations between donor and recipients. These problems could be overcome if the IMF ceases to be an institution funded by its members, and relies on SDRs for the resources needed.

Notes

1 First published as an UNCTAD research paper for the Intergovernmental Group of Twenty-Four on International Monetary Affairs and Development in November 2005. An earlier version was presented at a technical group meeting of G-24 in IMF on 16 September 2005. Comments and suggestions by Ariel Buira, Andrew Cornford, Richard Kozul-Wright and the participants of the G-24 Technical Group Meeting are greatly appreciated. The usual caveat applies.

2 The abolitionists include Walters (1994); Schultz, Simon and Wriston (1998); and Schwartz (1998). Friedman (2004) argues for closing down both the World Bank and the IMF on grounds that "they have done more harm than good, and have the capacity for continuing to do more harm than good."

3 See e.g., Clark (1990), Crook (1991), Schultz (1998), Burnham (1999) and Fischer (2004).

4 The list of reformists is much longer. The better known include the report by the Meltzer Commission (2000) and suggestions made by the former Chief Economist of the World Bank, a stern critique of the Fund, Joseph Stiglitz (2002, particularly chap. 9; and 2003). See also Boughton (2004) and a number of other articles in the same issue of Finance & Development prepared on the occasion of the 60th anniversary of the Bretton Woods Conference. For a review of several reports on the role and reform of the IMF see Williamson (2001). The Group of 24 research program has produced several papers on the reform of the IMF now jointly published by UNCTAD and G24 and placed on their respective websites. There are also many NGOs in the group of reformists demanding profound transformation of both the IMF and the World Bank.

5 For a discussion of the rationale for multilateral financial cooperation and the Bretton Woods institutions see Akyüz (2005a, Section 1).

6 According to Raymond Mikesell, who was actually given the task of calculating the quotas, "Assigning quotas in the Fund was the most difficult and divisive task of the conference [...] The quota formula was not distributed, and White asked me not to reveal it [...] I tried to make the process appear as scientific as possible, but the delegates were intelligent enough to know that the process was more political than scientific" (Mikesell 1994, 35–36).

7 For an excellent account of the rationale and evolution of IMF conditionality, see Dell (1981). For more recent trends see Jungito (1994), Kapur and Webb (2000), and Buira (2003a).

8 Performance criteria are specific preconditions for disbursement of IMF credit. Quantitative performance criteria include macroeconomic policy variables such as international reserves, monetary and credit aggregates and fiscal balances. Structural performance criteria vary widely, but could include specific measures to restructure key sectors such as energy, reform social security systems, or improve financial sector operations (IMF 2002).

9 After the 1969 amendment Article V, Sec. 3(c) stated that the "Fund shall examine a request for a purchase to determine whether the proposed purchase would be consistent with the provisions of this Agreement and the policies adopted under them, provided that requests for reserve tranche purchases shall not be subject to challenge".

10 This distinction is made by Helleiner (1999, 7) in the context of crisis lending. See also Mohammed (1999) who distinguishes between conditional and unconditional liquidity in the same context.

11 See Akyüz and Flassbeck (2002, 98). The last standby agreements with industrial countries were with Italy and the United Kingdom in 1977 and Spain in 1978; see IMF, Finance and Development, September 2004, 15.

12 In effect from 1974 to 1976, the oil facilities allowed the IMF to borrow from oil exporters and other countries in a strong external position and lend to oil importers; see Mohammed (1999, 53).

13 See Dam (1982, 284). For the implications of this mission creep for Bank-Fund relations see Ahluwalia (1999).

14 Mikesell (2001, 1). For a discussion of mission creep see Babb and Buira (2005).

15 For a view that the Fund does not provide development finance but payments support see Boughton (2005, 10).

16 See Rodrik (1995) and Gilbert, Powell and Vines (1999). However, it is not clear if the Bank really meets these expectations (Akyüz 2005a).

17 For an earlier call for merger see Crook (1991).

18 The most interesting example is the case of Korea. In that country financial restructuring undertaken with the support of the Fund in response to the 1997 crisis naturally resulted in an increase in government equities in financial institutions. This became a basis for a legal challenge in the WTO on grounds that such measures constituted actionable subsidies (WTO 2003, paras 8–10).

19 Yang (2005). See also Chauffour (2005). Interestingly the benefits claimed from liberalization are very small, around \$0.5 billion for entire sub-Saharan Africa excluding South Africa (Yang 2005, Table 7), or on average around \$10 million per country per annum, certainly not worth giving up policy options regarding tariffs. For a critical assessment of the costs and benefits of trade liberalization in the context of the current negotiations on industrial tariffs see Akyüz (2005b).

20 See UNCTAD TDR (1999, chap. 4); Santos-Paulino and Thirlwall (2004); UNCTAD TDR (2004, part 2, chap. 5); and Kraev (2005).

21 Keynes (1944, 5). The same point is made by Shultz (1998, 15) who suggested that the IMF should meet in WTO setting rather than with the World Bank since "exchange rates and trade rules are the two sides of the same coin."

22 IMF Press Release 99/14, 25 April 1999.

23 For an earlier assessment along these lines see Akyüz and Cornford (2002, 135). See also Goldstein (2000, 12, 13) and IMF (2003a).

24 The dissenting members of the Meltzer Commission pointed out that the most damaging proposals relate to the IMF's role in financial crises (Fidler 2000); see also Eichengreen and Portes

(2000) and Wolf (2000). In this respect the Commission Report is not consistent. As pointed out by DeLong (2000, 2) while it assigns a lender of last resort role to the Fund for solvent but illiquid governments, it condemns the Fund for its loans to Mexico in 1995 and recommends against any increase in the IMF's resources. See Meltzer (2001) for his comments on the critics.

25 A suggestion along these lines was made by the managing director of the IMF to the Copenhagen Social Summit in March 1995, when he stated that an effective response to financial crises such as the Mexican one depended on "convincing our members to maintain, at the IMF level, the appropriate level of resources to be able to stem similar crises if they were to occur," adding that this should lead to a decision in favor of "further work on the role the SDR could play in putting in place a last resort financial safety net for the world" (IMF Survey, 20 March 1995). See also Mohammed (1999).

26 See Ezekiel (1998); United Nations (1999); and Ahluwalia (1999).

27 For a survey of empirical evidence on the effect of IMF intervention on debtor and creditor incentives see Haldane and Scheibe (2003, 1) who "find concrete evidence of creditor-side moral hazard associated with IMF bail-outs." See also Mina and Martinez-Vazquez (2002) who conclude that IMF lending generates moral hazard in international financial markets from the perspective of the maturity composition of foreign debt.

28 The list of institutions and experts who put forward various proposals for mechanisms to overcome moral hazard and involve the private sector in the resolution of financial crises includes the Group of 22 (1998), the Council of Foreign Relations Independent Task Force (CFRTF 1999); the Emerging Markets Eminent Persons Group (EMEPG, 2001); and the High-Level Panel on Financing for Development (Zedillo 2001). For a discussion of issues in bailouts and reform see Goldstein (2000), Haldane (1999), Akyüz (2002) and Eichengreen (2002).

29 A proposal to apply bankruptcy principles was made by UNCTAD TDR (1986, annex to chap. 4) during the debt crisis of the 1980s. It was subsequently raised by Sachs (1995) and revisited by UNCTAD TDR (1998, 89–93) during the East Asian crisis. For a further discussion see Radelet (1999) and Akyüz (2002). The idea of establishing orderly workout procedures for international debt goes back even further. In 1942, in a report by the United States Council on Foreign Relations attention was drawn to interwar disputes between debtors and creditors and the need was recognized for exploration of the possibilities of establishing "a supranational judicial or arbitral institution for the settlements of disputes between debtors and creditors" (Oliver 1971, 20).

30 See IMF (2000). For further discussion of the debate in the IMF see Akyüz (2002, 123–28).

31 See IMF (2003b) for a description of the SDRM and background information.

32 Boom–bust cycles characterize not only the postwar experience, but almost the entire history of private capital flows to developing countries. The boom in private flows to Latin American countries that started soon after their independence around 1820 was followed by widespread defaults and disappearance of international liquidity to the region until around 1850. Again the boom of the 1920s was followed by widespread defaults and cutbacks in private lending in the 1930s. For a more detailed account of these cycles see UNCTAD TDR (2003, chap. 2, and 129–32), UNCTAD TDR (1998, part 1, chap. 3) and Kregel (2004).

33 A "harsh economic scenario" recently simulated by the IMF (2005c, 8–10) includes a 30 percent contraction in private flows to emerging markets, increased spread, disorderly dollar depreciation, lower growth and weak commodity prices.

34 This view is also held by the majority in the Meltzer Commission (2000, 11). See also Gilbert, Powell and Vines (1999, 622) who note that during the 1998 crisis "the Bank provided around $8 billion in short-term liquidity in the packages of lending to Thailand, Indonesia and Korea. This 'defensive' lending had little to do with promoting development (in the normal sense of that expression). If it were to be repeated, such emergency lending could severely destabilize the Bank's normal development lending".

35 See the joint paper by two senior officials of Bank of Canada and Bank of England, Haldane and Kruger (2001).
36 These include a high probability that debt will remain sustainable and good prospects for the member to regain access to private financial markets within the time Fund resources would be outstanding (IMF 2005c, 4) – conditions that failed to hold in the case of Argentina.
37 For a similar proposal see Kelkar, Yadav and Chaudhry (2004) who argue that contributions should be based on member's capacity to pay; access to resources should be based on need; and voting rights should balance the rights of creditors with the principle of sovereign equality.
38 See Executive Board Decision 5392-(77/63) adopted on 29 April 1977.
39 Group of Ten (1985, para. 40). For further discussion see Akyüz and Dell (1987).
40 IMF Interim Committee Communiqué of 16 April 1998, Washington, DC.
41 For the recent experience see Goldstein (2005b).
42 For a discussion of policy issues in securing greater financial stability see Kindleberger (1995), McCauley (2001), BIS (2001, chap. 7); and Akyüz (2004).
43 Because of such regulations Taiwan has so far been denied the developed market status by FTSE, the global index provider jointly owned by the *Financial Times* and the London Stock Exchange (Hille and Jung-a 2005, 3).
44 In a recent study of the vulnerability of emerging markets to adverse global financial conditions, potential exchange rate problems and fiscal and monetary policy challenges, Turkey heads the list (Goldstein 2005b, particularly table 11). On external financial fragility of the Turkish economy see also UNECE (2005, chap. 4).
45 Indeed management of external liabilities was a key part of the report of the Financial Stability Forum on capital flows. For a discussion see Cornford (2000).
46 See remarks by Camdessus on "How Should the IMF be Reshaped?" in *Finance and Development*, September 2004, 27.
47 For a discussion of these issues see Cottarelli (2005); van Houtven (2004); Kelkar, Chaudhry and Vanduzer-Snow (2005); and Kelkar, Chaudhry, Vanduzer-Snow and Bhaskar (2005) Some of these elements of governance reform have also been emphasized, to varying degrees, by the three former managing directors of the Fund, De Larosière, Camdessus and Köhler (*Finance and Devlopment*, 27–29).
48 See IMF Press Release 99/56, 23 November 1999.
49 See, e.g., Woods (1998, 2001), Mohammed (2000), Buira (2003b, and 2005), Kelkar, Yadav and Chaudhry (2004), and Kelkar, Chaudhry, Vanduzer-Snow, and Bhaskar (2005).
50 IMF (2004a, 72). For the definition of net financial position in the IMF see Boughton (2005, 4–5).
51 The former managing director Köhler argues that "it's critical for the IMF to maintain the spirit of consensus [...] [and] this is more important than numerical representation," while another former managing director, De Larosière, confirms that this is indeed the case: "During my years as a Managing Director, I do not remember that we ever counted votes." *Finance and Development*, 29.
52 See Buira (2003b, 4). Currently there are 30 developing countries represented by EDs from industrial countries (12 by Australia, 10 by Canada, 6 by Spain, and one by Italy and Belgium each).
53 Mohammed (2000, 208) uses "structural debtors" and "structural creditors" to make the distinction between industrial and developing countries.
54 For a brief history of the debate over IMF governance see Cottarelli (2005, 6–9).

References

Ahluwalia, Montek S. 1999. "The IMF and the World Bank in the New Financial Architecture." In *International Monetary and Financial Issues for the 1990s*, vol. 11. Geneva: UNCTAD.

Akyüz, Y. 2002. "Crisis Management and Burden Sharing." In *Reforming the Global Financial Architecture: Issues and Proposals*, edited by Yılmaz Akyüz. London: Zed Books.

______. 2004. "Managing Financial Instability and Shocks in a Globalizing World." Paper presented at a public lecture sponsored by Bank Negara and the University of Malaya, Kuala Lumpur. 6 February.

______. 2005a. "Rectifying Capital Market Imperfections: The Continuing Rationales for Multilateral Lending." In *The New Public Finance: Responding to Global Challenges*, edited by Inge Kaul and Ronald Mendoza. New York: Oxford University Press.

______. 2005b. "WTO Negotiations on Industrial Tariffs: What is at Stake for Developing Countries?" *TWN Trade & Development* Series 24. Penang: Third World Network.

Akyüz, Yılmaz, and Korkut Boratav. 2003. "The Making of the Turkish Financial Crisis," *World Development* 31 (9), September.

Akyüz, Yılmaz, and Andrew Cornford. 2002. "Capital Flows to Developing Countries and the Reform of the International Financial System." In *Governing Globalization*, edited by Deepak Nayyar. New York: Oxford University Press.

Akyüz, Yılmaz, and Sidney Dell. 1987. "Issues in International Monetary Reform." In *International Monetary and Financial Issues for the Developing Countries*. Geneva: UNCTAD.

Akyüz, Yılmaz, and Heiner Flassbeck. 2002. "Exchange Rate Regimes and the Scope for Regional Cooperation." In *Reforming the Global Financial Architecture. Issues and Proposals*, edited by Yılmaz Akyüz. London: Zed Books.

Atkinson, Anthony B., ed. 2003. "New Sources of Development Finance." *UNU-WIDER Studies in Development Economics*. New York: Oxford University Press.

Babb, Sarah, and Ariel Buira. 2005. "Mission Creep, Mission Push and Discretion: The Case of IMF Conditionality." In *The IMF and the World Bank at Sixty*, edited by Ariel Buira. London: Anthem Press.

Balls, Edward. 2003. "Preventing Financial Crises: The Case for Independent IMF Surveillance." Remarks made at the Institute for International Economics, Washington, DC. 6 March.

BIS (Bank for International Settlements). 2001. *71st Annual Report*. Basel.

Boughton, James M. 2004. "IMF at 60: Reflections on the Reform at the IMF and the Demands of a Changing World Economy." *Finance & Development*, September.

______. 2005. "Does the World Need a Universal Financial Institution?" IMF, Working Paper 116. Washington, DC.

Buira, Ariel. 2003a. "An Analysis of IMF Conditionality." UNCTAD G-24 Discussion Paper 22. Geneva.

______. 2003b. "The Governance of the IMF in a Global Economy," G24. Washington, DC.

______. 2005. "The Bretton Woods Institutions: Governance Without Legitimacy?" In *Reforming the Governance of the IMF and the World Bank*, edited by Ariel Buira. London: Anthem Press.

Burnham, James B. 1999. "The IMF and World Bank: Time to Merge." *The Washington Quarterly* 22 (2), Spring.

Chauffour, Jean-Pierre. 2005. "Ensuring Coherence between Africa's Trade Agenda and Long-Term Development Objectives." Introductory remarks made at the Workshop on Ensuring Coherence between Africa's Trade Agenda and Long-Term Development Objectives, Lausanne. 13–14 May.

Clark, Lindley H Jr. 1990. "Let's Merge the World Bank and the IMF." *Wall Street Journal*. 4 January.

CFRTF (Council on Foreign Relations Independent Task Force). 1999. "Safeguarding Prosperity in a Global Financial System: The Future International Financial Architecture." Washington, DC: Council on Foreign Relations.

Cornford, Andrew. 2000. "Commentary on the Financial Stability Forum's Report of the Working Group on Capital Flows." UNCTAD, G-24 Discussion Paper 7. Geneva.

______. 2002."Standards and Regulations." In *Reforming the Global Financial Architecture: Issues and Proposals*, edited by Yılmaz Akyüz. London: Zed Books.

Cottarelli, Carlo. 2005. "Efficiency and Legitimacy: Trade-Offs in IMF Governance." IMF, Working Paper WP/05/107. Washington, DC.

Crook, Clive. 1991. "Sisters in the Wood – A Survey of the IMF and the World Bank." *Economist*. 12 October.

Dam, Kenneth W. 1982. "The Rules of the Game: Reform and Evolution in the International Monetary System." Chicago: University of Chicago Press.

Das, Bhagirath Lal. 1999. "The World Trade Organisation. A Guide to the Framework for International Trade." Penang: Third World Network.

Dell, Sidney. 1981. "On Being Grandmotherly: The Evolution of Fund Conditionality." Essays in International Finance 144. Princeton, NJ: Princeton University Press.

______. 1985. "The Fifth Credit Tranche." *World Development* 13 (2): 245–49.

______. 1986. "The History of the IMF." *World Development* 14 (9): 1203–12.

DeLong, J. Bradford. 2000. Comment on "The Meltzer Report." http://www.j-bradford-delong.net/TotW/meltzer.html. Accessed 14 September 2005.

De Rato, Rodrigo. 2005. "Remarks at the Institute for International Economics Conference on IMF Reform." 23 September. http://www.imf.org/external/np/speeches/2005/092305.htm. Accessed 30 September 2005.

Eichengreen, Barry. 2002. "Financial Crises and What To Do About Them." New York: Oxford University Press.

Eichengreen, Barry, and Richard Portes. 2000. "A Shortsighted Vision for IMF Reform." *Financial Times*, 9 March.

EMEPG (Emerging Markets Eminent Persons Group). 2001. "Building the International Financial Architecture." Seoul: Korea Institute for International Economics.

Ezekiel, Hannan. 1998. "The Role of Special Drawing Rights in the International Monetary System." In UNCTAD, *International Monetary and Financial Issues for the 1990s*, vol. 9. Geneva.

Fidler, Stephen. 2000. "Report Urges Slimming Down of IMF and World Bank." *Financial Times*. 8 March.

Fischer, Fritz. 2004. "Thinking the Unthinkable: Combining the IMF and World Bank." *The International Economy*, Fall.

Fischer, Stanley. 1999. "On the Need for an International Lender of Last Resort." *Journal of Economic Perspectives* 13 (4): 85–104.

Friedman, Milton. 2004. "60 at 60: Is There a Need to Change the Structure of the IMF and World Bank?" IMF/World Bank 60th anniversary special. Emerging Markets. http://www.emergingmarkets.org/Article/1017839/Features/IMFWorld-Bank-60th-anniversary-special.html. Accessed 24 January 2005.

Gilbert, Christopher, Andrew Powell and David Vines. 1999. "Positioning the World Bank." *Economic Journal* 109 (459): 598–633.

Goldstein, Morris. 2000. "Strengthening the International Financial Architecture. Where Do We Stand?" Institute of International Economics, Working Paper 00-3. Washington, DC.

______. 2005a. "The International Financial Architecture." In C. Fred Bergsten, ed., *The United States and the World Economy: Foreign Policy for the Next Decade*. Institute for International Economics, Washington, DC.

______. 2005b. "What Might the Next Emerging-Market Financial Crisis Look Like?" Institute for International Economics, Working Paper 05-7. Washington, DC.

Group of Ten. 1985. "The Functioning of the International Monetary System." A Report to the Ministers and Governors by the Group of Deputies. Washington, DC.

Group of 22. 1998. Report of the Working Group on International Financial Crises, Washington, DC. http://www.bis.org/publ/othp01d.pdf. Accessed 2 March 2005.

Haldane, Andrew G. 1999. "Private Sector Involvement in Financial Crisis: Analytics and Public Policy Approaches." Bank of England, Financial Stability Review 9. London.

Haldane, Andrew G., and Mark Kruger. 2001. "The Resolution of International Financial Crises: Private Finance and Public Funds." Bank of Canada Working Paper 2001-20.

Haldane, Andrew G., and Jorg Scheibe. 2003. "IMF Lending and Creditor Moral Hazard." Bank of England, Working Paper 216. London.

Helleiner, Gerry. 1999. "Small Countries and the New World Financial Architecture." CIS Working Paper 2000-4. University of Toronto.

Hille, Kathryn, and Jung-a Song. 2005. "Reform Hurdles Still to be Jumped." Financial Times. Fund Management. 24 October.

IIF. (Institute of International Finance). 2005a. "Update on Capital Flows to Emerging Market Economies." 31 March. Washington, DC.

______. 2005b. "Tightened Monetary Conditions, Slowing Growth, Global Economic Imbalances Pose Challenges for Emerging Markets." Press Release. 26 May. Washington, DC.

IMF. (International Monetary Fund). 1969. *The International Monetary Fund 1945–1965*, vols 1–3. Washington, DC.

______. 2000. "Executive Board Discusses Involving the Private Sector in the Resolution of Financial Crisis." Public Information Notice 00/80. Washington, DC.

______. 2002. "IMF Conditionality: A Factsheet." Washington, DC. www.imf.org/external/np/exr/facts/conditio.htm.

______. 2003a. "IMF Concludes Discussion on the Review of Contingent Credit Lines." Public Information Notice 03/146. Washington, DC.

______. 2003b. Proposals for a Sovereign Debt Restructuring Mechanism (SDRM). A Factsheet. January.

______. 2004a. IMF Annual Report. Washington, DC.

______. 2004b. "Review of the Compensatory Financing Facility." Washington, DC.

______. 2004c. "IMF Concludes Review of the Compensatory Financing Facility." Public Information Notice 04/35. Washington, DC.

______. 2005a. IMF Financial Activities: Update June 2. Washington, DC.

______. 2005b. "The IMF's Trade Integration Mechanism." Washington, DC.

______. 2005c. "Review of Access Policy in the Credit Tranches, the Extended Fund Facility and the Poverty Reduction and Growth Facility, and Exceptional Access Policy." Washington, DC.

IMF/GIE (IMF Group of Independent Experts). 1999. External Evaluation of IMF Surveillance. Report by a Group of Independent Experts. Washington, DC.

IMF/IEO. (IMF Independent Evaluation Office). 2005. Report on the Evaluation of the IMF's Approach to Capital Account Liberalisation. Washington, DC.

IMF/WB. 2004. "Strengthening IMF-World Bank Collaboration on Country Programs and Conditionality: Progress Report." 24 February. Washington, DC.

Jungito, Roberto. 1994. "IMF-World Bank Policy Advice: The Coordination/ Cross-Conditionality Question." In UNCTAD, *International Monetary and Financial Issues for the 1990s*, vol. 4. Geneva.

Kapur, Davesh, and Richard Webb. 1994. "The Evolution of Multilateral Development Banks." In UNCTAD, *International Monetary and Financial Issues for the 1990s*, vol. 4. Geneva.

______. 2000. "Governance-Related Conditionalities of the International Financial Institutions." UNCTAD, G-24 Discussion Paper 6. Geneva.

Kelkar, Vijay L., Praveen K. Chaudhry, and Martha Vanduzer-Snow. 2005. "Time for Change at the IMF." *Finance and Development*, March.

Kelkar, Vijay L., Praveen K. Chaudhry, Martha Vanduzer-Snow, and V. Bhaskar. 2005. "Reforming the International Monetary Fund: Towards Enhanced Accountability and Legitimacy." In *Reforming the Governance of the IMF and the World Bank*, Ariel Buira. London: Anthem Press.

Kelkar, Vijay L., Vikash Yadav and Praveen K. Chaudhry. 2004. "Reforming the Governance of the International Monetary Fund." *The World Economy* 27, May: 727–43.

Keynes, J. M. 1980. John Maynard Keynes at the House of Lords, 23 May 1944. In *The Collected Writings of John Maynard Keynes*, vol. 26, "Activities 1941–1946: Shaping the Post-War World, Bretton Woods and Reparations." Cambridge: Cambridge University Press.

Kindleberger, C. P. 1995. "Asset Inflation and Monetary Policy." *Banco Nazionale del Lavaro Quarterly Review* 98, 192.

Kraev, Egor. 2005. "Estimating GDP Effects of Trade Liberalisation on Developing Countries." London: Christian Aid.

Kregel, Jan. 2004. "External Financing for Development and International Financial Stability." UNCTAD, G-24 Discussion Paper 32. Geneva.

Krueger, Anne O. 2001. "International Financial Architecture for 2002: A New Approach to Sovereign Debt Restructuring." Address given at the National Economists' Club Annual Members' Dinner, American Enterprise Institute. Washington, DC. 26 November.

______. 2005. "Trade Policy and the Strategy for Global Insertion." Speech at the Conference on Latin America in the Global Economy. Notre Dame, Indiana. 19 April. Washington, DC: IMF.

McCauley, R. N. 2001. "Setting Monetary Policy in East Asia: Goals, Developments and Institutions." Paper presented to the Conference on Financialization and the Global Economy," PERI, University of Massachusetts, Amherst, 7–8 December.

Meltzer, Allan H. 2001. "The Report of the International Financial Institution Advisory Commission: Comments on the Critics." Carnegie Mellon Graduate School of Industrial Administration. http://repository.cmu.edu/cgi/viewcontent.cgi?article=1029&context=tepper. Accessed 1 October 2002.

Meltzer Commission. 2000. Final Report of the International Financial Institution Advisory Commission. Washington, DC: U.S. Government Printing Office.

Mikesell, Raymond F. 1994. "The Bretton Woods Debates: A Memoir." Essays in International Finance Series 192. Princeton, NJ: Princeton University.

______. 2001. "The Bretton Woods Vision: From the Past to the Present." Special Commentary. *The Bretton Woods Committee Newsletter*, Summer.

Mina, Wasseem, and Jorge Martinez-Vazquez. 2002. "IMF Lending, Maturity of International Debt and Moral Hazard." International Studies Program, Andrew Young School of Policy Studies, Working Paper 03-01. Georgia State University, Atlanta.

Mohammed, Aziz Ali. 1999. "Adequacy of International Liquidity in the Current Financial Environment." In UNCTAD, *International Monetary and Financial Issues for the 1990s*, vol. 11. Geneva.

______. 2000. "The Future Role of the IMF: A Developing Country Point of View." In *Reforming the International Financial System: Crisis Prevention and Response*, edited by Jan J. Teunissen. Fondad: The Hague.

Oliver, Robert W. 1971. "Early Plans for a World Bank." *Princeton Studies in International Finance Series* 29. Princeton, NJ: Princeton University.

______. 1975. "International Economic Cooperation and the World Bank." London: Macmillan.

Radelet, Steven. 1999. "Orderly Workouts for Cross-Border Private Debt." In UNCTAD, *International Monetary and Financial Issues for the 1990s*, vol. 11. Geneva.

Rodrik, Dani. 1995. "Why Is There Multilateral Lending?" National Bureau of Economic Research, NBER Working Paper 5160. Cambridge, MA.

Sachs, Jeffrey D. 1995. "Do We Need an International Lender of Last Resort?" Frank D. Graham Lecture. Princeton University, vol. 8. 20 April.

______. 1998. "External Debt, Structural Adjustment and Economic Growth." In UNCTAD, *International Monetary and Financial Issues for the 1990s*, vol. 9. Geneva.

Santos-Paulino, Amelia, and A.P. Thirlwall. 2004. "The Impact of Trade Liberalisation on Exports, Imports and the Balance of Payments of Developing Countries." Economic Journal. 114: F50–F72.

Schneider, Benu, and Sacha Silva. 2002. "Conference Report on International Standards and Codes: The Developing Country Perspective." Conference held on 21 June 2002 at the Commonwealth Secretariat. London: Overseas Development Institute.

Schultz, George, P. 1998. "Merge the IMF and World Bank." *The International Economy* January/ February: 14–16.

Schultz, George P., William E. Simon and Walter B. Wriston. 1998. "Who Needs the IMF?" *Wall Street Journal*, 3 February.

Schwartz, Anna J. 1998. "Time to Terminate the ESF and the IMF." Cato Foreign Policy Briefing 48.

Stiglitz, Joseph E. 2002. "Globalization and Its Discontents." New York: W. W. Norton & Company.

_______. 2003. "Ethics, Market and Government Failure, and Globalization." Paper presented to the Vatican Conference at the Ninth Plenary Session of the Pontifical Academy of Social Sciences, Casina Pio IV, 2–6 May.

Summers, Lawrence H. 2000. "Testimony Before the Banking Committee of the House of Representatives." Treasury News, 23 March. Washington, DC.

Triffin, Robert. 1976. "Jamaica: 'Major Revision' or Fiasco". In E. M. Bernstein et al. eds., Reflections on Jamaica. Essays in International Finance Series 115. New York: Princeton University Press.

UNCTAD TDR (various issues). *Trade and Development Report.* Geneva: United Nations.

_______. 2004. The Least Developed Countries Report 2004. Linking Trade and Poverty Reduction. Geneva.

United Nations. 1999. Towards a New International Financial Architecture, Report of the Task Force of the United Nations Executive Committee of Economic and Social Affairs, January.

UNECE (United Nations Economic Commission for Europe). 2005. Economic Survey of Europe No.1. Geneva.

Van Houtven, Leo. 2004. "Rethinking IMF Governance." Finance and Development. September.

Wahl, Peter. 2005. *International Taxation: Regulating Globalization, Financing Development.* World Economy, Ecology and Development (WEED), Berlin.

Walters, Alan. 1994. *Do We Need the IMF and the World Bank?* London: Institute of Economic Affairs.

Williamson, John. 2001. "The Role of the IMF: A Guide to the Reports." In *Developing Countries and the Global Financial System*, edited by S. Griffith-Jones and A. Bhattacharya. London: The Commonwealth Secretariat.

Woods, Ngaire. 1998. "Governance in International Organizations: The Case for Reform in the Bretton Woods Institutions." In UNCTAD, *International Monetary and Financial Issues for the 1990s*, vol. 9. Geneva.

_______. 2001. Accountability, Governance, and Reform in the International Financial Institutions, Working Paper. Oxford: University of Oxford, University College.

Wolf, Martin. 2000. "Between Revolution and Reform – The Meltzer Commission's Vision." *Financial Times*, 8 March.

WTO. 2003. "Report of the Meeting. Working Group on Trade, Debt and Finance." WT/WGTDF/M/4. Geneva.

_______. 2004a. "Coherence in Global Economic Policymaking and Cooperation between the WTO, the IMF and the World Bank." WT/TF/COH/S/9. Geneva: WTO.

_______. 2004b. "Doha Work Program." Draft General Council Decision of 31 July 2004. WT/GC/W/535. Geneva: WTO.

Yang, Yongzheng. 2005. "Africa in the Doha Round: Dealing with Preference Erosion and Beyond." Paper presented at the Workshop on Ensuring Coherence between Africa's Trade Agenda and Long-Term Development Objectives, Lausanne, May 13–14

Zedillo, Ernesto. 2001. "Report of the High-Level Panel on Financing for Development." New York: United Nations.

Part Two

THE GLOBAL ECONOMIC CRISIS AND DEVELOPING COUNTRIES

Chapter VI

THE CURRENT GLOBAL FINANCIAL TURMOIL AND ASIAN DEVELOPING COUNTRIES[1]

A. Introduction

After almost six years of exceptional performance, the world economy has now entered a period of uncertainty due to a financial turmoil triggered by the subprime mortgage crisis in the United States. World economic growth and stability in the next few years will depend crucially on the impact of the crisis on the United States economy and its global spillovers. The resilience of emerging markets to direct and indirect shocks from the crisis will no doubt play an important role, since much of global growth in recent years has been due to expansion in these economies, notably in Asia. The extent to which growth and stability in Asian emerging markets can be decoupled crucially depends on prevailing domestic economic conditions as well as the policy response to possible shocks from the crisis.

This chapter takes up these issues. The following section posits the main theme of the paper that current difficulties in the United States economy and vulnerabilities in emerging markets are not unrelated to financial excesses that made a major contribution to global expansion in the past six years, including credit, asset and investment bubbles triggered by rapid expansion of global liquidity.

Section C takes up the causes, nature and the severity of the crisis in the United States, and the policy response already underway with a view to assessing their possible effects on growth and external adjustment. The role that regulatory shortcomings have played in the subprime crisis is examined in some detail because it provides useful lessons for emerging markets where such shortcomings are often seen as the root cause of crises.

This is followed in Section D by a discussion of key aspects of prevailing economic conditions in major Asian developing economies affecting their vulnerability to financial shocks from the crisis, examining the extent to which they have been successful in managing the surge in capital inflows and preventing the emergence of fragility and imbalances, drawing on the lessons from the 1997 crisis. Greater attention is paid to China and India since these two countries together account for about four-fifths of the total output and two-thirds of the total trade of developing countries in the region, and China has strong intraregional trade and financial linkages in East and Southeast Asia.

Section E looks at possible trade and financial effects of the crisis on Asian developing economies; makes an assessment of mainstream projections and scenarios; and discusses policy challenges and options. It is argued that the larger economies of the region, China and India, have fragility and imbalances which could be laid bare by shocks from the subprime crisis. However, in general, countries with strong fiscal and balance of payments positions, including China and several East and Southeast Asian countries, have adequate policy space to respond positively to shocks from the crisis. But others, including India, may face difficulties if the crisis leads to a reversal of direction of capital flows – an outcome which is not likely but which cannot be ruled out. There is a need to secure intraregional consistency in policy response, notably with respect to expansionary macroeconomic policies and currency adjustments. Consideration could also be given to establishing mechanisms for regional exchange rate cooperation on a more durable basis.

B. The Role of Finance in the Recent Global Expansion

To many observers the sudden turnaround in world economic prospects has come as a surprise in view of the strength and persistence of economic growth and stability since the early years of the decade. From 2002 until the end of 2007 world economic growth averaged 4.5 percent per annum compared to 3 percent in the 1990s. Growth has been particularly strong and broad-based in the developing world, reaching some 7.5 percent, twice the rate of the 1990s. Real commodity prices rose to levels not seen since the 1970s and developing countries as a whole started to run trade surpluses with advanced countries thanks to the strong export performance of China and trade surpluses of fuel exporters. After a short interruption in the early years of the millennium, private capital flows to developing countries recovered strongly and spreads on emerging market debt fell to historical lows. Price stability in the developing world has been unprecedented for many decades, with single digit inflation rates being the rule rather than the exception. There has been no major exchange rate and financial turmoil in the developing world, including in emerging markets with large and widening current account deficits.

Current economic difficulties and vulnerabilities, however, are not unrelated to forces driving this expansion. As a result of continued deregulation of financial markets and further opening of national borders to international capital flows, economic activity in both advanced and developing countries has come to be increasingly shaped by financial factors. The procyclical behavior of financial markets tends to reinforce expansionary and contractionary forces, amplifying the swings in investment, output and employment.[2] Risks are often underestimated at times of expansion, giving rise to a rapid credit growth, asset price inflation, overindebtedness and excessive spending, and adding to growth momentum. However, these also produce financial fragility which is exposed with a cyclical downturn in economic activity and/or increased cost of borrowing when incomes can no longer service the debt incurred, giving rise to defaults, credit crunch, asset price deflation and economic contraction – the kind of difficulties that the United States economy is now facing.

From the early years of the decade the world economy went through a period of easy money as policy interest rates in major industrial countries, notably the United States and Japan, were brought down to historically low levels and international liquidity expanded rapidly.[3] These, together with stagnant equity prices in most mature markets, led to a search-for-yield by creditors and investors. In the United States ample liquidity and low interest rates, together with regulatory shortcomings, resulted in a rapid growth of speculative lending and a bubble in the property markets, providing a major stimulus to growth, but also sowing the seeds of current difficulties. Low interest rates in some other advanced countries, notably in Japan, encouraged cross-currency flows toward countries with higher interest rates, including in the form of highly leveraged carry trades. The very same factors have played a major role in the strong recovery of capital flows to emerging markets, contributing to currency appreciations, asset bubbles and credit expansion, and stimulating spending and growth in the recipient countries. The credit crunch unleashed by the bursting of the subprime bubble and its global spillovers now threatens to reverse this process and produce a sharp slowdown in global growth.

C. Expansion and Crisis in the United States

1. The subprime boom and bust

Since the 1980s the United States economy has been increasingly driven by financial boom–bust cycles. Economic expansions are generally accentuated by credit and asset bubbles which eventually lead to credit crunch and debt deflation, and threaten to push the economy into a deep and long recession. Monetary policy largely ignores financial excesses at times of expansion, but tends to be deployed rapidly when the bubbles burst, and in doing so prepares the ground for the next bubble.

The United States economy had entered the 1990s with a recession deepened by a banking and real estate crisis produced by a combination of financial deregulation and deposit insurance in the previous decade. The response was a sharp reduction in policy interest rates to allow debtors to refinance debt at substantially lower rates and banks to build up capital by riding the yield curve – that is, by borrowing short term and investing in higher-yielding medium-term government securities.[4] This, together with advances in information technology, created the dot-com bubble in the second half of the 1990s. The Fed refrained from applying the brakes even though its chairman recognized that the United States economy was suffering from "irrational exuberance" as the stock market, led by the information sector, was booming. But when the bubble burst in the early 2000s, it came to the rescue, bringing policy interest rates to historical lows and expanding liquidity rapidly for fear of a credit crunch and asset deflation throwing the economy into a deep recession.

This, together with the continued deregulation of the financial system, resulted in another bubble, this time in the real estate market supported by subprime mortgage lending. Despite warnings, the Fed ignored the bubble and refrained from using monetary instruments and the regulatory authority it had been granted to stem speculative lending.[5] But, again, it has responded rapidly to the subprime crisis by large cuts in interest rates and massive expansion of liquidity, raising concerns that the United States economy may be poised to go through yet another boom–bust cycle.

A brief examination of the role that regulatory shortcomings have played in these boom–bust cycles helps reveal the nature and origin of the present crisis and produce valuable policy lessons. During the past few decades the banking industry in the United States and most other advanced countries has been losing its relative position in the financial sector as deposits became a less important source of funds for financial intermediaries. Furthermore, the margin between credit and deposit rates has been falling because of growing competition from nonbank financial intermediaries. In the United States the pressure on bank profits intensified during the 1980s with the removal of control over deposit rates, losing the banks the cost advantage at a time when accelerated growth of markets for commercial papers and junk bonds and increased securitization of assets put pressure on lending rates.[6]

The response was twofold. First, banks increasingly went into new, riskier areas of lending, notably for commercial and residential property and leveraged takeovers and buyouts. Second, they expanded their fee-based, off-balance-sheet activities in the capital market through subsidiaries and affiliates. Simultaneously, securities firms and insurance companies started engaging in traditional banking activities through various affiliates and these nonbank lenders have become increasingly important in the credit market, without, however, having access to insured deposits or being subject to conventional prudential restraints. These developments have strengthened the link between credit and asset markets whereby credit expansion has increasingly resulted in asset bubbles which have, in turn, provided the basis on which credit could grow thanks to the practice of mark-to-market valuation of assets.

Regulatory policies have not been adapted to this new financial environment even though there was considerable awareness of the risks involved.[7] Rather, the authorities submitted to pressures for further deregulation. Until recently, in the United States the banks' off-balance-sheet activities in nontraditional areas through affiliates and subsidiaries were subject to specific limits. In 1999, however, new legislation effectively demolished the firewalls between commercial banking and investment banking by allowing the former to expand into capital market activities and the latter to enter more deeply into the territory of traditional commercial banking – a step which has played a major role in the subprime boom–bust cycle.[8]

The new legislation allowed the banks to join mortgage companies and rapidly expand high-risk mortgage lending as well as credit card and car loans, and move them off their balance sheets through securitization. In search for yield in conditions of exceptionally low interest rates, many banks enticed households into taking up so-called "teaser loans" in very much the same way they had done in Asia in the run-up to the 1997 crisis; that is, loans for which a *borrower is qualified "based on an artificially low initial interest rate, even though he or she doesn't have sufficient income to make the monthly payments when the interest rate is reset in two years"* (Pearlstein 2007). They then put these into packages of mortgage-backed securities as collateralized debt obligations and sold in the capital market with the help of credit rating agencies, thereby eschewing capital charges while earning handsome fees and commissions. The special investment vehicles (SIVs) created for this purpose have acquired large amounts of securitized higher-yielding long-term loans with funds raised by issuing short-term commercial paper, often with the support of their sponsoring banks.[9]

As banks' profits from these nontraditional activities were boosted, there were strong incentives to expand such loans. This sustained the growth in demand for housing which, in turn, kept prices rising, thereby validating the underlying credit expansion.

It also provided a strong stimulus to investment in housing construction which became a main driving force of expansion: during 2002–2006 real residential private investment increased by almost one-third while nonresidential fixed capital formation rose by a mere 4 percent (OECD 2007, annex tables 6–7). However, as the housing market was satiated, prices levelled off and policy interest rates were raised, there was a sharp increase in foreclosures in the course of 2006, leading to declines in house prices, bursting the bubble.[10] The market for mortgage-based securities has totally seized up, as has the market for commercial paper issued by SIVs to fund securitized loans. Many of these securities have now been downgraded from triple-A ratings to the class of junk bonds.

High-risk financial operations concerning subprime lending, securitization and investment are not confined to the United States. Many of the banks involved are global banks operating in several mature and emerging markets. Banks in major European countries have been involved directly or indirectly by issuing or holding securitized subprime assets and running or sponsoring SIVs. The United Kingdom experienced a similar subprime bubble leading to serious difficulties in certain financial institutions of which Northern Rock is the most prominent. Several German and Swiss banks have also seen their solvency threatened because of large losses on subprime operations. Losses from the crisis are now generally recognized to be at least $1 trillion.

The mortgage-based securities have been marketed globally, in both mature and emerging economies, acquired by hedge funds, insurance companies, pension funds, foundations, nonfinancial firms and individuals so that the impact is felt more generally, across several sectors and even in countries which were not among the originators of such lending.[11] An important part of them was guaranteed by bond insurers, the so-called monolines, which joined the spree to benefit from the housing boom – something that is particularly revealing about the opaque nature of the operations, since bond insurers are expected to be in a better position to assess the risks involved. These insurers lack the necessary capital to cover the losses on defaulted securities and they have now started losing their credit ratings, with attendant consequences for bond ratings and values in other segments of the market.[12]

2. The policy response and prospects

The subprime bubble has left the United States economy with excessive residential investment which cannot be put into full use without significant declines in house prices. The household sector has ended up with debt in excess of equity represented by such investment. An important part of portfolios of banks and their affiliates is not performing. Bond insurers are faced with massive obligations they can no longer fulfil. And many investors across the world have found themselves holding worthless mortgage-based securities and commercial paper.

There is considerable uncertainty over whether the United States economy will succumb to this debt crisis brought on by years of profligate lending or be able to restore growth after a brief interruption. The evolution of economic activity will no doubt depend on the impact of the crisis on private spending. This will, in turn, depend on the ability and willingness of banks to provide adequate financing on appropriate terms and conditions, and of households and firms to expand consumption and investment.

In recognition of these two aspects of the problem, policymakers in the United States have responded to mitigate the difficulties in the financial system by large cuts in interest rates and provision of ample liquidity, and to support aggregate spending and incomes through a fiscal package.[13] Monetary easing is certainly helpful, but cannot fully resolve the difficulties the United States financial system is currently facing since this is, in essence, a solvency crisis. Lower policy rates and ample liquidity can help banks to gradually build up capital by riding the yield curve, but they cannot address the immediate problem of depleted capital. Beyond the arbitrage between the Fed and the Treasury, banks' ability to build up capital rapidly by investing in higher-yielding private securities is limited because, on current regulatory practices, this would necessitate spare capital in the first place.

The bailout provided by the "Big Bank" is thus incomplete even though the Fed has now gone further, accepting mortgage-based securities as collateral and lending directly to major investment banks. A more effective solution would be outright nationalization of nonperforming private debt.[14] This is what many governments in emerging markets hit by financial crises in recent years were forced to do, including in Asia where such operations added considerably to public debt.[15] However, such a solution would not only create moral hazard, but also sustain misalignments in asset prices, postponing the problems, possibly to come back with greater force.[16]

An alternative solution would be fire-sale foreign direct investment (FDI), as practised during the Asian crisis when collapse of currencies and asset prices created ample opportunities for foreigners to grab assets at drastically reduced prices (Krugman 1998). Many of the troubled banks have indeed been seeking injection of new capital from abroad, mostly from sovereign wealth funds (SWFs) in emerging markets, including China, Singapore and fuel exporters in the Gulf. So far the amount raised seems to be in the order of $40 billion, well below the capital losses (Gieve 2008). Misgivings about investment by SWFs from emerging markets, often considered as cross-border nationalization, have been put aside for the time being, but there are reasons for SWFs to become more cautious not only because the shares acquired do not always allow control and voting rights, but also because of large losses on their investments.[17]

The ability of the United States to continue lowering policy interest rates is circumscribed by the willingness of the rest of the world to absorb the excess liquidity since the dollar is an international currency. Continued depreciation of the dollar vis-à-vis the euro would hurt fragile growth in Europe while sharp declines against Asian currencies can generate strong inflationary pressures in the United States, creating serious dilemmas for monetary policy. A rise in long-term rates on expectations of higher inflation would not help growth even if it could support banks by steepening the yield curve. A "Goldilocks" scenario wherein the United States could raise its net exports to Asia without importing inflation is unrealistic. For the first time in the postwar era the United States may be seriously challenged in its ability to conduct independent monetary policy to the neglect of its external ramifications.

Table 6.1: United States household savings and indebtedness (percentage of disposable income)

	1992	1996	1998	2000	2002	2003	2004	2005	2006	2007
Savings	7.7	4.0	4.3	2.3	2.4	2.1	2.1	0.5	0.4	0.7
Liabilities	87.2	95.0	97.1	102.7	112.1	120.2	126.8	134.4	138.1	...
Mortgages	62.3	63.8	64.9	68.5	78.4	85.7	92.2	100.2	103.1	...
Debt as percentage of net worth	18.1	17.9	16.7	17.9	22.6	22.3	22.9	23.5	23.9	...
Memo item: CA[a]	–0.8	–1.6	–2.5	–4.3	–4.4	–4.8	–5.5	–6.1	–6.2	–5.6

Source: OECD Economic Outlook (December 2005; December 2007).
a. Current account balance as percent of GDP.

While loss of bank capital is likely to sustain tight credit conditions, even availability of credit at drastically reduced rates might not give a sufficient boost to household spending to reignite the economy, given the excessive levels of debt inherited from the two successive bubbles since the early 1990s. The debt accumulation has gone hand in hand with the expansion of private consumption ahead of disposable income, resulting in a drastic decline in household savings. While household savings reached 7.7 percent of disposable income in the early 1990s, they dropped to some 2 percent at the end of the decade and continued to fall in the new millennium during the housing bubble, disappearing altogether in the past two years. The household debt/income ratio now stands at around 140 percent compared to less than 90 percent in the early 1990s. There has been a rapid growth in mortgage debt since the beginning of the 2000s, which now exceeds disposable income (Table 6.1).

There is strong evidence that asset bubbles have played a major role in the decline of household savings and increased indebtedness. The dot-com bubble of the 1990s generated a strong wealth effect on private consumption because of increased household stock holding and greater access to credit. During the past two decades there has been a rapid increase in the share of households in stocks owned directly or through mutual funds, which has now reached 50 percent. On the other hand, financial deregulation has improved the access of households to credit, loosening the traditional budget (liquidity) constraint on consumption spending.[18] These account for the finding that the acceleration in the decline in the personal savings rate in the United States after 1994 was due to an increase in the propensity to consume of families whose portfolios benefited most from exceptional capital gains from the dot-com bubble (Maki and Palumbo 2001). This process was sustained by capital gains from rising house prices in the 2000s, as households increasingly extracted equity from the value of their houses to finance consumption. The mark-to-market practice greatly facilitated this process as rising market values provided the collateral needed for credit expansion.

With the decline in house prices many households now face negative equity and banks inadequate collateral for their outstanding claims. While household debt was around

18 percent of household net worth in the early 1990s, this went up to 24 percent in 2006. It is expected to increase further as household net worth falls as a result of continued declines in house prices as well as in stocks, which appear to be strongly correlated with the housing market.[19] According to the flow-of-funds figures released by the Fed in March 2008, the net worth of American households dropped during the last quarter of 2007 for the first time since 2002.

The decline in savings and increased indebtedness of households is mirrored by growing external deficits of the United States. While the current account was almost balanced in the early 1990s, it is now in deficit by over 6 percent of GDP, reflecting a greater savings gap. Since about 70 percent of the GDP is due to consumer spending, the deterioration in the current account is almost fully accounted for by the decline in personal savings.[20] In other words, asset bubbles have made a significant contribution to the widening of the national savings gap and the external deficit in the United States since the early 1990s. Consequently, any adjustment in household savings and indebtedness necessitated by the current process of asset deflation will have significant implications for the United States' external balances.

A sizeable decline in consumer spending now appears inevitable, leading to a sharp drop in growth. The fiscal package of some $170 billion introduced looks too small compared to the scale of the problem. Two-thirds of this stimulus is in tax rebates to consumers. It is difficult to predict how much of these would be translated into consumer spending rather than used for debt payments, but the amount to be spent is unlikely to exceed half of the total package. This would not make up for the decline in consumer spending that would result from the drop in house prices, which could lead to a loss of wealth as much as $6 trillion. Even on conservative estimates relating wealth to consumption, this could reduce consumer spending by $200–400 billion (Roubini 2008; Weisbrot 2008).

Not only would the crisis produce a large cut in household consumption, but any subsequent recovery may also see a reduced propensity to consume since balance sheet restructuring is a protracted process. In fact, United States recessions and recoveries following asset-bubble-driven expansions in the early 1990s and 2000s were generally associated with very weak spending in sectors with debt overhang. This was particularly the case during the recovery from the recession triggered by the dot-com bubble. Not only did nonresidential private investment drop considerably during the brief recession in 2001, but the recovery that followed was the weakest in terms of investment since 1949. The corporations which had overborrowed during the dot-com bubble were highly exposed to asset price declines during the recession. Efforts were directed in the subsequent recovery toward restoring the health of balance sheets. Thus, increased incomes were used for reducing debt rather than expansion of production capacity and employment. Industries that attracted too much investment during the boom were "paying it back" by reducing their workforce and structurally declining (Groshen and Potter 2003).

Certainly it is not possible to extrapolate linearly from corporate behavior to households in adjustment to overindebtedness. But it would not be unreasonable to expect that this crisis could well produce the much-awaited retrenchment in private consumption, a sustained upward shift in the household savings rate and a durable adjustment in the United States external deficits beyond what may be expected from a slowing economy. This adjustment could be a protracted process, resulting in erratic and slow growth, as in

Japan during the 1990s. The corollary is that the rest of the world would need to rely less on the United States' market for growth. Thus, the crisis is likely to bring a fundamental adjustment to global imbalances, but the key question is how orderly and rapid that would be.

D. Capital Flows and Vulnerability in Asia

1. Lessons from the 1997 crisis

There can be little doubt that the vulnerability of Asian developing countries to the current financial turmoil depends crucially on their prevailing macroeconomic and financial conditions. Experience from recurrent crises in emerging markets shows that these conditions are strongly influenced by international capital flows. Accordingly, the likelihood of contagion is closely related to how well the recent surge in capital inflows has been managed in the region. In this respect it is possible to draw on the lessons from the 1997 Asian crisis, focusing on four main areas of vulnerability associated with surges in capital inflows:[21]

- Currency and maturity mismatches in private balance sheets and exposure to exchange rate risks
- Rapid credit expansion, asset bubbles and excessive investment in property and other sectors
- Unsustainable currency appreciations and external deficits
- Lack of self-insurance against a sudden stop and reversal of capital flows, and excessive reliance on IMF help and policy advice

These lessons should generally be incontrovertible, at least among the policymakers in the region, but opinions may differ considerably about the ways and means of putting them into practice. In what follows, an assessment will be made as to whether the Asian developing countries have appropriately drawn on these in managing the recent surge in capital flows. The conclusion reached is that while most Asian countries have successfully avoided unsustainable currency appreciations and payments positions, and accumulated more than adequate international reserves to counter any potential current and capital account shocks without recourse to multilateral financial institutions, they have not always been able to prevent capital inflows from generating asset, credit and investment bubbles or maturity and currency mismatches in private balance sheets. This is in large part because they have been unwilling to impose sufficiently tight controls over capital inflows, even when they posed dilemmas in macroeconomic policy and generated fragility. These now expose them to certain risks, but not of the kind that devastated the region in the 1990s.

2. Capital flows

The search for yield triggered by ample liquidity and low interest rates has also played a central role in the recovery of capital flows to emerging markets, creating pressures on exchange rates and generating credit and asset bubbles. After falling to some $100 billion at the beginning of the millennium, private flows picked up rapidly, reaching an estimated level of $620 billion in 2007 (Table 6.2).[22] This has been accompanied by a rapid narrowing of spreads on emerging market debt. The average spread, which had reached 1,400 basis points after the Russian crisis and fluctuated between 600 and 1,000 basis points during the early years of the millennium, fell constantly from mid-2002 onwards, reaching 200 basis points in the first half of 2007 before starting to edge up with the deepening of the subprime crisis (World Bank 2007; IMF 2007a). That improvements in underlying economic fundamentals in the recipient countries are not always the main reason for this unprecedented decline in spreads is also recognized by the IMF:

> Very recent empirical work, including some undertaken by IMF staff for this report, appears to reinforce the widespread market view that liquidity and an increase in risk appetite have become relatively more significant influences on spreads than fundamentals in the emerging market debt rally that began in late 2002. Models based purely on fundamentals have found that recent emerging market bond spreads are generally tighter than can be justified by the models. (IMF 2004, 66)

Because of strong and favorable global push factors concerning liquidity and risk, recovery in capital flows has been broad-based, widely shared by all regions. But country-specific conditions (the pull factors) explain why inflows have been stronger in certain parts of the developing world than in others.[23] The pull factors have not always been linked to economic fundamentals such as growth and price stability, and external payments, debt or reserve positions. In fact international financial markets have made little differentiation among countries with respect to many of these factors, focusing instead on opportunities for short-term capital gains and arbitrage profits.

There have been considerable amounts of footloose capital motivated by speculative gains in all parts of the developing world, although the exact form it has taken has varied among countries depending on their individual circumstances. Such flows fall basically into three categories. First, capital attracted by carry trade profits due to large interest rate differentials with industrial countries, notably Japan, of which highly leveraged hedge funds have been among the main beneficiaries.[24] Second, capital inflows seeking gains from prospective currency appreciations in countries with undervalued exchange rates and large current account surpluses, notably China. Third, investment in asset markets, which have been a common feature of capital flows to emerging markets in different regions.

It is notable that during 2004–2007 emerging markets in Central and Eastern Europe received as much foreign private capital as those in Asia even though their total income is one-fifth of the total income of Asia, and their average growth has been much lower. The combination of high interest rates with independent floating has resulted in growing current account deficits which reached, on average, 7 percent of GDP in 2007.[25] High interest rates in some larger economies in Europe and Latin America (e.g., Turkey and Brazil) attracted large amounts of capital linked to carry trade. There have also been

Table 6.2: Private capital flows, current account balances and changes in reserves in emerging markets (billions of US dollars)

	Private Capital Flows				Current Account Balance				Reserve Increases			
	2004	2005	2006	2007[e]	2004	2005	2006	2007[e]	2004	2005	2006	2007[e]
Emerging markets	348.8	519.6	572.8	620.3	150.2	274.1	380.2	419.5	398.2	442.2	554.0	756.2
Asia	165.6	220.5	260.5	208.3	115.2	181.0	290.1	423.2	296.1	270.6	34.1	487.9
Latin America	41.8	70.0	52.6	106.0	22.3	41.1	51.6	26.5	22.5	29.7	50.3	95.2
Europe	131.1	204.1	234.0	276.1	5.7	35.8	23.7	–45.6	60.8	116.5	128.9	137.7
Africa/ Middle East	10.4	25.0	25.8	29.8	6.9	4.0	5.5	6.4	18.7	25.5	33.7	35.3

Source: IIF (September 2006; October 2007; March 2008).
e. estimate.

considerable intraregional carry trade activities in these regions where funds borrowed in low interest currencies have been invested in the same region in higher interest currencies, thereby providing some protection against intraregional contagion. High local interest rates have also attracted international investors to domestically issued local currency debt, as these investors have become more willing to assume the exchange rate risk in return for much higher yields.[26]

In gross terms capital inflows to Asia, as a proportion of GDP, have been close to historical highs, but in net terms they have been around the long-term average because of increased resident outflows (IMF 2007b; and IIF October 2007). Since 2003, about 60 percent of private capital inflows to the Asian countries in Table 6.2 have been in equity investment, compared to less than 40 percent in other emerging markets. Of these, two-thirds have been in direct equity and one-third in portfolio equity.[27] Equity flows have been particularly strong in China and, more recently, India. But in the latter country much of these are in portfolio equity rather than FDI. Hedge funds from the United States and the United Kingdom have been very active in equity markets, with assets managed by them being estimated to have grown sevenfold between 2001 and 2007.

Following the cutback in bank lending after the 1997 crisis, international bank inflows to Asia started to exceed repayments in the early years of the decade. The share of net international bank lending has been slightly over one-quarter of the total private inflows to Asia, and the remainder are other types of debt flows including bonds and carry-trade-related inflows, including those involving arbitrage among regional currencies. Sovereign bond issues have been relatively small in Asia because of strong fiscal and public debt positions. However, there has been a visible growth in syndicated loans privately placed by corporations in several countries. In many cases bank inflows have been encouraged by prospects of gains from currency appreciations.

However, private financial and nonfinancial corporations have also engaged in "carry-trade-style" short-term external borrowing in India, Korea and the Philippines, particularly through low interest yen-linked loans. Highly leveraged hedge funds are also known to be very active in carry trades in Asia. A relatively high volume of carry trade appears to be a reason why the category "other investment" accounts for a high share of total capital inflows to the region. While restrictions on foreign participation in domestic bond markets have generally been maintained, in Malaysia and Indonesia there have been marked increases in foreign holding of local currency debt instruments. In the region as a whole local claims of foreign banks, including local bond holdings, as a percentage of all foreign banks' claims, more than doubled since the beginning of the decade, suggesting a growing preference for international banks to lend in local currencies at higher rates.

3. Credit, asset and investment bubbles

The composition of capital inflows to Asian emerging markets is generally considered to be more favorable than other emerging markets because of a high share of equity flows. Foreign investment in equity and local currency debt is not considered as a serious potential threat to stability because the exchange rate risk is assumed by investors. Vulnerability to a sudden stop and reversal of capital flows is often assessed on the basis of short-term external liabilities in relation to reserves. Indeed, according to the so-called Guidotti–Greenspan rule formulated after the Asian crisis, in order to avoid a liquidity crisis international reserves in emerging markets should meet short-term external liabilities, defined as debt with a remaining maturity of up to one year.[28]

However, what matters for vulnerability to instability in capital flows is not simply currency denomination and maturity but also liquidity of liabilities. A run by nonresidents away from domestic equity and bond markets could create significant turbulence in currency and asset markets with broader macroeconomic consequences, even though declines in asset prices could mitigate the pressure on the exchange rate, and losses from asset price declines and currency collapses fall on foreign investors. This potential source of instability naturally depends on the relative importance of foreign participation in local financial markets. Extensive foreign participation not only increases market volatility, but also raises exposure to adverse spillovers and contagion from financial instability abroad. That such exposure has been on the rise is suggested by increased correlation between global and emerging market equity returns since 2004.[29]

Recent capital inflows have resulted in a rapid increase in foreign presence in Asian equity markets. Figures for net equity inflows understate this because, as noted, there has also been a rapid increase in resident outflows. Available evidence shows that nonresident holding of Korean equities reached almost one-half of market capitalization (McCauley 2008). According to a recent study on foreign net purchases and net sales of equities in Asian markets, the share of foreigner transactions in 2005 in average daily turnover was around 20 percent in Korea, 30 percent in Thailand and 75 percent in Taiwan (China) while in total holdings by foreigners accounted for between 20 and 30 percent in India,

Korea and Thailand and as high as 70 percent in Taiwan (China). There is also strong evidence that the entry and exit of foreigners to Asian equity markets are subject to a bandwagon effect – that is, foreign investors tend to move in and out of several Asian markets simultaneously – suggesting strong contagious influences across the region. Although equity inflows into this group of countries appear to have been driven not so much by gains from anticipated currency appreciations as by local market returns, they have put a strong upward pressure on exchange rates.[30]

A relatively large proportion of financial inflows to China appears to have been motivated by expectations of appreciation of the yuan (Setser 2008; Yu 2008). These have gone partly in equity and property markets, benefiting also from local price booms. Part of these are reported to have entered the country as investment or through trade, including overinvoicing of exports. According to some market participants, the so-called "hot money" amounted to $5–10 billion a month during 2007. The Chinese foreign exchange regulators felt obliged to take action against ten international banks for breaching capital account regulations by "assisting speculative foreign capital to enter the country disguised as trade and investment" (Anderlini 2007).

Large capital inflows to equity markets – together with the consequent expansion of liquidity – have both been the cause and effect of sharp increases in stock prices in several Asian markets. There is in fact a strong correlation between changes in net portfolio equity flows and stock prices in Asia – much stronger than that observed in Latin America.[31] For the region as a whole the equity market index tripled between 2002 and mid-2007, with increases exceeding 400 percent in China and India. The price–earnings ratios have also risen rapidly, resulting in a sharp drop in equity costs.[32] That such increases more likely reflect asset price bubbles than improvements in underlying fundamentals was actually cautioned a couple of years ago by the Institute of International Finance (IIF March 2005, 4): "there is a risk that the pickup in flows into some emerging market assets has pushed valuations to levels that are not commensurate with underlying fundamentals." It is notable that since then until mid-2007 the Asian markets rose by another 50 percent. China increased the stamp duty on stock market transactions in order to restrain the bubble, only to reverse it after the recent decline due to the fallout from the subprime crisis.

The two largest countries, China and India, which have seen the strongest surge in capital inflows and largest increases in stock markets and, to a lesser extent, Korea, have also experienced a boom in property markets. During 2002–2006 in real terms residential property prices rose by over 8 percent per annum in China and 10 percent in India.[33] In these countries the price-to-rent ratio rose by more than 20 percent during the same period while Korea saw an increase of more than 15 percent. The last couple of years have also seen acceleration of property price increases in Singapore and Vietnam. While these have not been as dramatic as increases in the United States – where the price-to-rent ratio rose by 30 percent over the same period – there are large pockets in China, India, Korea and the Philippines where increases have been comparable and even greater.[34] Concerned by the growing speculative spree, China has adopted a number of measures to stem increases in property prices, including higher interest rates and larger down-payments on both residential and commercial property loans (ESCAP 2007, 10).

In some cases house prices have also outstripped strong growth in incomes. Housing loans have expanded faster than other types of lending and have been a major factor in sharp increases in household indebtedness. In Korea, for instance, bank lending to households has been growing rapidly since 2005, and household debt has reached 140 percent of disposable income – above the level of household indebtedness in the United States (ADB 2007). While detailed data are limited, there are indications that speculative purchases motivated by strong prices as well as foreign demand for commercial space have made an important contribution to the boom in property markets in India and China.

Recent booms in housing and equity markets in Asia are a source of concern because of their potential adverse macroeconomic consequences. There is evidence, not only from industrial countries, but also from a number of Asian emerging markets, including Hong Kong (China), Indonesia, Japan, Korea, Malaysia, the Philippines, Singapore and Thailand, that such booms (defined as periods in which asset prices exceed their trend by more than 10 percent) significantly raise the probability of output being eventually pushed below its potential level and the price level above its trend (Gochoco-Bautista 2008). This implies that monetary and capital account policies should not neglect developments in asset markets since their longer-term consequences may undermine price stability and growth.

Rapid domestic credit expansion and low interest rates have played an important role in bubbles in equity and property markets in Asia. As in some mature economies, monetary policy has been highly expansionary and real interest rates have been considerably lower than those in other regions. However, the surge in capital flows is part of the reason for rapid expansion of liquidity since interventions in foreign exchange markets (discussed below) could not be fully sterilized. After 2003 private credit growth in real terms reached nearly 9 percent per annum in China and 5 percent in other countries.[35] Ample liquidity, low equity costs and loan rates together have made a strong impact on investment spending, occasionally pushing it to levels that may not be sustained over the longer term.

This is particularly the case in China and, to a lesser extent, India– investment rates in most other Asian countries did not fully regain their precrisis levels.[36] In China gross fixed capital formation has been growing 4–5 percentage points faster than real income, with the share of investment in GDP now reaching 46 percent. This increase appears to have been associated with considerable excess capacity and wastage of capital. Although 40 percent of China's state-owned industrial enterprises are reported to have been running losses and facing declining rates of return on capital, easy access to credit has been encouraging overinvestment (BIS 2007a, 56). In the event of a sharp upward adjustment in the exchange rate and a slowdown in exports, the capacity built in some industries may become unviable.[37] Similarly, in India growth in investment has been faster than GDP by more than 5 percentage points per annum with the investment ratio rising to over 30 percent of GDP from less than 24 percent in the early years of the decade. This has been greatly facilitated by capital inflows, credit and asset bubbles, and may not be sustained with the return of normal financial conditions.

4. Current account balances, exchange rates and reserves

While major Asian emerging markets have not been able to prevent capital inflows from leading to asset and investment bubbles, they have been more successful in managing their impact on exchange rates and the current account. Developing countries of the region taken together had a current account surplus of more than 7 percent of GDP in 2007, up from 1.5 percent in 2001. This is largely due to China's strong export performance, but a number of other countries have also been enjoying surpluses, including Malaysia and, to a lesser extent, Indonesia, Thailand and the Philippines. Among the newly industrialized economies (NIEs), Singapore continues to run a massive current account surplus while in Korea the current account has been broadly in balance. Current account deficits have been increasing in India, Pakistan and Vietnam in the past few years, but only in Pakistan has it been approaching the danger zone, expected to reach some 5 percent of GDP at the end of 2007. However, these trends reflect not so much the effects of currency appreciations as acceleration of growth from the first half of the decade.

Since the Asian crisis, several countries in the region have moved toward more flexible exchange rate arrangements. But they have followed various shades of managed floating rather than leaving their currencies entirely to the whims of international capital flows. Most countries have strived to absorb excess supply of foreign exchange generated by strong capital inflows and/or current account surpluses in reserves through interventions in foreign exchange markets, rather than allowing them to push up currencies to unsustainable levels and undermine their trade performance. To keep liquidity expansion and inflation under control, attempts have been made to sterilize such interventions, mainly by issuing government and/or central bank debt and by raising reserve requirements in the banking system.

Currency market interventions are generally believed to be ineffective in mature economies. The IMF has also drawn a similar conclusion from its research on developing countries; that is, sterilized intervention in emerging markets is likely to be ineffective when the influx of capital is persistent, and tends to be associated with higher inflation (IMF 2007c, 122–24). By contrast, recent work in the BIS (2005) shows that sterilized interventions in Asia have been reasonably effective in influencing the exchange rate without leading to loss of control over inflation.[38] There have been relatively sizeable appreciations in some countries, but these are moderate in comparison with those in other emerging markets where independent floating is practised. Moreover, appreciations in Asia have occurred under much more favorable current account positions and faster economic growth.[39]

The monetary impact of interventions has not been fully offset, particularly in China where large trade surpluses added to the glut of foreign exchange generated by the surge in capital flows. However, despite rapid expansion of liquidity generated by interventions and loose monetary conditions, inflation has been kept under control, though only in product markets, not in asset markets.

In China, government control over the financial system has allowed it to keep the fiscal cost of intervention down.[40] Reserve requirements of banks were constantly raised from 7 percent in 2003 to 15 percent in 2008, and banks have come to hold over

80 percent of central bank securities issued for that purpose, with their share in total bank assets exceeding 20 percent (Yu 2008). In India the cash reserve ratio was also increased in several steps, from 4.75 percent in 2003 to 7.5 percent in 2008, but because of higher interest rates, the cost of intervention reached 2 percent of GDP in 2007 – more than half of the central government deficits.[41]

As of the end of 2007, total reserves in developing Asia (excluding NIEs) exceeded $2 trillion and over 80 percent of these were generated after 2001 (Table 6.3). Asian reserves now account for more than half of total reserves of the developing world. The twin surpluses that the region as a whole has been running on its balance of payments (that is, on both current and capital accounts) have been fully converted into reserves.[42] Of the $1.7 trillion reserves accumulated after 2001, almost two-thirds are earned and one-third "borrowed".[43] Unlike other regions, therefore, reserve increases in Asia have come mainly from current account surpluses rather than capital inflows (Table 6.2).[44] Moreover, these reserves are earned in the context of rapid growth, rather than by sacrificing growth.[45] However, excluding China, two-thirds of Asian reserves in recent years are also from capital inflows. In India and other Asian countries with current account deficits, reserves are 100 percent "borrowed."

On the Greenspan–Guidotti rule noted above, Asian reserves are excessive. They are several times the total short-term external debt of the region, which stood at less than $300 billion at the end of 2007, and more than twice the total external debt of some $950 billion.[46] They now cover close to nine months of imports, much higher than the three months of imports traditionally considered as adequate for addressing the liquidity problems arising from time lags between payments for imports and receipts from exports.

A policy of accumulating reserves at times of strong capital inflows and using them during sudden stops and reversals appears to be a sensible countercyclical response to instability in international capital flows. By intervening in the foreign exchange market and accumulating reserves, a country facing a surge in capital flows can both reduce its external vulnerability by preventing appreciations and trade deficits, and secure self-insurance against possible speculative attacks. In other words, if inflows are believed to be temporary, it would be rational to resist an inward transfer by allowing the domestic consumption and/or investment to increase and the current account to run into deficits through faster growth and appreciations.[47]

However, such a strategy lacks a strong rationale because it implies that a country would borrow even if the funds thus acquired are not used to finance investment and imports, but held in short-term foreign assets. This is all the more so because reserves accumulated out of capital inflows are highly costly – that is, the return earned on reserves is less than the cost of foreign capital, including the cost of foreign borrowing and the foregone return on assets sold. In fact it is more so for portfolio equity and particularly FDI flows for acquisition of ownership rights of existing assets where rates earned by transnational companies exceed the cost of international borrowing by a very large margin (UNCTAD TDR 1999, chap. 5).

In previous decades the current account in Asia was generally in deficit so that a very large proportion of reserves held at the beginning of this decade was "borrowed" rather than earned reserves. If this is added to reserves accumulated from capital inflows since

Table 6.3: Current account and reserves (billions of US dollars)

	Asia	China
Reserves		
2007	2068.0	1559.5
2001	379.5	216.3
Increase	1688.5	1343.2
Current account[a]		
2002–2007	1067.8	939.9
Borrowed reserves[b]		
2002–2007	620.7	403.3
Import coverage[c]		
2001	4.9	6.6
2007	8.8	12.8

Source: IMF (2007b).
a. Cumulative current account balance over 2002–2007.
b. Difference between increases in reserves and cumulative current account balance over 2002–2007.
c. Months of imports covered by reserves.

2001, about half of the total stock of reserves in Asia now would be "borrowed" reserves. This is approximately equal to the existing stock of external debt of the region. Assuming a moderate 500 basis points margin between the interest cost on debt and the return on reserves, this would give an annual carry cost of $50 billion for the region as a whole.[48] This is how much the region as a whole could save per year by paying up its external debt by drawing on reserves.[49] The carry cost of reserves accumulated from debt creating and portfolio equity inflows since the beginning of the decade alone can be estimated to be as much as half of this amount. It would be much higher if FDI inflows for acquisitions are included. Furthermore, in view of the ongoing downward pressure on the dollar, countries with a large stock of dollar reserves stand to incur considerable losses.

The high carry cost of reserves in excess of possible liquidity needs, together with the risk of exchange-rate-related losses, raise the question of alternative investments in higher-yielding foreign securities, primarily through SWFs, as done by several fuel exporters. Like China, fuel exporters as a group also generate large current account surpluses, but unlike China, they run deficits in their capital accounts. About one-third of oil surpluses generated since 2002 have been used for investment abroad and two-thirds for reserve accumulation. In several of them investment is undertaken mainly by SWFs. According to some estimates, total assets of SWFs in fuel exporters exceed $1.5 trillion (IMF 2007e, annex 1.2; Truman 2007b). These funds come out of government earnings from oil exports rather than from reserves purchased from the private sector. In Asia, with the notable exception of Singapore, SWFs are relatively small. At some $200 billion, the assets of the recently established China Investment Cooperation (CIC) are only a fraction of the total reserves of the country, and only a small part of these appear to have been used for investment abroad.

As noted above, SWFs have recently been acquiring high-risk equity in Western banks hit by the subprime crisis, thereby acting as a global force for stability while suffering losses.

However, given the deep suspicion and misgivings about SWFs in some advanced countries, massive amounts of Asian reserves cannot be expected to be quickly translated into investment in more lucrative, less risky assets in these countries. An alternative would be to recycle them in the region for, inter alia, infrastructure projects in low income countries in need of development finance. This may best be achieved through a genuinely regional development bank, established among the developing countries of the region along the lines of the recent *Banco del Sur* in Latin America.

5. Capital account measures

Many Asian emerging markets are incurring high reserve costs and facing macroeconomic policy dilemmas mainly because they have chosen to keep their economies open to the surge in capital inflows, rather than imposing tighter countercyclical measures of control.[50] Indeed, capital accounts in the region are more open today than they were during the Asian crisis.[51] In China, for instance, one of the countries with the tightest restrictions, calculations based on an IMF formula are said to show that 80 percent of the capital account has been liberalized (Yu 2008).

In several cases the opening to inflows has been selective, such as raising the limits on the QFII (qualified foreign institutional investors) in China. Countries such as India have liberalized sectoral caps on FDI. Foreign banks have generally been allowed greater freedom to operate with many domestic borrowers receiving funding from such banks directly from abroad or through their local offices. However, there have been some efforts to bring greater transparency to capital inflows. For instance, in 2007 India adopted a proposal by the Securities and Exchange Board to restrict the foreign buying of shares through offshore derivatives despite an adverse initial reaction from the stock market– a move that was designed not so much to relieve the upward pressure on the rupee as to bring greater transparency by restricting the activities of hedge funds.

Efforts have no doubt been made to curb excessive inflows in order to ease the upward pressure on their currencies. In 2006 China extended to foreign banks the restriction over borrowing abroad to fund domestic dollar assets. At the end of 2006 Korea raised banks' reserve requirements from 5 percent to 7 percent in order to support the dollar vis-à-vis the won. Around the same time Thailand imposed a 30 percent reserve requirement on capital inflows held less than one year, including portfolio equity flows, in order to check continued appreciation of the currency. This provoked a strong reaction from the stock market, forcing the government to exempt investment in stocks from reserve requirements. The remaining restrictions were removed in March 2008. With continued surge in capital inflows, India reversed the liberalization of the limits on external commercial borrowing, tightening them in 2007. Similarly, Korea restricted external funding of domestic lending by foreign banks and reintroduced limits on lending in foreign currency to domestic firms.

However, the main response to the surge in capital inflows has been to liberalize outward investment by residents. This is partly motivated by a desire to allow national firms to expand abroad and become important players in world markets. This has particularly been the case in China and India. However, while in China assets acquired abroad are financed from trade surpluses, in India these are funded by capital inflows, in much the same way as Korean chaebols did in the run-up to the 1997 crisis.[52] As remarked by an observer, "the global flood of money (and attendant hubris) has enabled Indian companies like Tata to buy themselves a place on the world stage rather than earning it through export success or technological advance" (Bowring 2008a).

There has also been considerable liberalization of portfolio outflows. For instance China took a decision to permit investment by its residents in approved overseas markets and raised the limits on corporate and individual purchases of foreign currency for mitigating the pressure for appreciation through the so-called QDII (qualified domestic institutional investor) scheme. The share of portfolio investment in the total international assets of China in 2006 was three times that of FDI abroad; the former increased from under 10 percent in 2004 to about 15 percent in 2006 while the share of FDI fell to about 5 percent in the latter year (Hang Seng Bank 2008).

Korea has also liberalized rules limiting individual or institutional investment abroad, and even provided incentives for residents to invest in foreign securities and real estate assets. Thailand raised the limits on and extended the duration of deposits that could be held abroad by resident corporations, removed restrictions over foreign currency accounts in local banks by residents, allowed investment by local funds abroad, and abolished the surrender requirement for Thai exporters. The Philippines allowed residents to invest abroad without approval and raised the limits over such investment. India liberalized resident outflows, giving greater freedom for portfolio investment abroad and Malaysia increased the limit on foreign assets held by some institutional investors and investment trusts.

Capital account opening for residents as a response to a surge in inflows is clearly an alternative to sterilized intervention and has the advantage of avoiding carry costs for reserves. But, like interventions, it does effectively nothing to prevent currency and maturity mismatches in balance sheets, or instability and vulnerability to shocks associated with greater presence of foreigners in domestic asset markets. Its rationale as a longer-term strategy for closer integration with global financial markets is highly contentious. As a countercyclical measure, it can be even more problematic – once introduced for cyclical reasons, it may not be easily rolled back when conditions change. Besides in countries such as China where property rights are not clearly defined, liberalization of resident outflows could encourage asset stripping and money laundering (Yu 2008).

E. External Shocks and Policy Options in Asia

1. Growth prospects: projections and beyond

Asia is now facing external shocks triggered by the subprime crisis, coming on top of stagflationary pressures exerted by the upward trend in oil prices. However, there is a certain degree of compensation among the effects of these shocks. Unlike in the 1970s when oil price hikes resulted from supply shocks, the recent trend has been driven by growing demand in the face of a slow and limited supply response, declines in production in maturing fields and bottlenecks in refinery capacity.[53]

The weakness of the dollar has been a contributing factor since it means lower prices in currencies strengthening against the dollar and greater demand. There is also a strong speculative element, resulting in sharp increases in relatively short periods of time, as declines in property and equity prices tend to divert excess liquidity to commodity markets. However, to the extent that global growth slows down due to the subprime crisis, the demand pressure on oil prices could ease considerably even though a sharp reversal of the ongoing trend is quite unlikely. Furthermore, an upward adjustment in Asian currencies would relieve inflationary effects of higher international prices of food and oil.

Earlier projections for growth in 2008 in Asia and elsewhere of some of the more influential international and regional institutions made in the second half of 2007 appeared to assume that the subprime crisis would only cause a hiccup in global economic activity, just as it was initially believed to be the case during the Asian crisis in 1997. But even the most recent projections do not show a sharp deviation from the trend of rapid and broad-based growth that has been underway since the early years of the decade (Table 6.4).[54] For global growth, the drop projected in 2008 from 2007 lies between 0.3 and 0.8 percentage points. For the United States, the IMF and ADB project a 0.7 percentage point fall between 2007 and 2008, but the IIF sees no change. In these projections developing Asia is not expected to lose much momentum, with growth slowing down by no more than 1 percentage point.

Perhaps more important are the revisions made to growth projections for 2008 after the financial difficulties became more visible in the course of last autumn. Compared to projections made in July 2007, current projections for 2008 by the IMF show a 1.1 percentage point loss of growth for the world economy as a whole; 1.3 points for the United States; and 0.5 points for Asian developing countries.[55] Similarly, in March 2008 the ADB reduced its outlook for growth in the United States to 1.5 percent and in Asia to 7.6 percent from the earlier (September 2007) figures of 2.6 percent and 8.2 percent, respectively (ADB 2007).

These projections are subject to usual caveats and generally accompanied by warnings that risks are downside. Nevertheless, only the UN (2008) projections explore, under a "pessimistic scenario," what might happen if such risks were to materialize. The United States would go into a recession and growth in Asia and the world economy as a whole would both be more than halved. This scenario assumes a sharp decline in house prices in the United States and a hard landing of the dollar, leading to increases in dollar interest rates. Nevertheless, the United States recession would be quite mild compared to those in 1982 and 1991 when output contracted by three percent and one percent respectively. It is very much like the brief contraction in 2001, presumably reflecting counteracting influences from declines in house prices and sharp devaluation of the dollar on aggregate demand. Recession and the decline of the dollar would result in sharp cuts in imports in the United States, affecting major exporters. The dollar decline would also result in losses on dollar assets in countries with large holdings. This appears to be the main financial impact: no explicit reference is made to possible consequences of the crisis for asset prices and investment in emerging markets, or the policy response.[56]

Table 6.4: Growth estimates for 2007 and projections for 2008 (annual percentage change)

	2007			2008		
	World	US	Asia	World	US	Asia
IMF (01.08)	4.9	2.2	9.6	4.1	1.5	8.6
WORLD BANK (01.08)	3.6	2.2	10.0	3.3	1.9	9.7
ADB (03.08)	–	2.2	8.7	–	1.5	7.6
UN WESP (01.08)	3.7	2.2	8.1	3.4	2.0	7.5
(pessimistic)				(1.6)	(–0.1)	(4.8)
IIF (01.08)	3.5	2.3	9.1	3.1	2.3	8.6

Source: IMF (2008), World Bank (2008), ADB (2008), UN (2008) and IIF (2008).

2. Financial contagion and shocks

Asian economies do not appear to have large direct exposure to securitized assets linked to subprime lending, even though some losses have been reported in the region. The impact of the financial turmoil is likely to be transmitted through changes in the risk appetite and capital flows, in conditions of bubbles in domestic credit and asset markets in the larger economies of the region. The question of the sustainability of these bubbles had been raised before the subprime turmoil, and they have now become even more fragile.

There is considerable uncertainty about the impact of the crisis on asset markets and capital flows in emerging markets as financial markets have shown signs of both decoupling and recoupling in recent months (BIS 2007b). However, large drops in western equity markets caused by occasional bad news about financial losses have often been mirrored by similar changes in Asian markets. Should such difficulties continue unabated, the likelihood of a sharp and durable correction in Asian markets is quite high. By itself this may not lower growth by more than a couple of percentage points in China and India, and should not pose a serious problem since the recent pace of growth in these countries is generally viewed as unsustainable.[57] However, if combined with a sudden stop and reversal of capital flows and/or contraction of export markets, the impact on growth can be much more serious.

It is generally expected that bank-related flows would decline in view of the losses many international banks are now incurring. According to the most recent projections by the IIF (2008), total private flows to emerging markets would be broadly the same in 2008 as in 2007; there would be a decline of some $25 billion in bank lending, compensated by increases in equity flows. It is also argued that capital flows to emerging markets may even accelerate if Europe joins the United States in easy monetary policy. That this possibility cannot be ruled out is suggested by the most recent estimates for private capital flows for 2007 which have now put them above the earlier estimates by some $60 billion because of a stronger growth of equity flows and limited impact of the financial turmoil on investment in fixed income funds and international bank lending (IIF 2008, 19). The largest upward revision has been made for India, particularly for bank-related capital flows. If continued, this could also imply decoupling of Asian equity markets from the United States and Europe and the persistence of credit and asset bubbles in China and India.

It is quite likely that investors will now start differentiating among countries to a much greater extent than has been the case in recent years. Countries with large current account deficits, high stocks of external debt, inadequate reserves and appreciated currencies in Central and Eastern Europe and elsewhere may face a sudden stop and even reversal of capital flows and sharp increases in spreads, resulting in exchange rate and balance of payments crises.[58] Given large stocks of reserves, even a generalized exit from emerging markets would not create serious payments difficulties for most Asian countries, and the impact would be felt primarily in domestic credit and asset markets. Such an exit could be triggered by a widespread flight toward quality, with investors taking refuge in the safety of government bonds in advanced countries, or a need to liquidate their holdings in emerging markets in order to cover mounting losses and margin calls.[59]

The likelihood of a rapid exit of capital is difficult to assess, but it cannot be excluded. A number of countries in Asia experienced a withdrawal of foreigners from stock markets during the May–June 2006 global selloff. The amount of money taken out was small, in the order of some $15 billion, but it was the first reversal of capital flows after the Asian crisis and synchronized across all the countries studied.[60] Again there was a rapid liquidation by investors from advanced countries in several markets in Asia in summer 2007 as subprime losses started to surface. Thus the region may be susceptible to common adverse external financial shocks, quite independent of specific circumstances prevailing in individual countries.

3. Trade linkages and growth in Asia

The decoupling debate is often carried out in terms of linkages between trade and growth; that is, how the trade between Asia and the United States would be affected and what impact this would have on growth in Asia. These are contentious issues, but the weight of arguments leans toward the view that trade linkages would not result in a major adverse impact on growth in Asia, even allowing for a high degree of dependence on the United States market. Exports to the United States amount to some 8 percent of GDP in China and 6 percent in other Asian countries.[61] In value added terms these ratios are lower, particularly in China and a few other assembly platforms such as Malaysia where exports still have high import contents even though domestic value added contents have been rising in recent years as a result of upgrading.[62] Consequently, even if exports to the United States stop growing and even start declining in absolute terms as a result of a recession and weakening of the dollar, the Asian countries can still sustain rapid, albeit somewhat reduced, growth provided that other components of aggregate demand continue growing at their recent pace.

This line of thinking clearly focuses on the impact of exports on aggregate demand, rather than on the foreign exchange constraint. It is implicitly assumed that the countries affected can continue to maintain growth of imports despite reduced export earnings. This would pose no major problem for those running large current account surpluses such as China, Malaysia and Singapore. Others with deficits, such as India, however, would need to rely increasingly on capital inflows and/or draw on their reserves in order to finance the widening gap between imports and exports.

This simple arithmetic is complicated by a number of factors. First, the impact of a slowdown in the United States also depends on how Asian export markets elsewhere are affected. The effect on growth in Europe can be significant because of its direct exposure to the subprime crisis. Indeed, growth in the European Union is already falling below the levels of earlier projections. Since exports to the European Union are about 7 percent of GDP in China and even more in other Asian emerging markets, a sharp slowdown in Europe could have a relatively large impact. The Asian trade balance with the European Union could deteriorate even further if currencies in the region start rising against the euro.

Second, for some countries indirect exposure to a decline in growth of exports to the United States can be just as important because of relatively strong intraregional, intra-industry trade linkages.[63] More than two-thirds of Chinese imports consist of intermediate goods, and about a third of these are provided within the region, notably by Korea and Taiwan which individually account for around 10 percent of total imports by China. This means that a decline in Chinese exports to the United States would bring about a corresponding decline in imports of intermediate goods from the region. Thus countries exporting these goods to China would be affected by cuts not only in their direct exports to the United States, but also in their indirect exports through China. In these countries cuts in exports of intermediate goods to China would not entail an important offsetting decline in imports. Consequently, they could be affected even more than China by import cuts in the United States even when their direct exports to the United States are relatively small. For instance it has been estimated that a 10 percent slowdown in United States imports would reduce China's exports by 2.1 percent and Korea's exports by 1.5 percent. The consequent drop in China's imports from Korea would lower exports of that country by another 1.3 percent (BIS 2007a). Thus, Korea might be more vulnerable to a United States slowdown not only because its exports have higher value added, but also because it is indirectly exposed through exports to China. This is likely to be true for Taiwan as well.

Finally, domestic components of aggregate demand are not independent of exports. This is particularly true for investment. A deceleration in exports can lead to a sharp drop in investment designed to cater for foreign markets which can, in turn, aggravate the impact of contraction in exports on aggregate demand. This effect can be particularly strong in China where investment is a large component of aggregate demand and an important part of investment is linked to exports. This includes greenfield FDI which has been channeled to export sectors through various restrictions and incentives, including tax rebates and foreign-exchange balancing requirements as part of an aggressive export strategy (Yu 2007). The likelihood of a large drop in investment would be greater if contraction in export markets is accompanied by currency appreciations and asset price declines.

4. *Policy challenges*

A combination of severe external trade and financial shocks from the subprime crisis with domestic fragilities associated with credit, asset and investment bubbles could pose serious policy challenges in Asia, but above all in China and India. Whatever the nature and extent of contagion and shocks from the crisis, it is important to avoid destabilizing feedbacks between the real and financial sectors. A sharp drop in exports together with a rapid correction in asset prices could bring down growth considerably which can, in turn, threaten the solvency of the banking system given the high degree of leverage of some firms, particularly in China.[64] The appropriate policy response would be to expand domestic demand through fiscal stimulus, taking into account that a small dose of deceleration of growth toward more sustainable levels could be desirable. If difficulties emerge in the financial sector, it would also be necessary to provide lender of last resort financing. Nevertheless, it is important that policy interventions aim not at preventing but smoothing correction in asset prices and facilitating restructuring in sectors which have been overstretched thanks to easy financing conditions in recent years.

However, China would need not just a countercyclical macroeconomic expansion, but a more durable shift in the composition of aggregate demand from exports toward domestic consumption because, as noted above, the crisis is likely to bring a sizeable external adjustment in the United States.[65] Current economic conditions in China, including the twin balance of payments surpluses, growing reserves carried at high costs and risks, an undervalued currency, and an unprecedented growth in production capacity heavily dependent on external markets, cannot be defended on the grounds of economic efficiency or expediency. This combination is sometimes linked to China's development strategy. According to this view, a rapid reduction in unemployment through export-led growth calls for trade surpluses, undervalued exchange rates and capital controls. It is also argued that the viability of this strategy also depends on China's willingness to provide the external financing needed to the United States by translating its current and capital account surpluses into dollar reserves (Dooley, Folkerts-Landau and Garber 2004; Aizenman 2007).

However, as the experience of late industrializers, including first-tier NIEs and Japan, demonstrates, a development strategy emphasizing exports does not require generation of large and persistent current account surpluses through undervalued exchange rates. An undervalued currency often leads to terms of trade losses, and this seems to be the case in China (Yu 2007). It can also discourage technological upgrading and productivity growth. For these reasons many of the early industrializers in East Asia, including Japan, rarely resorted to cheap money for industrial development – by contrast they occasionally tolerated moderate appreciations in order to provide incentives for productivity growth.

A combination of current and capital account surpluses lacks a strong rationale. If capital inflows continue at their recent pace or accelerate, a policy of controlled appreciation of the yuan combined with much tighter control over inflows and a long-term strategy of expansion of Chinese investment abroad, including in developing countries, would appear to be a desirable response on several grounds. It would help achieve a soft landing by easing the upward pressures on asset prices, reducing the rate of liquidity expansion and enhancing monetary policy autonomy, and bringing down investment to sustainable levels. It would also ease inflationary pressures in product markets, particularly those linked to oil and food imports, and reduce the pace of reserve hoarding and associated costs and risks.

But perhaps a greater challenge would be to secure expansion of the internal market based on a much more rapid growth of consumption than has hitherto been the case. Since the early years of the decade, growth in consumption in China has constantly lagged behind income and investment. During 2002–2007, the average growth rate of consumer spending was around 8 percent per annum while gross fixed capital formation grew at a rate of 15 percent and exports 25 percent. Consequently, the share of consumption fell below 40 percent of GDP – almost half of the figure in the United States, and considerably less than the share of investment.[66] The imbalance between the two key components of domestic demand has meant increasing dependence of Chinese industry on foreign markets. Indeed, China appears to be trading a lot more than would be expected on the basis of observed historical patterns linking trade to population size, income levels and resource endowments.

The disparity between consumption and investment and the consequent dependence on foreign markets is largely a reflection of the imbalance between profits and wages. It is true that success in industrialization crucially depends on the pace of capital accumulation which, in turn, depends very much on the volume of profits and the extent to which they are used for investment rather than consumption. High corporate retentions and a dynamic profit–investment nexus, rather than high household savings, were indeed the key distinguishing components of successful industrialization in East Asia (Akyüz and Gore 1996). China is not an exception in this respect where corporate retentions exceed 20 percent of GDP due to a high share of profits in value added, the practice of nonpayment of dividends to the government by state-owned enterprises, and tax incentives for retentions and investment.[67]

In most late industrializers, particularly Japan and Korea, wages and household consumption grew in tandem with productivity and underpinned the expansion of productive capacity by providing a growing internal market. In China, by contrast, despite registering impressive increases, wages have lagged behind productivity growth and their share in value added has declined, and this is almost perfectly mirrored by the downward trend in the share of private consumption in GDP.[68] Since the early years of the decade labor productivity in the manufacturing industry has grown by some 20 percent per annum while nominal wage increases have been under 15 percent and real wage increases even lower. Profits rose faster than sales and the share of labor cost in total gross output in mining, manufacturing and utilities fell from 11.5 percent in 2002 to 7.1 percent in 2006; for the economy as a whole, the share of wages in GDP fell to about 40 percent after fluctuating between 50–55 percent in the 1990s. Furthermore, there are large precautionary savings out of wage incomes because of the absence of adequate public health, education and social security services. These savings are now increasingly held in stock trading accounts as the real return on bank deposits has been barely positive.

All these imbalances are presumably among the problems that Premier Wen Jiabao was referring to when he pointed out at the National People's Congress in March 2007 that "the biggest problem with China's economy is that the growth is unstable, unbalanced, uncoordinated and unsustainable." They need to be addressed independent of the shocks from the subprime crisis if China is to avoid the kind of difficulties that Japan faced during much of the 1990s following the asset and credit bubbles and excessive investment in the late 1980s.[69] Expansion of public spending in areas such as health, education and social security, as well as transfers to poorer households, financed, at least partly, by greater dividend payments by state-owned enterprises, can play an important role in lifting consumption spending. If needed, this expenditure policy can also be combined with tighter credit policy in order to check the rapid growth in investment. Any incentive that higher interest rates may generate for arbitrage flows may be offset by tighter capital controls including implicit and explicit taxes and administrative restrictions.

The shift toward a balance between domestic consumption and exports would necessitate a gradual restructuring of the industry so as to alter the product composition of supply to suit domestic tastes and preferences. China's export products are often designed for foreign markets and the existing capacity in some sectors cannot be fully utilized on the basis of expansion of domestic demand. On the other hand, since skills and equipment are often industry-specific, they cannot be easily shifted between industries. This means that adjustment in the production structure would be realized primarily by a reallocation of new investment and skills in favor of areas with domestic demand potentials. However, this should not cause a major difficulty given the state guidance of investment.

In East and Southeast Asian economies closely linked through production networks based on vertical integration, domestic stimulus would be needed to offset reduction in exports to advanced countries and China. Given too many burdens are already placed on monetary policy, including control over inflation and management of capital flows and exchange rates, the task falls again on fiscal policy. Most countries in the region have considerable scope to respond by fiscal expansion, in very much the same way as they were able to do during the weakness of global demand after 2000 (Akyüz 2006). The scope is somewhat limited in countries like India, Malaysia and Pakistan with relatively sizeable fiscal deficits. For these countries it is particularly important to design fiscal stimuli in such ways that they do not add to structural deficits. This is particularly important for India where budget deficits have been growing despite acceleration of growth, suggesting procyclical fiscal policy.

On the external side, Asian developing countries appear to have sustainable current account positions as well as relatively large stocks of reserves to weather any potential worsening of their trade balances as a result of a slowdown in exports. Countries such as India, Pakistan and Vietnam, which have recently been running current account deficits between 3 and 5 percent of GDP, could see their deficits rise further as exports slow down and growth of income and imports is sustained. Given the relatively high levels of reserves, this should cause no serious problems. However, if slowdown in markets abroad is accompanied by a sudden stop or reversal of capital flows, the ability of these countries to give a positive response to external shocks could be greatly compromized. In the case of India, the adverse impact on the economy could be aggravated by the bursting of the asset market bubble. The twin structural deficits in fiscal and external accounts thus need greater attention for reducing vulnerability to shocks.

Low income countries dependent on official financing are no doubt highly vulnerable to a sharp deterioration in global economic conditions, and many of them could see rapid increases in their current account deficits with a slowdown in trade in goods and services. Indeed, in several of them, including small island economies, current account deficits as a proportion of GDP are already in double digit figures. The external financing needs of these countries may well exceed the amounts available under normal access limits in the IMF, and they should be able to have access to additional financing through augmentation of resources made available under PRGF arrangements and the Exogenous Shocks Facility.

Finally, a reasonable degree of consistency would need to be ensured in the region among policy responses of individual countries to external financial and trade shocks from the subprime crisis. A coordinated macroeconomic expansion would certainly be desirable, but it would be even more important to secure cooperation and consistency in exchange rate policies. Despite a clear division of labor and complementarity of trade based on vertical integration, trade patterns in East and Southeast Asian emerging markets are becoming increasingly competitive as followers in industrial development are rapidly closing the gap with the more advanced economies through upgrading and building production capacity to substitute imported components and parts with domestic production. Under these conditions divergent movements in exchange rates can become highly disruptive and conflictual. Experience shows that such movements can become particularly intensive at times of severe external shocks and instability of trade and capital flows. If shocks are severe, some countries may even be tempted to respond by beggar-my-neighbor exchange rate policies.

It is, therefore, important to engage in regional consultations in exchange rate policies and explore durable currency arrangements. The experience of the European Union in exchange rate cooperation starting with the demise of the Bretton Woods system and culminating in the European Monetary Union holds valuable lessons, even though it may not be fully replicated since the region is not yet ready to float collectively vis-à-vis the G3 currencies (viz., the dollar, euro and yen). There are other, more flexible, options available including common pegs or a system of managed floating vis-à-vis G3 currencies with intraregional parity grids which deserve attention.[70] Complementary arrangements should also be considered, including common sets of measures to curb excessive capital inflows, formal arrangements for macroeconomic policy coordination, surveillance of financial markets and capital flows and effective short-term intraregional credit facilities based on an extension of the Chiang Mai initiative.

F. Conclusions

The world economy is going through difficult times. With financial turmoil rapidly deepening, it has now become quite likely that the United States will face economic contraction in the period ahead and, on some accounts, it may even experience the most serious recession since the Great Depression despite expansionary monetary and fiscal measures. There is no coordinated expansion by the G7 in sight. Spillovers from this crisis to developing countries will certainly surpass the adverse international repercussions of crises in emerging markets in the 1990s. However, for the first time in modern history, hopes seem to be largely pinned on developing countries, particularly in Asia, for sustaining stability and growth in the world economy. On the one hand, the SWFs from emerging markets are increasingly looked at as stabilizing forces in financial markets by providing capital to support troubled banks in the United States and Europe. On the other hand, economic prospects in the world economy seem to hinge, more than ever, on the ability of Asian developing countries to decouple their growth and continue surging ahead despite adverse spillovers from advanced countries.

In Asia the impact of these spillovers will be felt at a time when the region is facing fragility and imbalances resulting from trade and financial policies and strategies pursued in recent years, including credit, asset and investment bubbles and excessive reliance on foreign markets. However, economic fundamentals in the region are generally strong enough to allow a positive response to trade shocks from contraction of markets abroad and swings in exchange rates. Countries with weak fiscal and current account positions look somewhat vulnerable to a sudden stop and reversal of capital flows, but this is not seen as likely to occur. On balance, therefore, Asian developing countries can be expected to continue with rapid, albeit somewhat reduced, growth provided that they undertake countercyclical and structural measures needed to address domestic fragility and imbalances and counter the adverse effects of external shocks from the subprime crisis.

Current conditions demonstrate once again that when policies falter in regulating financial institutions and markets, there is no limit to the damage that they can inflict on an economy. Furthermore, in a world of closely integrated markets, every major financial crisis has global repercussions. This means that shortcomings in national systems of financial rules and regulations are of international concern – more so for those in major advanced economies than in emerging markets because of their greater global repercussions. So far piecemeal initiatives and efforts in international fora such as the IMF, the BIS and the Financial Stability Forum have not been able to prevent recurrence of virulent global financial crises. A fundamental collective rethinking with full participation of developing countries is thus needed for harnessing financial markets and reducing systemic and global instability.

Notes

1 Paper prepared for the United Nations Economic and Social Commission for Asia and the Pacific (ESCAP) and presented at the Ministerial segment of its 64th commission session in Bangkok on 29 April 2008, and first published in *ESCAP Series on Inclusive & Sustainable Development*. I am grateful to Andrew Cornford, Martin Khor and staff members of ESCAP for comments and suggestions on an earlier draft and to Ka-Min Lean of the Third World Network for editorial assistance. The usual caveat applies.

2 This is the essence of the financial instability hypothesis developed by Minsky (1978) following in the footsteps of Fisher and Keynes. Minsky starts from the proposition that stability (tranquility), including that of an expansion, is destabilizing since it increases confidence, reduces the value placed on liquidity and raises the acceptable debt-to-equity ratios. He sees financial instability as an intrinsic feature of market economies and financial fragility as endogenous. For a discussion of the relevance of this analysis to boom–bust cycles in emerging markets see, Akyüz (2008).

3 See IMF (2007c) for the notion of global liquidity and the role of monetary policy in advanced economies and financial innovation in global liquidity expansion and risk appetite. See also BIS (2007a, 8–10) for a similar discussion.

4 On financial deregulation, banking and real estate crisis in the United States in the 1980s and the policy response in the early 1990s see UNCTAD TDR (1991; 1994; and 1997).

5 On the reluctance of the Fed to use the direction and authority given in 1994 to clamp down on dangerous and predatory lending practices, see Kuttner (2007).

6 On the decline of traditional banking and earlier response see Kaufman and Mote (1994) and Edwards and Mishkin (1995).

7 This was clearly stated by one of the present members of the Federal Reserve Board in a co-authored article in 1995: "The decline of traditional banking entails a risk to the financial system only if regulators fail to adapt their policies to the new financial environment that is emerging" (Edwards and Mishkin, 1995, 42).

8 In the new legislation depository institutions are permitted to own other financial institutions or to be affiliated with them through financial holding companies. On the role of deregulation, notably the repeal of the Glass–Steagall Act, in the subprime crisis, see Kregel (2007) and Kuttner (2007).

9 SIVs are like banks in respect of maturity transformation between long-term assets and short-term liabilities, but unlike banks they are not regulated; nor do they have access to lender of last resort financing. They are thus exposed to liquidity risk. Their solvency can also be threatened if the value of their assets falls below that of their liabilities as a result of short-term interest rate hikes or default on their assets, as is now happening with mortgage-backed securities.

10 The underlying assumption that the spread between short and long rates would remain stable or widen failed to materialize as the yield curve flattened with increases in policy rates after 2004, slowing the demand for mortgage-based securities and squeezing SIVs.

11 The Bank of China is reported to have lost some $2 billion on its holdings of collateralized securities, including those backed by United States mortgages (Pearlstein 2008). Standard Chartered, in which Singapore's sovereign wealth fund, Temasek, owns a 19 percent stake, is reported to have been walking away from its $7.5 billion SIVs sold in Asia and the Middle East (Bowring 2008b).

12 Monolines are bond insurers which guarantee repayment of principal and interest in case of default of the issuer. They are so named because originally they were engaged in a single line of business– namely, insuring municipal bonds. The triple-A credit rating they enjoy is passed on to any bond they insure so that downgrading will affect the ratings and values of all the bonds insured by monolines. Banks are now reported to own some $850 billion of securities guaranteed by bond insurers, and the failure of monolines to pay out the principals and interest on insured bonds would require additional funds for banks, estimated in the order of some $150 billion.

13 This is very much in line with what Minsky (1986) proposed to resolve such crises and prevent deep and prolonged recessions – that is, a "Big Bank" as a lender of last resort, and a "Big Government" as a spender of last resort – even though their effectiveness at the present juncture is contentious.

14 A recent proposal by a former chairman of the Council of Economic Advisers, Feldstein (2008), comes close – that is, the federal government should lend each mortgage holder 20 percent of the value of the mortgage with a 15 year payback period at the rates on two year Treasury debt.

15 The assumption of private sector liabilities through recapitalization of insolvent banks in financial crises has made a significant contribution to growth of public debt in emerging markets. In Indonesia, these raised public debt by more than 50 percent of GDP (IMF 2003, 28n), creating problems of fiscal sustainability despite a good track record. For Thailand and Korea corresponding figures are 42 percent and 34 percent respectively (Hoggard and Saporta 2001, 162).

16 It is notable that warnings are coming from some financial market participants that bailouts would prevent the much-needed correction in asset prices and compound the problems (Roach 2007).

17 See Weisman (2007). Several commentators including Summers (2007b) and Truman (2007a) call for greater transparency and accountability – something visibly missing in the case of Western institutional investors and hedge funds. Others such as Wade (2007) see SWFs as "a partial redress to the unlevel playing field built into 'global system' through a panoply of international rules [...] which confer structural advantages on western companies."

18 See Debelle (2004) who also mentions low interest rates among the reasons for increased household indebtedness.

19 Van Eeden (2006) shows that the S&P 500 stock index closely follows a forward-looking Housing Market Index with a one-year lag.

20 A decline in the personal savings rate by 7 percentage points of disposable income corresponds to a 5 percent decline in terms of GDP. The much-publicized fiscal deficits have had very little to do with this deterioration – before the dot-com bubble fiscal deficits were in the order of 5 percent of GDP compared to some 3 percent in recent years.

21 Not all Asian countries hit by the crisis manifested vulnerability in all these areas (UNCTAD TDR 1998, Akyüz 2000).

22 The underlying figures in Table 6.2 are on net–net basis for equity flows and gross basis for debt flows; that is, net outflows of FDI and portfolio equity by residents are deducted from net inflows by nonresidents. Thus, the current account balance plus private capital flows minus net lending by residents (and errors and omissions) would give changes in reserves – see IIF (October 2007, box 3). The countries included are China, India, Indonesia, Malaysia, Philippines, South Korea and Thailand in Asia; Argentina, Brazil, Chile, Colombia, Ecuador, Mexico, Peru, Uruguay and Venezuela in Latin America; Bulgaria, Czech Republic, Hungary, Poland, Romania, Russian Federation, Slovakia, Turkey and Ukraine in Europe; and Algeria, Egypt, Morocco, South Africa and Tunisia in Africa/Middle East.

23 That the push factor is generally more important in boom–bust cycles in international capital flows is also noted by the World Bank (2003, 26): the "dynamics of net capital inflows and the changes of official reserves over the cycle do indeed indicate that the push factor is more important for middle income countries, while the pull factor dominates in high income countries."

24 On different forms of carry trade and interest differentials, see BIS (2007a, 83–88); UNCTAD TDR (2007, chap. 1) and IIF (October 2007).

25 For current account and growth figures in Central and Eastern Europe (excluding the Russian Federation) see IMF (2007c, Tables A4 and A12).

26 The proportion of domestic-currency sovereign debt held by nonresidents in emerging markets is estimated to have reached 12 percent – Mehl and Reynaud (2005) and De Alessi Gracio, Hoggarth and Yang (2005). The expansion appears to be particularly rapid in Latin America due to high levels of sovereign debt. Available data shows that foreign investment in local-currency government securities went from less than $15 billion at the beginning of 2003 to $200 billion by the end of 2006– see Tovar and Quispe-Agnoli (2008). Moreover, some Latin American countries have been able to issue local-currency-denominated global bonds at rates below those in domestic markets because of lower jurisdiction spreads (Tovar, 2005; IMF, 2005).

27 For further discussion of components of capital flows to Asian emerging markets see BIS (2007a), IMF (2007d and 2007e) and McCauley (2008).

28 For a discussion of adequate level of reserves see UNCTAD TDR (1999, chap. 5). For an attempt to empirically determine the optimum level of reserves based on welfare criteria see Jeanne and Rancière (2006).

29 See BIS (2007a, 51) which points out that this correlation has been higher during the most recent periods of global market volatility.

30 For the evidence cited in this section see Chai-Anant and Ho (2008). The evidence is from six emerging Asian markets– India, Indonesia, Korea, the Philippines, Taiwan (China) and Thailand.

31 See IIF (October 2007, Chart 13). IMF (2007e), however, finds that institutional investors appear to have little impact on equity prices in emerging markets, but introduce considerable volatility because of herd behavior.

32 Data on equity prices and price–earnings ratios are from IMF (2007e).

33 For an analysis of developments in Asian housing markets see IMF (2007b) which somewhat underplays the extent of the bubble and the risks involved, but nevertheless points out that speculative dynamics cannot be ruled out, notably in China, India and Korea.

34 Korean and the United States data from OECD (2007, annex, table 60). For the others see BIS (2007a, 50) and IMF (2007b).

35 For credit conditions and interest rates in Asia see BIS (2007a, 39–41), Mohanty and Turner (2006, 43), and IMF (2007c, 5).

36 For a discussion of why boom–bust-recovery cycles harm investment see Akyüz (2008).

37 See Goldstein and Lardy (2004), Nagaraj (2005) and Branstetter and Lardy (2006) on excess capacity, waste and sustainability of the investment boom in China.

38 See notably Disyatat and Galati (2005), Mihaljek (2005) and Mohanty and Turner (2006), and for a general survey of the issues involved see Sarno and Taylor (2001).

39 Most Latin American and European emerging markets have experienced sizeable appreciations in real effective exchange rates – see UNCTAD TDR (2007) and IIF (October 2007). According to UNCTAD figures, real effective exchange rates were relatively stable in India and China during 2002–2006 while Indonesia saw an appreciation of over 20 percent and Malaysia close to 10 percent. Appreciations in Korea and Thailand were in the order of 10 percent – see also BIS (2007a, 41, 81). India, the Philippines and Thailand saw relatively strong appreciations in 2007.

40 The fiscal (or quasi-fiscal) cost of each dollar of reserves acquired through intervention can be written as: $ig - ir = (ig - ix) + (ix - ir)$ where *ig*, *ir* and *ix* are the rates, in common currency, on government domestic debt, reserve holdings and external borrowing, and typically $ig > ix > ir$. The margin between *ix* and *ir* is determined mainly by the credit risk and between *ig* and *ix* by the exchange rate risk. When nonresident claims are only in foreign currencies, the first term on the RHS is captured by the holders of public debt at home and the second term is the net transfer abroad – what Rodrik (2006) calls the social cost of foreign exchange reserves. For the distinction between the two types of transfers and costs see UNCTAD TDR (1999, chap. 5). Mohanty and Turner (2006) provide some estimates of fiscal cost of intervention in emerging markets.

41 Fiscal cost from ESCAP (2007, 21) and central government deficits from IMF (2007d, 20).

42 Here capital account surplus is used in the conventional sense; that is, surplus on nonreserve financial account.

43 Borrowed in the sense that they accompany increased claims by nonresidents in one form or another, including direct and portfolio equity investment, which entail outward income transfers.

44 In most emerging markets in Table 6.2 reserves are fully borrowed since the current account is broadly balanced. In some, notably in Europe, however, net capital inflows are used partly to finance current account deficits and partly to add to reserves.

45 For instance Brazil also earns reserves by running a current account surplus, but this is accompanied by sluggish growth. Because of a high degree of vulnerability to deterioration in the market sentiment, monetary and fiscal policies have been kept tight, restraining growth and imports. With the recent acceleration of growth toward 6 percent, the Brazilian current account has indeed started to run deficits.

46 On external debt see IMF (2007c). According to BIS (2007a, 94), at the end of 2006 reserves in China were 13 times the short-term debt, defined as bank debt with a maturity up to and including one year plus international debt securities with a maturity of up to one year.

47 See Williamson (1995) on the rationality of reserve accumulation under such conditions. Polak and Clark (2006, 555) refer to the fear of floating in explaining reserve holding in China, Korea and Singapore.

48 This figure appears quite modest if one takes the average spread over the full boom–bust cycles in capital flows to emerging markets. For instance the average spread of emerging market bonds exceeded 700 basis points during the 1990s and never fell below 400 basis points.

49 Since "borrowed" reserves of some countries fall short of their total external debt, realization of this aggregate benefit would require lending by countries with excess reserves to those with deficits at rates earned on reserves.

50 These include direct restrictions over foreign borrowing by residents and access of nonresidents to domestic securities markets, supplemented by market-based or administrative restrictions over maturity and currency mismatches in banks' balance sheets and restrictions designed to limit exchange-rate- related credit risks – for a discussion see Akyüz (2008).

51 For recent measures in Asia see BIS (2007a); IMF (2007b and 2007e); and McCauley (2008).

52 For a discussion of inward and outward FDI in India see Chandrasekhar (2008).

53 For comparison with the 1970s and the factors driving the recent hikes in oil prices see UNCTAD TDR (2005) and for current market conditions and prospects IMF (2007c, chap. 1).

54 Large differences between growth rates for world output given by the IMF and other institutions in Table 6.4 are due to the use of purchasing power parity by the IMF.

55 Just as this paper was being finalized the IMF cut its outlook for global growth for 2008 for the second time this year, to 3.7 percent, and argued that a global recession – defined as a global growth rate below 3 percent – was a possibility. The projection for developing Asia is also cut from 8.6 percent to 8.2 percent, and the United States is expected to slip into a mild recession in 2008 (IMF World Economic Outlook April 2008).

56 The World Bank (2007, table 1.3) simulates the impact of what it calls a prolonged recession in the United States on the world economy, triggered by a sharp fall in residential investment wherein growth in the United States would fall to 1 percent. This would cause a deceleration of growth in developing countries by no more than 0.6 percentage points.

57 On some accounts it might reduce the Chinese growth to 8 percent (Chancellor 2008).

58 According to a World Bank (2007, table 1.2) simulation, a once-and-for-all increase of 200 basis points in emerging market spreads could bring down growth in developing (low and middle income) countries by 1.7 percentage points in 2008 and 0.9 percent in 2009.

59 McCauley (2008, 1) argues that a systematic withdrawal of funds from Asia in the latter sense requires a new image whereby "Asian markets *provide* liquidity under stressed conditions to portfolios managed in the major markets."

60 See Chai-Anant and Ho (2008). The countries concerned are India, Indonesia, Korea, the Philippines, Taiwan (China) and Thailand.

61 As of the end of 2006 China's exports were just under 40 percent of its GDP with slightly over 20 percent of total exports going to the United States. For the remainder of the region the average export–GDP ratio is somewhat higher, above 40 percent, but the share of the United States in total exports is much lower.

62 Increases in the domestic content of exports render China more vulnerable to external trade shocks. On upgrading and delinking of China's exports from imports see Cui and Syed (2007) and Cui (2007).

63 That is, imports and exports within the same product categories– see UNCTAD TDR (2005), ADB (2007a), and IMF (2007d) for trade patterns and intraregional trade in Asia.

64 BIS (2007a, 56) notes that in China the bulk of recorded profits are earned by relatively few enterprises while the rest has high leverage, so that if growth slows significantly, a substantial proportion of bank loans can become nonperforming.

65 For a simulation of the trade impact of a sizeable adjustment in the United States deficits on countries in the Americas see Weisbrot, Schmitt and Sandoval (2008). In a high adjustment scenario where the United States' trade deficit falls to 1.0 percent of GDP by 2010, declines in exports of some of the countries heavily dependent on the United States such as Canada and Mexico are quite high, reaching 4 percent of GDP. However, these countries' exports to the United States as a proportion of GDP are more than twice the level of China.

66 Figures on growth in the components of aggregate demand are from the WB CQU (August 2005; September 2007; February 2008). See also Aziz and Dunaway (2007) on the evolution of the shares of private consumption and investment in GDP.

67 See WB CQU (August 2005), Kuijs (2005), Yu (2007), and Aziz and Dunaway (2007).

68 On recent behavior of labor productivity, profits and wages and consumption see Kim and Kuijs (2007), and WB CQU (August 2006; and February 2007).

69 On parallels between China today and Japan in the late 1980s, see Summers (2007a) and BIS (2007a, 150) which argues that "given the recent rates of credit expansion, asset price increases and massive investment in heavy industry, the Chinese economy also seems to be demonstrating very similar, disquieting symptoms." On the role of sluggish wage growth in Japan see UNCTAD TDR (2002 and 2003).

70 Such a regime was proposed in a paper jointly prepared by staff of the French and Japanese Ministries of Finance: "A possible solution for many emerging market economies could be a managed floating exchange rate regime whereby the currency moves within a given implicit or explicit band with its center targeted to a basket of currencies. [...] Managed free-floating exchange rate regimes may be accompanied for some time, in certain circumstances, by market-based regulatory measures to curb excessive capital inflows" (Ministry of Finance, Japan 2001, 3–4).

References

ADB (Asian Development Bank) (various issues). *Asian Development Outlook*. www.adb.org.

Aizenman, J. 2007. "Large Hoarding of International Reserves and the Emerging Global Economic Architecture." NBER Working Paper 13277.

Akyüz, Y. 2000. "Causes and Sources of the Asian Financial Crisis." Paper presented at the Host Country Event: Symposium on Economic and Financial Recovery in Asia, UNCTAD X, Bangkok. Reprinted in *TWN Global Economy Series* 1.

______. 2006. "From Liberalization to Investment and Jobs: Lost in Translation." ILO Working Paper 74. Geneva.

______. 2008. "Managing Financial Instability in Emerging Markets: A Keynesian Perspective." *METU Studies in Development* 35 (1): 177–208.

Akyüz, Y., and C. Gore 1996. "The Investment–Profits Nexus in East Asian Industrialization". *World Development* 24 (3).

Anderlini, J. 2007. "China Hits out over 'Hot Money.'" *Financial Times*, 27 June.

Aziz, J. and S. Dunaway. 2007. "China's Rebalancing Act." *Finance and Development* 44 (3).

BIS (Bank for International Settlements). 2005. "Foreign Exchange Market Intervention in Emerging Markets: Motives, Techniques and Implications." *BIS Papers* 24. Basel.

______. 2007a. *Annual Report*. Basel.

______. 2007b. *Quarterly Review*, December. Basel.

Bowring, P. 2008a. "Asia Won't Get Away Clean." *Asia Sentinel*, 25 January.

______. 2008b. "StanChart Leaves Investors out in the Cold." *Asia Sentinel*, 12 February.

Branstetter, L., and N. Lardy. 2006. "China's Embrace of Globalization." NBER Working Paper 12373.

Chai-Anant, C., and C. Ho. 2008. "Understanding Asian Equity Flows, Market Returns and Exchange Rates." BIS Working Paper 245.

Chancellor, E. 2008. "Bursting Chinese Bubble Could Hurt." *Independent Investor*, 18 January.

Chandrasekhar, C. P. 2008. "India and the World Economy." http://www.networkideas.org/news/jan2008/news25_World_Economy.htm. Accessed 1 February 2008.

Cui, L. 2007. "China's Growing External Dependence." *Finance and Development* 44 (3).

Cui, L., and M. Syed. 2007. "The Shifting Structure of China's Trade and Production." IMF Working Paper 07/214.

De Alessi Gracio, C., G. Hoggarth and J. Yang. 2005. "Capital Flows to Emerging Markets: Recent Trends and Potential Financial Stability Implications." *Bank of England Financial Stability Review*, December: 94–102.

Debelle, G. 2004. "Macroeconomic Implications of Rising Household Debt." BIS Working Paper 153. Basel.

Disyatat, P., and G. Galati. 2005. "The Effectiveness of Foreign Exchange Intervention in Emerging Market Countries." *BIS Papers* 24, May: 97–113.

Dooley, M., D. Folkerts-Landau and P. Garber. 2004. "The Revived Bretton Woods System: The Effects of Periphery Intervention and Reserve Management on Interest Rates and Exchange Rates in Center Countries." NBER Working Paper 10332.

Edwards, F. R., and F. S. Mishkin. 1995. "The Decline of Traditional Banking: Implications for Financial Stability and Regulatory Policy." FRBNY *Economic Policy Review*, July: 27–45.

ESCAP (Economic and Social Commission for Asia and the Pacific). 2007. *Key Economic Developments in the Asia-Pacific Region 2008*. Bangkok: United Nations.

Feldstein, M. 2008. "How to Stop the Mortgage Crisis." *Wall Street Journal*, 7 March.

Gieve, J. 2008. "Sovereign Wealth Funds and Global Imbalances." *BIS Review* 31.

Gochoco-Bautista, M. S. 2008. "Asset Prices and Monetary Policy: Booms and Fat Tails in East Asia." BIS Working Paper 243.

Goldstein, M., and N. R. Lardy 2004. "What Kind of Landing for the Chinese Economy?" Policy Brief 04-7. Institute for International Economics. Washington, DC.

Groshen, E. L., and S. Potter. 2003. "Has Structural Change Contributed to a Jobless Recovery?" Federal Reserve Bank of New York, *Current Issues in Economics and Finance* 9 (8): 1–7.

Hang Seng Bank. 2008. "Mainland China's Overseas Investment Escalating." *Economic Focus*, 5 February.

Hoggard, G., and V. Saporta. 2001. "Costs of Banking System Instability: Some Empirical Evidence." *Bank of England Financial Stability Review*, June: 148–65.

IIF (Institute of International Finance) (various issues). *Capital Flows to Emerging Markets*. www.iif.com.

______. 2008. *Global Economic & Capital Markets Forecasts 2008*. 10 January. http://www.google.ch/url?sa=t&rct=j&q=&esrc=s&source=web&cd=1&cad=rja&ved=0CCYQFjAA&url=http%3A%2F%2Fwww.iif.com%2Fdownload.php%3Fid%3DgBnYBJziXIU%3D&ei=gezgUq--MOqe7Abcl4HoCQ&usg=AFQjCNEtq4ZkWzzrm-dcjcjsaoC1mShzXA&bvm=bv.59568121,d.bGQ. Accessed 1 March 2008.

IMF (International Monetary Fund). 2003. "Sustainability Assessments – Review of Application and Methodological Refinements." Discussion Paper. June.

______. 2004. *Global Financial Stability Report*. April. Washington, DC.

______. 2005. *Global Financial Stability Report*. April. Washington, DC.

______. 2007a. *World Economic Outlook*. April. Washington, DC.

______. 2007b. *Regional Economic Outlook. Asia and Pacific*. April. Washington, DC.

______. 2007c. *World Economic Outlook*. October. Washington, DC.

______. 2007d. *Regional Economic Outlook. Asia and Pacific*. October. Washington, DC.

______. 2007e. *Global Financial Stability Report*. October. Washington, DC.

______. 2008. *World Economic Outlook Update*. January. Washington, DC.

Jeanne, O., and R. Rancière. 2006. "The Optimal Level of International Reserves for Emerging Market Countries: Formulas and Applications." IMF Working Paper 06/229.

Kaufman, G. G., and L. R. Mote. 1994. "Is Banking a Declining Industry? A Historical Perspective." *Federal Reserve Bank of Chicago Economic Perspectives*, May–June: 2–21.

Kim, S. Y., and L. Kuijs. 2007. "Raw Material Prices, Wages and Profitability in China's Industry – How Was Profitability Maintained When Input Prices and Wages Increased So Fast?" World Bank China Research Paper 8. Beijing.

Kregel, J. A. 2007. "The Natural Instability of Financial Markets." Working Paper 523. The Levy Economics Institute of Bard College.

Krugman, P. 1998. "Fire-Sale FDI." http://web.mit.edu/krugman/www/FIRESALE.htm. Accessed 1 March 2008.

Kuijs, L. 2005. "Investment and Saving in China." World Bank Policy Research Working Paper 3622.

Kuttner, R. 2007. "1929 Redux: Heading for a Crash?" 8 October. http://www.alternet.org/story/64684/1929_redux%3A_heading_for_a_crash. Accessed 1 December 2007.

Maki, D. M., and M. Palumbo. 2001. "Disentangling the Wealth Effect: A Cohort Analysis of Household Saving in the 1990s." FEDS Working Paper 2001-21. Washington, DC.

McCauley, R. 2008. "Managing Recent Hot Money Flows in Asia." ADBI Discussion Paper 99. Tokyo.

Mehl, A., and J. Reynaud. 2005. "The Determinants of 'Domestic' Original Sin in Emerging Market Economies." Working Paper 560. European Central Bank.

Mihaljek, D. 2005. "Survey of Central Bank Views on Effectiveness of Intervention." *BIS Papers* 24, May: 82–96.

Ministry of Finance, Japan. 2001. "Exchange Rate Regimes for Emerging Market Economies." Discussion Paper prepared by staff of the French and Japanese Ministries of Finance. Tokyo. 16 January. http://www.mof.go.jp/english/international_policy/convention/asem/asem_2001/aseme03e.htm. Accessed 4 March 2001.

Minsky, H. P. 1978. "The Financial Instability Hypothesis: A Restatement." North East London Polytechnic, *Thames Papers in Political Economy*. Reprinted in H. P. Minsky, *Can "It" Happen Again? Essays on Instability and Finance*. Armonk, New York: M. E. Sharpe, 1984.

______. 1986. *Stabilizing an Unstable Economy*. New Haven and London: Yale University Press.

Mohanty, M. S. and P. Turner. 2006. "Foreign Exchange Reserve Accumulation in Emerging Markets: What are the Domestic Implications?" *BIS Quarterly Review*, September: 39–52.

Nagaraj, R. 2005. "Industrial Growth in China and India: A Preliminary Comparison." *Economic and Political Weekly*, 21 May.

OECD Economic Outlook (various issues).

Pearlstein, S. 2007. "'No Money Down' Falls Flat." *Washington Post*, 14 March.

______. 2008. "More Room to Fall." *Washington Post*, 22 January.

Polak, J. J., and P. B. Clark. 2006. "Reducing the Costs of Holding Reserves: A New Perspective on Special Drawing Rights." In *The New Public Finance: Responding to Global Challenges*, edited by I. Kaul and P. Conceição. New York: Oxford University Press.

Roach, S. 2007. "America's Inflated Asset Prices Must Fall." *Financial Times*, 7 January.

Rodrik, D. 2006. "The Social Cost of Foreign Exchange Reserves." NBER Working Paper 11952.

Roubini, N. 2008. "The Rising Risk of a Systemic Financial Meltdown: The Twelve Steps to Financial Disaster." http://www.economonitor.com/nouriel/2008/02/05/the-rising-risk-of-a-systemic-financial-meltdown-the-twelve-steps-to-financial-disaster/. Accessed 2 March 2008.

Sarno, L., and M. P. Taylor. 2001. "Official Intervention in the Foreign Exchange Market: Is It Effective and, If So, How Does It Work?" *Journal of Economic Literature* 39 (3): 839–68.

Setser, B. 2008. "The Debate over the Pace of Hot Money Flows into China." 20 February. http://blogs.cfr.org/setser/2008/02/20/the-debate-over-the-pace-of-hot-money-flows-into/. Accessed 14 March 2008.

Summers, L. H. 2007a. "History Holds Lessons for China and its Partners." *Financial Times*, 25 February.

______. 2007b. "Funds that Shake Capitalistic Logic." *Financial Times*, 29 July.

Tovar, C. E. 2005. "International Government Debt Denominated in Local Currency: Recent Developments in Latin America." *BIS Quarterly Review*, December: 109–18.

Tovar, C. E., and M. Quispe-Agnoli. 2008. "New Financing Trends in Latin America." *BIS Papers*, 36.

Truman, E. M. 2007a. "Sovereign Wealth Funds: The Need for Greater Transparency and Accountability." Peterson Institute of International Economics. Washington, DC.

______. 2007b. "The Management of China's International Reserves: China and a SWF Scoreboard." Peterson Institute of International Economics. Washington, DC.

UN (United Nations). 2008. *World Economic Situation and Prospects 2008*. New York.

UNCTAD TDR (various issues). *Trade and Development Report*. Geneva: United Nations.

Van Eeden, P. 2006. "Consumer Spending, Real Estate and the Economy." http://www.paulvaneeden.com/Consumer.spending.real.estate.and.the.economy. Accessed 15 January 2007.

Wade, R. H. 2007. "Sovereign Funds a Useful Weapon for Poorer Nations." Letter to the Editor. *Financial Times*, 10 August.

WB CQU (various issues). *China Quarterly Update.* World Bank Beijing Office, China.

Weisbrot, M. 2008. "Proposed Stimulus Package Not Enough." Center for Economic and Policy Research. 19 February. http://www.alternet.org/story/76166/proposed_stimulus_package_not_enough. Accessed 10 February 2008.

Weisbrot, M., J. Schmitt and L. Sandoval. 2008. "The Economic Impact of a U.S. Slowdown on the Americas." Issue Brief. Center for Economic and Policy Research.

Weisman, S. 2007. "U.S. fears overseas funds could 'buy up America.'" *International Herald Tribune*, 21 August.

Williamson, J. 1995. "The Management of Capital Flows." *Pensamiento Iberoamericano*, January–June.

Wolf, M. 2007. "The Brave New World of State Capitalism." *Financial Times*, 26 October.

World Bank. 2003. *Global Economic Prospects*. Washington, DC.

______. 2007. *Global Development Finance.* Washington, DC.

______. 2008. *Prospects for the Global Economy.* 9 January. Washington, DC.

Yu, Y. D. 2007. "Global Imbalances and China." *The Australian Economic Review* 40 (1): 3–23.

______. 2008. "Managing Capital Flows: The Case of the People's Republic of China." ADBI Discussion Paper 96. Tokyo.

Chapter VII

THE GLOBAL ECONOMIC CRISIS AND ASIAN DEVELOPING COUNTRIES: IMPACT, POLICY RESPONSE AND MEDIUM-TERM PROSPECTS[1]

A. Introduction

After several years of impressive growth, the world economy encountered an equally impressive downturn starting in the third quarter of 2008, triggered by financial fragility and imbalances generated by speculative lending and investment and debt-driven spending in major advanced economies (AEs), notably the United States. Initially, there was widespread optimism that growth in developing and emerging economies (DEEs) of East Asia[2] would be decoupled from the difficulties that pervaded AEs and the region would continue to surge ahead as an autonomous growth pole. Sound balance of payments positions and self-insurance provided by large international reserves accumulated from current account surpluses and/or private capital inflows were expected to protect them against the kind of financial shocks that had devastated the region during 1997–98. In the event, however, the region could not avoid a significant drop in growth, in large part because of a sharp contraction in exports. Growth fell even in countries such as China which responded to fallouts from the crisis with massive countercyclical fiscal packages and aggressive monetary easing, while in many others growth fell to negative territory for the first time since the 1997 crisis.

Like the earlier episodes of instability, this crisis too has revealed certain structural weaknesses and vulnerabilities among various DEEs in Asia. As a result of the growth strategies pursued, economic activity has come to depend heavily on exports to major AEs or international capital flows or remittances from workers abroad and hence become highly vulnerable to their interruption. Furthermore, despite the measures taken in response to the lessons drawn from recurrent crises, almost all Asian DEEs now manifest increased susceptibility to financial boom–bust cycles and gyrations in equity, property and currency markets because of their closer integration with major financial centers through liberalization of the capital account and significantly increased presence of foreign financial institutions and investors in their markets.

There is now increased agreement that the dependence of countries in the region on foreign markets and/or external financing needs to be reduced, particularly since the world economy is unlikely to go back to the conditions prevailing before the outbreak of the crisis, characterized by rapid expansion of exports to AEs and plenty of footloose capital and cheap money. Moreover, the original enthusiasm about bringing international financial markets and institutions under tighter global regulation and control has so far yielded little result and in all likelihood instability in international financial markets and capital flows will continue unabated. Thus, a key lesson from this crisis is that DEEs ought to look for a strategic rather than full and close integration with markets in AEs, in both trade and finance, and need to rebalance domestic and external sources of growth.

This chapter is produced as part of a research project sponsored by the Third World Network (TWN) and coordinated by this author on the impact of the global crisis on Asian DEEs and the policy issues that need to be addressed for securing sustained growth and stability over the medium term. The countries studied in the TWN project include China (Yu 2010), India (Chandrasekhar 2009), Korea (Lee 2010), Malaysia (Goh and Lim 2010), Pakistan (Haque 2010), the Philippines (Lim 2010), Singapore (Lim and Jaya 2010) and Turkey (Uygur 2010). While drawing on the findings of these studies, discussions in this paper are organized around issues rather than countries, also using data and information provided by other studies and for other countries in the region.

The following section explores the link between the current crisis and the forces driving the preceding economic expansion. It is argued that the property and consumption surges in the US and elsewhere after the turn of the millennium produced not only a strong economic expansion, but also financial fragility and global trade imbalances that culminated in the subsequent crisis. Section C examines the transmission of the impact of the crisis through three main channels: finance, remittances and trade. This is followed by a discussion of the policy response to fallouts from the crisis and its role in recovery. Medium-term growth prospects and policy challenges are examined in Section E. It is argued that a return to "business as usual" is not a viable option and coming years are likely to see tightened global economic and financial conditions in comparison with precrisis expansion, including an external adjustment in the US based on export expansion and instability and sluggish growth in the European Union. This means that medium-term growth prospects of the Asian DEEs hinge crucially on their success in reducing their dependence on foreign markets and/or capital flows. Assessed on the basis of possible evolution of the global economic environment and domestic policy spaces and options, the Asian DEEs are not expected to go back, over the medium term, to the kind of rapid and sustained growth they enjoyed in the years before the crisis. Slowdown in growth is expected to be greater in countries suffering chronic current account and budget deficits. The concluding chapter summarizes the systemic and structural strengths and weaknesses of the countries in the region and the policy approaches needed in order to reduce vulnerability to external shocks.

B. The Great Financial Bubble, Global Expansion and Imbalances

After the turbulent years of the 1990s and early 2000s, characterized by recurrent financial crises in emerging economies, financial instability and sluggish and erratic growth in Japan and the dot-com boom–bust cycle in the US, the world economy enjoyed a period of exceptional growth and stability until the outbreak of the global crisis in 2008. Average growth of the world economy during 2002–2007 exceeded that of the 1990s

Table 7.1: Real GDP growth (annual percentage change)

	1991–2000	2002–2007	2008	2009	2010*
World	3.1	4.4	3.0	–0.6	4.2
AEs	2.8	2.5	0.5	–3.2	2.3
DEEs	3.6	7.0	6.1	2.4	6.3
Asian DEEs	7.4	8.9	7.9	6.5	8.7
China	10.4	10.7	9.6	8.7	10.0
India	5.6	8.0	7.3	5.7	8.8
Indonesia	4.0	5.3	6.0	4.5	6.0
Philippines	3.0	5.7	3.8	0.9	3.6
Korea	6.1	4.8	2.3	0.2	4.5
Malaysia	7.1	5.9	4.6	–1.7	4.7
Thailand	4.4	5.6	2.5	–2.3	5.5
Singapore	7.6	6.8	1.4	–2.0	5.7
Pakistan	3.9	5.9	2.0	2.0	3.0
Turkey	3.7	6.8	0.7	–4.7	5.2

Source: IMF WEO Database.
* Projections

by almost one-half (Table 7.1). This was entirely due to acceleration in DEEs where growth was twice as fast as in the 1990s, exceeding even the rates attained during the golden age. Almost all developing regions and countries enjoyed faster growth than in the 1990s and many Asian DEEs with already high growth rates also saw a significant acceleration. All this took place in conditions of a high degree of price stability, with average consumer inflation hovering around 2 percent in AEs, 6 percent in DEEs and less than 4 percent in Asian DEEs.

This period also witnessed a rapid expansion of international trade and capital flows. World exports of goods and services in dollars increased by 2.5 times during 2002–2007, with most Asian DEEs experiencing double digit export growth rates. From the beginning of the decade the DEEs as a whole started to run growing current account surpluses with the AEs, notably the US where current account deficits exceeded 6 percent of GDP on the eve of the crisis. The current account surplus of DEEs was as high as $660 billion in 2007 and almost two-thirds of this was due to East Asian DEEs and the rest to fuel exporters (FEs).

After falling to some $50 billion in 2002, net private capital flows to DEEs (that is, net nonresident inflows minus net resident outflows) rose to $620 billion in 2007, and the Asian DEEs were one of the main recipients. The twin surpluses on current and capital accounts allowed the DEEs to accumulate large amounts of international reserves which increased fivefold during 2002–2008 and reached $5 trillion; more than half of these belonged to Asian DEEs. The period also saw a rapid increase in workers' remittances, from less than $100 billion at the beginning of the decade to some $330 billion on the eve of the crisis, ranking only behind foreign direct investment (FDI) as a source of external financing for DEEs (Ratha et al. 2009).

This above-trend performance of the world economy and widening global trade imbalances were greatly helped by the factors that subsequently led to the most severe postwar global financial crisis and recession. At the center of the crisis were the financial bubbles that were allowed to drive the US economy from the mid-1990s onwards. The combination of advances in information technology and sharp reduction in policy rates in response to the 1990–91 recession created the dot-com bubble in the second half of the 1990s when equity prices rose to unsustainable levels. This was also accompanied by a housing bubble. Exceptional capital gains on stocks gave a major boost to spending on consumption and property, and this made a major contribution to the decline in household savings, bringing it down from 7.7 percent of disposable income in the early 1990s to 2 percent at the end of the decade.[3]

The US housing bubble continued with even greater force with the bursting of the dot-com bubble in the early years of the present decade for several reasons. First, the US Federal Reserve responded to the bursting of the dot-com bubble and the collapse in equity markets by bringing policy rates to historical lows for fear of asset deflation and recession. Second, the collapse of the stock market made investment in property even more attractive. Finally, a new piece of legislation introduced in the late 1990s allowed greater room for banks to engage in and expand speculative lending through securitization. All these combined to produce a massive expansion in lending for property investment as well as for household consumption. Capital gains from the property boom helped bring down personal savings even further, as homeowners increasingly extracted equity to finance consumption, making it disappear altogether in the middle of the decade and raising the household debt to some 140 percent of disposable income.[4]

The policy of easy money and low interest rates in the US was also mirrored in several other AEs. Interest rates in Japan were brought down to almost zero as a result of efforts to break out of deflation. Even the otherwise conservative European Central Bank joined in and brought interest rates to unusually low levels.

Low interest rates, stagnant equity prices and ample liquidity played a major role in redirecting private capital flows to DEEs in search of quick windfall gains and arbitrage profits. Oil surpluses also added considerably to the surge in capital flows. Unlike China which has run twin surpluses on current and capital accounts and used them entirely for investment in international reserves, FEs have had deficits on their capital account. They used about one-third of oil surpluses generated after 2002 for investment abroad, mainly through sovereign wealth funds, and two-thirds for reserve accumulation. Unlike in the 1970s, the oil surpluses were not recycled through commercial banks, but were used for direct equity and portfolio acquisitions, including in DEEs. These investments supported widening current account deficits and appreciating exchange rates in some DEEs in Europe and elsewhere, including Turkey.

The global financial bubble and widening trade imbalances in the run-up to the 2008–2009 crisis are occasionally explained in terms of a global savings glut rather than monetary and regulatory slippages in the US, including by former and present governors of the Fed (Bernanke 2009; Greenspan 2009). According to this view, high savings in several Asian emerging economies, notably in China, brought down long-term interest rates globally, thereby reducing incentives for private savings in the US and some other economies. At the same time, investment of these savings in the US markets resulted in significant increases in funds available for domestic lending, creating aggressive competition for borrowers and lowering lending standards. Briefly, according to this view, the global savings glut resulting from export-led growth strategies of Asian DEEs was responsible for the build-up of financial fragility, excessive debt-driven spending and collapse of household savings, and for rising current account deficits in the US in the run-up to the crisis.

It is true that low interest rates and the surge in consumer spending in the US were supported by exchange rate, balance of payments and reserve policies of surplus East Asian countries, notably China. These policies were motivated by the lesson drawn from the 1997 crisis that at times of turbulence DEEs cannot rely on support from the International Monetary Fund (IMF) and they would need to secure self-insurance by sustaining sound current account positions and accumulating large amounts of international reserves. They thus managed their currencies in close pegs to the dollar, avoiding appreciations, achieving growing trade surpluses and investing them – and their net private capital inflows – in US Treasuries and the debt of government-sponsored agencies such as the mortgage firms Fannie Mae and Freddie Mac. On the eve of the crisis around 90 percent of China's and 65 percent of FEs' holdings of US Treasuries were long term. Consequently, when the Fed started to tighten monetary policy after 2004, long-term rates moved only a little and the yield curve flattened, giving rise to what is known as Greenspan's conundrum. Thus, monetary policy lost its effectiveness in checking private borrowing and spending, notably for investment in property.[5]

There can be little doubt that without large inflows from China and FEs, the financial bubble in the US could not have been sustained for long. Both the dollar and long-term interest rates would have eventually come under strain. This would have made it difficult for the US to pursue lax monetary and regulatory policies and ignore the spending boom and mounting current account deficits.

However, the link between savings and current account imbalances on the one hand, and the financial bubble in the US, on the other hand, is much more complex than is typically portrayed by the proponents of the "savings glut" argument. First, as noted, the housing and consumption boom in the US started long before China began running large trade surpluses. Second, low interest rates do not always give rise to surges in consumer spending. For over a decade the Japanese economy suffered from underconsumption despite historically low interest rates, which often became negative in real terms. Furthermore, personal savings have been strong in some other surplus countries, notably Germany, where interest rates were also low. US households were willing to incur a growing amount of debt not so much because of low interest rates as because of widespread and firmly held expectations that property prices would keep on rising. Expansionary monetary policy and regulatory shortcomings allowed the banks to expand lending while spreading the risks widely to investors both inside and outside the country through exotic and opaque instruments.

Capital inflows helped to keep a lid on long-term rates, but it was excessive household debt and overinvestment in property, not a cutback in the supply of Chinese savings, that brought an end to speculative lending, the housing bubble and the consumption spree in the US.

Indeed, without profligate American consumers and reckless lending by American banks, China would not have been able to run large and growing trade and savings surpluses. As discussed subsequently, in the event of the US starting to live within its means, it would be very difficult for China to maintain simultaneously strong growth, large and growing trade surpluses and exceptionally high savings. In such an event a return to growth of some 10 percent would depend very much on a considerably faster growth of consumption in China than has been the case so far and sizeable declines in the shares of national savings and current account surpluses in GDP.

C. Asian Vulnerabilities and Spillovers from the Crisis

Contrary to the initial hype about decoupling, Asian DEEs have been severely affected by shocks and contagion from the financial turmoil in AEs, to a much greater extent than during the 1997 crisis. Growth slowed down sharply everywhere at the end of 2008 and about half of the countries examined here are estimated to have registered negative growth in 2009, with the swing from the average growth attained during 2002–2007 ranging between 5 and 12 percentage points in Korea, Malaysia, Thailand, Singapore and Turkey (Table 7.1).

With few exceptions, the exposure of Asian DEEs to shocks and contagion from the crisis has its origin in their growing financial and economic linkages with the AEs, rather than their domestic macroeconomic imbalances and financial fragilities. Closer and deeper integration with major financial centers and rapidly growing gross assets and liabilities positions of DEEs with the AEs have intensified the transmission of financial stress to asset, banking and currency markets in the region. Large stocks of assets invested in AEs have exposed the Asian DEEs to losses resulting from declines in asset prices and increased defaults. Similarly the surge in private capital inflows exposed them to withdrawal of funds from equity and debt markets, putting pressure not only on international reserves and exchange rates, but also on domestic asset prices. The crisis led to a contraction of credit in DEEs due to cutbacks in international bank lending and local lending by foreign banks' affiliates in DEEs as well as declines in interbank cross-border lending for funding by domestic banks (Cetorelli and Goldberg 2010). Strong fiscal, balance of payments and reserve positions did not insulate the East Asian DEEs against adverse spillovers and shocks, but helped to contain their impact on the real economy, by allowing, inter alia, considerable space for countercyclical policy response.[6]

Trade has been the principal channel of transmission of deflationary impulses from the crisis, particularly in countries where exports have been growing faster than domestic components of aggregate demand. In others, declines in exports impinged on economic activity not so much by reducing aggregate demand, but by tightening the payments constraint and thereby narrowing the space for countercyclical policy response.

1. Losses on foreign asset holdings

The period since the early 2000s has seen an unprecedented accumulation of foreign assets by Asian DEEs invested in AEs, due to a surge in private capital inflows and the emergence of large and growing current account surpluses. Countries such as China have enjoyed twin surpluses on their current and capital accounts while in many others with current account deficits such as India, capital inflows have exceeded by a very large margin the needs for current account financing.

Most Asian countries followed a policy of stable and competitive exchange rates, not only as part of an export-led growth strategy, but also to avoid the kind of difficulties that were laid bare during the 1997 crisis resulting from currency appreciations, large and growing current account deficits and lack of self-insurance.[7] As a result, they intervened heavily in currency markets in order to absorb the excess supply of foreign exchange, thereby preventing large appreciations and accumulating large amounts of international reserves. A few others, notably Turkey, chose to float independently and accumulated reserves only to the extent deemed necessary to meet external payments rather than to prevent appreciations. Most of the reserves – at least some 60 percent of the total – are held in dollar-denominated public sector liabilities, including those issued by government-sponsored agencies in the US.

As capital inflows and/or current account surpluses continued to grow, many countries found it extremely difficult and costly to fully sterilize the impact of interventions on domestic liquidity. Rather than checking capital inflows through tighter direct and indirect controls, they chose to liberalize resident outflows for both direct and portfolio investment abroad. Private portfolio investment abroad by Asian DEEs in AEs, excluding reserves, rose from less than 5 percent of GDP in the late 1990s to over 10 percent in 2007, while international reserves held by central banks increased even more rapidly, exceeding on average 40 percent of GDP.

The increased holding of foreign assets has no doubt resulted in greater exposure of Asian DEEs to instability in their market valuations as well as exchange rate swings. There is no readily available information on the exposure of commercial banks and institutional investors in Asia to toxic derivatives and on counterparty risks with respect to their asset holdings in AEs. However, the amounts involved appear to be small compared to the global scale of the problem. On the eve of the outbreak of the crisis, Chinese commercial banks' holding of bonds issued or guaranteed by the US mortgage firms Fannie Mae and Freddie Mac is estimated to have been in the order of some $25 billion. The Bank of China is reported to have lost some $2 billion on its holdings of collateralized securities, including those backed by US mortgages (Pearlstein 2008; Yu 2010). The investment portfolio of Temasek, Singapore's state-owned investment company, fell by over 30 percent in 2008 due to losses on Western banks, and further losses were reported on assets sold during 2008–2009 (Bowring 2008).

More importantly, Asian central banks appear to have invested large amounts of their international reserves in debt issued or guaranteed by Fannie Mae and Freddie Mac which had combined liabilities of around $5.5 trillion. Holdings by central banks outside the US of such debt are estimated to be in the order of $1 trillion, and large amounts are also known to be held in private portfolios. China's holding of US agency debt is estimated to be at least 10 percent of its GDP, mostly in Fannie and Freddie assets (Pesek 2008). Had the US government not taken over these institutions, losses could have been severe. Central banks are also known to have invested in equities in AEs as well as bonds. For instance, the loss of $6.3 billion incurred by the Monetary Authority of Singapore in the fiscal year ending in March 2009 on assets invested in the US, Europe and Japan was partly due to equity price declines.

2. Capital flows and financial and currency instability

During 2002–2007 cumulative net private capital flows to Asian DEEs added up to only $500 billion, but this was associated with a massive gross cumulative inflow of $2.5 trillion (IMF WEO May 2009). A large proportion of these inflows were in direct and portfolio investment and only a small proportion in bank loans. At the end of 2007, the stock of portfolios held by the residents of AEs in Asian DEEs was about 25 percent of the GDP of these economies (Balakrishnan et al. 2009). This represents a significant increase in foreign presence in the securities markets of Asian DEEs, making them highly susceptible to changes in market sentiments in AEs. In Korea, for instance, nonresident holding of equities reached almost one-half of market capitalization (McCauley 2008). In China foreign share as a percentage of market capitalization increased from 2.5 percent in 2001 to 23.2 percent in 2006 and in India from 6.6 percent to 10 percent in the same period (BIS 2009). The share of foreigner transactions in 2005 in average daily turnover was around 20 percent in Korea, 30 percent in Thailand and 70 percent in Taiwan (Chai-Anant and Ho 2008). The share of nonresidents in long-term local-currency-denominated bonds rose in Indonesia and Malaysia to reach 15–20 percent in 2007 (World Bank 2009, 29).

The surge in nonresident capital inflows was associated with rapid credit expansion in several Asian countries. On the one hand, low interest rates in AEs and large and continued inflows of capital encouraged governments in several DEEs to lower interest rates and expand domestic credit without facing the risk of external liquidity problems and exchange rate pressures. On the other hand, the impact of interventions in foreign exchange markets on domestic liquidity could not always be fully sterilized, particularly in countries where the banking sector was not closely controlled. Thus, in several Asian emerging economies too monetary conditions became extremely expansionary, leading to a rapid credit expansion.

The increased foreign presence associated with the surge in nonresident capital inflows and domestic liquidity expansion played a major role in generating stock, property and investment bubbles and currency appreciations in several Asian DEEs. Stock market bubbles were most marked in China, India, Turkey and Korea where equity prices in dollar terms rose between 135 and 500 percent during 2003–2007 (Table 7.2). These countries also experienced property bubbles, driven partly by foreign acquisition and partly by domestic credit expansion. From the early 2000s investment in India and China started growing much faster than income, with its share in GDP rising by 10 and 7 percentage points, respectively. Exchange rates saw significant nominal and real

Table 7.2: Equity prices in US dollars (period-to-period percentage change)

	2003–2007	2007–2008	2008–2009
China	502.1	−51.9	58.8
India	349.5	−65.1	100.5
Indonesia	30.4	−57.6	120.8
Korea	136.9	−55.9	69.4
Malaysia	67.5	−43.4	47.8
Pakistan	28.2	−75.7	78.1
Philippines	25.4	−53.8	60.2
Taiwan	55.2	−48.7	75.1
Thailand	78.0	−50.3	70.0
Turkey	332.1	−63.4	92.0

Source: IMF GFSR (September 2003; September 2004; September 2005; September 2006; September 2007; September 2008; October 2009).

Table 7.3: Exchange rate swings (percentage change in nominal bilateral rates)

	Dollar rates			Yuan rates		
	Boom	Bust	Recovery	Boom	Bust	Recovery
Chinese Yuan	9.4	10.8	0.1	–	–	–
Indian Rupee	18.6	−17.1	10.7	8.4	−25.1	10.7
Indonesian Rupiah	−1.8	−20.5	24.6	−10.1	−28.3	24.4
Malaysian Ringgit	11.8	−3.6	7.6	1.3	−13.2	7.6
Pakistan Rupee	−5.3	−24.0	−4.5	−13.2	−31.3	−4.6
Philippine Peso	17.4	−2.9	4.4	7.5	−12.3	4.3
Singapore Dollar	13.8	0.4	9.3	5.0	−9.1	9.5
S. Korean Won	28.5	−34.8	25.3	17.6	−41.2	25.1
Taiwan Dollar	5.6	−3.6	6.2	−3.2	−13.0	6.6
Thai Baht	40.5	−10.4	7.6	28.8	−19.0	7.5
Turkish Lira	28.3	−21.1	13.2	17.2	−23.7	13.6

Source: OANDA Historical Exchange Rates. http://www.oanda.com/currency/historical-rates/ (accessed 10 February 2010).
Boom: January 2003–July 2007.
Bust: August 2007–February 2009.
Recovery: March 2009–December 2009.

appreciations not only in countries pursuing independent floating (Korea, the Philippines and Turkey) but also managed floating (India, Singapore and Thailand) (Table 7.3).[8]

These bubbles came to an end with spillovers from the global crisis. Capital inflows to emerging markets, including bank-related flows, initially kept up, but after the collapse of Lehman Brothers and the deepening of the credit crunch, there was a sharp decline starting in September 2008. Redemption by highly leveraged hedge funds in the US and the UK which had been very active in Asian equity markets in earlier years was a main driver of withdrawal of nonresident investment. In a way emerging economies in Asia and elsewhere were providing liquidity to portfolio managers and institutional investors in mature markets in order to cover their mounting losses and margin calls and to reduce debt.

As the crisis deepened, resident outflows increased while nonresident inflows declined, and for 2008 as a whole both gross and net private capital flows to Asian DEEs were significantly lower than in 2007 (IMF WEO April 2010). These fluctuations were closely followed by sovereign spreads on foreign and local currency bonds. Premium on credit default swaps (CDS) was between 100 and 200 basis points for most of the Asian DEEs before the outbreak of the crisis and withdrawal of funds from the region. From late 2008 they started shooting up, reaching 500 basis points for Malaysia and Thailand, 700–800 for Korea and the Philippines and 1,200 for Indonesia. The increase in spreads on domestic bonds was even steeper, particularly in countries with sizeable financing needs. In Indonesia, spreads on ten year government local currency bonds surged to 1,260 points over US Treasuries (World Bank 2009, 30). However, they stabilized gradually after the first quarter of 2009, with spreads on CDS falling to a range of 250–500 basis points.

With the rapid exit of foreign and resident investors and global retrenchment of risk appetite, equity and currency markets came under pressure in Asia. Equity markets lost more than half of their values in 2008 in most countries examined here (Table 7.2). Booms in property markets also came to an abrupt end, with house prices declining in China in December 2008 for the first time since the government started releasing the data in 2005 and urban fixed asset investment falling after September 2008, forcing the government to take measures to revive the property market.[9] In Korea the slump that started in 2008 threatened to set off a process of debt deflation, reminiscent of the 1997 crisis when housing prices fell by some 13 percent (Citigroup 2009).

Because of the sharp slowdown in net capital flows, several currencies that had faced strong upward pressure against the dollar after 2003, particularly the Indian rupee, Indonesian rupiah, Korean won, Thai baht and Turkish lira, started falling sharply during summer 2008 (Table 7.3). Given the strong deflationary trade impulses from the crisis, this was often seen as a welcome development. Indeed, unlike in 1997, governments were unwilling to use their reserves for stabilizing their currencies. However, in some of these countries, notably India and Korea, reserves declined sharply as a result of rapid exit of capital and widening current account deficits.[10]

After the first quarter of 2009, however, these trends have been reversed. With aggressive monetary easing in the US and sharp cuts in interest rates across the AEs generally, capital flows to DEEs soon recovered, driven to an important extent by dollar carry trade (Roubini 2009). This, together with significant easing of monetary policy in several DEEs, gave rise to new bubbles in asset markets and put upward pressures on currencies and commodities. In all Asian economies, equity prices stood at much higher levels at the end of the year than at the beginning (Table 7.2). In some cases – India and Indonesia – they fully recovered the losses incurred earlier. However, as doubts mounted about the strength of the recovery in major AEs toward mid-2010, stock markets again came under severe pressure in many Asian countries, notably in China.

Similarly, from March 2009 almost all currencies in the region started to go up against the dollar, with appreciations being generally stronger for countries which had faced stronger declines previously, notably Korea, Indonesia and Turkey (Table 7.3). This reflected in part the general weakening of the dollar after the first quarter of 2009 vis-à-vis other major reserve currencies, notably the euro, after considerable strengthening in the second half of 2008 and the early months of 2009. Nevertheless, in most cases the decline of the dollar vis-à-vis Asian currencies has been steeper.

An important consequence of these large swings in Asian currencies against the dollar is increased instability of intraregional exchange rates of East Asian countries closely connected through trade and investment, notably China, Korea and the major member countries of the Association of Southeast Asian Nations (ASEAN), as indicated by the swings in regional currencies vis-à-vis the yuan (Table 7.3). Before the outbreak of the financial crisis, most currencies in East Asia appreciated against the yuan, and the Thai baht appreciated against other ASEAN currencies along with their growing strength against the dollar. This was sharply reversed after mid-2007 when almost all currencies fell against the yuan. More recently, after early 2009, this was reversed once again with all currencies – except the Pakistan rupee – rising against both the dollar and the yuan.

These sharp swings in intraregional exchange rates have no doubt been greatly influenced by differences in capital flows, current account positions and overall macroeconomic conditions in different countries. Nevertheless, their origin also lies in differences in currency regimes pursued by the countries in the region, which now span the entire spectrum between the two corners. At one corner there are economies with independent floating – Korea, the Philippines and Turkey. At another there is Hong Kong with a currency board. While India, Thailand and Singapore have been using relatively flexible regimes, China and Malaysia followed very tightly managed pegs (IMF 2008). Whether or not the change introduced in June 2010 in the yuan peg policy in China would result in more flexible exchange rates remains to be seen.

3. Remittances

Both East and South Asia are among the main recipients of remittances from workers abroad, together accounting for more than 40 percent of total inflows to DEEs. According to World Bank estimates, among the top five recipients of remittances in 2008, there were three Asian countries – India ($52 billion), China ($49 billion) and the Philippines ($19 billion) (Table 7.4). These countries retained their positions as top recipients of remittances in 2009 (Ratha et al. 2010). In the Philippines remittances made it possible to generate current account surpluses despite large and persistent trade deficits (Lim 2010). In Pakistan during 2002–2007, remittances amounted to $25 billion, exceeding net capital inflows by more than 50 percent and accounting for about 20 percent of total foreign exchange receipts (Haque 2010).

Remittances add to growth in two ways. First, they help ease the balance of payments constraint, thereby allowing domestic spending to rise without facing foreign

Table 7.4: Remittances (billions of US dollars)

	2003	2007	2008	2009	As % of GDP 2007
China	15.1	38.8	48.5	47.0	1.0
India	21.0	37.2	51.6	47.0	3.3
Indonesia	1.5	6.2	6.8	6.6	1.4
Korea	0.8	1.1	3.1	2.9	0.1
Malaysia	1.0	1.8	1.9	1.9	1.0
Pakistan	4.0	6.0	7.0	8.6	4.2
Philippines	10.2	16.3	18.6	19.4	11.3
Thailand	1.6	1.6	1.9	1.8	0.7
Turkey	0.7	1.2	1.4	1.3	0.2

Source: World Bank, *Migration and Remittances Factbook* (November 2009).

exchange shortage. This is particularly important in countries which run structural trade deficits such as India, Pakistan and the Philippines. Second, income from workers abroad is often translated into domestic consumption, thereby adding to effective demand, output and employment. This is identified to be a main source of growth in the Philippines in recent years where remittances boosted incomes by some 10 percent (Lim 2010).

The crisis tends to reduce remittances because of falling employment and wage incomes and declines in the flow of migration. Where migrant workers are employed in cyclically sensitive sectors such as construction, the impact can be felt disproportionately by foreign workers.[11] However, despite the rapid increase in unemployment in the major host countries, notably in construction, remittances to DEEs have been more resilient than both private capital flows and export receipts. They grew strongly during 2008, but slowed down in the last quarter of the year. According to recent estimates by the World Bank, in 2009 they fell by 6 percent to $316 billion. The decline is mostly concentrated in Latin America because of close linkages with the US, notably in construction, while for South and East Asia they continue to register modest increases (Ratha et al. 2010).

In Pakistan remittances rose by $1 billion in 2008 while portfolio investment disappeared and FDI remained unchanged (Haque 2010), and there was a further increase in 2009, despite the slowdown in transfers from the US, thanks to continued growth from the Gulf. The Philippines also saw increases in 2008 and 2009, with higher remittances making up for declines in other sources of foreign exchange (Lim 2010). In India there was a large increase in 2008, by some $12 billion, despite the contraction in the US and Europe which together account for close to 60 percent of total remittances to that country, particularly from workers in IT-related sectors, linked closely to the export of software services (Chandrasekhar 2009). Part of these transfers to India seem to have been used for investment in local markets, attracted by currency depreciations and declines in asset prices, including property.

Despite the continued relative strength of remittance flows to South and East Asia, over the medium term they are unlikely to return to the rapid growth experienced in precrisis years, particularly if recovery in the US and Europe turns out to be sluggish and jobless, creating not only unemployment but also xenophobia and discrimination against foreign workers, and construction activities in the Gulf continue shrinking with persistent weakness of oil prices.[12] Indeed, the most recent World Bank projections for remittances in 2010–2011 suggest faster growth than earlier projections, but weaker than in precrisis years (Ratha et al. 2010).

4. Export shocks

Trade has been by far the most important channel of transmission of deflationary impulses from the global crisis.[13] After growing by close to 10 percent per annum during the years before the crisis, world trade volume started to fall sharply in the last quarter of 2008 and throughout the first half of 2009. Despite the subsequent recovery, it registered a decline of close to 13 percent for the year as a whole (WTO 2010).

In most Asian DEEs in the years preceding the crisis exports were the most dynamic component of aggregate demand, growing faster than domestic investment and consumption and at double digit rates in China, India, Indonesia, Korea, Singapore and Turkey. With the downturn of the global economy, this rapid growth was followed by a sharp downturn in the last quarter of 2008, with exports falling at double digit rates in most countries until the last quarter of 2009 (Table 7.5).

The impact of export contraction on economic activity has varied according to the importance of exports in the income generation process in comparison with the components of domestic demand. To account for the contribution of different components of demand to income and growth, one needs to go beyond the conventional growth accounting based on ex post national income identity. The trade balance or net exports (that is, exports minus imports) describe the ex post contribution of trade to income, but do not provide a correct measure of dependence of income on exports because all imports are deducted from exports and imports used for domestic consumption and investment are not accounted for. They thus underestimate the contribution of exports and overestimate the contribution of domestic demand to GDP.

On the other hand, the standard exports X–GDP ratio overestimates the income (value added) generated by exports because it ignores the foreign (import) content of exports. Since exports use, directly or indirectly, imported intermediate goods, parts and components, any contraction in exports would bring, pari passu, a contraction in imports used for the production of exportables, thereby tempering the impact of export declines on income and growth. Thus, in order to correctly assess the impact of export shocks on income and growth, it is necessary to identify direct and indirect import contents of exports, using input–output linkages.

Furthermore, a contraction in exports reduces income not only directly but also indirectly, through its effects on domestic consumption and investment. The Keynesian multiplier establishes an indirect link between exports and income through consumption. There are also strong knock-on effects of exports on investment, particularly where an important part of manufacturing is export-oriented.

Table 7.5: Real export of goods and services

	2004–2007 Average growth		2008		2009 [a]
	Growth (Y-o-Y)	As % of GDP	Growth (Y-o-Y)	As % of GDP	
China	24.1	37.8	8.6	36.5	– 15.9
India	17.0	20.4	12.8	22.7	– 26.4[b]
Indonesia	12.0	31.7	9.5	29.8	– 19.4
Korea	12.9	40.5	5.7	52.9	– 14.3
Malaysia	8.9	115.0	1.3	103.6	– 24.9
Pakistan	9.1	15.2	17.9	12.8	– 22.1[b]
Philippines	9.7	47.1	– 1.9	36.9	– 29.2[b]
Singapore	13.0	233.6	1.3	234.3	– 20.2
Thailand	7.5	72.8	5.5	76.4	– 12.0
Turkey	16.1	22.6	20.7	23.9	– 22.6

Source: WB China Quarterly Update (December 2008; November 2009; March 2010), ADB Key indicators (2009) and IMF IFS Database.
a. Merchandise exports.
b. Average for the first three quarters of 2009.

Estimates for import contents of different components of aggregate demand and spillovers from exports to domestic demand are not always readily available for DEEs. However, it is known that a common feature of East Asian DEEs closely linked to international production networks is that not only their X–GDP ratios but also the import content of their exports are high.[14]

Evidence suggests that the import content of Chinese exports is between 40 and 50 percent; that is, domestic value added generated by exports is less than 60 percent of their gross value. In value added terms the share of exports in GDP is no more than 20 percent. A very large proportion of the foreign content of exports consists of imported parts and components directly used in sectors producing exportables. Almost two-thirds of domestic value added contained in exports are generated in industries supplying inputs to sectors producing exportables. Around 60 percent of imports are used, directly and indirectly, for exports; less than 15 percent for consumption; and some 20–25 percent for investment.

Despite high import content, one-third of growth of income in China in the years before the outbreak of the global crisis is estimated to have been due to exports because of their phenomenal growth of some 25 percent per annum. This figure goes up to 40 percent if spillovers to domestic consumption are accounted for and further to 50 percent if knock-on effects on domestic investment are added. The sharp contraction of exports in 2009 is estimated to have dragged down GDP by more than 3 percent, without allowing for spillovers to domestic demand.[15] This meant a sharp swing of more than 6 percentage points in the contribution of exports to GDP compared to precrisis years. Despite massive government intervention, this is only partly offset by faster growth of domestic demand so that GDP growth in 2009 is estimated to have remained some 3 percentage points below the 2002–2007 average.

Available evidence suggests that the import content of exports is lower in Indonesia, Korea, the Philippines and Thailand than in China. With the exception of Indonesia, these countries also have higher X–GDP ratios (Table 7.5). Consequently, in value added terms the share of exports in GDP is higher in these countries than that in China, reaching 30–40 percent. This means that they are more susceptible to export shocks. Thus, it is estimated that the impact of export contraction in these countries during 2008 on GDP varied between 4 and 6 percent. Malaysian and Singaporean exports have higher import contents than Chinese exports, but these countries also have much higher X–GDP ratios than China. Consequently, in value added terms their exports account for a higher share of GDP than not only China but also the first group of countries. Accordingly, export shocks in 2009 had a stronger impact on GDP growth in these countries, possibly reaching double digit figures.

All in all, it can be estimated that, on average, contraction of exports during 2008–2009 reduced GDP in East Asian DEEs by 5–6 percent. When spillovers to domestic demand are accounted for, this figure is likely to be much higher. Indeed, according to an estimate by the United Nations Economic and Social Commission for Asia and the Pacific (ESCAP 2010, box 1) for East Asian DEEs and Japan, the impact of the 2009 shortfall in exports on GDP reaches 7.8 percent, accounting for both direct and indirect effects.

India, Pakistan and Turkey also suffered significant drops in exports from the last quarter of 2008. However, in the run-up to the crisis, growth in these countries was not as dependent on exports as in East Asia. They are less integrated into international production networks and their X–GDP ratios are much lower – in India and Turkey less than half the average X–GDP ratio in East Asia, and in Pakistan less than one-third. While data and information on import content of exports are not readily available for these countries, in value added terms the share of exports in GDP is likely to be around 15 percent in India and Turkey and 10 percent in Pakistan.[16] This would mean that the contraction in exports during 2008–2009 pulled down GDP by some 4–5 percent in India, 3–4 percent in Turkey but less than 2 percent in Pakistan.

These considerations suggest that the more successful exporters of manufactures with very high X–GDP ratios have been hit particularly hard by trade shocks emanating from the global crisis even when the import content of their exports is relatively high. These include not only countries which enjoyed large current account surpluses such as China, Malaysia, Singapore and Thailand, but also Korea where the current account was broadly in balance in the run-up to the crisis, but an important part of the manufacturing industry was export-oriented.

By contrast, countries which are not so closely integrated into the global trading system and international production networks in manufacturing suffered relatively less from contraction in exports. These include India, Indonesia and, to a lesser extent, the Philippines where domestic demand played as important a role in precrisis economic expansion as exports. In India, both domestic consumption and investment grew rigorously. Consumption, particularly of upper income groups, was stimulated by a credit boom resulting from financial deregulation and rapid inflow of capital, while investment in property rather than industry was the most dynamic component of domestic demand

(Chandrasekhar 2009). In the Philippines rapid expansion of private consumption supported by growing remittances resulted in an above-trend growth during 2002–2007 despite the falling share of investment in GDP (Lim 2010). All three countries maintained broadly sustainable external positions, running small current account surpluses or deficits. Turkey, which also enjoyed above-trend growth based on domestic demand, was externally more vulnerable to export shocks because of a large current account deficit and heavy dependence on capital inflows. Consequently it has been hit hard by the combination of sharp declines in capital flows and export earnings.

D. Policy Response and Recovery

The growth outcome during 2008–2009 naturally depended not only on the incidence of shocks but also on the policy response. The space for countercyclical policy varied considerably among countries. The East Asian economies have generally been able to respond by expansionary monetary and fiscal measures, but growth losses could not be prevented even where strong stimulus packages have been put in place. Thus, despite the original hype that growth in East Asia would decouple from advanced economies and could even help prevent the world economy plunging into recession, many countries in the region could not avoid negative GDP growth in 2009. For the sample of DEEs in Table 7.1, growth for 2009 was around 5 percentage points below the average growth over 2002–2007.

The reaction to the reversal of capital flows and the hike in risk premia after the collapse of Lehman Brothers was quite different from the response to the exodus of capital in previous emerging market crises, including the East Asian crisis of 1997. Although Indonesia initially succumbed to the Washington Consensus instinct and resorted to interest rate hikes in an effort to stabilize the currency, this was soon reversed. The large stock of reserves accumulated from current account surpluses and capital inflows in precrisis years was not used to any significant degree for exchange rate stabilization. Rather, as already noted, currencies were allowed to fall, as this was seen to provide some buffer against the severe drop in exports.

Unlike in the 1997 crisis, no country resorted to control over capital outflows, neither for residents nor for foreigners. Instead, several measures were announced to boost confidence and increase the resilience of the financial system to shocks. Indonesia, Korea, Malaysia, the Philippines and Thailand expanded deposit insurance. Korea also provided guarantees on interbank transactions and external debt of domestic banks up to $100 billion. Singapore introduced a Deposit Insurance Scheme in October 2008 to avoid erosion of bank deposits, guaranteeing all Singapore dollar and foreign currency deposits of individual and nonbank customers in banks, finance companies and merchant banks licensed by the Monetary Authority of Singapore until 31 December 2010 (Lim and Jaya 2010). China, Korea, India and Thailand injected capital into financial institutions.

With the stabilization of capital flows, monetary authorities in almost all countries started to cut policy rates from the last quarter of 2008, including those with relatively high inflation such as Turkey, in order to stimulate domestic demand. In addition, quantitative easing has been sought in several ways. Reserve requirements have been reduced in several countries in order to increase liquidity in the banking system. In India, Indonesia and Korea central banks not only provided liquidity support to financial institutions in local currency, but also used international reserves to lend in foreign currency in order to offset the reduction in external financing, notably to exporters. Moreover, as capital flows recovered, currency interventions were no longer sterilized, unlike in the period before the outbreak of the crisis (Akyüz 2008). In the third quarter of 2008 China stopped issuing central bank bills to sterilize the impact of dual surpluses on its current and capital accounts, adding significantly to credit expansion (Yu 2010).

East Asian countries with favorable combinations of current account and reserves positions faced no balance of payments constraint in pursuing expansionary macroeconomic policies to offset the impact of drastic declines in exports by increasing domestic consumption and investment, particularly since capital flows quickly stabilized after the initial reversal. Nor did they face fiscal constraints since their central government budgets were either in surplus or moderate deficits and debt and debt burden were quite moderate compared to most other DEEs. India too had significant policy space despite a higher sovereign debt ratio than East Asian countries.[17] Its current account deficit was relatively small compared to reserves despite some large initial losses due to capital outflows. At some 4 percent of GDP, its central government budget deficit was moderate and its debt burden was not onerous.

The main exceptions among the countries examined here were Turkey and Pakistan, with current account deficits in the order of 5–6 percent and declining reserves (Uygur 2010 and Haque 2010, respectively). In the face of sharp declines in export earnings and reduced and unstable capital flows, both countries saw the payments constraint tighten considerably. Use of tariffs and other trade measures to alleviate the payments constraints was not part of the accepted thinking of policymakers in these countries, as in most other DEEs, even though doing so would have been quite legitimate under current multilateral rules (Akyüz 2009b).

Both Pakistan and Turkey had little scope for fiscal expansion. Pakistan had already a large budget deficit of some 6 percent of GDP and resorted to procyclical fiscal tightening. In the event, it managed to grow moderately in 2009 under an IMF program, by one-third of its average growth after 2002, while its current account deficit doubled. In Turkey the main concern was to secure sovereign debt sustainability by generating a primary surplus of some 5 percent of GDP. Besides, the government was quite confident that the crisis would bypass Turkey. In any case, given the dependence of the economy on foreign capital and a high level of indebtedness, a strong countercyclical fiscal expansion could have undermined market confidence, thereby curtailing access. In the event the fiscal incentives came too late and too little. Growth collapsed in 2009, with a swing of about 12–13 percentage points from the 2002–2007 average. As expected, the current account deficit fell as imports contracted faster than exports while the central budget deficit rose sharply to exceed 5 percent of GDP.

In East Asia the countercyclical fiscal response was unprecedented, not only for the region alone but also the developing world as a whole.[18] On some estimates, the fiscal package in 15 DEEs in East, South and Central Asia amounted to 7.5 percent of 2008 GDP, almost three times the average level in the G7 major industrial countries. China introduced the largest fiscal package, close to $600 billion, but in terms of share of GDP some smaller countries implemented even bigger packages; e.g., the Thai fiscal stimulus package amounted to some 17 percent of GDP compared to 13 percent in China. Fiscal packages were also relatively large, in excess of 5 percent of GDP, in Malaysia, Singapore and Korea, but somewhat smaller in the Philippines, India and particularly Indonesia.[19]

Unlike in advanced economies, countercyclical fiscal packages in Asia placed much less emphasis on tax cuts and focused on increases in spending, particularly in infrastructure investment. Since public works are politically easier to control than current spending and tax cuts, this approach is consistent with the Keynesian approach to countercyclical fiscal intervention which calls for fiscal consolidation at times of expansion (Akyüz 2006). The main exception was Indonesia where over 80 percent of the fiscal stimulus package consisted of tax breaks and subsidies to consumers and business. India also used taxes and subsidies while China, Malaysia, Korea and Singapore focused on infrastructure spending. Although some attention has been paid to rural infrastructure and building schools and hospitals and public housing projects, in general spending targeting the poor, including social transfers, has been a relatively small part of stimulus packages.

In China less than 20 percent of the fiscal package has been allocated to social spending, with the rest going mainly into infrastructure investment in roads, railways, ports and airports. It has pushed the investment rate to 50 percent of GDP, and aggravated the problem of excess capacity that had pervaded several sectors and increased the dependence of growth on exports. Policies designed to revive real estate demand and an unprecedented growth of mortgage lending to households created a bubble in the property market, with real estate investment growing by close to 40 percent. While private consumption held up thanks to several incentives, particularly for car purchases, it did not provide much impetus to offset the sharp decline in exports. The increase in investment is estimated to have contributed between 80 and 90 percent of growth in 2009 (Wolfe and Ziemba 2009a and 2009b; Hung 2009).

Large as they may have been, stimulus packages have not always been adequate to deal with the consequences of export shocks for economic activity.[20] According to estimates by ESCAP (2010), only in less than half of East Asian DEEs (i.e., China, India, Korea and Thailand) were the announced fiscal packages sufficiently large to offset the overall impact of the decline in exports on GDP. However, this did not prevent loss of growth compared to precrisis years even though these countries also pursued highly expansionary monetary policy.

There are several reasons for the absence of a very strong correlation between the size of fiscal stimulus packages and growth performance across countries, even allowing for diversity in the incidence of export shocks. First, there appear to have been considerable variations in the impact of trade and financial shocks on private domestic demand, notably investment. The impact has been particularly strong in Korea, Taiwan, Malaysia, Thailand and the Philippines where private investment, notably in durable equipment, slowed down or contracted significantly. This, together with a slowdown in FDI, is the main reason for sharp drops in the share of domestic investment in GDP during 2008–2009 in these countries even though in most cases government investment spending rose as part of the countercyclical policy response to the crisis (ADB ADO 2010). Second, there are slippages in the implementation of announced measures. Third, infrastructure investment projects take a long time to implement fully. Finally, in most cases, fiscal packages were introduced from late 2008 onwards to be implemented in several steps, extending into 2010 and even beyond. In Thailand, for instance, the second package introduced in 2009 was for implementation in 2010–2012. Nevertheless, it is beyond doubt that countercyclical fiscal policy in Asia has been highly effective in stabilizing output and promoting recovery in the face of severe external shocks, both directly through its impact on aggregate demand and indirectly by helping maintain confidence among consumers and investors.

While recovery is stronger than expected at the outset of the global crisis, current projections for 2010 put growth well below the average rates attained in precrisis years (ADB ADO 2010, table 1). Without doubt much of that growth is coming from monetary and fiscal stimulus packages introduced from the last quarter of 2008. With exit from stimulus packages, growth will depend on private spending. A main concern is that a premature exit, in both major industrial and developing economies, could short-circuit recovery, leading to sluggish growth or even another dip in economic activity.

In this context, exit can refer to two different things: ending or reversing reflationary measures. In the former sense, exit would mean ending cuts in interest rates or quantitative easing on the monetary front, and phasing out tax cuts and additional discretionary spending on the fiscal front. In the case of reversal, there would be monetary tightening and interest rate hikes and fiscal consolidation designed to reduce structural budget deficits.

Central banks have ended interest cuts and liquidity expansion in almost all major developing and developed economies. In AEs there are signs of the beginning of monetary tightening, with the US Fed raising the interest rate it charges on short-term loans to banks and Canada raising policy rates. In several DEEs in Asia, including China, monetary tightening has started as interest rates and/or banks' reserve requirements are raised gradually with the upturn in growth and inflation. On the fiscal side, there appear to be no plans for new packages even though some spending programs introduced earlier extend to the current year and the next. While fiscal consolidation is not yet in sight anywhere in the developing world, in view of large deficits that emerged, Asian DEEs are urged to go back to fiscal prudence, rather than maintaining fiscal activism in response to continued growth slowdown (ADB ADO 2010). While the US administration appears to be reluctant to undertake fiscal retrenchment before recovery is strongly in place and growth is restored, sovereign debt problems and pressures from currency and bond markets are forcing premature fiscal adjustment in Europe.

Even without a monetary and fiscal policy reversal, the current pace of recovery may not be maintained if stimulus programs so far put in place do not lead to sustained increases in private spending. Indeed, the 1990s witnessed several failed fiscal pump-priming attempts in Japan in conditions of financial fragility whereby recovery stalled when fiscal injection came to an end. Such an outcome cannot be entirely ruled out in the current recovery. Since precrisis growth in East Asia was driven mainly by exports, a central issue over the medium term is whether they can go back to export-led growth and the kind of policy challenges they face in the likely case that there may be no return to business as usual. This clearly depends not only on policies in China and Asian DEEs, but also on the evolution of the global economy and policy and performance of major AEs.

E. Medium-Term Prospects and Policy Challenges

1. Adjustment and growth in major advanced economies

A return of the global economy to the kind of rapid and broad-based expansion enjoyed from the early years of the decade until 2008 is no doubt desired by all, but the main question is how to achieve this without the accompanying financial fragilities and trade imbalances that led to the most severe postwar global economic crisis.[21] There is wide agreement that a return to "business as usual," with the US continuing to consume beyond its means and absorbing Chinese exports by issuing growing amounts of dollar liabilities, is not a sustainable option – it is a recipe for heightened international monetary and financial instability and disorderly and deflationary adjustment to global economic imbalances.

The prospects for global stability and growth are thus believed to depend crucially on rebalancing the US and China – the largest deficit and surplus countries, respectively. In view of the central place occupied by the dollar in the international reserves system, it is recognized that international monetary and financial stability crucially depends on spending discipline by the US, in line with its income, allowing for a fundamental and sustained balance of payments adjustment. However, in order to maintain growth, the US should not simply cut domestic absorption but also shift to export-led growth. An orderly US adjustment would also require, inter alia, a shift by China from export-led to consumption-led growth and the realignment of the exchange rate of the yuan against the dollar. In this way, prospects for global stability are expected to improve without sacrificing growth.[22]

A significant adjustment by US consumers is already underway, brought about by massive losses of personal wealth caused by the subprime crisis. Personal savings have moved into positive territory and, on recent trends, may reach 10 percent of disposable income in coming years.[23] By contrast, stimulus and bailout packages have resulted in a significant increase in fiscal deficits, which now exceed 10 percent of GDP, pushing the public debt ratio toward 100 percent. Clearly, with consumer spending staying behind income growth, attempts to reduce public deficits and debt through tax increases and spending cuts would be highly deflationary.

Given consumer retrenchment, a growth-driven US fiscal adjustment would require strong export growth. Indeed, a shift from consumption-led to export-led growth is the main objective of the National Export Initiative (NEI) launched by President Obama in his State of the Union Address, which targets a doubling of exports in five years.[24] However, even with rapid export expansion, US growth is likely to be sluggish due to the decline in potential growth brought about by the crisis.[25] Actual growth may fall even further if bond markets force a swift fiscal adjustment. In other words, the US may have to pay the cost of decades-long bubble–bust cycles and aggressive monetary and fiscal policy easing in response to consequent crises by going through slow and unstable growth for some years to come. But, whether or not growth slows down over the medium term, net demand stimulus from the US to East Asian DEEs is likely to be significantly lower than in the years preceding the financial crisis. This means that domestic demand in surplus countries, including China, needs to expand much faster than in the past in order to maintain a relatively rapid global growth.

Germany and Japan are also among the major surplus countries that need to adjust and add to global demand. Although these countries often escape attention because their bilateral trade surpluses with the US are much smaller than that of China, they have also been running large amounts of current account surpluses – $250 billion in Germany and $210 billion in Japan before the onset of the crisis, compared to $370 billion in China. They have both been siphoning off global demand without adding much to global growth. During 2002–2007, exports grew 25 times faster than domestic demand in Germany and 8.5 times in Japan while this figure was less than 3 for China. In both countries, the contribution of exports to growth was much higher than that in China during the years preceding the crisis. This lack of dynamism in domestic demand has been due to the falling share of consumption in GDP along with stagnant or falling real wages, slow employment growth and the downward trend in the share of wages in GDP.

In Germany reliance on exports for growth through wage restraints (or the so-called "competitive disinflation") at the expense of consumer demand has been compromising growth and stability in other eurozone countries which are unable to restrain wages to the same extent, but locked into a common currency. It has played a major role in growing external imbalances and debt accumulation in several eurozone countries including Greece, Portugal and Spain where current account deficits as a percentage of GDP have been hovering around double digit figures and debt ratios have been rising rapidly. The region is highly vulnerable to financial turmoil due to the combination of large and what looks like unsustainable sovereign debt in these countries and a high degree of exposure of European banks to sovereign default.

Avoiding such an outcome would call for strong growth, but this has been severely constrained by continued beggar-my-neighbor policies of Germany. The deflationary policy bias would be aggravated by premature fiscal consolidation which the countries in the region seem to be determined to pursue under the pressure of bond and currency markets, posing the risk of a double dip. According to the IMF (2010 and WEO April 2010), potential growth in the euro area, currently at zero, will only reach 1.5 percent over the medium term and actual growth would remain below the rates attained during precrisis years. With increased concerns over sovereign insolvency and premature fiscal retrenchment, the figure may even be lower, if positive at all. Under these conditions, even if the specter of a double-dip recession could be averted, Europe is unlikely to provide a rapidly expanding market for East Asian exporters for several years to come.

Japanese growth prospects look as bleak as Europe's, expected to be the worst among the G7 by the Organization for Economic Cooperation and Development (OECD) (Fujioka 2010). Sluggish markets in the US and the EU would cut down Japan's growth not only directly but also indirectly since Japan provides over 15 percent of China's total intermediate imports used in the production for exports. Indeed, a very large proportion of negative export shocks to China during 2008–2009 were passed on to Japan alongside Taiwan and Korea, as the main suppliers of parts and components to China. Therefore, Japan is unlikely to provide much independent growth stimulus to lesser developed countries in the region.

2. Sustaining rapid growth in Asia

With consumer retrenchment and external adjustment in the US and sluggish growth or stagnation in the EU and Japan, it will be very difficult for the world economy to return to the kind of rapid growth enjoyed in the years preceding the global economic crisis. This means considerably dampened export prospects for Asian DEEs. Fiscal and balance of payments adjustment and monetary tightening in the US could also lead to considerably tightened global financial conditions over the medium term. They could result in significant increases in interest rates, strengthening the dollar and leading to a rapid unwinding of dollar carry trade. By triggering rapid and sustained capital outflows, these could wreak havoc in DEEs heavily dependent on foreign capital flows.[26]

The impact of these possible changes in the global economic environment on the countries under study would vary considerably depending on their underlying macroeconomic and structural conditions. The growth outcome will also depend on the policy response, the space for which also varies significantly across countries. In these respects, a distinction can be made between, on the one hand, the South and West Asian countries, India, Turkey and Pakistan, where domestic demand has been a more dynamic component of growth than exports and external accounts are in structural deficits, and, on the other hand, China and the East Asian DEEs linked to the Sinocentric production network where growth is export-led and much less dependent on foreign capital inflows.

3. South and West Asia

Turkey and Pakistan need to overcome a number of structural weaknesses in order to be able to return to the kind of rapid and sustained growth they enjoyed in the years before the global crisis. This may be difficult to achieve rapidly even under drastic policy changes. Turkey suffers from a fundamental disequilibrium in its current account balance. Even though its current account deficit has narrowed since the last quarter of 2008, it will certainly start climbing with any acceleration of growth based on domestic demand. Thus, it could need, inter alia, a major currency alignment to help achieve external adjustment without facing deflation. It is important that this takes place in an orderly way, rather than through a rapid exit of capital and an attack on its currency that may be triggered by postponing adjustment, which would lead to defaults in the private sector with extensive liability dollarization as well as severe difficulties in servicing domestic public debt.

Turkey also needs to raise national savings in order to reduce its dependence on foreign capital. Currency adjustment can play a role in this since there appears to be an inverse correlation between real appreciations and private savings (Uygur 2010).

However, the country also needs to raise its fixed investment rate significantly – from some 20 percent of GDP before the crisis and 17 percent now – in order to accelerate structural change through upgrading and moving out of labor-intensive manufactures. This is absolutely essential because its markets are wide open to cheaper Asian exporters of manufactures and it has very little room for trade policy measures in view of its customs union agreement with the EU. With its national savings rate hovering around 16 percent of GDP since 2003, closing the external gap while raising investment is a daunting task. Thus, Turkey can face severe problems regarding stability and growth if the global economic environment in coming years does not turn out to be as favorable as in precrisis years.

Much of this is also true for Pakistan. From 2002 onwards Pakistan enjoyed above historical growth, driven primarily by inflows of capital and remittances: during 2002–2007 net capital flows and current transfers accounted for as much as 45 percent of total foreign exchange receipts, with exports covering less than three-quarters of imports (Haque 2010). However, the country had been facing serious difficulties in maintaining growth and keeping deficits under control long before the onset of the global crisis – a process which culminated in an IMF program. Medium-term prospects regarding capital inflows and remittances do not look very bright. In all likelihood, recovery in advanced economies will continue to be jobless for some time to come and activity in the Gulf cannot pick up without a sustained upturn in oil prices. Therefore, following the modest recovery in sight over 2010–2011, the Pakistan economy may well return to the more moderate growth rates of the 1990s.

Although India has been running current account deficits constantly since the middle of the decade, the contribution of its exports to growth is much greater than is commonly appreciated. As noted, the share of value added exports in GDP is in the range of 15–17 percent. With Indian real exports growing, on average, by 17 percent per annum during 2004–2007, it can be estimated that around one-third of GDP growth in that period was due to exports, even without accounting for spillovers to domestic demand.[27] It would be difficult to replicate this export performance over the medium term. With unchanged pace and pattern of domestic demand, Indian growth over the medium term is thus likely to be about some 2 percentage points below the average enjoyed in the years before the crisis, coming down to around 7 percent. This is still respectable – more than twice the so-called Hindu growth of the 1960s and 1970s. It could be possible to push this up by faster expansion of domestic demand, but this would widen the current account deficit, possibly to 5 percent of GDP. Coming at a time when global financial conditions can become quite tight, this could make the economy highly vulnerable to sudden stops and reversal of capital flows. Thus, it might be wiser to settle at a somewhat lower growth rate than try to replicate the 9–10 percent growth of the earlier period and expose the economy to such risks.

4. *China*[28]

For countries closely linked to the East Asian production network, the policies and performance of China, as well as major AEs, hold the key for medium-term growth prospects, given the sheer size of China and their close trade linkages. For the reasons already discussed, China cannot go back to precrisis export growth rates in excess of 25 percent per annum, more than three times the projected medium-term growth in world trade volume (IMF WEO April 2010, table A17). An aggressive export push in the markets of AEs or DEEs is likely to meet strong resistance, creating conflicts in the trading system. If, on the other hand, the rate of expansion of Chinese exports comes down to a more acceptable level, say to 10 percent, then, without a fundamental change in the pace and pattern of domestic demand, its growth may barely reach 7 percent. Growth may drop a lot more if the credit-driven investment bubble bursts, exposing bad loans and giving rise to difficulties in overstretched banks and, eventually, to a financial crisis.

One option is to expand rapidly in the markets of poorer economies where imports are constrained by foreign exchange availability, by simultaneously providing them the necessary financing through lending and/or direct investment. However, there are limits to what these economies could absorb while securing sustainable external debt and asset positions. For instance, total merchandise imports of least developed countries (LDCs) are less than 10 percent of Chinese exports and for sub-Saharan Africa the ratio is less than one-to-five. Besides, Chinese expansion in these markets could threaten the domestic industry in certain sectors such as clothing, a main manufactured export item of several low income countries, including the larger ones such as Bangladesh and Vietnam. While such an option would certainly help both the poorer countries and China in expanding trade, it should be seen as a step in the transition from export-led to domestic-demand-led growth, rather than as a way of postponing the necessary adjustment.

Another option would be to lower the foreign content of exports by upgrading and import substitution of high-tech parts and components so as to enhance their contribution to growth. Such a transformation has been underway, but even if accelerated considerably, it will take a long time to have its effects felt on domestic content of exports. Besides, it would imply continued growth of the Chinese trade surplus, thereby aggravating global imbalances.

The solution should be sought primarily in raising domestic consumption much faster than has been the case so far. Since the beginning of the decade until the global financial crisis, investment in China went ahead of consumption and the demand gap was filled by rapidly growing exports. The share of private consumption in GDP fell from over 50 percent in the 1990s to around 36 percent on the eve of the crisis while that of investment rose to 45 percent. Consumption as a share of GDP remained stable during the 2008–2009 downturn while the investment rate has been pushed up to 50 percent by the stimulus package. With a sustained slowdown in the pace of exports, a return to a path of some 9–10 percent growth will require reversing the downward trend in the share of private consumption and the upward trend in the share of investment in GDP.

The main reason for underconsumption in China is not excessive household savings. They are no doubt high, but not always higher than those in other DEEs. In the past few years they have remained around 20 percent of GDP, broadly the same as household savings in Malaysia in the 1980s and in India in recent years. As a proportion of household disposable income, they are in the order of 28 percent compared to 32 percent in India. However, at more than 50 percent of GDP, the Chinese national savings rate exceeds that of India by a large margin because of significantly higher corporate savings or profit retentions – over 20 percent of GDP compared to 10 percent in India. Chinese corporate profits and savings are also much higher than those in late industrializers in Asia. While household savings as a proportion of disposable income have been rising in recent years, their share in national savings has been declining because of sharply rising corporate savings.[29]

The disparity between consumption and investment and the consequent dependence of China on foreign markets is largely the outcome of the imbalance between wages and profits. Wages in China constitute a very large proportion of household income because government transfers and investment income, including dividends, are very small. Despite registering impressive increases, wages have lagged behind productivity growth and their share in value added has been declining. The downward trend in the share of wages in GDP is almost perfectly mirrored by the share of private consumption in GDP.[30] This has no doubt been a factor in the recent labor unrest in China.

A return to trend growth in China thus crucially depends on a sizeable increase in the share of household income in GDP and a corresponding decline in corporate profits and investment, which are boosted by tax incentives and the practice of nonpayment of dividends to the government by state-owned enterprises. This calls for a higher share of wages in value added and significantly greater government transfers to households, particularly in rural areas where incomes remain depressed. Greater public spending on social infrastructure in health, housing and education would not only improve social welfare but also serve to reduce relatively high precautionary household savings. These expenditures and income transfers can be financed with dividend payments by state-owned enterprises.

As noted, with its emphasis on investment, the recent policy response in China to fallouts from the crisis has done little to address the problem of underconsumption. It will be in a weaker position to give a similar positive response to fallouts from a possible second dip in global economic activity that may result from debt difficulties and premature fiscal tightening in Europe. Indeed, the longer the adjustment to underconsumption is delayed, the greater the vulnerability of China to instability of economic activity in its main markets in AEs. Instability in the latter economies is likely to persist since the crisis response has not eliminated its root causes – namely, excessive indebtedness and rapid liquidity expansion.

5. China's East Asian suppliers

As noted, the dependence of growth on exports is greater in East Asian DEEs closely participating in the Sinocentric production network than in China. These economies have direct exposure to a sustained slowdown in exports to the US and the EU, which together account for more than a quarter of total exports of some of these countries. They also have a significant indirect exposure through China. Although China has become the largest export market for an increasing number of East Asian DEEs, an important part of Chinese imports from them is used for inputs into exports of final consumer goods to the US and the EU. For every \$100 worth of processing exports of China to the US and the EU, about \$35 to \$40 accrue to East Asian DEEs.

As an export hub to the US and the EU, China is a major importer from East Asian DEEs, but it is not a major market for them since an important part of Chinese imports is destined to exports rather than used internally. Domestic consumption in China generates proportionately much less demand for imports from East Asian DEEs than its exports to the US and the EU. Consequently, a shift by China from export-led to consumption-led growth could result in a significant slowdown of its manufactured imports from East Asian DEEs. Thus, at its current pattern of domestic spending, the Chinese market is not a good substitute for US and EU markets for East Asian DEEs. It cannot replace the US even if it maintained GDP growth of some 10 percent based on domestic consumption rather than exports; its GDP is about one-third of the US, the share of households in GDP is much smaller, they save a much higher proportion of disposable income and the import content of household consumption is much lower than in the US. Briefly, a China–US rebalancing can make it quite difficult for East Asian DEEs to sustain rapid export-led growth.

To become a regional locomotive, China would need to raise not only its domestic consumption as a proportion of GDP, but also its import content and, in particular, its imports of final goods from the region. While the share of such goods in Chinese imports from the region has been increasing in recent years (Athukorala 2008; Kim et al. 2009), production sharing continues to dominate the intraregional trade. Moreover, even if there is a rapid increase in domestic consumption and its import content in China, many East Asian DEEs may not be able to expand their exports rapidly because intraregional network trade is crucially different from trade in final goods. A shift from the former to the latter would call for industrial restructuring and a significant change in the mix of exports. For the same reason a shift to alternative markets may prove to be difficult even for smaller countries supplying parts and components to China. The same problem would also be encountered in reducing dependence on exports by shifting to domestic markets.

Outside China a main reason for excessive reliance on exports is underinvestment. In several economies including Malaysia, Singapore, the Philippines, Taiwan and Indonesia, investment rates have been hovering around 20 percent of GDP in recent years, less than half the rate in China. In none of these economies have investment rates recovered to the levels attained before the 1997 crisis (Table 7.6).[31] Even recognizing that the precrisis investment boom was an unsustainable bubble driven by massive capital inflows, recent investment rates are too low to generate rapid growth of either productive capacity or effective demand.

Exceptionally high investment in China and low rates of investment in the rest of East Asia are related. Generous incentives provided by China to export-oriented FDI play an important part in attracting large amounts of investment from the region. There is a need to redistribute aggregate investment within East Asia, from China toward the rest. This would be greatly helped if China were to start focusing on domestic markets and dismantling incentives to export-oriented FDI.

Private consumption has also been weak in most East Asian countries. In Korea, Malaysia, Taiwan and Thailand its share in GDP barely reaches 55 percent – much below the rates in more affluent countries such as the US (over 70 percent) and the EU

Table 7.6: Investment in Asia (percentage of GDP)

	1994–97	2003–2007
Indonesia	31.4	24.4
Korea	36.5	30.0
Malaysia	42.3	21.7
Thailand	39.1	27.7
Philippines	23.2	15.4
Singapore	35.9	20.0

Source: ADB ADO (2000; 2008).

(some 60 percent). Singapore is another underconsumption economy in the region where the share of private consumption in GDP has been declining since the beginning of the decade – it is now below 40 percent while national savings are as high as 53 percent of GDP, very much as in China. In some of these cases too underconsumption has its origin, in part, in low and/or declining shares of wages in income.[32] They thus face the dual task of raising both consumption and investment while allowing wages to grow faster.

F. Conclusions: Policy Issues and Lessons

The global crisis has uncovered systemic and structural weaknesses and vulnerabilities in certain areas in the Asian economies examined here and strengths in others. Given that global economic conditions are likely to be less favorable than those prevailing before the outbreak of the crisis, it is important to address these weaknesses and vulnerabilities in order to be able to return to the rapid and sustained growth enjoyed in the earlier part of the decade.

First, start with strengths. In almost all countries the financial sector has shown a significant degree of resilience to shocks from the subprime crisis. This is in part due to various measures taken in the aftermath of financial crises of the late 1990s and early 2000s. Exposure of the banking system to toxic assets has been limited. This has been so also for indigenous institutional investors which were allowed greater freedom to invest in foreign securities from the early years of the decade in order to, inter alia, ease the pressure of the surge in capital inflows and growing current account surpluses on currencies. Losses on reserves invested in mortgage-based securities of government-sponsored institutions in the US have also been limited.

Self-insurance provided by large stocks of international reserves and strong payments positions have certainly been a key element in the resilience of the financial system to shocks. These not only prevented any threat to financial stability during the rapid exit of capital in the early months of the crisis, but also allowed implementation of strong countercyclical policies without facing a payments constraint.

Korea could not demonstrate the same degree of resilience to financial shocks as other East Asian countries in large part because it had chosen to liberalize the capital account almost fully in the aftermath of the 1997 crisis and allowed considerable build-up of external financial fragility in much the same way as it had done in the run-up to the 1997 crisis. However, large reserves and a sustainable payments position helped avoid financial meltdown. Turkey and Pakistan found themselves with large and growing current account deficits on the eve of the crisis, in large part because they had allowed their economies to be driven by easy money from abroad. Both countries had already faced difficulties in sustaining growth before the outbreak of the global crisis. With these two exceptions, all countries have had adequate fiscal and balance of payments space to respond to shocks through countercyclical policies.

A common feature of the countries examined here is their high degree of susceptibility to financial boom–bust cycles and gyrations in equity, property and currency markets. This is in large part due to excessive and widespread capital account liberalization for both residents and nonresidents. Indeed, in all East Asian countries the capital account is much more open and integration into the global financial markets is much closer today than was the case on the eve of the 1997 crisis (Akyüz 2008). This crisis has shown the risks of full integration with markets in global financial centers and the need to adopt a strategic approach to financial opening and integration. Both the capital account regimes and policies regarding rights of establishment of foreign financial institutions thus need to be reassessed, particularly since the initial enthusiasm for tightening the control over major players in global financial centers has died away.

The subprime boom–bust cycle has also entailed gyrations in intraregional exchange rates in East Asia. A main reason is the co-existence of inconsistent exchange rate regimes in the region, ranging from hard pegs to various brands of soft pegs and independent floating. This is a potential source of conflict and not a sound basis for deepening regional economic integration. Quite apart from reorienting their integration into the international financial system, the region also needs relatively close cooperation over exchange rate policies (Akyüz 2009a).

Finally, the crisis has uncovered a high degree of vulnerability of East Asian DEEs to trade shocks, raising the question of whether the end of export-led growth has been reached. This echoes the dilemma that Arthur Lewis pointed out in his Nobel Lecture three decades ago (Lewis 1980), that dependence of growth in DEEs on AEs through trade would make it difficult to catch up and close the income gap. The solution proposed by Lewis was to develop an internal market in DEEs and South–South trade. East Asia has ample space in these respects. Traditionally the balance of payments constraint is seen as the main reason for the dependence of DEEs on exports. But East Asian DEEs export not simply to earn foreign exchange for imports needed for capital accumulation and utilization of productive capacity, but to find markets for goods for which there is little or no domestic demand because of imbalances between investment and consumption and profits and wages. The solution is not to turn inward, away from world markets, but to stop relying on cheap labor and cheap currency and start allowing wages and private consumption to grow in tandem with productivity and underpin the expansion of productive capacity by providing growing internal and regional markets in final goods, very much as in the first tier newly industrialized economies.

Notes

1 First published in *TWN Global Economy Series* in 2010. The author is grateful to Joseph Lim and Irfan Haque for comments and suggestions on an earlier draft, to Xuan Zhang for assistance with the data used in this paper, and to Lean Ka-Min of the Third World Network for editorial assistance.

2 For the purpose of this study East Asian DEEs are defined to include the newly industrialized economies (NIEs; Korea, Taiwan, Singapore and Hong Kong), China and members of the Association of Southeast Asian Nations (ASEAN). Asian DEEs include, in addition, South and West Asian countries.

3 On the contribution of the dot-com bubble to the decline in the personal savings rate in the United States, see Maki and Palumbo (2001).

4 On the housing boom, see Baker (2008), and on expansion and crisis, see Akyüz (2008).

5 This lending behavior by China and FEs also created problems for the so-called special investment vehicles (SIVs) which operated on the assumption that the yield curve would remain steep, borrowing short and lending long.

6 Balakrishnan et al. (2009) measure the pass through by means of a financial stress index that combines correlation between banking stocks and overall market stocks, stock market returns and volatility, sovereign debt spreads and an exchange market pressure index comprising currency depreciations and declines in reserves, and find that transmission of shocks to emerging economies has been very rapid and financial stress experienced has been more severe than that during the 1997–98 Asian crisis, particularly in countries with larger stocks of foreign liabilities to AEs.

7 For a detailed discussion of the issues taken up in the next two paragraphs, see Akyüz (2008).

8 This distinction between independent and managed floating is based on the classification by the IMF (2008) based on actual, de facto arrangements, not officially announced arrangements.

9 See Xinhuanet (2009) and Forbes (2008). In earlier years, concerned about the growing speculative spree, China had adopted measures to stem increases in property prices (ESCAP 2007, 10).

10 On the behavior of reserves in India and Korea during 2008, see Obstfeld et al. (2009).

11 This was observed during the Asian crisis in Malaysia where rising unemployment mostly affected migrant workers (Akyüz 2006).

12 According to Ratha and Mohapatra (2009), almost all major destination countries have tightened controls against migrant workers.

13 This section draws on Akyüz (2010b), using more up-to-date data on exports for more recent years.

14 These include China, the newly industrialized economies (NIEs; Korea, Taiwan, Singapore and Hong Kong) and the members of ASEAN.

15 The impact of export contraction on GDP is estimated using $g_x (1 - \delta) (X/Y)$, where g_x is the growth rate of exports, δ is the import content of exports and X/Y is the share of exports in GDP as conventionally measured (Akyüz 2010b).

16 Agarwala (2009) assumes that in India the import content of exports is no more than that of domestic demand. This gives a figure of 20 percent for 2007–2008. On this assumption, in value added terms the share of exports in GDP would be around 17 percent.

17 The average sovereign (central government) debt in East Asia is less than 40 percent of GDP. The only major economy with a high debt ratio is the Philippines where it is close to 60 percent. The average ratio in South Asia is much higher, with Indian central government debt exceeding 60 percent of GDP and general government debt 80 percent.

18 On fiscal stimulus packages, see United Nations (2010), Khatiwada (2009), ESCAP (2009 and 2010), ADB ADO (2010), IMF WEO (October 2009) and IMF REOAP (October 2009).

19 Difficulties in identifying fiscal stimulus measures are revealed by widely different figures given by different international organizations for some East Asian countries; cf. United Nations (2010, table I.4), ADB ADO (2010, Figure 2.4.1) and ESCAP (2009, table 1).

20 Khatiwada (2009) reaches the same conclusion on the adequacy of fiscal measures for a sample of 32 countries including the G20 major economies where stimulus spending in 2009 was 1.7 percent of GDP as compared to the 2 percent recommended by the IMF.

21 For a further discussion of the issues taken up in this section, see Akyüz (2010a).

22 This was broadly the plan promoted by the IMF in its multilateral consultations to reduce global imbalances on the eve of the crisis. Although the crisis has resulted in sizeable changes in external positions and savings patterns, the Fund recognizes that imbalances are not a problem of the past and there is still a need to remove global imbalances (Blanchard and Milesi-Ferretti 2009).

23 On US consumer adjustment in the coming years, see Glick and Lansing (2009).

24 Achieving this target would require, inter alia, an active industrial policy to redirect investment in export sectors. For a discussion of the main ingredients of the NEI, see Akyüz (2010a).

25 According to the IMF (WEO October 2009), after a sharp decline during 2008–2009, potential output growth will pick up only slowly to about 2 percent over the medium term; see also IMF (2010).

26 On the possible impact of dollar carry trade on assets and currencies, see Pineda et al. (2010).

27 Agarwala (2009) estimates that the contribution of exports to GDP growth during 2003–2008 in India was *at least* 26 percent. With spillovers to domestic consumption, this figure is raised to 31 percent.

28 This and the following sections draw on Akyüz (2010b) which contains further analysis and evidence on the issues discussed here.

29 On household and corporate savings in early industrializers, see Akyüz and Gore (1996) and UNCTAD TDR (1997, table 44). On savings in China and India, see Prasad (2009). See also Anderson (2007) for a discussion of household and corporate savings in China.

30 On the behavior of labor productivity, profits and wages and consumption, see Kim and Kuijs (2007), WB CQU (August 2005, August 2006 and February 2007), Kuijs (2005), Yu (2007), and Aziz and Dunaway (2007).

31 See Akyüz (2009a). Singapore experienced a property boom in 2007 which took investment to some 30 percent of GDP (Lim and Jaya 2010).

32 This is most clearly the case in Singapore – see Lim and Jaya (2010) who reiterate that Singapore has a First World per capita income level but a Third World income distribution profile.

References

ADB (Asian Development Bank). ADO (various issues). *Asian Development Outlook*. www.adb.org.

Agarwala, R. 2009. *On Managing Risks Facing the Indian Economy: Towards a Better Balance between Public and Private Sectors*. RIS Discussion Paper 158, New Delhi, September.

Akyüz, Y. 2006. *From Liberalization to Investment and Jobs: Lost in Translation. TWN Global Economy Series* 8. Penang, Malaysia.

______. 2008. *The Current Global Financial Turmoil and Asian Developing Countries. TWN Global Economy Series* 11, Penang, Malaysia.

______. 2009a. *Exchange Rate Management, Growth and Stability: National and Regional Policy Options in Asia*. Columbo: UNDP.

______. 2009b. "Policy Response to the Global Financial Crisis: Key Issues for Developing Countries." South Centre, Research Paper 24.

______. 2010a. "Global Economic Prospects: The Recession May Be Over but Where Next?" South Centre, Research Paper 26.

______. 2010b. "Export Dependence and Sustainability of Growth in China and the East Asian Production Network." South Centre, Research Paper 27.

Akyüz, Y., and C. Gore. 1996. "The Investment–Profits Nexus in East Asian Industrialisation." *World Development* 24 (3): 461–70.

Anderson, J. 2007. "Solving China's Rebalancing Puzzle." *Finance and Development* 44 (3).

Athukorala, P-C. 2008. China's Integration into Global Production Networks and Its Implications for Export-Led Growth Strategy in Other Countries in the Region. Australian National University, Working Paper 2008/04. April.

Aziz, J., and S. Dunaway. 2007. "China's Rebalancing Act." *Finance and Development* 44 (3).

Baker, D. 2008. "The Housing Bubble and the Financial Crisis." *Real-World Economics Review* 46: 63–81.

Balakrishnan, R., S. Danninger, S. Elekdag and I. Tytell. 2009. "The Transmission of Financial Stress from Advanced to Emerging Economies." IMF Working Paper WP/09/133. Washington, DC.

Bernanke, B. 2009. "Four Questions about the Financial Crisis." Speech given at Morehouse College, Atlanta, Georgia, April 14, Board of Governors of the Federal Reserve System.

BIS (Bank for International Settlements). 2009. "Capital Flows and Emerging Market Economies." CGFS Paper 33. Basel.

Blanchard, O., and G. M. Milesi-Ferretti. 2009. "Global Imbalances: In Midstream?" IMF Staff Position Note SPN/09/29, December 22. Washington, DC.

Bowring, P. 2008. StanChart Leaves Investors out in the Cold. *Asia Sentinel*, 12 February.

Cetorelli, N., and L. S. Goldberg. 2010. Global Banks and International Shock Transmission: Evidence from the Crisis. Federal Reserve Bank of New York Staff Report 446. May. New York.

Chai-Anant, C., and C. Ho. 2008. Understanding Asian Equity Flows, Market Returns and Exchange Rates. BIS Working Paper 245.

Chandrasekhar, C. P. 2009. *The Costs of "Coupling": The Global Crisis and the Indian Economy. TWN Global Economy Series* 19. Financial Crisis and Asian Developing Countries. Penang, Malaysia.

Citigroup. 2009. "Korea: Asset Deflation Impact on Construction and Banking.' *The Asia Investigator*. 19 January. http://www.theiafm.org/publications/370_SAP23775.pdf. Accessed 14 March 2009.

ESCAP (Economic and Social Commission for Asia and the Pacific). 2007. *Key Economic Developments in the Asia-Pacific Region 2008*. United Nations, Bangkok.

______. 2009. *Economic and Social Survey of Asia and the Pacific 2009: Year-End Update*. http://www.unescap.org/pdd/publications/survey2009/download/index.asp. Accessed 10 January 2010.

______. 2010. *Economic and Social Survey of Asia and the Pacific 2010*. http://www.unescap.org/pdd/publications/survey2010/download/index.asp. Accessed 1 May 2010.

Forbes. 2008. "China Seeks to Revive Property Market." 30 December. http://www.forbes.com/2008/12/29/china-cisis-property-cx_1230oxford.html. Accessed 2 February 2010.

Fujioka, T. 2010. "Japan Growth Prospects Are Worst Among G-7, OECD Says." 26 March. http://www.bloomberg.com/apps/news?pid=newsarchive&sid=aUPM2kBbZBcY. Accessed 31 March 2010.

Glick, R., and K. J. Lansing. 2009. "US Household Deleveraging and Future Consumption Growth." *Federal Reserve Bank of San Francisco Economic Letter*, 2009–16. 15 May.

Goh, S. K. and M. M.-H. Lim. 2010. *The Impact of the Global Financial Crisis: The Case of Malaysia. TWN Global Economy Series* 26. Financial Crisis and Asian Developing Countries. Penang, Malaysia.

Greenspan, A. 2009. "The Fed Didn't Cause the Housing Bubble." *Wall Street Journal*, 11 March.

Haque, I. 2010. *Pakistan: Causes and Management of the 2008 Economic Crisis. TWN Global Economy Series* 22. Financial Crisis and Asian Developing Countries. Penang, Malaysia.

Hung, H.-F. 2009. America's Head Servant? The PRC's Dilemma in the Global Crisis. *New Left Review* 60, November–December.

IMF (International Monetary Fund). 2008. De Facto Classification of Exchange Rate Regimes and Monetary Policy Framework. April 31. Washington, DC.

______. 2010. G-20 Mutual Assessment Process – Alternative Policy Scenarios. G-20 Toronto Summit, Toronto, Canada. 26–27 June.

IMF GFSR (various issues). *Global Financial Stability Report*. Washington, DC.

IMF REOAP (various issues). *Regional Economic Outlook: Asia and Pacific*. Washington, DC.

IMF WEO (various issues). *World Economic Outlook*. Washington, DC.

Khatiwada, S. 2009. "Stimulus Packages to Counter Global Economic Crisis: A Review." International Institute for Labour Studies Discussion Paper 196. www.ilo.org/public/english/bureau/inst/publications/. Accessed 10 November 2010.

Kim, S., J.-W. Lee and C.-Y. Park. 2009. "The Ties that Bind Asia, Europe and the United States." Presentation made at the ADB-BNM-EC Joint Conference, Beyond the Global Crisis: A New Asian Growth Model?, Kuala Lumpur, Malaysia. 18–20 October.

Kim, S.-Y., and L. Kuijs. 2007. "Raw Material Prices, Wages and Profitability in China's Industry: How Was Profitability Maintained when Input Prices and Wages Increased so Fast?" World Bank China Research Paper 8. Beijing.

Kuijs, L. 2005. "Investment and Saving in China." World Bank Policy Research Working Paper 3622.

Lee, K.-K. 2010. *The Post-Crisis Changes in the Financial System in Korea: Problems of Neoliberal Restructuring and Financial Opening After 1997. TWN Global Economy Series* 20. Financial Crisis and Asian Developing Countries. Penang, Malaysia.

Lewis, A. 1980. "The Slowing Down of the Engine of Growth," Nobel Lecture. *American Economic Review* 70 (4): 555–64.

Lim, J. A. 2010. *The Impact of the Global Financial and Economic Turmoil on the Philippines: National Responses and Recommendations to Address the Crisis. TWN Global Economy Series* 23. Financial Crisis and Asian Developing Countries. Penang, Malaysia.

Lim, M. M.-H., and M. Jaya. 2010. *Financial Liberalization and the Impact of the Financial Crisis on Singapore. TWN Global Economy Series* 24, Financial Crisis and Asian Developing Countries. Penang, Malaysia.

Maki, D. M., and M. Palumbo. 2001. "Disentangling the Wealth Effect: A Cohort Analysis of Household Saving in the 1990s." FEDS Working Paper 2001-21. Washington, DC.

McCauley, R. 2008. "Managing Recent Hot Money Flows in Asia." ADBI Discussion Paper 99. Tokyo.

Obstfeld, Maurice, Jay C. Shambaugh and Alan M. Taylor. 2009. "Financial Instability, Reserves, and Central Bank Swap Lines in the Panic of 2008." American Economic Association, *American Economic Review* 99 (2): 480–86.

Pearlstein, S. 2008. "More Room to Fall." *Washington Post*, January 22.

Pesek, W. 2008. "Asia is About to Give U.S. a Kick in the Fannie." http://www.bloomberg.com/apps/news?pid=newsarchive&sid=aqu59cnYfsFY. Accessed 1 September 2008.

Pineda, M., et al. 2010. "Carry Trade Hotspots: A Currency by Currency Forecast for 2010." Roubini Global Economics, 4 January. www.roubini.com/analysis/94821.php. Accessed 10 February 2010.

Prasad, E. 2009. "Rebalancing Growth in Asia." *Finance and Development* 46 (4).

Ratha, D., and S. Mohapatra. 2009. "Migration and Development Brief 9." World Bank, Washington, DC.

Ratha, D., S. Mohapatra and A. Silwal. 2009. "Migration and Development Brief 10." World Bank, Washington, DC.

______. 2010. "Migration and Development Brief 12." World Bank, Washington, DC.

Roubini, N. 2009. "Mother of All Carry Trades Faces an Inevitable Bust." *Financial Times*, 1 November.

UNCTAD TDR (various issues). *Trade and Development Report.* Geneva: United Nations.

United Nations. 2010. *World Economic Situation and Prospects 2010.* January. New York: United Nations.

Uygur, E. 2010. *The Global Crisis and the Turkish Economy. TWN Global Economy Series* 21. Financial Crisis and Asian Developing Countries. Penang, Malaysia.

WB CQU (various issues). *China Quarterly Update.* World Bank Beijing Office, China.

Wolfe, A., and R. Ziemba. 2009a. "Chinese Monetary Policy: Little Effect on Overcapacities, and Risks of Blowing a Property Bubble." Roubini Global Economics, 10 October. http://www.economonitor.com/analysts/2009/10/21/chinese-monetary-policy-little-effect-on-overcapacities-and-risks-of-blowing-a-property-bubble/. Accessed 5 February 2010.

______. 2009b. "What is China's Exit Strategy?" Roubini Global Economics, 11 November. http://www.roubini.com/analysis/85913. Accessed 3 February 2010.

World Bank. 2009. *Battling the Forces of Global Recession. East Asia and Pacific Update.* 15 April. Washington, DC.

WTO (World Trade Organization). 2010. "World Trade 2009, Prospects for 2010." Press Release, Press/598. 26 March.

Xinhuanet. 2009. "Chinese Housing Prices Decline for the First Time Since 2005." 10 January. http://news.xinhuanet.com/english/2009-01/10/content_10634712.htm. Accessed 20 January 2009.

Yu, Y. 2007. Global Imbalances and China. *The Australian Economic Review* 40 (1): 3–23.

______. 2010. *The Impact of the Global Financial Crisis on the Chinese Economy and China's Policy Response. TWN Global Economy Series* 25, Financial Crisis and Asian Developing Countries. Penang, Malaysia.

Chapter VIII

THE STAGGERING RISE OF THE SOUTH?[1]

A. Introduction and Summary

In the early days of the global economic crisis, growth in developing and emerging economies (DEEs) was widely expected to be decoupled from the difficulties facing advanced economies (AEs). Strong growth that many DEEs had been enjoying since the early years of the millennium was expected to continue with some moderation and prevent AEs and the world economy from falling into recession. In the event, however, growth in DEEs slowed considerably in 2009 as a result of contraction of exports and financial contagion. AEs fell into recession and world income declined for the first time in several decades.

Nevertheless DEEs recovered rapidly, with many emerging economies restoring growth rates close to those enjoyed before the crisis. By contrast, growth in the US has been anaemic and erratic, and deepened debt difficulties and financial fragility in the eurozone have raised the spectre of a second dip. This two-track world economy, the widening growth gap between the South and the North, has resuscitated the decoupling hypothesis that growth dynamics of emerging economies have gained considerable autonomy. While it is generally recognized that it may take several years for AEs to overcome their debt overhang and return to stable and rigorous growth, it is also believed that the rise of the South will generally continue unabated in the coming years and income levels in several DEEs will converge rapidly to those in early industrializers. Thus, the global crisis is seen as a turning point in the economic balance of power between the North and the South, with many emerging economies such as China, India and Brazil gaining a greater presence and role in the world economy.

Strictly speaking, decoupling means desynchronization of business cycles. This is not really consistent with increased global integration of markets or "globalization." Indeed, evidence shows that the deviations of economic activity from underlying trends continue to be highly correlated between DEEs and AEs. This was also evident during the post-Lehman downturn when a large majority of DEEs experienced a significant slowdown despite strong countercyclical policy responses.[2]

There is, however, a more important question of whether trend growth in the developing world has shifted up relative to that in AEs. Even though business cycles are synchronized, a significant rise in trend growth in DEEs could still result in a rapid increase in living standards and convergence to income levels of AEs. This was basically the issue raised by Arthur Lewis in his Nobel Lecture:

> For the past hundred years the rate of growth of output in the developing world has depended on the rate of growth of output in the developed world. When the developed grow fast, the developing grow fast, and when the developed slow down, the developing slow down. Is this linkage inevitable? More specifically, the world has just gone through two decades of unprecedented growth, with world trade growing twice as fast as ever before. [...] During these prosperous decades, the less developed countries (LDCs) have demonstrated their capacity to increase their total output at 6 percent per annum, and have indeed adopted 6 percent as the minimum average target for LDCs as a whole. But what is to happen if the more developed countries (MDCs) return to their former growth rates, and raise their trade at only 4 percent per annum: is it inevitable that the growth of the LDCs will also fall significantly below their target? (Lewis 1980, 555).

Lewis thus saw trade as the main link between growth in the South and the North. His main concern was that since the growth gap between the two was small, some 2 percentage points, a significant deceleration in AEs and hence in world trade would mean that the South would not be able to make significant progress in development. He then went on to propose that DEEs should develop internal and regional markets to gain greater autonomy.

Growth in the South no doubt shows a rapid shift in the new millennium compared to previous decades, including even the postwar golden age which Lewis was referring to. The central question in this paper is thus whether and to what extent this rapid rise of the South constitutes a shift in the trend growth of DEEs relative to AEs. This calls for an explanation of the sudden surge of growth in the South, to identify the factors and conditions driving it and to assess whether they can be sustained over the longer term. In making such an assessment, discussions here will focus on major emerging economies which constitute a large part of the developing world both in population and income, and particularly on China because of its strong impact on other DEEs. However, many of the conclusions also apply to smaller economies, exporters of both manufactures and commodities.

A correct assessment of the respective roles played by domestic and external factors in the acceleration of growth in DEEs is necessary in order to avoid complacency and reduce exposure to shocks. In this respect the main conclusion here is that while there have been significant improvements in economic management in DEEs after the recurrent crises of the 1990s and early 2000s and these may have somewhat raised the trend growth in some, the exceptionally favorable international economic conditions made a major and in many cases much greater contribution to the general acceleration of growth in the South. These conditions were shaped mainly by policies in AEs. The only emerging economy which has had a major impact on global conditions, notably on commodity prices and hence on commodity exporting countries, is China, but its own growth depends very much on exports to AEs because of its development strategy and underlying structural characteristics.

Until the outbreak of the global crisis, policies in AEs created, directly or indirectly, a favorable global environment for DEEs in trade and investment, capital flows and commodity prices. But the credit, consumption and property bubbles resulting from the same policies led to financial fragility and global imbalances which culminated in the Great Recession. The crisis brought to an end the expansion of markets in the North, the boom in commodity prices and capital flows to DEEs. However, sharp cuts in interest rates and quantitative easing in response to the crisis in AEs has restored the surge in capital flows to DEEs. This, together with a strong countercyclical policy response in major emerging economies, notably in China, has restored growth in the South and reversed the downturn in commodity prices. Consequently, growth in major emerging economies, including in export-oriented economies, has increasingly come to depend on domestic demand and this is reflected by a sharp reduction in current account surpluses in East Asia and growing deficits elsewhere.

The pace and pattern of domestic-demand-driven growth that emerging economies have been enjoying since 2009 cannot be sustained. First, in deficit countries such growth depends on continued and, in fact, increased inflows of capital, but the conditions driving the recent surge in capital inflows cannot be expected to last forever. There are already strong signs of growing nervousness among international investors and lenders, creating heightened instability in capital flows to emerging economies and asset and currency markets. Second, the major growth pole in the South, China, cannot keep on creating investment bubbles in order to fill the demand gap triggered by the slowdown of its exports to AEs, as it has done since the outbreak of the crisis. Furthermore, even if AEs can return to rigorous and sustained growth, it would not be possible for China to go back to the precrisis pattern of growth, rapidly increasing its penetration of markets of AEs, with the US acting again as a global locomotive and running growing deficits and debt. Such a process is not sustainable and could seriously destabilize the international trading and monetary systems.

Emerging economies such as BRICS and others need to reconsider their development strategies in order to gain considerable autonomy in growth and become major players in the global economy, rather than remaining as *markets* for Goldman Sachs and the like. First, starting with China, the East Asian surplus economies need to reduce their dependence on markets in AEs by promoting national and regional markets. They need to expand domestic consumption rapidly and this calls for a significant increase in the share of household income in GDP. China has already become a major driver of growth in commodity-rich economies because of its growing demand for commodities. It can also become an important market for manufactures from other DEEs provided that it shifts from export-led to consumption-led growth and increases the import content of its consumption.

Second, deficit DEEs need to reduce their dependence on foreign capital. Most of them also need to increase investment significantly. The majority of these countries are commodity exporters and the two key determinants of their economic performance, capital flows and commodity prices, are largely beyond their control. Reducing vulnerability on both fronts crucially depends on their progress in industrialization. This is also true for deficit countries relying on export of services and remittances, such as India.

B. The Growth Record

At the end of the 1990s and the early 2000s, many economies in the developing world were in disarray. East Asia was still recovering from the 1997 crisis while a host of other emerging economies were falling into payments and financial crises one after another; Brazil and Russia in 1998, Turkey 2000–2001 and Argentina 2001–2002. The prospects for the global economy were dimmed by the bursting of the dot-com bubble in the US at the beginning of the decade, coming on top of prolonged deflation in Japan and uneven growth in the EU.

For the entire period from 1990 to 2002, the average growth in DEEs exceeded the average growth in AEs by just over 1 percentage point and in per capita terms there was hardly any income convergence. The picture was even worse in the 1980s when a large number of DEEs were suffering from severe payments difficulties caused by a debt overhang and sharp declines in commodity prices. Until the new millennium the only major economy in the South that was able to close the income gap with AEs by leaps and bounds was China, with an average growth rate close to 10 percent during 1990–2002 compared to less than 4 percent in the rest of the developing world (Table 8.1).

All these changed in the new millennium. From 2002 until the outbreak of the subprime crisis, the growth difference between the DEEs and AEs shot up to 5 percentage points. This was not because of deceleration in AEs, but an unprecedented acceleration in DEEs where the average growth rate almost doubled from the 1990s. The global crisis led to a loss of momentum in DEEs during 2008–2009, but their growth difference with AEs widened further because of a severe recession in the latter countries. Despite subsequent recovery in AEs, growth in DEEs has continued to be faster by about 4 percentage points in 2010–2011 – a margin still considerably larger than those during the 1980s and 1990s. Taking the whole decade from 2002 until 2012, the average growth in DEEs exceeds the average growth in AEs by more than 5 percent per annum. This is unprecedented. As noted, during the postwar golden age DEEs also grew at a very fast pace, by some 6 percent per annum, but growth in AEs was also high, with the gap being no more than a couple of percentage points.[3]

However, there has been considerable diversity in the pace of acceleration of growth among DEEs. During precrisis years acceleration was faster in Africa than the two other main regions even though the African growth rate remained below that of Asia. By contrast, the Western Hemisphere saw only a modest rise in average growth compared to the 1990s. Among analytical groups, fuel exporters saw faster acceleration than either the exporters of nonfuel commodities or manufactures – from just over 1 percent in the 1990s to 7.5 percent between 2003 and 2008. Among the major emerging economies, Russia, Argentina, Turkey, India and South Africa enjoyed much faster acceleration than the others. In the first three countries this was due to rapid recoveries from severe crises which had caused large output losses at the end of the 1990s and the early 2000s.

The acceleration of growth in DEEs since the beginning of the new millennium is not due to China. Indeed, growth in China during the 1990s was almost as fast as that in the 2000s.[4] However, it is notable that in the 1990s China was not widely perceived as an

Table 8.1: Real GDP growth in selected economies (annual percentages of constant price)

	1990–2002 average	2003–2007 average	2008	2009	2010	2011
All AEs	2.7	2.7	0.1	–3.5	3.0	1.6
All DEEs	3.9	7.6	6.1	2.7	7.4	6.2
Developing Asia	7.0	9.6	7.9	7.0	9.5	7.8
Latin America and the Caribbean	2.6	4.8	4.2	–1.5	6.2	4.5
Sub-Saharan Africa	2.9	6.3	5.6	2.8	5.3	5.1
Selected DEEs:						
Argentina	1.9	8.8	6.8	0.9	9.2	8.9
Brazil	1.9	4.0	5.2	–0.3	7.5	2.7
China	9.6	11.6	9.6	9.2	10.4	9.2
India	5.4	8.6	6.9	5.9	10.1	6.8
Indonesia	4.2	5.5	6.0	4.6	6.2	6.5
Mexico	3.0	3.4	1.2	–6.0	5.6	3.9
Russia	–0.9	7.5	5.2	–7.8	4.3	4.3
South Africa	1.9	4.8	3.6	–1.5	2.9	3.1
Turkey	3.5	6.9	0.7	–4.8	9.2	8.5
Malaysia	6.6	5.9	4.8	–1.5	7.2	5.1
Korea	6.6	4.3	2.3	0.3	6.3	3.6
Thailand	4.8	5.6	2.6	–2.3	7.8	0.1

Source: IMF WEO (October 2012).

emerging economic power capable of challenging the US dominance until it had started running growing trade surpluses with the US and accumulating large dollar reserves.

C. Global Economic Conditions

1. International trade and investment

The new millennium witnessed a rapid growth in world trade which increased, in nominal dollars, by 2.5 times by 2008, with the average annual growth in total exports reaching twice the rate of growth of world output. This period also saw a significant increase in the share of DEEs in world trade, rapid expansion of South–South trade and growing global imbalances. The current accounts of AEs as a whole, which had already turned into red at the end of the 1990s, constantly deteriorated until the outbreak of the crisis. This was entirely due to mounting deficits of the US and to a lesser extent the UK, as the eurozone was broadly in balance, and Japan and the remaining AEs were running surpluses. This was reflected in growing surpluses of DEEs, which came to exceed $600 billion in 2007, of which two-thirds belonged to China and smaller East Asian DEEs and the rest to Fuel Exporters (FEs). This, together with large inflows of capital, resulted in an unprecedented rise in the international reserves of DEEs, which reached $5 trillion in 2007 despite substantially increased capital outflows (Chart 8.1).[5]

The rapid expansion of exports and growing current account surpluses of DEEs owe a great deal to US spending extravaganza. The US private savings had already began to fall and current account deficits to rise in the mid-1990s largely because of a strong wealth effect of the dot-com equity market bubble on private consumption and a boom in the property market. The spending spree continued with greater force in the 2000s when the Fed responded to the bursting of the dot-com bubble by bringing down policy rates to historical lows for fear of asset deflation and recession, and new legislation introduced in the late 1990s allowed greater room for banks to expand high-risk lending for property. Capital gains from rising house prices in the 2000s sustained the spending boom as homeowners increasingly extracted equity to finance consumption. As a result, household savings, which formed some 6 percent of GDP in the early 1990s, started to fall rapidly and disappeared altogether on the eve of the 2008 crisis. This was mirrored by growing external deficits – the US current account was broadly balanced in the early 1990s, but it registered a deficit of over 6 percent in 2007. Indeed the evidence provided by research in New York Fed shows a strikingly strong positive correlation between house price appreciations and current account deficits not only in the US but also in other countries that have subsequently experienced the highest degree of financial turmoil (Ferrero 2012).

In Europe, the UK went through a similar property bubble, but was running a relatively small current account deficit. In the eurozone, deficits in peripheral countries were rising not only vis-à-vis the core economies, notably Germany, but also the rest of the world, reaching on average 7 percent of GDP in Spain and 9 percent in Portugal and Greece. These deficits resulted from loss of competitiveness due to wage settlements in excess of productivity increases in conditions of rising private consumption and property spending. The participation of these countries in the European Monetary Union facilitated the financing of these deficits by significantly lowering the risk premium. Banks in Germany, France and elsewhere in Europe were more than willing to pump in funds to finance these deficits – a process which culminated in the eurozone crisis, in much the same way as the boom–bust cycles in lending to several emerging economies in the past. Germany pursued a policy of wage deflation – competitive disinflation – running surpluses against most other eurozone members and the rest of the world, including the US. Japan was in a similar situation, relying for growth on exports and generating current account surpluses which reached 5 percent of GDP in 2007. Thus, the US was acting as a locomotive not only to export-led East Asian DEEs but also to Japan and Germany (Akyüz 2011b).

The increased outsourcing to the Sinocentric production network by transnational corporations from AEs has made a significant contribution to growing exports from East Asia. China's accession to the WTO in December 2001 significantly accelerated this process by granting that country a Permanent Normal Trade Relations status in the US and eliminating discriminatory, WTO-inconsistent measures against its exports. This removed the uncertainties regarding the issuance of the yearly waiver by the US president, and played a central role in the rapid increase in FDI to China, which doubled the levels of the late 1990s to reach $80 billion in 2007. Thus, China and other East Asian DEEs

Chart 8.1: Balances of payments in DEEs

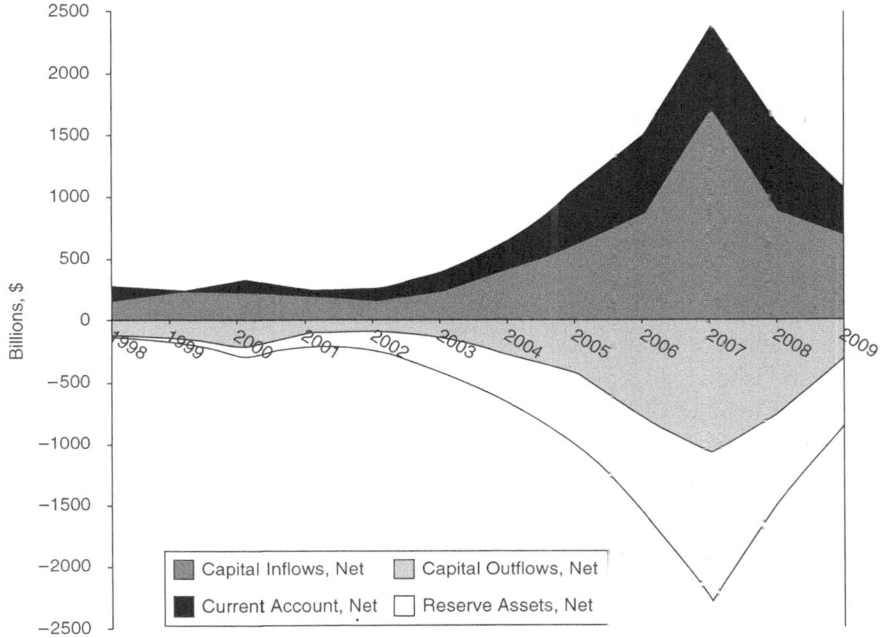

Source: IMF, WEO database. BOP databases.
Notes: A minus sign indicates an increase.
Capital flows comprise direct investment, portfolio investment and other official and private financial flows, exclude changes in reserves.
Capital inflows are adjusted by net official flows.

participating in the Sinocentric production network benefited not only from growing exports to AEs, but also from investment and technology brought in by transnational corporations to expand exportables.[6] Until the global crisis, Chinese exports to AEs and FDI inflows reinforced each other. After 2008, when exports slowed down considerably, FDI inflows to Chinese manufacturing remained sluggish, even though China was able to restore growth on the basis of expansion of domestic demand.[7]

2. *Capital flows and remittances*

The new millennium witnessed the beginning of the third postwar boom in capital flows to DEEs, mainly as a result of exceptionally low interest rates and rapid expansion of liquidity in AEs, including the US, the EU and Japan.[8] Both net flows and net inflows to DEEs peaked in 2007 before the outbreak of the subprime debacle (Charts 8.1 and 8.2). The surge in capital inflows was accompanied by rapidly narrowing spreads on emerging market debt, brought about by significantly improved risk appetite. This, together with low interest rates in AEs, resulted in a sharp decline in the cost of external financing for DEEs. Most DEEs enjoyed the increased risk appetite and shared in the boom in capital inflows irrespective of their underlying fundamentals.

Although capital flows among DEEs have also been increasing rapidly and China has become a major investor in some resource rich DEEs, a very large proportion of capital came to DEEs from lenders and investors in AEs. However, China contributed to the expansion of capital inflows to DEEs by investing its twin surpluses in current and capital accounts in reserves, mostly in dollars.[9] Large acquisitions of US Treasuries by China and FEs helped to keep long-term rates relatively low even as the US Fed started to raise short-term rates. Thus, while growing US external deficits were being financed "officially" there was plenty of highly leveraged private money searching for yield in DEEs. A mutually reinforcing process emerged between private flows to DEEs and official flows to the US – the former were translated into reserves of DEEs and constituted an important part of official flows to the US, and supported lower rates there and private flows to DEEs.

Private capital inflows to DEEs held up initially during the subprime debacle despite growing strains in credit and asset markets in the US and Europe. However, with the collapse of a number of leading financial institutions in the US, notably the Lehman Brothers, the boom came to a halt in the second half of 2008. The rapidly growing volatility in financial markets led to an extreme and generalized risk aversion, pushing up spreads on emerging market debt and triggering a flight to safety into US Treasuries and appreciation of the dollar vis-à-vis other major currencies, even though the US was the epicenter of the crisis.

However, the contraction of private capital inflows to DEEs was short-lived. They started to recover in the first half of 2009, driven by historically low interest rates and rapid expansion of liquidity in major AEs brought about by monetary policy response to the crisis as well as better growth performance in DEEs and a shift in risk perceptions against AEs. In the second half of 2011, a generalized increase in risk aversion led to the exit of capital from several DEEs (IMF WEO 2012 January, update), but according to the latest available projections by the IMF (WEO September 2011), both net private inflows and net flows will continue to remain strong in 2012, though still below the 2007 peaks.

DEEs also enjoyed a rapid growth of workers remittances, at an average annual rate of some 20 percent between 2002 and 2008, rising from less than $100 billion at the beginning of the decade to more than $320 billion in 2008, exceeding all categories of capital inflows except FDI (Chart 8.3). Much of these also came from AEs, with Europe accounting for almost half of total inflows followed by the US. Some major emerging economies were among the top receivers, including India, China, Mexico and Indonesia. In 2007 remittances amounted to 1–1.5 percent of GDP in China and Indonesia, around 3 percent in India and Mexico, over 4 percent in Pakistan and 11 percent in the Philippines. In many of these countries they led to a significant improvement in the current account, reducing deficits and even generating surpluses despite large trade deficits.

With the outbreak of the crisis remittances registered a moderate decline in 2009. However, the subsequent recovery has been weak; during 2010–11 they are estimated to have grown by less than half of the rate observed during precrisis years. According to recent projections by the World Bank (Mohapatra et al. 2011) they would grow by 7–8 percent per annum in the coming years, subject to serious downside risks associated with persistent unemployment in Europe and the US and hardening political attitudes toward new migration.

Chart 8.2: Net private capital flows to developing countries, 2000–2010

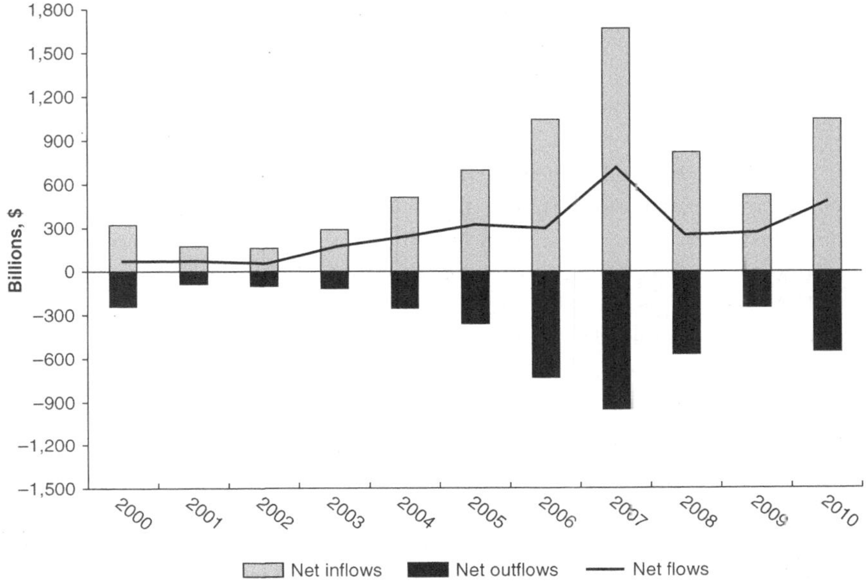

Source: IMF WEO (September 2011 and September 2010).

Chart 8.3: Remittances flows in developing countries, 2000–2010

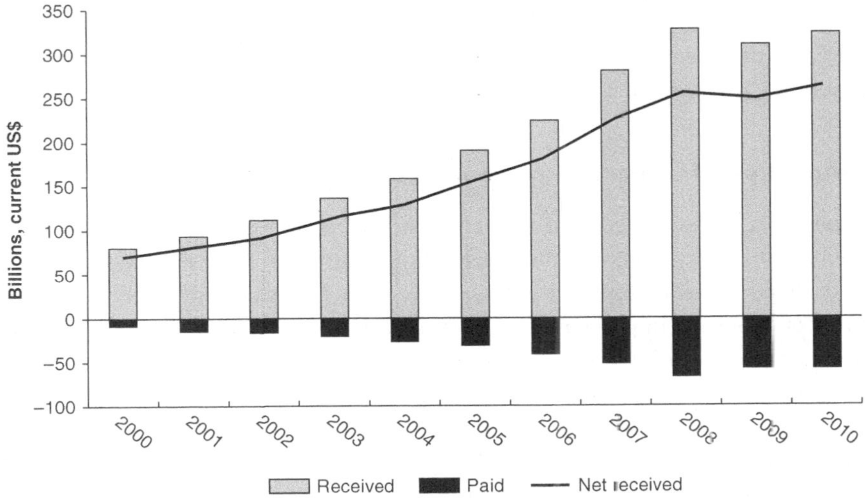

Source: World Bank, *World Development Indicators.*

3. Commodity prices

With rapid liquidity expansion and acceleration of growth in the global economy, commodity prices started to rise in 2003, gaining further momentum in 2006 (Chart 8.4). The factors driving the boom included a strong pace of activity in DEEs, notably in China, where commodity intensity of growth is high, low initial stocks, weak supply response and the relatively weak dollar. These markets also became increasingly financialized after the beginning of the decade as financial investors sought to diversify into commodity-linked assets and low interest rates led to a search for yield in commodity markets (UNCTAD TDR 2011). In the case of food, diversion to biofuels and rising cost of fertilizers and transport due to high oil prices also played a role.

Despite growing financial strains in the US, commodity prices continued to increase before they made a sharp downturn in August 2008. This boom–bust cycle in commodity prices in the middle of the subprime crisis was largely due to shifts in market sentiments regarding the future course of prices. Initially, the subprime crisis was seen as a hiccup and the downturn in economic activity was expected to be short-lived, including by the IMF (WEO July 2008), followed by a rapid and robust recovery. However, with mounting financial difficulties in the US and the collapse of the Lehman Brothers, sentiments turned sour and growth prospects were dampened. Investors pulled out large amounts of money from oil and non-oil futures, more or less at the same time as capital flows to DEEs were reversed and the dollar started to strengthen. By the end of October 2008, food was 27 percent and oil 45 percent below their peaks.

Again the downturn in commodity prices was short-lived and the upturn in 2009 coincided with the recovery of capital flows to DEEs and the decline of the dollar. After falling in late 2008 and early 2009, index trading also started to gain momentum as commodity prices turned up in spring 2009 as a result of increased demand from DEEs, notably China, in conditions of continued expansion of international liquidity and historically low interest rates. Investment in commodities recovered rapidly while the number of exchange traded options and futures rose to unprecedented levels (BIS 2010). Despite recent weakening of markets for metals and minerals and several agricultural commodities, prices remain significantly above the levels of the early 2000s.

D. Impact on Macroeconomic Balances in DEEs

The past ten years have witnessed considerable improvements in macroeconomic conditions in DEEs. Alongside the acceleration of growth, fiscal and payments deficits have declined considerably and inflation has been brought under control in a large majority of countries. Improvements in economic management and institutions, following a number of policy errors resulting from adherence to the Washington Consensus, have no doubt played an important role in bringing these about. However, extremely favorable global conditions have also made a major contribution and indeed played a more crucial part in many countries.

DEEs have generally manifested greater fiscal discipline in recent years. Average central government deficits were hovering around 3.5 percent of GDP at the beginning of the 2000s (IMF WEO October 2007). By 2006–2007 they came down to around 0.5 percent. During the same period, the average external debt of DEEs declined from around 40 percent of GDP to 25 percent. Total public debt as a proportion of GDP also declined considerably in many highly indebted emerging economies, particularly on account of rapidly falling external debt. In the seven largest Latin American economies, the public debt fell, on average, from over 50 percent of GDP in the early 2000s to

Chart 8.4: Commodity prices and commodity imports of China, 2000–2010

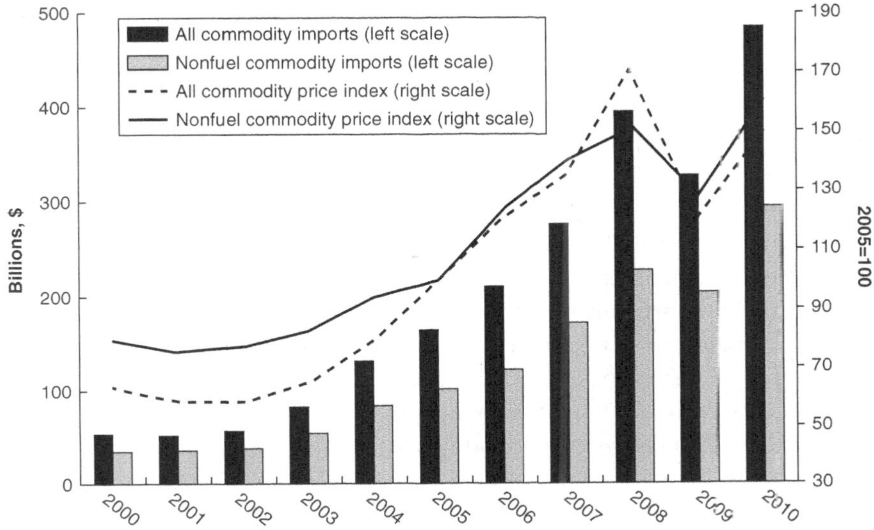

Source: UNCTAD, UNCTADstat and IMF WEO (September 2011).

35 percent in 2007 while the share of the foreign currency debt fell from some 60 percent to less than 40 percent in the same period (IDB 2008). Securing the conditions for overall debt sustainability has become an overriding objective in fiscal management, even though it has occasionally resulted in highly regressive tax regimes relying increasingly on indirect taxes.[10]

Considerable progress has also been made in bringing inflation under control since the beginning of the decade. Average consumer inflation in DEEs was close to 30 percent per annum throughout the 1990s. It came down to single digit levels, just over 6 percent during 2003–2007. This is largely because of sharp declines in inflation in Latin America toward the levels of more stable Asian economies.

Drawing on the lessons from past crises, DEEs have generally been more successful in managing exchange rates, capital flows and balance of payments, even though there are notable exceptions, including many countries in Central and Eastern Europe, Turkey and South Africa – those more seriously affected by the 2008–2009 crisis. Almost all emerging economies moved away from fixed currency pegs which had proved highly damaging by encouraging boom–bust cycles in capital flows, exchange rates and current account balances, with severe impact on employment and growth. Many DEEs, particularly in Asia, followed various shades of managed floating, heavily intervening in currency markets in pursuit of strong payments and reserve positions. Even though several DEEs, notably in Latin America, have adopted inflation targeting and left their currencies largely to markets, they have nevertheless paid greater attention to their current account positions and the adequacy of reserves in meeting short-term external obligations. The resilience of domestic financial institutions and markets to shocks has also been improved through tighter prudential regulations and supervision, and significantly increased capitalization. All these have been reflected in significantly improved credit ratings of major emerging economies.

However, improvements in macroeconomic balances in DEEs have not been independent of the favorable international economic environment. In Latin America, an important part of the decline in budget deficits after 2002 was due to rising commodity prices, with revenues from commodity taxes, profits and loyalties accounting for as much as 50 percent of the total increase in the fiscal revenue ratio in some countries (Cornia et al. 2011). Indeed, the fiscal record was less impressive in terms of structural balances since several governments in the region pursued procyclical expansion in spending. According to the IMF (REO November 2007) during 2006–2007 structural primary (noninterest) balances in the region were weaker than actual primary balances while the IDB (2008) finds that only Chile was in structural fiscal surplus. Similarly, an ECLAC report (Jiménez and Gómez-Sabaini, 2009) argued that much of the improvement in the fiscal situation after 2002 was the result of the steady increase in commodity prices and warned that a sharp decline in these prices could seriously jeopardize the fiscal achievements. Indeed, the fiscal space gained during the subprime expansion was largely lost with the reversal of commodity prices in 2008–2009, when budgets went into deficits in the region by some 3 percent of GDP (ECLAC 2010).

The situation is much the same for current account balances in commodity exporters in Latin America and Africa. At the end of the 1990s and early 2000s current accounts in these regions registered deficits in the order of 3–4 percent of GDP. By 2007, both regions had moved to a surplus, at a rate of some 1 percent of GDP in Latin America and over 3 percent in Africa. Again, an important reason was the increase in oil and non-oil commodity prices, which resulted in a 50 percent improvement in the terms of trade in Latin America between 2002 and 2006. It is estimated that without terms of trade gains from commodity price increases, the current account of the region would have shown a deficit of about 4 percent of GDP, more or less at the same rate as that observed before the Tequila crisis (Calvo and Talvi 2007; Ocampo 2007). Indeed, external deficits started to grow after 2008 with the decline in commodity prices and increased reliance on domestic demand for growth.

In several cases, success in bringing inflation under control also owes a greater deal to favorable international financial conditions and the generalized surge in capital flows. Even though fixed pegs were abandoned and floating was adopted along with inflation targeting, the exchange rate operated as an anchor for inflationary expectations, as net capital flows exceeded current account deficits and led to nominal appreciations. In countries such as Brazil and Turkey high interest rates did not bring inflation under control by restricting credit expansion and domestic spending – in both cases credits expanded by 20–30 percent per annum and growth was driven by consumer spending. Rather, they accelerated capital inflows, particularly carry trade, resulting in significant appreciations of the nominal exchange rate. In such cases currency appreciations also played an important part in reducing the ratio of foreign currency denominated debt to GDP.

Finally and more importantly, not all DEEs enjoying the acceleration of growth in the 2000s have seen commensurate improvements in domestic savings, capital accumulation or productivity – a factor which raises considerable doubt about the sustainability of strong growth. The average savings rate in middle income countries during 2000–2008 was lower than the rate in the 1990s while the record on investment and productivity was mixed (World Bank 2011).

Among the major emerging economies, apart from China, only India has registered large increases in domestic savings and investment alongside rapid growth (Table 8.2). However, despite reforms designed to promote manufacturing, almost three-quarters of Indian growth in the 2000s came from services while the share of manufacturing has stagnated at around 15 percent of GDP, more or less the same level as in the early 1990s. In manufacturing and services the well-performing export sectors are capital- or skill-intensive rather than labor-intensive, manifesting a vent-for-surplus style expansion based on the mobilization of a backlog of underutilized skills (Gupta et al. 2008). Infrastructure bottlenecks top the list of impediments to manufacturing development. Unless these are removed and manufacturing starts expanding rapidly, the Indian resurgence may well remain a one-off miracle of the kind seen in some countries in past decades, such as Brazil in the late 1960s and the early 1970s and Turkey in the 1980s.

In Latin America the average savings rate has shown a moderate increase, largely on account of improvements in fiscal balances resulting from the commodity bonanza. In Argentina the increase is sizeable but in Brazil the savings rate has continued to remain at too low a level to provide a reliable basis for capital accumulation needed for rigorous and sustained growth. In Turkey, despite rapid growth and improvements in public savings, domestic savings declined substantially and an important part of investment was financed by capital inflows as the savings gap reached almost 6 percent of GDP during the boom years of 2006–2007 (Uygur 2011).

Again there is considerable diversity in the pace of capital accumulation among the DEEs which enjoyed a significant acceleration of growth in the 2000s. In Latin America private investment rose as a share of GDP, but remained well below the levels in other regions (IMF REO October 2008). As noted by IDB (2008), Latin American private investment and productivity during the post-2002 expansion did not perform significantly better than during the previous expansion of the 1990s even though external conditions were exceptionally more favorable – with world growth stronger by 1.4 percentage points, commodity prices higher by 76 percent and emerging market bond spreads lower by some 400 basis points. In Brazil, at less than 20 percent of GDP, investment has remained too low to provide a rapid increase in productive capacity. High real interest rates, extremely low public investment as well as the long-standing problem of lack of a strong animal spirit among the entrepreneurial class have been major factors. [1] Low rates of investment in Brazil, as well as some other DEEs in the region, is a major reason why Latin America continues to have a poor record in productivity compared to East Asia (Palma 2011). The average total factor productivity growth in the seven largest Latin American countries during 2003–2006 is found to have been lower than that during the 1991–94 expansion (IDB 2008).

In several economies in East Asia, including Malaysia, Singapore, the Philippines, Taiwan (China) and Indonesia, investment rates have been hovering around 20 percent

Table 8.2: Gross national savings, investments and current accounts in selected DEEs (percentage of GDP)

Year	2000			2002			2007			2010		
	Savings	I	CA	Savings	I	CA	Savings	I	CA	Savings	I	CA
Argentina	13.0	17.5	–3.1	20.5	10.8	8.5	26.6	24.1	2.4	22.8	24.4	0.8
Brazil	14.5	18.3	–3.8	14.7	16.2	–1.5	18.4	18.3	0.1	17.0	19.3	–2.3
China	36.8	35.1	1.7	40.3	37.9	2.4	51.9	41.7	10.1	53.4	48.2	5.2
India	23.3	24.3	–1.0	25.5	24.1	1.4	36.7	37.4	–0.7	34.2	36.8	–2.6
Indonesia	27.1	22.2	4.8	25.4	21.4	4.0	27.3	24.9	2.4	33.3	32.5	0.8
Korea	33.3	30.6	2.8	30.5	29.2	1.3	31.5	29.4	2.1	31.9	29.2	2.8
Malaysia	35.9	26.9	9.0	32.7	24.8	8.0	37.5	21.6	15.9	32.9	21.4	11.5
Mexico	22.8	25.5	–2.8	21.5	23.5	–2.0	25.7	26.5	–0.9	24.4	25.0	–0.5
Russia	36.7	18.7	18.0	28.5	20.0	8.4	31.3	25.4	5.9	25.1	20.3	4.8
South Africa	15.6	15.7	–0.1	16.7	15.9	0.8	14.3	21.2	–7.0	16.5	19.3	–2.8
Thailand	30.4	22.8	7.6	27.5	23.8	3.7	32.8	26.4	6.3	30.6	25.9	4.6
Turkey	17.0	20.8	–3.7	17.3	17.6	–0.3	15.2	21.1	–5.9	13.6	20.1	–6.6

Source: IMF WEO (September 2011).

of GDP in recent years, less than half the rate in China. Large current account surpluses in some of these economies reflect low rates of domestic investment rather than exceptionally high domestic savings rates. For instance, in recent years savings rates have been quite similar in India and Malaysia, but while the current account in India has been in balance or deficit, Malaysia has had a surplus reaching double digit figures as a percentage of GDP. In none of these East Asian economies have investment rates recovered the levels attained before the 1997 crisis.[12] Even recognizing that the precrisis investment booms were unsustainable bubbles driven by massive capital inflows, recent investment rates have been too low to produce rapid and sustained growth of the kind many of these economies had enjoyed during the earlier phases of their industrialization, creating concerns that some of them run the risk of getting caught in a middle income trap (Radhi and Zeufack 2009).

E. Impact on Growth in DEEs

The exceptionally favorable global economic conditions prevailing before the outbreak of the crisis not only improved internal and external balances and stability in DEEs, but also contributed to the expansion of economic activity, directly or indirectly. China and other export-oriented East Asian DEEs benefited significantly from credit, consumption and property bubbles created by speculative lending and investment in the US and Europe, growing rapidly based on exports to these markets, running increasing current account surpluses and accumulating large amounts of reserves. In most DEEs in Latin

America and Africa, the combination of increasing commodity prices and declining cost of external financing significantly reduced the payments deficits and allowed to expand domestic demand and accelerate growth. In oil-importing emerging economies such as India and Turkey, capital inflows were more than sufficient to meet the deficits created by oil price shocks, again allowing rapid growth based primarily on domestic demand. India additionally enjoyed a rapid growth in workers' remittances which reached 3.3 percent of GDP in 2007.

Low interest rates in AEs and the surge in capital inflows also allowed most emerging economies to pursue expansionary monetary policies and maintain historically low interest rates, stimulating domestic demand. Large inflows of capital in excess of current account needs in deficit countries or coming on top of current account surpluses in surplus countries, contributed to expansion by creating asset bubbles. Equity prices rose sharply between 2002 and 2007 both in dollar and local currency terms. The increase was particularly strong in Brazil, China, India and Turkey, and many of these also experienced credit and property booms both due to increased entry of nonresidents to domestic asset markets and the impact of capital inflows on domestic monetary conditions (Akyüz 2010). In several countries, growing workers' remittances from abroad were also translated into domestic consumption, thereby adding to demand, output and employment.

It is not always easy to identify precisely the relative contributions of global conditions and domestic policies to growth in DEEs. However, evidence strongly suggests that extremely favorable global conditions played a much more predominant role in the acceleration of growth in DEEs in the new millennium than is typically appreciated in the popular debate on the rise of the South. This is particularly true for commodity-rich economies of Latin America and Africa which, together with India and Turkey, account for much of the recent acceleration of growth in the South.

Empirical research in the Inter-American Development Bank on the role of external factors in boom–bust cycles in Latin America over 1990–2006 has come to the conclusion that an important part of growth in the period after 2002 could be explained by improved global conditions (Izquierdo et al. 2008; IDB 2008). Using industrial production in AEs, US interest rates, the terms of trade and risk spreads on international sovereign debt as proximate measures of international economic conditions, it is found that growth in Latin America after 2002 would have been lower by 2 percent had these variables remained at the levels predicted in the late 1990s on the basis of their historical patterns. Growth would have been lower even by a greater margin if the unfavorable global economic conditions (high risk spreads and interest rates, low commodity prices and severely depressed capital inflows) that were prevailing in the aftermath of the Russian crisis had persisted. Cohan and Yeyati (2012) have reached similar conclusions on the impact of external conditions on the performance of Latin America, using a Global Wind Index consisting of three basic indicators of the external environment – risk appetite, commodity prices and global growth.

Until the outbreak of the crisis, growth in East Asian DEEs relied heavily on exports. In China during 2002–2008 exports grew on average by 25 percent per annum while domestic consumption lagged income growth (Table 8.3). During this period, about

Table 8.3: Growth of real GDP and its components in China (in percent)

	GDP	Consumption	Gross Capital Formation	Exports	Imports
2002	9.1	7.4	13.2	29.4	27.4
2003	10.0	6.6	17.2	26.8	24.9
2004	10.1	7.1	13.4	28.4	22.7
2005	10.4	7.3	9.0	24.3	11.4
2006	11.6	8.4	11.1	23.8	15.9
2007	13.0	10.1	11.4	19.9	14.0
2008	9.6	8.8	10.2	8.6	5.1
2009	9.1	8.5	19.8	−10.4	4.3
2010	10.3	8.0	11.6	27.6	21.8
2011	9.3	8.0	10.7	12.4	13.2

Source: WB CQU (November 2005; December 2008; November 2009; and November 2010).

Table 8.4: Manufactured exports of China to various regions

Partner	2005		2007		2010	
	$, billions	% of total	$, billions	% of total	$, billions	% of total
Africa	10.4	1.5	19.7	1.7	29.8	2.0
Latin America	17.2	2.5	40.0	3.5	70.7	4.8
Asia	92.0	13.2	169.5	14.9	248.0	16.8
Total DCs (Africa +LA+Asia)	119.6	17.1	229.3	20.2	348.5	23.6
The rest[a]	579.2	82.9	904.8	79.8	1125.7	76.4
World	698.7	100.0	1134.0	100.0	1474.3	100.0

Source: UNCTADstat.
Note: regions are defined according to Global System of Trade Preferences countries (GSTP).
a. Includes AEs, emerging countries in Central and Eastern Europe and CIS.

one-third of GDP growth in China was due to exports, taking into account their direct and indirect import contents. If the multiplier effect of exports on domestic consumption and knock-on effect on domestic investment are added, this proportion goes up to almost 50 percent.[13] Much of these exports went to AEs (Table 8.4).

Exports of East Asian DEEs closely linked to the Sinocentric production network, including Korea and Taiwan (China) and the major ASEAN countries (Indonesia, Malaysia, Philippines, Singapore, Thailand and Vietnam) also grew rapidly during this period, but except Vietnam, not as rapidly as China's. The share of exports in GDP is higher in the majority of these countries than in China, both in gross value and value added terms. This, together with relatively rapid growth of exports, meant that precrisis growth in ASEAN+2 depended even more on exports than in China. Indeed estimates suggest that during 2003–2007 about 60 percent of growth in Korea, Taiwan (China) and Thailand and even a greater proportion of growth in Malaysia, Singapore and Vietnam came from exports, taking into account their import contents. Most of the exports went to AEs, directly or through China by providing the latter country parts and components for its exports to AEs.

F. The Role of South–South Trade and China

Rapid growth in DEEs in the new millennium has not only resulted in a significant increase in their share in world income, but has also been associated with a sizeable increase in their share in world trade and an unprecedented expansion of South–South trade. These are often taken as a manifestation of decoupling of the South from the North and the increased capacity of major DEEs such as BRICS to provide growth impulses to other developing countries and even to AEs. However, a closer examination shows that the picture is much more nuanced than is portrayed by this popular presentation of the increased role of the South in the world economy.

There is no doubt that the share of DEEs in world income has increased rapidly in the new millennium as a result of their significantly faster growth than AEs regardless of how it is measured (Table 8.5). However, the measurement of the shares of economies in world income in Purchasing Power Parity (PPP) as an indication of their relative importance is highly misleading. It is the market (exchange) values of goods and services, not the PPP values, that determine the economies' contributions to global supply and demand and the expansionary and deflationary impulses they transmit to others. The share of DEEs in world income is considerably smaller when measured in market exchange rates, both in current or constant (2005) dollars, than when measured in PPP. In fact, despite a large increase, in constant dollars the share of DEEs taken together is still less than the share of the US. In current dollars, their share is considerably higher because of a sharp appreciation of the currencies of most major DEEs against the dollar. China is the only country with a significant share in world income in comparison with AEs; in current dollars it is second only to the US. Its share would be considerably higher if it had allowed its twin surpluses to appreciate the yuan faster than has been the case.

The share of DEEs in world trade has also increased significantly, in the order of 10 percentage points between 2000 and 2010, both for imports and exports, to reach around two-fifths of total world trade (Table 8.5). China accounts for the bulk of the trade by DEEs. It exports more than any other economy in the world and it comes second after the US in imports. The shares of other DEEs, including Brazil and India, in world imports and exports are much smaller.

South–South trade as a proportion of world trade has also seen a significant increase in the new millennium (Table 8.6). East Asia accounts for three-quarters of South–South trade and China's share is around 40 percent. China also comprises close to 60 percent of South–South imports in Asia and 58 percent and 65 percent of Asian DEEs' imports from Africa and Latin America, respectively (ADB 2011). Again, the shares of other DEEs in South–South trade are small – for India it is around 5 percent and for the rest of the developing world, including Latin America and Africa, it is around 25 percent.

These imply that major DEEs other than China, including India and Brazil, cannot act as a driving force for the South. In any case, the expansionary impulses that these economies could generate for other DEEs depend very much on large and continued inflows of capital, because they tend to run current account deficits except at times of strong growth in the rest of the world.

There is considerable double counting in the estimated shares of DEEs and South–South trade in world trade. Since trade is conventionally measured in gross value not in value added terms, a country's exports contain imports from and, hence, value added generated in other countries. Typically, the import content of exports of DEEs has been growing as a result of their increased participation in international production networks supplying final goods to AEs. It is also greater than the import content of exports of AEs (Koopman et al. 2010; Akyüz 2011a; Riad et al. 2011). This is particularly true for East Asian DEEs participating in the Sinocentric production network as well as for Mexico which has become an assembly hub in NAFTA. This means that in value added terms, the share of DEEs in world exports would be lower and that of AEs higher than the shares indicated by official figures.

The Sinocentric East Asian production network involves considerable South–South trade in intermediate goods, parts and components closely linked to final exports to AEs. In that region goods in process often cross borders several times before reaching their final destinations while in NAFTA – as well as in the European production network – foreign inputs usually come directly from AEs and there are little imports from other DEEs for exports to AEs (Riad et al. 2011). It is estimated that only 22 percent of exports of major East Asian DEEs to each other are destined to final demand in these economies while 60 percent go to final demand in the US, Europe and Japan (Lim and Lim 2012).

In China, imported parts and components and other intermediate goods that are directly or indirectly used in the production of exportables reach 40 percent of gross value of exports. By contrast, the import content of consumption in China is much lower than that in AEs – about a quarter of the import content of US consumption. During 2003–2007, around 60 percent of total Chinese imports are estimated to have been used for exports, under 15 percent for consumption and some 20–25 percent for investment.

Chinese merchandise imports are dominated by manufactures (Table 8.7). More than half of these come from DEEs. East Asian DEEs account for a large proportion of these imports, mostly in parts and components used in China's export industries (Athukorala 2011; Lee, Park and Wang 2011). China also imports intermediate parts and components from AEs. In fact, Japan is its largest supplier, with a share of 17 percent of such imports by China.

High import content of exports means that a relatively important part of Chinese exports receipts accrues to countries that provide direct and indirect inputs to export industries in China. In processing exports, which constitute close to 80 percent of China's total exports to the US, more value added is earned by East Asian economies

Table 8.5: Share of selected economies in world income, exports and imports in 2000 and 2010 (percent)

	GDP						Exports		Imports	
	In constant dollars (2005)		In current dollars		In PPP		In current dollars		In current dollars	
	2000	2010	2000	2010	2000	2010	2000	2010	2000	2010
United States	28.6	26.1	30.9	23.1	23.5	19.5	12.1	8.4	18.9	12.8
EU	31.9	28.5	26.4	25.8	25.0	20.4	38.0	33.9	37.7	34.2
Japan	10.9	9.3	14.5	8.7	7.6	5.8	7.4	5.1	5.7	4.5
DEEs	18.5	25.8	20.3	34.2	37.2	47.9	31.9	41.8	28.8	39.1
Argentina	0.4	0.5	0.9	0.6	0.8	0.9	0.4	0.5	0.4	0.4
Brazil	2.0	2.2	2.0	3.3	2.9	2.9	0.9	1.3	0.9	1.2
China	3.6	7.6	3.7	9.3	7.1	13.6	3.9	10.4	3.4	9.1
India	1.5	2.4	1.5	2.6	3.7	5.5	0.7	1.5	0.8	2.1
Indonesia	0.6	0.8	0.5	1.1	1.2	1.4	1.0	1.0	0.6	0.9
Mexico	2.0	1.8	2.1	1.6	2.5	2.1	2.6	2.0	2.7	2.1
South Africa	0.5	0.6	0.4	0.6	0.7	0.7	0.5	0.6	0.5	0.6
Turkey	1.0	1.1	0.8	1.2	1.2	1.3	0.4	0.8	0.8	1.2

Source: GDP in current dollars and PPP terms from IMF WEO (September 2011), GDP in constant 2005 dollars from World Bank database; and exports and imports data from UNCTAD, UNCTADstat.

supplying parts and components to China than by China itself. China has become the single most important market for many of them, particularly for Korea and Taiwan (China) – the two main suppliers of parts and components other than Japan. In the precrisis years only about 12 percent of exports from Korea and Taiwan (China) went directly to the US and EU each, but as much as 25 percent to China. However, a large proportion of the latter also ended up in the US and EU as inputs in Chinese exports to them.

This means that growth in many East Asian DEEs depends on exports to AEs directly and through China, even to a greater extent than growth in China itself. Although East Asian DEEs absorb about one-fifth of Chinese manufactured exports (Table 8.4), these are partly in parts and components for exports to AEs, not for domestic consumption. More importantly, economic activity in these countries and hence their imports from China depend very much on their exports to AEs, both directly and through China. Many of these economies suffer from underconsumption as well as sluggish investment noted above. Thus, they do not provide a strong autonomous market for China's exports and an alternative to AEs. A slowdown in AEs would reduce their exports to them both directly and through China, thereby slowing economic activity and hence reducing their imports from China.

Table 8.6: South–South trade (percent)

	2000–2001	2006–2007	2009
South–South trade as share of world trade			
Exports	10.2	15.0	17.7
Imports	9.6	14.1	16.1
Trade	9.9	14.5	16.9
Developing Asia's share of South–South trade			
Exports	79.8	79.8	80.3
Imports	71.6	69.3	68.5
Trade	75.7	74.6	74.4
China's share of South–South trade			
Exports	35.1	40.8	41.6
Imports	36.9	37.8	38.4
Trade	36.0	39.3	40.0
India's share of South–South trade			
Exports	3.1	3.7	4.9
Imports	1.6	2.4	5.8
Trade	2.4	3.0	5.4
Other South's share of South–South trade			
Exports	20.2	20.2	19.7
Imports	28.4	30.7	31.5
Trade	24.3	25.4	25.6

Source: ADB, *ADO* (April 2011).

The share of oil and non-oil commodities in China's imports has been growing. It now exceeds one-third of the total, compared to less than 20 percent in the early 2000s (Table 8.7). Over 60 percent of these now come from DEEs, including Africa and Latin America. Although they are also used as inputs into exports, it can be expected that the commodity import content of Chinese exports is less than their manufacturing import content. Thus, a greater proportion of commodity imports are used to meet domestic demand than manufactured imports in China.

China has started to exert a strong and growing influence on commodity prices since the beginning of the new millennium (Farooki and Kaplinsky 2011; Farooki 2012). As seen in Chart 8.4, there is a close correlation between the evolution of Chinese imports and commodity prices. After hovering around 4 percent of world commodity imports in the late 1990s and early 2000s, China's share started to rise, doubling by 2007 when the global growth and commodity prices peaked and reaching almost 11 percent

Table 8.7: Manufactured and commodities imports of China from various regions (billions, $)

a) Commodities imports of China from various regions

Partner	2003		2007		2010	
	Nonfuel	Fuel	Nonfuel	Fuel	Nonfuel	Fuel
Africa	2.3	4.9	7.9	26.1	19.5	41.5
Latin America	10.0	0.4	37.5	5.3	66.7	13.0
Asia	15.5	19.5	48.3	56.1	66.6	100.0
Total DCs (Africa +LA+Asia)	27.8	24.9	93.7	87.6	152.8	154.5
The rest	27.3	4.3	80.3	17.6	146.0	34.5
World	55.1	29.2	174.1	105.1	298.9	189.0

b) Manufactured imports of China from various regions

Partner	2003		2007		2010	
	$, billions	% of total	$, billions	% of total	$, billions	% of total
Africa	0.8	0.3	1.8	0.3	2.6	0.3
Latin America	4.4	1.4	8.1	1.2	11.4	1.3
Asia	161.1	49.2	373.3	55.3	473.1	53.2
Total DCs (Africa +LA+Asia)	166.3	50.8	383.2	56.8	487.1	54.7
The rest	160.9	49.2	291.2	43.2	402.6	45.3
World	327.2	100.0	674.5	100.0	889.8	100.0

Source: IMF, *Direction of Trade,* and UNCTAD, UNCTADstat.
Note: Hong Kong, Korea, Macau, Taiwan and Singapore are defined as developing countries and reported externally. Nonfuel commodities are defined as industrial metals, food, beverages and agricultural raw materials in terms of the SITC (Revision3) classification groups with codes 0, 1, 2, 4, 67 and 68, also including precious metals and stones (667+971); the manufactured goods (SITC 5 to 8 less 667 and 68); fuels (SITC 3).

in 2010. In 2009, total world demand, Chinese imports and commodity prices all fell. By the end of 2010, total world demand was still below the peak of 2008, but commodity prices went up along with a strong recovery in Chinese imports, which surpassed its 2008 peak by 22 percent.

Empirical evidence suggests that the impact of China on Latin American business cycles is stronger through rising commodity prices and demand spillovers to third markets than through bilateral trade, and much greater than that of India (Lederman et al. 2009). It is also found that because of these indirect effects, since the mid-1990s, the impact of shocks to Chinese GDP on Latin America has grown by three-times while that of shocks to US GDP has declined by half (Cesa-Bianchi et al. 2011). Still, it should be borne in mind that until the crisis, a large part of China's growth itself depended on its exports to AEs.

G. Crisis and Recovery

With the outbreak of the crisis, the international economic environment deteriorated rapidly in all areas that had previously supported expansion in DEEs. Capital inflows were reversed and net flows turned negative. Commodity prices made a sharp downturn, losing much of the gains recorded after the beginning of the decade. Economic activity contracted rapidly in AEs, leading to a sharp drop in world trade and exports of DEEs.

The reversal of capital flows created a generalized downward pressure on the currencies of almost all DEEs. India, Korea, Turkey and South Africa experienced sharp depreciations and suffered large reserve losses. Equity markets of all major DEEs came under heavy selling pressures and lost over 80 percent of the gains made during the earlier boom in a matter of a few months. However, the reduced exposure to currency risks, large stock of reserves accumulated during the boom, greater readiness of international financial institutions to provide liquidity to countries threatened by contagion and, above all, the quick recovery of capital flows prevented the instability from being translated into a fully fledged financial crisis even in economies heavily dependent on foreign capital.[14]

Trade has been by far the most important channel of transmission of deflationary impulses from the global crisis, both for exporters of manufactures and commodities. After growing by close to 10 percent per annum during the years before the crisis, world trade volume started to fall sharply in the last quarter of 2008 and throughout the first half of 2009. Despite the subsequent recovery, it registered a decline of close to 13 percent for the year as a whole.

The impact of export contraction on economic activity varied according to the contribution of exports to growth in comparison with domestic demand. Exports of East Asian DEEs, including China, made a sharp downturn in the last quarter of 2008, falling at double digit rates in 2009 (Table 8.3). On average this reduced GDP by 5–6 percentage points. With spillovers to domestic demand, the figure reaches almost 8 percentage points.[15] Loss of output due to declines in exports was more moderate in India and Turkey, in the range of 3–4 percentage points. In these countries declines in exports were comparable to those in East Asia, but export ratios were much lower both in gross value and value added terms and growth had relied more on domestic demand. This was also true for some major commodity exporters such as Brazil. In other words, the more successful exporters with high exports–GDP ratios were hit particular hard by the crisis.

The growth outcome depended not only on the incidence of shocks but also on the policy response. The policy space was limited in countries which were running large current account deficits on the eve of the crisis, such as Turkey and South Africa where the combination of sharp declines in capital flows and export earnings resulted in large drops in GDP. However, even where there was a rigorous countercyclical policy response, growth rates were lower during 2008–2009 than in precrisis years, in some cases by a very large margin. Among the regions the largest drop was in Latin America, which went into recession in 2009 (Table 8.1).

There has been widespread resort to cuts in policy interest rates and monetary and fiscal expansion, but the policy response in East Asia, notably in China, played a central role in the subsequent recovery not only in the region alone but also in a wider range of DEEs. The countercyclical fiscal response was unprecedented, not only for the region alone but also the developing world as a whole.[16] On some estimates, the fiscal package in 15 Asian DEEs amounted to 7.5 percent of 2008 GDP, almost three times the average level in G7 countries (ESCAP 2009). China introduced a large package, close to $600 billion or 13 percent of GDP. Fiscal packages were also relatively large in Thailand, Malaysia, Singapore and Korea, but somewhat smaller in India.[17] Unlike in AEs, they placed much less emphasis on tax cuts but focused on increases in spending, particularly in infrastructure and property investment.

In China less than 20 percent of the fiscal package was allocated to social spending with the rest going mainly to investment. It pushed the investment rate toward 50 percent of GDP financed by rapid credit expansion and debt accumulation by local governments. This has created unused capacity in infrastructure and added to excess capacity that had already existed in several industries such as steel because of overinvestment in previous years. More importantly, policies designed to revive real estate demand and an unprecedented growth of mortgage lending created a bubble in the property market with real estate investment growing by close to 40 percent. While private consumption held up thanks to several incentives such as subsidies for vehicle and appliance purchases, it did not provide much impetus to offset the sharp decline in exports. Around 80 percent of growth in 2009 was due to investment. As the effects of this package started to fade out, another investment boom emerged, with fixed investment growing by 26 percent and property investment by 33 percent year-on-year in the first half of 2011 (Xinhuanet 2011). As of the end of 2011, property investment doubled as a share of GDP from the early 2000s, accounting for more than half of the rise in total investment.

The Chinese stimulus package gave a strong push to economic activity in Latin America and Africa by helping reverse the decline in commodity prices. Indeed, changes in the composition of demand from exports toward domestic investment generated especially strong spillovers to commodity exporters. This is because while China's exports have very high import contents in manufactured parts and components supplied by East Asian DEEs and Japan, property and infrastructure investment has typically higher import contents in commodities.[18] For this reason, in 2010 commodity imports of China stood 75 percent higher than those in 2007 while the increase in manufactured imports was just over 30 percent (Table 8.7).

This means that the new demand pattern driving Chinese growth after 2008 has helped commodity exporters more than that during the precrisis expansion when Chinese growth was driven mainly by exports. Indeed, this is found to be the reason why Latin America recovered much faster than was initially anticipated: "the evidence shows that Latin American growth owes more to a fast-growing economy that enacted a powerful fiscal stimulus during the global crisis (China), and relatively less to the economy that was at the epicenter of the crisis (United States)" (Cesa-Bianchi et al. 2011, 4).

The shift from exports to investment resulted in a steep reduction in the current account surplus of China, from over 10 percent of GDP in 2007 to 4–5 percent in 2010–11. Again, many East Asian countries saw sizeable declines in their surpluses as a result of slowdown of their exports to AEs as well as exports of parts and components to China. In the same vein, in DEEs which had been relying predominantly on domestic demand for growth, such as Brazil, India and Turkey, current account deficits started to grow.

However, so far, growing current account deficits have not posed serious payments difficulties because of rapid recovery of capital inflows. In fact, as during the subprime expansion, from early 2009 net flows started to exceed current account deficits, creating currency appreciations and asset bubbles. Equity markets recovered sharply and in most major emerging economies including Brazil, China, India and Turkey, private sector borrowing started rising faster than GDP, posing the risk of overheating (IMF 2011). Major deficit economies, Brazil, India, Turkey and South Africa, started appreciating faster than East Asian surplus countries. Unlike during the subprime expansion, some of these such as Brazil, as well as several others with sound payments positions, became less willing to see their currencies appreciate as their exports were slowing. They did not only intervene in currency markets more vigorously, but also resorted to market-based capital control measures, though often without much effect on the size of inflows (Akyüz 2012).

As a result of countercyclical stimulus packages, the recovery in commodity prices and capital flows, growth in DEEs resumed after a brief interruption during 2008–2009 despite the sharp slowdown in AEs. In Argentina, Brazil, India, Korea and Turkey, average growth during 2010–2011 approached or exceeded the levels achieved before the subprime crisis (Table 8.1).

H. Sustainability and Vulnerabilities

However, there are a number of reasons to believe that the forces that have been driving growth in DEEs since 2009 cannot be sustained over the medium term. Nor is it possible to return to the extremely favorable international economic conditions prevailing before the outbreak of the global crisis. This means that unless fundamental changes take place in the way DEEs are integrated into the world economy – unless they reduce their dependence on foreign markets and capital – the recent staggering ascendancy of the South may prove to be a passing phenomenon and the speed of their convergence to income levels of AEs could slow considerably in the coming years.

China is now widely recognized to be suffering from underconsumption due to low shares of wages and household income in GDP and high precautionary savings. The share of wages in GDP has been constantly falling since the mid-1990s, bringing down the share of household income from almost 70 percent of GDP to less than 60 percent (Akyüz 2011b). Virtually in every year since the beginning of the 2000s, consumption has lagged GDP, resulting in continued reduction in its share (Table 8.3). This has also been the case after the outbreak of the global crisis. On the eve of the crisis private consumption accounted for around 36 percent of GDP, it is now less than 34 percent – a figure one would expect to see only during war times! The need to raise consumption is recognized by policymakers in China, but the main problem is that they have been trying to raise consumption primarily by reducing the household propensity to save rather than by lifting the share of household income in GDP. Cuts in interest rates generally fail to make a dent in consumption spending, adding, instead, to the property bubble. It is also unlikely that increased availability of consumer credit would boost private consumption.

A reduction in precautionary savings would depend very much on adequate public provisioning of health, education and housing services. Recent focus on investment in social housing is certainly a step in the right direction, but much more is needed in all social areas, including health and education, in order to expect a significant drop in precautionary savings. In any case, even a relatively large drop in the savings rate would not bring much increase in the share of consumption in GDP in the absence of a significant increase in the share of household income in GDP.

Export prospects are equally dim. None of the three major markets for Chinese manufactures, the US, Europe and East Asia, offer much room for expansion. In the US consumers continue to deleverage as the ratio of household debt to GDP still hovers around the levels of 2003 and unemployment remains at historic levels despite recent improvements. The US itself is seeking export-led growth, trying to hit the target set by President Obama in 2010 to double exports over five years. Japan went into recession in 2011 and growth prospects in the coming years are not bright (World Bank 2012a). Even if Europe avoids a severe recession, its growth is widely expected to remain anaemic and unbalanced for several years to come. China's exports to the eurozone have already shown double digit declines in the last months of 2011, leading to a decline in total exports in November on a quarterly basis (Plowright 2012). East Asian DEEs as a major market for Chinese exports are even more vulnerable than China to a slowdown in the US and Europe because of their dependence on these markets, directly or through China. The rest of the developing world does not provide an important market for China – in any case, many commodity exporters themselves depend on strong growth in China to maintain momentum. Therefore, China will have to rely increasingly on domestic demand to maintain its stellar growth.

Nor is the slowdown in exports a temporary, cyclical problem that could disappear with an eventual return of the US and Europe to rigorous and sustained growth. A full recovery in AEs will no doubt give some room to China for faster expansion of its exports. However, it is quite unrealistic to expect that China can go back to a precrisis pattern of expansion when its growth was driven primarily by exports to AEs. With Germany and Japan continuing to adhere to export-led growth, this would also mean a return of the US to precrisis conditions, acting as a locomotive for the rest of the world. That would be a recipe for the breakdown of the international monetary and trading system. If, on the other hand, China cuts the rate of expansion of its exports to a more acceptable level, say to 10 percent, then, without a fundamental change in the pace and pattern of domestic demand that prevailed before the outbreak of the global crisis, its growth might barely reach 7 percent (Akyüz 2011a).

In China a stop-gap strategy of offsetting the slowdown in exports with accelerated investment cannot work indefinitely. Investment in social housing may appear to be a way out, but it is unlikely to compensate for declining investment opportunities in other areas including manufacturing, infrastructure and commercial real estate (Pettis 2011b). Continuing to invest in the latter areas despite excess capacity may help postpone the underconsumption crisis, but only for it to come back with greater force. A debt-driven investment bubble at a rate of 50 percent of GDP is no less fragile than the US-style consumption and property bubbles or the investment bubbles that several East Asian countries were experiencing before the 1997 crisis. It cannot avoid ending up with massive overcapacity and nonperforming loans. The boom in the property sector has already come to an end with property prices falling in a large number of cities, with strong adverse spillovers to other sectors. The increased debt difficulties have prompted the government to call for a rollover of local government loans by creditor banks (Rabinovitch 2012).

A sharp slowdown in China resulting from a contraction in investment or exports would also mean the end of favorable conditions in commodity markets. There is already a softening of commodity prices. Even though oil prices have been relatively stable, non-oil commodity prices, including metals and minerals and several agricultural commodities, have declined since summer 2011, and both oil and non-oil prices are projected to decline further in 2012 (IMF WEO 2012, January Update; World Bank 2012a). A steep fall would no doubt result in sizeable losses for commodity exporters in Latin America and Africa. On the other hand even if commodity prices remain high, growth in Latin America (and Africa) could still fall since commodity prices may affect the level rather than the growth rate of GDP – that is, to maintain a high rate of growth, commodity prices would need to keep on rising (IDB 2008). Growth losses would be more severe if commodity declines are accompanied by worsened global financial conditions. Estimates on the impact of external factors on Latin American business cycles suggest that a combination of terms of trade and financial shocks – reversal in capital flows and hikes in risk spreads – could produce a steep decline of growth in Latin America or even push the region into outright recession (IDB 2010; Izquierdo et al. 2008).

The risk–return configuration that has so far sustained strong inflows of capital to DEEs is indeed susceptible to sudden changes. Even though it is almost impossible to predict the timing of stops and reversals and the events that can trigger them, it must be clear that the conditions that have been driving the surge in capital flows, historically low interest rates in AEs and favorable risk appetite for investment in DEEs cannot last forever. The immediate threat is a sharp increase in global risk aversion due to prospects of falling growth and increasing imbalances in major emerging economies, economic contraction and financial fragility in the eurozone, the political stalemate in the US over fiscal policy and geopolitical oil supply risks. Any combination of these could lead to a sharp reversal of capital flows to DEEs and a hike in risk spreads, very much in the same way as seen during the Lehman collapse.

Indeed, growing risks in many of these areas have been making international investors highly nervous, creating considerable instability in capital flows and asset and currency markets. After mid-2011 many emerging economies saw sizeable capital outflows and sharp drops in asset and currency markets (Chart 8.5). India has seen FDI disappear and even China is reported to have experienced net capital outflows during October and November 2011 (Fleming 2012). For the first time since the Asian crisis, Chinese reserves fell in the last quarter of 2011, by almost $100 billion. At the end of 2011, the MSCI equity index was lower by 16 percent in Mexico and South Africa, 23 percent in China and Brazil, and over 35 percent in Turkey compared to the peaks reached in summer 2011.

Chart 8.5: Equity prices and nominal exchange rates, September 2008 – December 2011

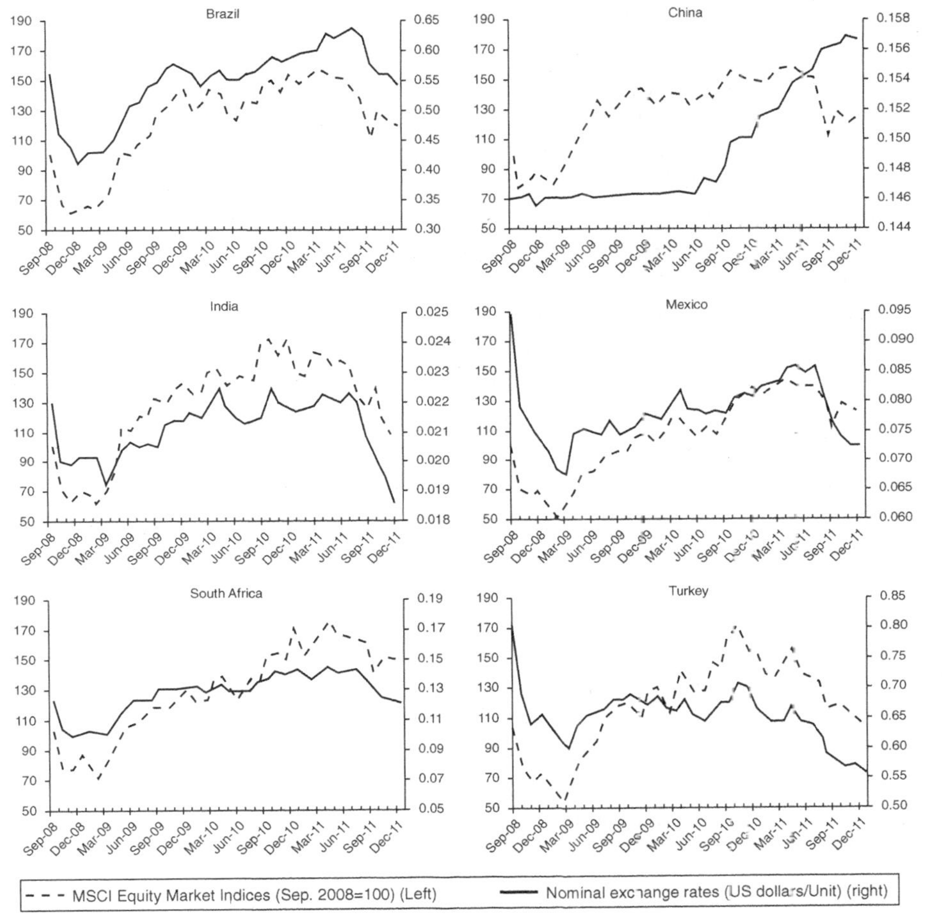

Source: MSCI & OANDA Historical Exchange Rates (http://www.oanda.com/currency/historical-rates/).

Again, in the second half of 2011, the nominal effective exchange rates dropped by 10 percent in Brazil and India, 15 percent in Mexico, and 18–20 percent in South Africa and Turkey, following strong appreciations after 2009 with the recovery of capital flows. Declines against the dollar were even steeper – about 25 percent in Turkey and between 15 and 20 percent in the rest.

These declines have partly been reversed at the beginning of 2012 with improvements in the US economy and perceptions of reduced risk of default in the eurozone. In view of continued expansion of liquidity and historically low interest rates in Europe and the US, this upturn may persist, leading to a renewed surge in capital inflows to DEEs. However, continued global economic and financial fragility could tilt the balance and lead to a rapid flight to safety and liquidity well before monetary conditions and interest rates return to normalcy in the US and EU.

In the event of persistent and sharp declines in capital inflows and commodity prices, the most vulnerable countries are commodity exporters with large current account deficits. Other deficit countries such as India and Turkey are less vulnerable because they could benefit from falling energy bills. Even though most deficit DEEs have relatively large international reserves, these are borrowed reserves accumulated from capital inflows, rather than earned from current account surpluses. They have thus their counterparts in equally large net foreign exchange liabilities, often in the form of liquid portfolio flows and short-term loans, which present a potential threat in the event of loss of confidence. The East Asian DEEs with strong current account and reserves positions may not face severe payments and currency instability even in the event of a generalized and rapid flight from emerging economies. However, their financial markets are highly exposed to destabilizing impulses from abroad because of increased foreign presence and closer integration into the international financial system, as seen during the Lehman collapse. In both deficit and surplus countries, the consequent damage could be more severe since the reversal may last much longer and the policy space in responding to renewed instability and downturn is now significantly narrower.

These latent destabilizing and deflationary impulses are already weighing down on the outlook in DEEs. The latest (January 2012) projections by both the World Bank (2012a) and the IMF (WEO 2012, January Update) have Europe going into a mild recession in 2012 and global growth falling below 3.5 percent in PPP or some 2.5 percent in constant dollars. EIU (2012) projects 2.0 percent growth in world output at market exchange rates for 2012, gradually rising to 3.0 percent by the middle of the decade. IMF downside scenario for deepened financial instability and severe recession in Europe puts global growth in 2012 at below 2 percent in PPP.

It now appears that growth in emerging economies has passed its apex. Current projections by the World Bank (2012a) and the IMF (WEO 2012, January Update), put growth in China at less than 8.5 percent in 2012 for the first time since 2002. The Chinese government has now lowered the growth target for 2012 to 7.5 percent, half a percent below the targets set in the previous seven years, with an export growth target of 10 percent. Although such targets have generally been exceeded in the past, this reflects the recognition of the difficulties faced in sustaining rapid growth and the need to improve its quality (*Economist* 2012; Xinhuanet 2012a and 2012b). Growth could be much lower if exports and/or investment falter. According to the IMF (2012), a deep recession in Europe could bring China's growth to some 4 percent in the absence of a strong domestic policy response. Again, it is estimated that with zero growth in property investment, *ceteris paribus*, GDP growth in 2012 could fall to 6.5 percent, but with a 10 percent decline, it could come down to 5.3 percent (Chovanec 2012). On some accounts the crisis has not yet hit China. When it does, the slowdown can be much more severe, with growth coming down to 3 percent and even less by 2015–16 (Pettis 2011a, 2012). A recent report jointly produced by the World Bank and Development Research Center of the State Council of China (World Bank 2012b) also warns of the risk of a rapid deceleration and crisis but argues that China can maintain over 8 percent growth until 2015 and between 6 and 7 percent in the coming two decades, provided that it undertakes the reforms recommended in the report and that it can avert the risk of hard landing in the short term with countercyclical measures supportive of long-term structural reforms. It appears that these contrasting prognostications differ not so much in the risks facing China but its ability to give an appropriate and timely response and the nature of the reforms that need to be introduced.

According to recent projections, India may barely reach 7 percent instead of climbing to China-like double digit rates as previously intended by its policymakers. The Indian government is reported to be planning a fiscal stimulus for FY2013 to jumpstart the economy (Lamont 2012). After reaching an Asian-like rate of 7.5 percent in 2010, Brazil is rapidly decelerating and seems to be poised to go back to its historical average of some 3 percent. This is also true for the other major economies of Latin America, Argentina and Mexico, with projected growth rates under 4 percent. Turkey is coming down sharply from 8–9 percent toward 3–4 percent and South Africa seems to be sticking to its paltry recovery from the 2009 recession with a similar growth rate.

I. Conclusions: Reconsidering Policies and Strategies

Developing countries face two interdependent challenges which call for rethinking their development policies and strategies. First, in the immediate future, they face the risk of a significant drop in their growth rates which can be quite severe if Europe falls into a deep recession, bringing down the US. Second, over the medium term, DEEs cannot go back to the pace and pattern of growth they enjoyed during the subprime expansion and since 2009 even if AEs succeeded in recovering fully and settling on a rigorous and stable growth path.

DEEs now have narrower policy space for a countercyclical response to deflationary and destabilizing impulses than they had after the Lehman collapse. In many emerging economies fiscal and external imbalances have widened significantly in the past few years. Nevertheless, they need to deploy all possible means to prevent a sharp slowdown of economic activity and a hike in unemployment. Many DEEs, notably in Latin America, have some space in trade policy since their bound tariffs are above the applied tariffs, but the margins are generally quite narrow for the majority of DEEs. A way out would be to invoke, as a last resort, GATT (and GATS) balance of payments safeguard provisions, designed to address payments difficulties arising from a country's efforts to expand its internal market or from instability in its terms of trade. If used judiciously, such measures would not necessarily restrict the overall volume of imports but their composition. Selective restrictions over nonessential, luxury imports, as well as of imports of goods and services for which domestic substitutes are available, could ease the payments constraint and allow increasing imports of intermediate and capital goods needed for the expansion of domestic production and income, thereby facilitating expansionary macroeconomic policies.

Provision of adequate international liquidity by multilateral financial institutions could naturally alleviate the need for restrictive trade measures, even though it would not be wise for many DEEs, notably poor countries, to use such liquidity for importing nonessential goods and services. This could be done through a sizeable SDR allocation, in proportion to the needs, not the IMF quotas of DEEs, or lending without procyclical conditionality. Liquidity provision by multilateral institutions should be designed to support income, trade and employment in DEEs, rather than international creditors to them. This means that in the event of continued and large outflows of capital, countries should be prepared to impose exchange restrictions and even temporary debt standstills, and these should be supported by the IMF through lending into arrears.

China cannot introduce another massive investment package to maintain an acceptable pace of growth without compromising its future stability. Any countercyclical policy response should be consistent with the longer-term adjustment needed to maintain rigorous growth and should address the underlying problem of underconsumption. An immediate increase in private consumption could be achieved through large transfers from the public sector, especially to the poor in rural areas, and sharply increased public provision of health and education – the former would raise the purchasing power of households and the latter would help reduce precautionary savings. These expenditures and income transfers can be financed by dividend payments by state-owned enterprises, thereby simultaneously curbing excessive investment. China also needs to raise the share of wages in GDP a lot faster than is promised by recent measures in order to shift to a consumption-led growth path (Akyüz 2011a).

Through its growing demand for commodities, China is already playing a key role in growth in commodity-dependent economies. However, it is not an important market for exporters of manufactures. At present, the size of its consumer market is less than 20 percent and its total (direct plus indirect) imports for consumption is less than 10 percent of those in the US, even though Chinese GDP is around 40 percent of the US GDP. This is not only because of the exceptionally low share of household income in GDP and a high household savings rate, but also extremely low import content of consumption. Therefore, to provide an important market for DEEs, China needs not only to raise the shares of wages and household income in GDP and lower precautionary savings, but also to increase the import content of consumption.

A shift to wage-cum-consumption-led growth does not mean that China ceases to be a major exporter of manufactures to finance its growing imports. Even though an important part of the increased consumption demand might be met by domestic producers, such a shift would entail a significant increase in imported manufactured consumer goods. China also needs to export manufactures in order to finance its growing commodity imports which have now reached almost 10 percent of GDP, and imports of capital goods from more advanced economies. In other words, a shift to consumption-led growth by China may not significantly reduce the share of imports and exports in GDP. These may in fact remain at much higher levels than would be expected for such a large economy.

For other DEEs policy challenges vary, but they are all linked, one way or another, to accumulation and productivity growth. Commodity exporters in Latin America have little control over the two key determinants of their economic performance, namely capital flows and commodity prices, and their main policy challenge is how to break out of this dilemma and gain greater autonomy in growth. They need to reduce dependence on foreign capital. Even though the wealthy in Latin America receive a greater proportion of national income than those in Asia, they save and invest a much lower proportion of their incomes. Low levels of investment and productivity growth are the main reasons for Latin American deindustrialization, somewhat aggravated by recent booms in commodity markets and capital flows. In Brazil the need for reversing this process and moving into high-tech manufacturing is widely recognized, but it seems that the country is poised to deepen its dependence on commodities by pinning its hopes on oil in the deep waters of the South Atlantic (Gall 2011). Low public and private investment and high dependence on foreign capital is the very first problem that needs to be addressed, not only in Latin America but also in some exporters of manufactures such as Turkey. As seen in Southeast Asia, a high rate of savings does not always translate into an equally high level of investment and, as seen in India, a high level of aggregate investment does not necessarily translate into a rapid industrial growth. Overcoming all these difficulties calls for targeted public interventions, including a judicious use of macroeconomic and industrial policy tools.

Notes

1 Paper prepared for the United Nations Economic and Social Commission for Asia and the Pacific (ESCAP) and presented at the ministerial segment of its 64th session in Bangkok on 29 April 2008. Published in *ESCAP Series on Inclusive and Sustainable Development* in 2008 and in *TWN Global Economy Series* in 2010. The author is grateful to Korkut Boratav, Richard Kozul-Wright, Jörg Mayer, Manuel Montes, Rubens Ricupero, Bob Rowthorn and Juan Somavia for comments and suggestions, and to Xuan Zhang for statistical assistance. The usual caveat applies.

This paper argues that the unprecedented acceleration of growth in the developing world in the new millennium in comparison with advanced economies is due not so much to improvements in underlying fundamentals as to exceptionally favorable global economic conditions, shaped mainly by unsustainable policies in advanced economies. The only developing economy which has had a major impact on global conditions, notably on commodity prices, is China. However, growth in China has been driven first by a rapid expansion of exports to advanced economies and more recently, after the global crisis, by an investment boom, neither of which is replicable or sustainable over the longer term. To maintain a rapid growth, export-led Asian economies need to reduce their dependence on foreign markets. For Latin American and African commodity exporters, gaining greater autonomy and achieving rapid and stable growth depend on their success in reducing reliance on capital flows and commodity earnings – the two key determinants of their growth which are largely beyond national control.

2 Kose, Otrok and Prasad (2008) find decoupling between AEs and DEEs, but increased coupling within each group. Wälti (2009) argues that assessment of decoupling should not be based on actual growth rates but deviations from trend (or potential output) and on that basis there is no decrease in the synchronicity between DEEs and AEs. Rose (2009) comes to broadly the same conclusion while Yeyati (2009) argues that the 2000s witnessed an increase in the correlations of DEEs and G7 cycles. For further discussion see also Kose and Prasad (2010).

3 For an account of long-term historical trends, see Nayyar (2009).

4 Nevertheless, the increased weight of China in DEEs raises the average growth of DEEs since Chinese growth has been considerably faster than the rest during both periods.

5 Here *capital inflows* refer to the acquisition of domestic assets by private nonresidents while sale of assets are negative inflows. *Capital outflows* refer to the acquisition of foreign assets by private residents, including foreign companies and individuals that have established residence in DEEs, and sales are defined as negative outflows. *Net private capital flows* is the difference between net capital inflows and net capital outflows.

6 Reduction of tariffs and nontariff barriers in China after its accession to the WTO also facilitated the emergence of East Asian trade networks and growing intraregional trade (ADB 2011).

7 FDI inflows to China peaked in 2008 before falling in 2009. In 2010 they were still below the level of 2008 (UNCTAD WIR 2011). Moreover, there was a sharp increase of foreign investment in property, with the share of FDI going into real estate rising to 23 percent in the latter year (SAFE 2011).

8 This and the following section draw on Akyüz (2012).

9 Here capital account surplus is used for surplus on nonreserve financial accounts.

10 This has been the case in Turkey where special consumption and value added taxes account for a growing proportion of total tax revenues. By contrast, there have been improvements in the distributional impact of taxes as well as the tax–GDP ratio in Latin America (Cornia et al. 2011).

11 A measure of this is the ratio of private investment in GDP to the income share of the top 20 percent. This ratio was around 25 percent in Brazil both in the 1980s and 1990s compared to 70 percent in Korea in the former period and over 53 percent in the latter (UNCTAD TDR 2003). Palma (2011) uses private investment as a percentage of the income share of the top decile and finds that in 2009 this ratio was twice as high in Asia, including Korea, China, India and Vietnam as in Latin America, including Brazil, Mexico, Argentina and Chile.

12 Except for a property boom in Singapore (Lim and Maru 2011).

13 On the estimation of import content of exports and the contribution of the exports to growth in GDP in the East Asian countries discussed in this section, see Akyüz (2011a).

14 According to IDB (2010), the increased readiness of international financial institutions to provide liquidity played a central role in restraining financial instability in Latin America.

15 According to an estimate by ESCAP (2010, box 1) for East Asian DEEs and Japan, the impact of the 2009 shortfall in exports on GDP reached 7.8 percentage points, accounting for both direct and indirect effects.

16 For fiscal stimulus packages, see United Nations (2010), Khatiwada (2009), ESCAP (2009 and 2010), ADB (2010), and IMF WEO (October 2009).

17 Difficulties in identifying fiscal measures are revealed by widely different figures given by different organizations for some East Asian countries; see UN (2010, table 1.4), ADB (2010, figure 2.4.1), and ESCAP (2009, table 1).

18 It has been reported that the property sector accounts for almost half of Chinese steel use and is a major driver of demand for other commodities, such as copper (Plowright 2012).

References

ADB (Asian Development Bank) (various issues). *Asian Development Outlook*. www.adb.org.

Akyüz, Y. 2009. "Policy Response to the Global Financial Crisis: Key Issues for Developing Countries." South Centre Research Paper 24. May.

———. 2010. "The Management of Capital Flows and Financial Vulnerability in Asia." In *Time for a Visible Hand: Lessons from the 2008 World Financial Crisis*, edited by S. Griffith-Jones, J. A. Ocampo and J. E. Stiglitz. New York: Oxford University Press, IPD.

———. 2011a. "Export Dependence and Sustainability of Growth in China and the East Asian Production Network." *China and World Economy* 19 (1), January.

———. 2011b. "Global Economic Prospects: The Recession May be Over but Where Next?" *Global Policy* 2 (2), May.

———. 2012. "The Boom in Capital Flows to Developing Countries: Will It Go Bust Again? *Ekonomi-tek* 1 (1).

Athukorala, P. 2011. "South–South Trade: An Asian Perspective." ADB Economics Working Paper 265, July. Manila: ADB.

BIS. 2010. *Quarterly Review*, December. Basel.

Calvo, G., and E. Talvi. 2007. "Current Account Surplus in Latin America: Recipe Against Capital Market Crises." RGE, 18 May. http://www.economonitor.com/blog/2007/05/current-account-surplus-in-latin-america-recipe-against-capital-market-crises/. Accessed 25 January 2012.

Cesa-Bianchi, A., M. H. Pesaran, A. Rebucci, and T. T. Xu. 2011. "China's Emergence in the World Economy and Business Cycles in Latin America." IDB Working Paper 266, September.

Chovanec, P. 2012. "Further Thoughts on Real Estate's Impact on China GDP." 20 January. http://www.economonitor.com/blog/2012/01/further-thoughts-on-real-estate%e2%80%99s-impact-on-china-gdp/. Accessed 2 September 2011.

Cohan, L., and E. L. Yeyati. 2012. "What Have I Done to Deserve This? Global Winds and Latin American Growth." http://www.voxeu.org/index.php?q=node/7519. Accessed 20 January 2012.

Cornia, G. A., J. C. Gómez-Sabaini and B. Martorano. 2011. "A New Fiscal Pact, Tax Policy Changes and Income Inequality: Latin America during the Last Decade." UNU-WIDER Working Paper 2011/70.

ECLAC (various issues). "Preliminary Overview of the Economies of Latin America and Caribbean." Santiago.

Economist. 2012. "China's New Growth Targets: Year of the Tortoise. China Seeks (slightly) Slower Growth," March 10. www.economist.com/node/21549977. Accessed 8 March 2012.

EIU (Economist Intelligent Unit). 2012. "Global Forecasting Service February 2012." http://gfs.eiu.com/PastReports.aspx. Accessed 26 February 2012.

ESCAP. 2009. "Economic and Social Survey of Asia and the Pacific 2009: Year-end Update." Bangkok. http://www.unescap.org/pdd/publications/survey2009/download/index.asp. Accessed 10 January 2010.

———. 2010. "Economic and Social Survey of Asia and the Pacific 2010." http://www.unescap.org/pdd/publications/survey2010/download/index.asp. Accessed 1 May 2010.

Farooki, M. Z. 2012. "China's Metals Demand and Commodity Prices: A Case of Disruptive Development?" *European Journal of Development Research* 24 (1): 56–70.

Farooki, M. Z., and R. Kaplinsky. 2011. *The Impact of China on Commodity Prices.* London: Francis and Taylor.

Ferrero, A. 2012. "House Price Booms, Current Account Deficits, and Low Interest Rates." Staff Report 541. Federal Reserve Bank of New York. January.

Fleming, S. 2012. The Brics' Growth Story Start to Lose its Way. *Times*, 2 January 2012.

Gall, N. 2011. "Oil in Deep Waters." Fernand Braudel Institute of World Economics, Braudel Papers 45.

Gupta, P., R. Hasan and U. Kumar. 2008. "What Constrains Indian Manufacturing? Indian Council for Research on International Relations Working Paper 211." March.

IDB (Inter-American Development Bank). 2008. "All that Glitters may not be Gold. Assessing Latin America's Recent Macroeconomic Performance." Research Department. April.

———. 2010. "The Aftermath of the Crisis. Policy Lessons and Challenges Ahead for Latin America and the Caribbean." March.

IMF WEO (various issues). *World Economic Outlook*, Washington, DC.

IMF REO (various issues). *Regional Economic Outlook: Western Hemisphere.* Washington, DC.

IMF. 2011. "Global Economic Prospects and Policy Challenges." Prepared by Staff of the International Monetary Fund, Meeting of G-20 Deputies, July 9–10, Paris. http://www.imf.org/external/np/g20/070911.htm. Accessed 4 August 2011.

———. 2012. "China Economic Outlook." IMF Resident Representative Office, People's Republic of China, Beijing. 6 February. www.imf.org/external/country/CHN/rr/2012/020612.pdf. Accessed 13 February 2012.

Izquierdo, A., R. Romero and E. Talvi. 2008. "Booms and Busts in Latin America: The Role of External Factors." IDB, Working Paper 631. February.

Jiménez, J. P., and J. C. Gómez-Sabaini. 2009. "The Role of Tax Policy in the Context of the Global Crisis: Consequences and Prospects." ECLAC (LC/L.3037) Montevideo, 19–20 May.

Khatiwada, S. 2009. "Stimulus Packages to Counter Global Economic Crisis: A Review." International Institute for Labor Studies Discussion Paper 196.

Koopman, R., W. Powers, Z. Wang and S.-J. Wei. 2010. "Give Credit Where Credit Is Due: Tracing Value-Added in Global in Global Production Chains." NBER Working Paper 16426. September.

Kose, A., C. Otrok, and E. Prasad. 2008. "Global Business Cycles: Convergence or Decoupling?" NBER Working Paper 14292.

Kose, M. A., and E. Prasad. 2010. *Emerging Markets: Resilience and Growth amid Global Turmoil.* Brookings Institution.

Lamont, J. 2012. "India to Launch $35bn of Public Investment." *Financial Times*, 18 January.

Lardy, N. R. 2012. "China's Rebalancing Will Not Be Automatic. Economic Monitor, February 24th. http://www.economonitor.com/piie/2012/02/24/. Accessed 28 February 2012.

Lederman, D., M. Olarreaga and G. E. Perry. 2009. *China's and India's Challenge to Latin America: Opportunity or Threat?* Washington, DC : The World Bank Press.

Lee, H.-H., D. Park and J. Wang. 2011. "The Role of the People's Republic of China in International Fragmentation and Production Networks: An Empirical Investigation." ADB Working Paper on Regional Economic Integration 87. September.

Lewis, A. 1980. "The Slowing Down of the Engine of Growth." *American Economic Review* 70 (4). September.

Lim, M. M.-H., and J. Maru. 2011. "Financial Liberalization and the Impact of the Financial Crisis on Singapore." In *The Financial Crisis and Asian Developing Countries*, Y, Akyüz. Penang: TWN.

Lim, M. M-H., and J. Lim. 2012. "Asian Initiatives at Monetary and Financial Integration: A Critical Review." South Centre Research Paper 46, July.

Miroudot, S., and A. Ragoussis. 2009. Vertical Trade, Trade Costs and FDI. OECD Trade Policy Working Paper 89.

Mohapatra, S., D. Ratha and A. Silwal. 2011. "Outlook for Remittance Flows 2012–14." Migration and Development Brief 17. World Bank, Washington, DC. http://siteresources.worldbank.org/INTPROSPECTS/Resources/334934-1110315015165/MigrationandDevelopmentBrief17.pdf. Accessed 12 February 2012.

Nayyar, D. 2009. "Developing Countries in the World Economy: The Future in the Past?" WIDER Annual Lecture 12, UNU-WIDER, Helsinki.

Ocampo, J. A. 2007. "La Macroeconomía de la Bonanza Económica." *Revista de la CEPAL* 94, December.

Palma, J. G. 2011. Is Brazil's Recent Growth Acceleration the World's Most Overrated Boom? Presentation made in the UNCTAD-South Centre Workshop, The Rise of the South and the New Opportunities and Challenges for Development, South Centre, 21 November.

Pei, M. 2009. "Looming stagnation." *The National Interest,* March–April.

Pettis, M. 2011a. "Some Predictions for the Rest of the Decade," 28 August. www.creditwritedowns.com/2011/08. Accessed 15 December 2011.

———. 2011b. "How Do We Know that China is Overinvesting?" 3 December. http://www.economonitor.com/blog/2011/12/how-do-we-know-that-china-is-overinvesting/. Accessed 20 January 2012.

———. 2012. "When Will China Emerge from the Global Crisis?" 22 February. www.ecomonitor.com/2012/02. Accessed 28 February 2012.

Plowright, M. 2012. "Growth Fears Cast Shadow over Emerging World. Emerging Markets," 9 January. www.emergingmarkets.org/Article/2958146/News/Growth-fears-cast-shadow-over-emerging-world.html. Accessed 18 January 2012.

Radhi, N. A., and A. G. Zeufack. 2009. "Malaysia: Escaping the Middle Income Trap." Unpublished paper. Khazanah Research and Investment Strategy, Khazanah Nasional Bhd. Kuala Lumpur, April.

Riad, N., L. Errico, C. Henn, C. Saborowski, M. Saito and J. Turunen. 2011 *Changing Patterns of Global Trade: Strategy, Policy, and Review Department.* IMF, Washington, DC.

Rabinovitch, S. 2012. "China Tells Banks to Roll over Loans." *Financial Times* 12 February. www.ft.com/intl/cms/s/0/dc7035dc-553b-11e1-b66d-00144feabdc0.html#axzz1mZB0JVcP. Accessed 13 February 2012.

Rose, A. K. 2009. "Business Cycles Become Less Synchronized over Time: Debunking 'Decoupling.'" http://www.voxeu.org/index.php?q=node/3829. Accessed 14 January 2012.

SAFE (State Administrator of Foreign Exchange). 2011. "Monitoring Report: 2010 Cross-Border Capital Flows in China." 7 February.

UNCTAD TDR (various issues). *Trade and Development Report.* Geneva United Nations.

UNCTAD WIR (various issues). *World Investment Report.* United Nations: Geneva.

United Nations. 2010. *World Economic Situation and Prospects 2010.* New York: United Nations. January.

Uygur, E. 2011. "Domestic Savings in Turkey: Policy, Institutional and Legislative Framework," background study for the World Bank CEM, Ankara.

Wälti, S. 2009. "The Myth of Decoupling." 27 July. http://www.voxeu.org/index.php?q=node/3814. Accessed 12 December 2012.

WB CQU (various issues). *China Quarterly Update.* World Bank Beijing Office, China.

World Bank. 2011. "Domestic Saving and Growth." Turkey CEM Synthesis Report, 6 June.

———. 2012a. *Global Economic Prospects: Uncertainties and Vulnerabilities.* January, Washington, DC.

———. 2012b. *China 2030: Building a Modern, Harmonious, and Creative High-Income Society.* The World Bank and Development Research Center of the State Council, the People's Republic of China. Washington, DC.

Xinhuanet. 2011. "China's Fixed Asset Investment up 25.6% in H1." Xinhua News Agency, 13 July. http://news.xinhuanet.com/english2010/business/2011-07/13/c_13981891.htm. Accessed 31 October 2011.

———. 2012a. "FACTBOX: China's Economic and Social Development." 5 March. http://news.xinhuanet.com/english/china/2012-03/05/c_131447759.htm. Accessed 6 March 2012.

———. 2012b. "China Cuts 2012 GDP Growth to 7.5% for Quality Development. 5 March. http://news.xinhuanet.com/english/china/2012-03/05/c_131445684_3.htm. Accessed 6 March 2012.

Yeyati, E. L. 2009. "On Emerging Markets Decoupling and Growth Convergence." 7 November. http://www.voxeu.org/index.php?q=node/4172. Accessed 12 November 2011.